JÁN LACIKA

BRATISLAVA

DAJAMA
VYDAVATEĽSTVO

BRATISLAVA
1st edition, 2000

Author of the text: Ján Lacika
Reviewers: Štefan Holčík and Silvia Seitzová
Editors: Peter Augustini and Daniel Kollár
Responsible editor: Daniel Kollár
Technical editor: Ján Lacika
Author of the hiking tours: Ján Lacika
Author of the bike tours: Ján Hanušin
Author of tourist information: Ada Motyková
Translation: Mgr. Hana Contrerasová
Language editor: Martin Styan B.A.
Photographs: Ján Lacika, Ivan Kostroň
Plans and maps: Ján Lacika
Extracts of maps: Vojenský kartografický ústav, š.p. Harmanec
Illustrated map: Pegas, Považská Bystrica
Design and layout: Jagus DTP
Print: Kníhtlačiareň Svornosť a.s. Bratislava

This guidebook is also available in the Slovak, German and Hungarian languages.

This book was published with financial assistance from the State Fund for Culture Pro Slovakia

ISBN 80-88975-16-6

Dear readers

The purpose of the DAJAMA publications since the very beginning of their existence is the promotion of the regions of Slovakia and publishing of guidebooks. In the series of Regions Without Frontiers the book "The Slovak-Austrian Basin of the River Morava" was published in the Slovak and German languages in 1996, "The Slovak-Polish Tatras" in the Polish, Slovak, German, English and Hungarian languages was published in 1998. Translation into several foreign languages is an indispensable part of the publisher's activity and his principal aim is to introduce the Slovak regions to foreigners.

This was also why the publisher started a new series called Visiting Slovakia. His primary effort is to prepare and progressively elaborate a book on every region. In 2000 as a part of this project the guidebook to Bratislava appears in four languages: Slovak, English, German, and Hungarian. These tourist guidebooks contain:

- Basic characteristics of the natural setting of the city
- Detailed history of the city
- The Old Town, its most important cultural and historical monuments
- The most beautiful walks in the centre of the Old Town
- Characteristics of the individual urban districts
- The most beautiful hiking and bike tours
- Practical information for visitor

The texts concerning the Old Town and other parts of the city describe the history and landmarks enriched by various legends, stories, myths and other interesting details, which complement the general picture of the mentality and way of life of Bratislavians. The division of the chapters and walks in the Old Town should contribute to better understanding of Bratislava with its intimate corners and sights. As a matter of fact, there are few cities on the map of Europe with such unique situation and rich history as those of Bratislava. Its situation on both banks of the Danube and on the foothills of the Little Carpathians provides numerous wonderful views of the individual parts of the city. The pride of Bratislava is the Danube, the second greatest river of Europe, which is typical of many of its sights. We have tried to offer them to you by means of historical and recent photographs and illustrations in an effort to inspire you to visit the capital of Slovakia and to make its most beautiful spots accessible to the public.

Daniel Kollár and Peter Augustini

TABLE OF CONTENTS

ACKNOWLEDGEMENT

The most cordial thanks go to our closest collaborators: Ján Lacika, Ján Sepp and Erika Mészárošová and all those who participated in the preparation of the texts and graphic form of the book. Precious suggestions of the historian Štefan Holčík, who contributed so far unpublished results of his research and generously mediated the pictorial documents of the old engravings and paintings of the Municipal Museum, the Slovak National Museum, Archaeological Museum, the Slovak National Gallery and the Gallery of the city of Bratislava deserve special thanks. The drawings and illustrated maps of the city were borrowed from the PEGAS Ltd. company Považská Bystrica, the biggest producer of illustrated maps of cities in the Slovak and Czech Republics. Cordial thanks for them! We are also thankful for the city plan and the map extracts to VKÚ Harmanec, to the Office of the Mayor of Bratislava, and the Bratislava Information Service for providing the topical database of practical information about the city.

Let us also express gratitude to our wives Zuzka and Danica, because without their support it would have been impossible to realize this project. We dedicate the publication to all natives of Bratislava and especially to our children Peťka, Kamilka, Miško, and Danielka so that they do not forget where they grew up and where they come from.

Daniel Kollár & Peter Augustini

SITUATION AND ADMINISTRATIVE DIVISION

The geographical position of Bratislava is very similar to that of the neighbouring Vienna or Budapest. These three Central European metropolises lie on the banks of the river Danube in places, where the great river leaves behind mountain ranges. Bratislava is only 65 kilometres from Vienna and only 50 from the Vienna's international airport of Schwechat. The distance between Bratislava and Budapest is 180 km, and that between Bratislava and Prague is 330 km.

The territory of Bratislava is crossed by the 17th meridian of the Eastern Hemisphere. It runs across the municipal part of Devín and the 48th geographical parallel almost touches the southern border of the city near the municipal part of Čunovo. The geographical co-ordinates of Bratislava are 17° 7' east for longitude and 48° 9' north for latitude.

The position of Bratislava is eccentric with regard to the territory of the Slovak Republic. It is situated at its extreme south-western corner. A comparatively long section of the city border coincides with the frontier, a rare phenomenon in comparison to other European capitals. It is a long way to Bratislava from any point of the country. In spite of this, Bratislava is relatively near the economically and culturally advanced western part of the Old Continent. The city is part of Euroregion constituted by the triangle between Bratislava, Vienna and the Hungarian town of Györ, estimated by an international expert group as the one with the best outlooks within Europe.

Bratislava and Pressburg

Bratislava and Pressburg are two names of the same city used in different historical periods. The older name of Pressburg *was used for more than a thousand years. It was first mentioned in the Salzburg annals in connection wit the battle between the Bavarian and Old Hungar-*

Right: Bratislava seen from the New Bridge

ian armies in 907 below the castle of Brezalauspurc. *The castle probably bore the name of one of its lords or administrators. It might have been either the Slav prince Braslav or a man called Predslav quoted in the list of Great Moravian nobles of the famous Cividal Evangeliary. It must be emphasised though, that any connection of these two figures with Brezalauspurc is purely hypothetical. Besides the German name Pressburg and Slovak name Prešpork, the Latin name* Posonium *or its Hungarian form* Poszony *was also long used. It is referred to in various derived forms like* Bassan *or* Posana *from the* 12th *century. Matej Bel, the* 18th *century enlightened scholar attributed the origin of this name to the Roman general Pison. More recent historians rather believe that it derived from the name of a less known Old Slav noble Božan. The modern name Bratislava has been the official name of the city since the end of the First World War. The author of its primitive form* Břetislav *is the Slovak scientist Pavol Jozef Šafárik who published it in 1837. Later Štúr's followers modified it to* Bratislav.

Right: Sandberg

Bratislava is one of the youngest European capitals. It was capital during the short existence of the Slovak State in the years 1939-1945. Later in 1993 it again became the capital of the independent Slovak Republic. The territory also referred to as Greater Bratislava has an area of 367.5 square kilometres with population 451,400 (to December 31st 1998) equalling to about eight per cent of Slovakia's total population. Pursuing the new administrative arrangement of 1996 Bratislava became the part of province Bratislava and out of the eight districts of the smallest Slovak province five are inner administrative units of the capital. They are the districts of Bratislava I, Bratislava II, Bratislava III, Bratislava IV, and Bratislava V.

The smallest district not only of Bratislava, but also of the whole Slovak

Republic with an area of 9.6 square kilometres is the district of Bratislava I. Greater Bratislava consists of 17 municipal parts and 266 town wards. The body of local self-government is the municipal council chaired by the Mayor. The municipal parts have their mayors and local representations.

Natural setting

Although Bratislava can be denoted as a prevailingly lowland city one must take into consideration the inseparable part of its silhouette, the Little Carpathian Mountains. The oldest history of Bratislava started on a peripheral hill of the Carpathians, where stands the castle of Bratislava. The medieval town was formed on the Danube's alluvial plain at the foot of this hill. The modern and dynamically growing city expanded its area to the slopes of former vineyards of the Little Carpathian foreland and it also "jumped" over the Danube and "spilled" over the edge of the Záhorská nížina lowland.

Approximately one quarter of Bratislava's territory is on the flanks of the forested **Little Carpathians** (Malé Karpaty). This mountain range between the Danube and Záhorská lowland is the south-western edge of the massive Carpathian Arc, which returns back to the Danube after running 2,000 kilometres across Slovakia, western Ukraine and Romania. The eastern and central parts of the mountain range consist of extensive granite massifs. The granite is of poor quality and it is not suitable for stonemason use in contrast to, for example, the Scandinavian or Czech granites. On the western side of the Little Carpathians there is a narrow belt of folded sediments with sandstone, dolomite and shale rocks. For instance, the rock of Devín is mostly sandstone with small karstic formations. Slate can be seen in the old quarry on the north-western edge of Bratislava. Many old houses in Bratislava have their roofs covered by shingles made of the slate extracted from this quarry.

The core of the mountain range from which today's Little Carpathians originated was formed in the Upper Tertiary about thirty million years ago. Tectonic movements uplifted the plain dry land, which became a flat peninsula spreading between two warm seas existing in the area of today's Danube and Záhorská lowlands. Tiny remains of the coastal cliffs of this sea are preserved on the western slope of the Devínska Kobyla Mountain. An ideal spot for the detailed study of the remains is the locality called **Sandberg** south of the village of Devínska Nová Ves.

On the shore of the Tertiary sea

Sandberg (German for Sand Hill) is a very appropriate name of the old sand pit where fine sea sand was extracted for several centuries. However, Sandberg became a well-known place above all thanks to the finding of bones of an animal that lived here some 15 million years ago. During the geological periods, which the scientists call the Badenian and Sarmatian, the local landscape was quite different from what we see there now. Sandberg was a sea bottom for a while, maybe a beach or coastal cliff. Sea currents brought the sand now showing in the bizarre yellow rock face here. Their marine origin is proved by unusually rich paleontological finds of various remains of the sea fauna. More than three hundred species of fossils were found here. In the sand pit nearby called Hlavica, which is the remnant of the dismantled sand hill, a remarkable bone weighing about two kilograms was found in 1976. The experts recognized in it a part of back bone of a prehistoric whale. Remains of dry land mammals that were

brought here by an unknown prehistoric river were also found on Sandberg. Bones of rhinos, antelopes, cave bear, and a monkey, presumably the predecessor of the gibbon, were discovered. However, the most valuable find was that of the primate of dryopithecus *type.*

The southern part of the Little Carpathians is called the **Devínske Karpaty**. The tallest mountain here is **Devínska Kobyla**, which with its 514 metres above sea level is also the highest point in Bratislava. In the south this bulky hill drops into **Devínska brána**, the gate between the mountains, which the river Danube uses to cross the Carpathians. In the east the relief of the Devínske Karpaty passes to the **Bratislavské predhorie**, which is divided by the Dolná Mlynská dolina valley into Staré grunty in the west and Bratislavské vŕšky in the east. Round hills and ridges do not exceed an altitude of 250 metres above sea level. In the north the Devínske Karpaty Mountains are limited by another lowering, the Lamačská brána Gate. The **Lamačská brána** Gate is especially windy as it acts as a sort of funnel for the winds blowing from the Záhorská nížina lowland.

North of the Lamačská brána Gate is the southern part of the Pezinské Karpaty Mts. running to the north-east far beyond the northern border of Bratislava. The **Pezinské Karpaty** is a massive mountain range with comparatively extensive central plateaux. Central plateaux also called planated surfaces are in fact relicts of the little dissected Tertiary relief. They were formed in different climatic conditions favourable to planation of the surface forms. Later, when the mountain range was uplifted by tectonic activity, the river network intersected the flat mountain ranges. The valleys formed by erosion of the Carpathian brooks progressively divided the originally continuous planated surface into several isolated plateaux. The altitude of the plateaux above sea level is arranged into several steps increasing from 330 metres near Kačín Mt. to 500 m near Biely kríž Mt. South of Biely kríž almost original remnants of old Little Carpathian valleys are discernible. They are shallow with wide wet bottoms and moderate inclination. A good example is the spring section of the **Horná Mlynská dolina** valley with the little meandering river of **Vydrica**. The valley becomes gradually deeper and gains a more dynamic form. With its lakes it is one of the most romantic spots in the territory of Bratislava. The Horná Mlynská dolina valley is the only one among the Little Carpathian valleys in the territory of the Pezinské Karpaty Mts. that does not end in the neighbouring lowlands. It is oriented to the lower part of Devínska brána Gate. East of the Horná Mlynská dolina valley above the plateaux and flat ridges is the mountain of **Kamzík** (439 m a.s.l.) with the TV tower on its top. It is the landscape dominant and a typical symbol of Bratislava.

The Little Carpathians are mostly covered by broad leafed forests and are the most compact and most extensive forested territory of Bratislava. Oaks and hornbeams prevail in lower positions, while beeches are typical of the higher parts. However, vineyards replaced the forests on the eastern side of the Little Carpathians and those of Devínske Karpaty had to make the way to construction of residential quarters. The **Protected Landscape Area** (CHKO) **of the Little Carpathians** statute has protected the preserved Little

Left: Adonis vernalis
Right:: Devínska Kobyla Mountain

Carpathian forests since 1976. The administration of the protected area is located in Modra. The Little Carpathians are the most important recreation zone for the citizens of Bratislava who can enjoy it for the whole year round. The hills become especially attractive on hot summer days when it is more pleasant to pass the day in the forest than in the street. In winter they offer the possibility of winter sports. Often when there is not a trace of snow down in the city, the Carpathians boast a typical white winter. In spite of the fact that the forests are frequently visited, there is comparatively abundant wild life there including deer, fox, hare, squirrel, and numerous species of fowl. An occasional encounter with boar is not impossible either. In the part of the Little Carpathians around Bratislava there are nine small protected areas. The oldest one, established in 1964, is the **National Nature Reserve Devínska Kobyla**. It protects the thermophile flora and fauna. An instructive path through the area provides information about its specific features.

The southernmost tip of the **Záhorská nížina lowland** reaches as far as the territory of the city. There is the shallow Bystrická depression west of the village of Záhorská Bystrica and a flat river terrace north of the village of Devínska Nová Ves, where the Volkswagen car factory stands. The alluvial forest along the **river Morava** is a special and well-preserved natural landscape. The landscape conserved its unique natural value only due to the fact that it was strictly guarded as the frontier territory shared with Austria. It is also in the **protected landscape area** (CHKO) called **Záhorie** since 1988. The Záhorská nížina lowland lies in a warm climatic zone. Due to a large share of forests it is a little bit cooler and wetter than the Danube lowland. Typical trait of this part of Bratislava is windiness, as it is open to the winds coming from the north and north-west blowing along the Morava's riverbed. By the end of the winter season even sand storms occur here. Strong wind is capable to set in motion large amounts of blown sands and to create an unpleasant yellow veil.

The centre of tectonic sinking in the **Danube lowland** (Podunajská nížina) moved to the area of Žitný ostrov that became the core of today's **Danube plain** in the Quaternary. The **river Danube** formed this plain landscape. The second largest European river with its sediments gradually over millennia filled the vast natural hole between Bratislava and Komárno. In the course of two million years it created a big inland delta here. The thickness of the Quaternary sediments rapidly increases from the west to the east from 10-15 metres in the Old Town of Bratislava to 60-70 metres near Čunovo. In the centre of this depression, that is Dunajská Streda, it reaches as much as 500 m. Under the Žitný ostrov island an enormous amount of ground water of the best quality has accumulated. It represents the largest reservoir of drinking water in Central Europe.

Left: The spilled Morava
Right:: The Danube
Mean mothly temperatures and precipitation

The part of Bratislava stretching onto the Danube lowland is the **warmest and driest climatic area of Slovakia**. The mean annual temperature here is 10.3 °C, the annual rainfall total is 642 mm and the sun shines here an average of 2,100 hours a year. The favourable climatic conditions are appreciated by the local gardeners and cultivators of vineyards, as well as by holiday-makers bathing in Zlaté piesky, Kuchajda, Veľký Draždiak or other artificial lakes. The bathing seasons starts by the end of May and ends in September. The warmest month of the year is July with a mean monthly temperature over 20°C.

The Danube was the major force that ruled over the extensive alluvial forests until the 18th century. Man did not intervene at all. The great river shifted its bed and branched into uncountable arms. It flooded immense areas each year by the end of the spring season. In the past the Danube also tortured the town of Pressburg with destructive floods. The oldest flood referred to occurred in 1445. The water in the Danube rises every year. The cause is the thawing of snow in the Austrian Alps. An unusually abundant rainfall assisted the flood in 1445. The history of Bratislava also recorded numerous winter floods. One of the biggest winter floods struck the city on February 5th 1850. The lines engraved on the facade of the tower on Hlavné námestie square and other buildings in the city prove it.

The Danube in 1965

The last disastrous flood on the Slovak reach of the Danube took place in 1965. The abundant June rainfall caused rises of the Danube. Population had to be evacuated from the threatened Austrian territories. The panic seized Bratislava as well. Crowds of curious people hurried to the embankment of the Danube to see the rising water level and the gauging apparatus. It displayed the value of 855 cm and it was still rising. The water reached as high as the upper edge of the concrete wall skirting the embankment. The water flooded the parking lot next the Old Bridge and on the other side of the river the trees, benches and roundabouts were standing in water. It took several days before the water retreated. As a matter of fact the water did not actually enter the city. But several tens of kilometres lower down the stream, near the village of Čičov, the water broke the dykes and easily flooded half of Žitný ostrov. Fifty thousand people had to leave their homes and the damage caused by the flood was estimated at three billion crowns.

History

The history of creative presence of man in the territory of today's Bratislava goes back several thousand years. To know the first inhabitants of the town, we should go back as far as the **Older Stone Age**. It is more than probable that the area around the middle part of the Danube was attractive enough for groups of prehistoric hunters wandering in the country in pursue of game or other means of subsistence. Some of these prehistoric people were using ancient tools dug out in Bratislava's Mlynská dolina valley. The Palaeolithic hunters did not build permanent settlements. One could say that we had Bratislavians but not Bratislava. Early human settlements in the territory of the modern Slovak metropolis sprung out many thousand years later. They were the products of the oldest farmers and shepherds who settled here about seven thousand years ago. Finds of at least four localities in the inner medieval town, in Mlynská dolina, Lamačská brána and Devín date back to the **Younger Stone Age**. There were probably more of them in a densely populated space, but the majority of them are lost under the mantle of buildings and asphalt. In the discovered Neolithic localities various simple work tools of farmers and earthen pots used for storing the crops, which belonged to farmers or shepherds were found. In the **Late Stone Age** probably the oldest fortified settlements originated on the castle hills of Bratislava and Devín. The advantageous position of both settlements offered their population good control over the movement on the ancient trade routes heading to fords over the Danube. The people of furrow decorated pottery living in these settlements more than four thousand years ago mastered some crafts and traded their products.

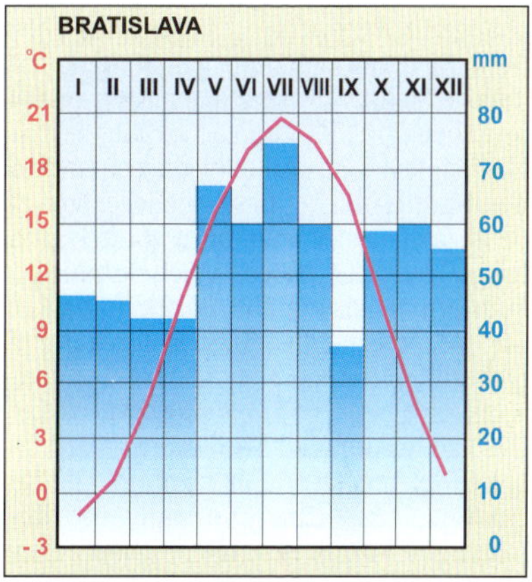

The first copper objects announcing the arrival of the **Bronze Age** found in the soil of Bratislava, are some of the oldest in Central Europe. They testify to the participation of this region in lively trade with the near and distant parts of Europe. Contacts with the Mediterranean are proved by the Tyrrhenian sword found near Bratislava (deposited in the National Museum of Budapest). The Baltic amber found in the graves of rulers of the Mycenae was most probably transported via the **Amber Route**.

The Iron Age in the history is one of the most important periods for Bratislava. The older time often denoted as Hallstatt period is documented by the traces of the people of **Calenderberg culture**. Several lowland settlements, for instance in Devínska Nová Ves, Trnávka, and Ivanka pri Dunaji (next to Bratislava airport) were found. In addition there are two high-situated settlements on the castle hills of Bratislava and Devín. A single-room hut dug out into rock was found in the area of Bratislava Castle. It documents the level of housing of the people belonging to the lower social class. Moreover, a wonderful little statue of a horse was found in the Calenderberg settlement in the area of Devín Castle.

The Celts brought a revolutionary change in the history of Bratislava. They were the first inhabitants whom we do not have to identify by means of pottery or the way they buried their dead as they left us written texts (so far only on coins) and who lived in the first predecessor of Bratislava, which can be regarded as a town. The Celtic tribes, which subdued a substantial part of the northern half of Europe, also settled in the territory of modern Bratislava. They maintained contacts with more civilized southern half of the Old Continent. They were often inspired by progressive elements of Classical times, imitating especially the Romans. The towns were one of them. They

Left: Bratislava Castle
Right: Devín Castle

built up a large settlement which the experts call the **Oppidum of Bratislava**, the nature of which was undoubtedly urban as the Celtic finds testify. It means that Bratislava with its two thousand years old municipal tradition is one of the oldest towns in Central Europe. Traces of Celtic settlement were found in the territory extending over sixty hectares, which was larger than an average medieval town. The majority of Celtic artefacts are concentrated in the space of the historical centre, which constituted the core of the oppidum. For the time being it is not sure whether the localities situated out of the centre (for instance the square of Námestie slobody), were its part. It is also possible that this was an agglomeration of settlements. Another imported item from the Classical world was money, heartily welcomed by the Celts. As the Central European Celts possessed admirable skills for work with metals, they were able to produce coins of high quality comparable with those of the Romans or Greeks. The Celtic coins bear the oldest writing used in the territory of Slovakia, including the territory of Bratislava. The texts on these coins are easy to read as the writing is practically identical with ours taken over from the Romans. The inscription BIATEC frequently appears on the reverse of the coins and this is why the coins are called **biatecs**.

The biatecs of Bratislava

When in 1923 the building of Tatra bank was under construction in the SNP square of modern Bratislava, the workers discovered 399 Celtic coins. As this treasure is not unique in the territory of Bratislava, the experts believe that the coins were struck at the local mint. This was confirmed by the later find of 223 smelting forms and 16 fragments of dozing plates discovered under the Palffy's Palace on Panská Street. In total eight such treasures and more than a thousand Celtic coins were found in Bratislava and its close environs. Practically all of them are made with extraordinary precision and artistic style. The old Celtic craftsmen imitated the Greek-Macedonian patterns from the time of the rulers Philip II and Alexander the Great. They struck silver tetradrachmas, starters or small coins of Simmering type. They were inspired most probably by the Celtic expansion to the Balkans. The unknown artist has drawn some remarkable images of aristocrats, horsemen and animals on a small coin with diameter of 1.5 to 3 cm. They usually bear various inscriptions such as DEVIL, NONNOS, COISA, AINORIX, TITTO, and MACCIUS. BIATEC is the most frequent one. It is presumed that it derives from the name of the prince of the Celtic tribe of Boii tribe, who ruled over the Bratislava oppidum. Prince Biatec presumably struck the coins for the local market place.

There was a Celtic settlement near Devín as well. It probable formed one unit with the elevated spot of Braunsberg at the opposite bank of the Danube. The rule of the Celtic Boii on the middle reach of the Danube was suddenly ended by inva-

sion of the Dacians. The impact must have been so strong that the authors of old chronicles named the Celtic settlements *the Boii desert*. After a short Dacian episode, which took place short before the arrival of new era, another important period of Bratislava's history started, which can be called after the prevailing ethnicities the **German-Roman period**. As the Romans were not able to push the frontiers of the Empire up to the crests of the Carpathians, the territory of Bratislava became part of the turbulent contact zone separating often hostile Romans living south of the Danube and Germans ruling over the areas north of this great European river. For approximately four centuries the area immediately neighbouring the Danube found itself on the border between two different worlds, which meant permanent political and economic instability. The part of modern Bratislava lying south of the Danube belonged to the Roman province of Pannonia administered by the Roman legions settled nearby in *Carnuntum* (today Bad Deutsch Altenburg in Austria). There were (within the territory administered now by the village of Rusovce) a Roman fort called **Gerulata** (→ 221) with a settlement bigger than usual and a market place. It was the departure point for expeditions to the territory beyond the frontier of the Empire lying on the left bank of the Danube. The Roman legions entered this territory for the first time in 9 BC. They crossed the river in the territory of modern Bratislava. Tiberius, step-son of Augustus and later Roman Emperor, proceeded with a great army to Záhorie pursuing the Barbarian enemy. The successors of the Tiberius´ legionaries went even further. Their another and more important mission was to found a system of guard stations on the other side of the river with permanent military garrisons, which warned in case the German warriors were coming too close. Along with the forts on the right bank of the middle reach of the Danube these guard stations represented an important part of the fortifications known as the **Limes Romanus**. Advanced Roman units stationed on the Bratislava and Devín castle hills fulfilled yet another task. They protected important fords over the Danube used by the traders travelling on the Amber Road. Two rivals were interested in the castle hill of Devín. It is presumed that it is the site of a border fort of the Quadi kingdom, which belonged to the rebellious vassal king Vannia. The Romans owned the strategic elevation point most of the time. Even the Emperor Valentinian I visited it personally in 375. When he came to the Danube, he found there the town of Carnuntum destroyed by the Germans and this was the reason why he was accommodated in the nearest Roman station which must have been the one at Devín. The Emperor died shortly after at Brigetio near Komárno. His death actually meant the end of the Roman-German period of Bratislava's history. Under

Left: The Roman pottery from Gerulata
Right: The Roman thombstone
Biatecs

pressure from the German Visigoths, the Romans left Pannonia forever in 378.

The fall of the Roman Empire was followed by a cultural, economic and political vacuum. Several waves of migration passed over the territory of Bratislava during the **migration period** of the 4th to 6th centuries. The new inhabitants of the Central European region were not able to continue the Roman cultural and social traditions. Chaos and violence replaced them. Ostrogoths, Vandals, Huns, Longobards, Alamans and other tribes rode over the country. The first Slavs came to the territory of Bratislava by the end of the migration period.

The beginnings of settlement of the area by the **Slavs** are not certain. There were no Roman chroniclers to note down the facts and events. Anyone, who tries to study the pre-Great Moravian and Great Moravian periods of Bratislava's history has to rely on the meticulous work of the archaeologists. Avar tribes invaded Central Europe and influenced the history of the region for at least three centuries. The Avars gradually settled down and mixed with the original, prevailingly Slav population. In the seventh century the development reached the point when a joint Avar-**Slav state** was created and **ruled by the Frankish merchant Samo**. Historians have been long discussing the actual situation of the administrative centre of Samo's realm. The hypothesis of the archaeologist J. Eisner that Samo had his seat somewhere in south-western Slovakia is widely supported at the moment. Some historians even believe that Samo's famous city called *Wogastigburg*, which

was saved by the Slav army from the Frankish king Dagobert could have been situated somewhere near Devínska Nová Ves. Maybe it was next to the local 7th century burial ground, where the archaeologists discovered more than 600 Slav and Avar graves. The Avars left the area of Bratislava after 791 under the pressure of the Frankish army, which advanced along both banks of the Danube heading to the east. The Franks drove the Avars to the Tisa.

Agitated Europe politically calmed down in the 8th and 9th centuries. The fact that the eastern frontier of the Frankish realm united by Charles the Great stabilized amidst the territory inhabited mostly by the Slavs was especially important for Bratislava. Now it was in a boundary position. Charles´ descendants fighting between them for the crown of the successor state of the Western Roman Empire tried to conquer this territory. But they met with resistance from the Slav princes Mojmír and Pribina, who were not on particularly good terms with each other either.

When the Moravian prince defeated his rival Pribina from Nitra and drove him out of the country, he built the stable foundations of the powerful though not long existing **Empire of Great Moravia**. A large portion of the populations of this new state formation, which reached its apex in the second half of the 9th century, inhabited forts, and two of them were constructed in the territory of Bratislava. One was situated below the Devín castle rock, and the second occupied the castle hill of Bratislava. The old Slavs built a massive **fortified settlement** above the confluence of the Morava and Danube, which is connected in old historical sources with the name of prince Rastislav. It is mentioned in the **Fulda annals** in 864 under the Slavic name *Dowina*, an Old Slavic word for girl. The Frankish chronicler renders an interesting testimony about the siege of Rastislav´s castle at Devín by the Frankish king Louis the German. Judging by the oldest of the graves next to the church of the Bratislava fort, this second Great Moravian settlement originated presumably by the end of Mojmír´s or the beginning of Rastislav´s reign. In 863 the Thessalonikan brothers Constantine (Cyril) and Methodius, the ambassadors of the Byzantine Emperor Michal III crossed the territory of Bratislava. Their suite bringing Christianity and writing to the Great Moravian Empire had to avoid the dangerous territory of Bulgaria and use the safer Amber Road crossing Pannonia and heading towards the Bratislava fords over the Danube. Another valuable **document** related to the Great Moravian period of Bratislava **originated in Salzburg**, Austria. The famous annals of Salzburg mentioned an important battle between the Hungarians and Bavarians, which took place in 907 near Bratislava, particularly the castle called *Brezalauspurc*, owned by the local Slav aristocrat Breslav. It is the oldest known written reference to the existence of today's Bratislava.

The end of the Great Moravian Empire is still a great mystery. The Salzburg annals do not mention it at all. This is the reason why it is believed that by 907 it did not exist as a state anymore. The country ruled by continuously fighting nobles was first smothered by Hungarian tribes, which were brought to the wide plains of central Danubian lands by the tribal chieftain and founder of the oldest Hungarian royal dynasty, Arpád. How it happened, we do not know, as the chronicles do not mention the event. Great Moravia disappeared but the people stayed on Bratislava castle hill and it seems that their position was not altered too much by these mentioned political "earthquakes". The local fort was included into the settlement structure of the arising early feudal **Hungarian Kingdom**.

Arpád's direct descendant **Stephen I** elected as the first King of Hungary in 1000 was even seated at the Bratislava castle for some time. The fortified hill over

Left: Remains of church in Castle
Right: A button from the Great Moravian period
A model of old church in Devín Castle

the Danube repeatedly became a good shelter for rulers of Hungary looking for a safe haven during the bloody quarrels between the Stephen´s successors for crown of Hungary. Salomon in the 11th century and likewise, Stephen III in the 12th century fled to the castle. While dividing Hungary into **royal comitats** or counties, King Stephen also remembered the castle of Pressburg when he chose it as the seat of a *comes*, the royal official, who administered these medieval administrative units. The fact that the Slav element preserved itself also after the fall of the Great Moravian Empire is proved by the Slav names such as Lavka, Ivanka or Jaroslav on the list of the counts, who lived at the Pressburg Castle. They were probably the representatives of the domestic Slav nobility. After the invasion of Hungary by the German Emperor Henry III of in 1042 when he forced the Hungarian king Abu Samuel to give up the town of Hainburg and territories beyond the Leitha river in Austria, the castle of Pressburg was pushed into the background. As a border fort it had to resist numerous attacks against the Arpád realm undertaken by its powerful western neighbour. The raids of the Emperor Henry III continued in the years 1044, 1051, and 1052. Henry's last military adventure though, was unexpectedly solved in front of the gates of Pressburg Castle.

The oldest picture of Bratislava castle

The illustrated chronicle of Vienna from the 14th century depicts a romantic image of Pressburg castle. It represents an event, which took place about three centuries before, during the siege of the castle by the troops of the Emperor Henry III. After two months of unsuccessful siege things developed in unexpected manner. One of the defenders of the castle got unnoticed to the enemy's boats anchoring nearby and drove holes into them. The boats sank and the parties had to negotiate peace. Pope Leo IX was mediator in these negotiations. The whole story ends just like in a fairy tale, with the wedding of the Emperor's daughter to son of Andrew, the King of Hungary.

The castle of Pressburg with the settlement lying below its walls experienced also other military events in the course of the 12th and 13th centuries. Although in May 1189 its environs were thronged with troops, their arms were not aiming at the castle walls. Pressburg witnessed the gathering of the Third Crusade. The armies were drawing closer to the castle in several currents. The individual armies were commanded by the French King

Philip II August, the English King Richard the Lion Heart and German Emperor Fridrich. The smaller Hungarian detachment was under the command of the king's younger brother Gejza after German Emperor's intervention released from prison for the occasion. The Emperor himself, nicknamed Barbarossa for his red beard, became the leader of the joint army, which started the journey after long preparations and waiting. But he never arrived in the Holy Land. He was drowned while he was bathing in some Asian mountain river.

The castle of historic Bratislava or Pressburg has seen various coronation ceremonies and royal engagements. The castle lodgers were present when the King **Přemysl Otakar II** of Bohemia married Kunhuta, the granddaughter of the King Belo IV of Hungary on 25th October 1265.

Left: King Henry III bellow Pressburg Castle
Right: Coronation festival
The mediaval sketch of Castle

Five years later the feared Czech ruler "paid back" Pressburg its hospitality by conquering the castle and burning down the townlet around it. Hungary breathed with relief only after Přemysl Otakar II died on the Marchfeld on 26th August 1278. His death on the battlefield not far from Pressburg opened the way to the throne to the Habsburgs, who held the St. Stephen's crown until 1918.

Apart from the castle the medieval town around it was also important in time of the House of Arpad. At the beginning it was a small settlement, but it quickly grew to a little town. The main stimulus to its development was moving of Church buildings from the castle area into its environs. The first to move was the parish church in 1202, because the castle lords feared that enemy spies could hide among the believers and visitors to the Church offices and could easily penetrate to the castle premises. Then in 1221 the Pope granted permission to the provost of Pressburg to also move out the **Church of the Most Holy Saviour** in the 11th century built on the foundations of the Great Moravian basilica along with the provost's house and the seat of the chapter. When the Church left the castle hill, construction works started and the result was a well-fortified Romanesque castle. With the removal of churches a group of priests and church clerks including their servants came to live in the settlement below the castle. The clergy mostly settled around the Romanesque church then under construction on Kapitulská street, which is also today the home of priests and theology students. The settlement was expanding and progressively changing into a market town. The oldest preserved written reference to the market place is from 1151, but trade probably existed there even before. If not, how could the abbot of a Benedictine monastery collect one third of the Pressburg's toll in 1002. Thriving **centre of trade and crafts** under the castle of Pressburg was quickly expanding to the east. German "guests", the colonists invited in by King Belo IV after the Tartar invasion needed new houses. The population number was also increasing thanks to the Jews and monks. Bad experience from the time of the devastating raids of the Asian warriors taught the inhabitants of Pressburg a lesson. More efficient defence against the enemy was needed. On one side the castle strengthened its fortifications and on the other the town itself realized that it needed protection. Its walls were probably palisades. Fortifications were not either perfect or complete, because rich burghers cared individually for their protection, building of what were called tower houses.

Kapitulská street and the contiguous Zámocká street leading to the castle represented the centre of the town. The Germans and other immigrants built their houses along the old trade roads heading to the ford next to Vodná veža tower, laying foundations of today's Ventúrska and Panská streets. The Franciscan and Cistercian monasteries and the Jewish quarter were outside the fortified town. In the 13th century the hospice of St. Anton was added to them. In front of the eastern town walls a big space was formed occupied by several Romanesque yards and houses with towers. The entire town was subject to the castle until 1291 and the royal clerk or *comes* did not live at the castle from 1267. From 1267, the *comes* (governor of the county) in Pressburg Castle was not appointed by the king. As a result of the increasing power of the aristocrats, he was elected by the aristocracy.

The lost Romanesque Pressburg

None of the buildings from the Romanesque period of Pressburg, comparable to the rotunda of St. Juraj in the town of Skalica or the old church at Kostoľany pod Tribečom, has survived. Seven centuries of repeated adjustments and reconstruction, which were incessantly changing the architectural face of the town, completely wiped away its oldest Romanesque appearance. Every fashionable building style, which arrived in Pressburg with more or less delay after passing through Vienna, has destroyed something from the older and obsolete ones. This is why we have negligible and usually well-hidden fragments of Romanesque buildings from the 12th and 13th centuries. These include the remains of several stone buildings around Kapitulská and Ventúrska streets, parts of the southern facade of St. Martin's Minster and the staircase window in a

house on Panská street. We should not forget the Romanesque Vodná veža tower built on foundations of an older building, which as a military structure was not built in a too decorative manner. The elements of Late Romanesque architecture are hidden also under the facade of what was originally a tower house from the 13th century standing at the corner of Hlavné námestie square and Radničná street. The find of the remains of St. Jakub´s Chapel in front of Stará Tržnica in the SNP square contributes to our imaginations of Romanesque architecture. The lapidary of the Town Museum contains sandstone capitals from a now disappeared house of the lost Romanesque Pressburg.

The date of **December 2nd 1291** is not the date of birth of Pressburg. One should take it rather as the date of its school leaving certificate, which confirms the aptness of its inhabitants to become the free citizens of a royal borough. The last king of the Arpad dynasty **Andrew II** granted the town several **privileges** usual for the Hungarian towns directly ruled by the king. Royal clerks ran Pressburg in the same way as other Hungarian towns. Some groups of population, above all the **German "guests"**, enjoyed special personal privileges even before 1291. The domestic inhabitants were unprivileged subjects. All burghers got their privileges from King Andrew. The town had its own administration and judicial system. They elected their **mayor** and twelve counsellors every year on April 24th (St. George's day). They were entitled to administer the municipal matters, to judge the accused and solve arguments with foreigners. Only the mayor could judge the citizens of the town. The royal privileges also regulated the relation of nobility to the town, only the Church preserved its autonomy and the provost decided all its matters. Another important group of privileges provided for the economic development of the town. It concerned **trade and the crafts**. The citizens were entitled to free use of the port and ford on the Malý Dunaj river near Vrakuňa, the ford over the Morava river, etc. Sale of wine was facilitated by exemption from the fees for vineyards, both existing and ones, which would be created in future. Another municipal privilege worth mentioning concerned the defence of the town. Only the royal boroughs were allowed to have **municipal fortifications**, while the king himself approved their construction. Pressburg obtained this privilege in 1297. The principle was to fortify the smallest possible area, as it was easier to defend. This has slowed down the development of the town a lot, since the town had to squeeze into the limited space for safety reasons. Further constructions made use of material from the demolished suburb Széplak (today Obchodná street). The church of St. Andrew, which used to stand near Laurinská brána gate also had to be pulled down. Four gates served as entrances to the

Left: The Zámocké schody stairs
Right: Historic centre of the city

town. The only gate preserved up to the present time is Michalská brána. Bastions played an important role in the defence. Also the river Danube with its four arms flowing under the town walls on the southern side contributed to the passive defence. A water filled moat was a part of the defensive system.

The town walls of Pressburg restricted a comparatively small medieval town. Between the 14th and 16th centuries inside the fortifications a **Gothic town** had developed, from which much more had survived than from its Romanesque predecessor, more than only fragments covered by younger facades. It includes complete architectural gems such as the burial chapel of St. John next to the Franciscan church and some old Gothic burgher houses.

What was the Gothic Pressburg like?

The ground plan of the Gothic town under Pressburg Castle was irregular, but very roughly triangular. Such shape can be found on the oldest ground plan representation of the town included in the Gothic plan of Vienna from 1438-1455. The street pattern of Pressburg was fork-shaped and it traced the old trade roads. The original spindle-shaped square of the Romanesque settlement was reduced to two smaller central squares in the 14th century. An irregular Františkánske námestie square was formed in front of the Franciscan church and it communicated with the almost square-shaped Hlavné námestie. They were especially used by merchants. When the area became too small, the market transactions and stands spread to the contiguous streets, gates and even suburbs. At the inner municipal market place, normally the square of Hlavné námestie, only selected assortment of goods was sold. Cattle, timber and grain were sold outside of the town walls. Apart from the main street and squares there were circular streets running around the square. At the very edge the lanes facilitated access to any part of the town walls (for instance, the streets of Baštová or Zámočnícka). First

there were no buildings there. The people generally avoided the narrow lane running between the town walls and fences of the gardens. It was used only in time of siege. Transverse streets connected the square with circular streets or they led out to the bastions of the fortifications (Klobučnícka or Zelená streets). The basic spatial unit was the house plot. In the Romanesque period the churches were built on top of hills or even outside the settlements. The Gothic churches in turn were built in the municipal centres.

When medieval Pressburg obtained the privileges of a free royal borough in 1291 practically nothing prevented it from development especially with the **forthcoming century of peace**. After the war years of 1302-1304 when the inhabitants of the town had to put up with fights for the throne of Hungry between Matúš Čák and the followers of Charles Robert of Anjou, a period of peace came, which ended only with the Hussite Graceful Rides. The crafts and trade throve and tense relations with neighbouring Vienna did not affect too much the atmosphere of prosperity. Likewise, the creation of what was called the Czech road which avoided Pressburg thus depriving it of many traders, who travelled between the Kingdom of Bohemia and the lower Hungarian provinces did not have a negative impact either.

A special and above-standard relation originated between Pressburg and the **King Sigismund of Luxembourg** who ascended to the throne in 1387 and reigned for fifty years, longer than any other Hungarian ruler. Too many obligations and shortage of finances had the result that King Sigismund, who was also elected the Holy Roman Emperor by the end of his life, had to delegate many of his duties and pawn towns or entire counties. This was how the county of Pressburg along with another two counties came into the hands of counts Jošt and Prokop from Margraviate of Moravia, who lent their cousin Sigismund two thousand florins. This pawn did not last as long as the one of the Spiš towns lent to the Polish crown. They were not returned until the mid-18th century. It was returned to the King of Hungary after four years. The causes of Sigismund´s financial troubles included the high expenditure of the royal court and an acute need of to strengthen the defence capacities of the country. There were two dangers threatening Hungary. The Turks were constantly in the south, but Sigismund concentrated more on the enemy coming from the north-west. They were the Czech Hussites. The ruler headed the anti-Hussite forces and sent a punitive expedition to Bohemia in 1420. But when the Czech warriors won over his troops, Sigismund started to prepare for further fights. The role of main pillar of the country's defence had to be played precisely by Pressburg. The special inter-

Left: The tower of St. Clara church
Right: Bridge of St. Michael
Gothic windows of the Old Town Hall

est of the ruler in this town grew. He progressively granted it various privileges. The first of them, awarded in 1402, was very important for the economic life of the town. It was the **right of storage** often attributed such importance that the towns carried on years of armed conflict to obtain it. In 1430 Pressburg received another privilege, the **right to strike coins** in its own mint. The prestige of the town grew with the granting of a coat of arms in 1436. The **municipal coat of arms of Pressburg** (used until today) was taken over from the burgher seal *Sigillum civium de Posonium* depicting three towers. The

seal was used for sealing official acts from the first half of the 13th century.

Sigismund dedicated special attention to the castle of Pressburg. It also had to be prepared for the attack of Hussites. It was properly fortified but also made more comfortable. The result of Sigismund´s reconstruction thanks to numerous adjustments was an impressive **Gothic palace** respectable enough to become the home of the German Emperor. The ruler also supported an extensive Gothic reconstruction of **St. Martin's Minster**.

The quarters beyond the town walls were quickly expanding but they often had to be demolished. They were pulled down either by the burghers themselves in an effort not to provide shelter to enemy or they were demolished by conquerors. The people from the suburbs sought protection within the town walls. However, Pressburg's suburbs were expanding in spite of the disadvantages. Around the outer walls new market places sprang, such as today's squares of Župné námestie, or Námestie SNP, Rybné, and

Hviezdoslavovo. The ground plan of the suburbs was determined by the trade roads, which departed from the centre of historic Bratislava in fan-like manner. The packed inner town could not take in more people living in the suburbs and that was why the town started to build **outer fortifications** in Sigismund's time. The overall defence of the town was strengthened by the construction of a massive earthwork protecting the suburbs. The outer side of this rampart was fixed by a stone wall and palisades heightened its upper part. Small earth forts were constructed on the Danube islands in the southern suburb. There were five gates in the ring of outer fortifications. Kozia brána gate was the entry from the vineyards and the road heading to Moravia entered the town through the gate at Suché mýto. At the upper end of the former Széplak settlement was the Schöndorfská brána gate and the more southerly Špitálska brána. The fifth gate was built near the Danube arm approximately in the place of today's Dunajská street. More squares, for instance, Hodžovo and Kollárovo originated within the fortifications next to the gates. The outer walls were partially restored in 1670, but they mostly disappeared along with the inner walls during the rule of Maria Theresia.

The expected **Hussite graceful rides** finally arrived at Pressburg. They drew closer to the town for the first time in 1427 when the standard with the Chalice flapped over the Austrian town of Marcheg. Sigismund was at Pressburg castle and immediately hurried the strengthening of the municipal and castle's fortifications. The next year the Hussite troops led by Prokop Holý crossed the Little Carpathians and reached Pressburg. In February the townlet under the castle did not resist their attack and was burnt down as were some of the suburbs. In spite of good fortifications Sigismund

Left: The coat of arms document
Right: The armour-bearers
The western town walls

preferred to negotiate. However, after eleven days of negotiations no agreement was reached. The Hussites well-aware of their force did not agree with the king's peace proposals also because of the offensive tone of the proud ruler. Summer negotiations were not successful either. In the meantime Hussites conquered several towns in Hungary including Skalica and Trnava. It was very probable that Pressburg´s fate would be similar. But an unexpected and lucky betrayal of a plot prepared by the burghers who sympathized with the Hussites saved the town from conquest (→ 106).

After the battle at Lipany in 1434 the political situation still did not calm down. When the King Sigismund of Luxembourg died the Hungarian nobility favoured Albrecht of Hapsburg in the argument over the empty throne. Abrecht, like his predecessor, dedicated attention to historic Bratislava. He had a bridge over the Danube constructed (it lasted until 1445) and the town was granted the **privilege of toll for the goods transported over the river**. The fights for the crown revived after his death. Albrecht´s widow Elizabeth, who was trying to win the crown for their under-aged son **Ladislav the Posthumous** chose Pressburg for her residence because of its proximity to Vienna. The burghers offered her the town as residence and declared support for her interests in exchange for her promise to repair the town walls and expand the mint. The queen settled in the royal curia. In spite of the assistance provided by a Bratrik army (Bratriks were independent military units, often of Hussite origin) she was not successful and **Vladislav Jagelonsky** supported by the Transylvanian magnate Ján Hunyady became king. The conflict did not divide only the country, but also the town of Pressburg. Pressburg was drawn into a small civil war in 1440. The burghers supported Queen Elizabeth and the castle was supporting Vladislav. The castle garrison led by the powerful family of Rozgoň refused to hand over the castle to Elisabeth. Fire was opened. The cannons fired against the town and its defenders responded. The siege of the castle lasted two years. In 1442 the army of King Vladislav came to Pressburg and captured it. Elisabeth fled to Austria and ended up at the court of Emperor Fridrich. The Emperor attacked Vladislav and compelled him to retreat as far as Trnava. Pressburg and its castle remained divided. The town was in hands of queen's followers and the castle belonged to Jagelonsky. The castle garrison surrendered only after King Vladislav was killed in Varna in a battle against the Turks. Ladislav the Posthumous, later King Ladislav V never really

ruled Hungary. It was rather Ján Hunyady, who rewarded Pressburg for its constancy and entrusted it with the administration of taxes and a salt trade monopoly. He also granted it a series of important privileges in 1453 and approved the construction of a new bridge over the Danube. Ladislav´s uncle, the Emperor Fridrich permitted the merchants of Pressburg to trade freely all over Austria.

Ladislav's successor was Hunyady's son **Matthias Corvinus**. Traditional sympathy of the Hungarian sovereigns to Pressburg also continued during his thirty-year reign. Ceremonious confirmation of the privileged position of the town by **The Golden bull of King Matthias** in 1464 and the addition of a new **privilege**, that of **the sword**, in 1468 manifested it. The name of King Matthias is connected with the penetration of humanistic ideas into Central Europe. The king's second wife Beatrix of Naples was an enthusiastic fan of humanism and the Renaissance. The arrival of this Neapolitan princess in Buda was accompanied by that of numerous scholars who later inspired the king on numerous occasions. The result of one such inspiration was the opening of university, which followed the example of the oldest university at Bologna. Pressburg was chosen for the seat of this university and its name was **Universitas Istropolitana** (often and incorrectly referred to as Academia Istropolitana). In spite of its short duration, Pressburg became known in the cultural Europe of that time. The Renaissance as an artistic expression of humanistic ideas arrived in Pressburg with considerable delay many years after the king's death.

Arrival of the Renaissance in Pressburg

Humanism, which spread in Hungary during the reign of king Matthias Corvinus created favourable atmosphere for adoption of Renaissance. It arrived at Pressburg via Austria considerably influenced by the Late Gothic thinking and feelings. In architecture the best example of this style is the

southern porch of St. Martin's Minster from 1510, which is the oldest example of the beginnings of the Renaissance style in Slovakia. The Renaissance style fully unfolded only in the reconstruction of Pressburg Castle initiated by Ferdinand I Habsburg in the mid-16th century. The Renaissance left Pressburg with the same sluggishness, and the straight lines of Late Renaissance buildings prevailed in the town even in the mid-17th century, when the rest of Europe was captivated by the curves of Baroque.

During the reign of the two Jagelonian kings (1490-1526) Pressburg again became the place of important negotiations and meetings of statesmen. In 1491 it was on occasion of signature of the **treaty** between King Vladislav II of Hungary and the German Emperor Maximilian I, which would bring then unforeseen consequences for Hungary. In accordance with

Left: The Old Town Hall
Right: A house on Michalská street

this treaty, the Hungarian crown would be given to the Habsburg family if the Jagelonian dynasty died out. The succession derived from a family relationship between the two houses. In less than a half of century the subject of the Pressburg treaty became topical. Young king Louis died on the battlefield in 1526 and left no successors. The sovereign house from the Swiss castle of Habsburg applied its right.

Another important treaty was signed in Pressburg in 1499. It concerned the western neighbour, the Kingdom of Bohemia. A **congress of the Czech estates was called to Pressburg** where they agreed on various political resolutions concerning the Kingdom of Bohemia. During the congress fire broke out in the inner town and destroyed many houses.

The defeat of combined Hungarian forces at the **battle of Mohács** in 1526 was disastrous for the country. The army of the Ottoman Sultan Süleyman II first deprived the country of its king and then of its freedom. But Pressburg paradoxically benefited from the situation. Two weeks after the national tragedy, which the battle of Mohács certainly was, the Turks occupied Buda, and Hungary had to look for another city to serve as the seat of the royal offices. It was easy to decide. Pressburg with its Golden Bull of King Matthias was practically the only one able to assume the role of capital of the heavily stricken state. Pressburg at the beginning of the 16th century was a comparatively prosperous Hungarian town situated near Vienna and still saved from any massive Turkish attacks. The next priority was the problem of vacant throne. The devastated country urgently needed a new ruler and there were two to choose from. Finally, the Transylvanian Duke Ján Zápoľský was crowned in November 1526 in the town of Székesfehérvar. In the meantime, the Habsburgs remembered the old Pressburg treaty from 1491 about succession rights and summoned their supporters to the **congress of the Hungarian estates in**

Left: Pressburg in the 16th century
Right: Statue of Maxmilian II.

Pressburg. The estates elected the Austrian Archduke Ferdinand of Habsburg as their king on December 17th, 1526. He too, was crowned in Székesfehérvar by the Bishop Štefan Podmanický of Nitra. After the period of anarchy the country had all of a sudden two rulers. The situation lasted until Zápoľský's death in 1540. Pressburg became the centre of events again and it was the place, where the European history was written, as its favourite Ferdinand eventually won the race for the crown. The town witnessed the beginnings of one of the most powerful royal houses in Europe, which showed its crowned rivals what absolutism was about. Ferdinand of Habsburg, confirmed by repeated coronation in Székesfehérvar a year after the Pressburg congress, compensated the town for its goodwill and promoted it to the capital of Hungary by the law approved by the Hungarian Parliament in 1536. It was a temporary act. It would be in force only until the entire territory was won back from the Turks. This is how Pressburg kept its position of metropolis until the end of the 18th century. Joseph II terminated this favourable period when he moved the last Hungarian central institutions out of Pressburg in 1783. On the other hand, Pressburg became the seat of palatine, supreme judge, chancellor, the royal exchequer, and other royal officials in 1536. Shortly after also the archbishop of Esztergom, who was at the same time the **Primate** (head of the Catholic Church in Hungary), joined them as its town of Ezstergom too fell into the hands of the Turks. In the new political circumstances the frontier town found itself in the **centre of the new state** of the Austrians, Hungarians and numerous other nations. The ever more intense attacks of the Turks compelled Ferdinand to concentrate all forces and means in defence of his state. Pressburg due to its proximity to Vienna should become the most important part of this defence. It was predestined to fulfil the role of buffer against the attack of Turkish forces aimed at the seat of the Emperor's court.

The Emperor invited Italian architects to **reconstruct Pressburg Castle** built in the Gothic style by Sigismund of Luxembourg, and give it a Renaissance form. The town strengthened the municipal fortifications, and new and more massive walls replaced the old ones. Everything that might provide shelter to an enemy in the suburbs was pulled down. The space in front of the walls was cleared of buildings, churches, hospices, and even trees. The inhabitants of Pressburg prepared themselves for the forthcoming military events. And the future showed that the preparations were more than appropriate. Ferdinand's Danube fleet, built by the local shipwrights, proved to be very useful as well.

The Turks preferred to avoid Pressburg

The Turks came close to Pressburg for the first time in 1529 while marching to Vienna. Luckily for the town it was not the main stream of the army which progressed between the Alps and Leitha Mountains in

Austria. The castle garrison surprised the Turkish fleet advancing upstream the Danube with cannon fire, causing it great damage. The infantry did not get close to town at all as they were stopped by the Imperial troops. During a big campaign in 1532 Pressburg became one large military camp where the soldiers of Imperial Army and allied Christian princes concentrated. About 40 thousand soldiers came from Bohemia, Ferdinand's brother Charles V sent 25 thousand infantry soldiers and 5,000 cavalrymen. There was a military force counting about 120,000 infantry and cavalry soldiers moving in the wide environs of the town. The Turkish attack of Vienna was proceeding more southerly through today's Hungarian town of Köszeg. Vienna resisted for the second time and the Turks preferred to avoid well-fortified Pressburg.

The fall of Székesfehérvar meant that Hungary lost its traditional coronation town. This is how Pressburg won another **privilege, the one of coronation of the Hungarian kings** and their spouses. It was another, though temporary function to be kept until 1830 and used nineteen times. The first king crowned in St. Martin's Minster in Pressburg was Ferdinand's son Maximilián II on September 8th, 1563.

The first **immigrants from Croatia** fleeing from the Turks came to the Pressburg county at the time of Maximilian's reign. They settled mostly in four trans-Danubian villages and part of them came to the villages in the southern Záhorie region (Devínska Nová Ves, Záhorská Bystrica, and Dúbravka). They also founded a new village of Lamač. Others found refuge in the villages situated north-east from Pressburg around Svätý Jur and Pezinok (Rača, Vajnory, Slovenský Grob, Chorvátsky Grob, and Šenkvice) and in the communities of the neighbouring county of Mosony (Rusovce, Jarovce, and Čunovo). During the reign of Rudolf I, another king of Hungary

Left: Coronation of Maria Theresia
Right: Coronation festival

crowned in Pressburg, the Hungarian Parliament met on November 1st, 1587 and adopted an important resolution to use what was called the Gregorian calendar. It was adopted with a five year delay after Pope Gregory XIII's bull *Inter gravissima* was issued for the matter. In the second half of the 16th century, the first news about the reformed teaching of Martin Luther was brought to Pressburg by students and merchants. The **Reformation** quickly found its enthusiastic followers among the burghers. The refugees from Germany, Italy and Bohemia only helped the promotion of the idea. The brothers Michael and Baltazar Segner, who founded a respectable Protestant family in Pressburg, were also originally refugees from the persecution by the Catholic Church. (→ 51).

The years of precarious armistice signed with the Turkish Sultan by Emperor Maximilian II terminated in a fifteen year war during the reign of Rudolf I. Fortunately, it did not directly affect Pressburg. However, peace did not last and in 1605 fighting burst out again in the town. This time it was not the Turks in front of the gates but the rebels led by the Transylvanian prince **Štefan Bocskay**, the leading opponent of the Habsburgs. His soldiers plundered the environs of Pressburg, destroyed the suburbs but did not enter the town. In 1606 the Imperial troops broke up the camp in front Schöndorfská brána gate, and drove back Bocskay's troops as far as Trnava. The citizens of Pressburg could recover from the nightmare of the siege. The rebellion was definitely terminated by the signing of what is called the Vienna Peace on June 23th 1606. Among other things it fostered religious freedom and the members of Protestant churches were now allowed to practice in public. Especially the Hungarian estates adhering to the Reformation improved their position. Another anti-Habsburg rebel, **Gabriel Bethlen** was one of them. He conquered the town in 1619, while the castle was still held by the Imperial troops. However, the defenders of

castle headed by palatine Žigmund Forgáč surrendered after heavy fighting and Bethlen enjoyed a precious war booty: the royal crown deposited in the Coronation Tower. The Protestant citizens of Pressburg immediately made use of the situation and had the Parliament approve that St. Martin's Minsterl would now belong to them. It was given back to the Catholics only in 1621, when the imperial general Buquoi drove Bethlen and his people out of Pressburg.

The turbulent May of 1621

After the Battle at Biela hora, the White Mountain in November 1620, the Czech national tragedy, Emperor Ferdinand II gathered a sufficient military force to face the rebellious army of Gabriel Bethlen. The Imperial Army came to the gates of Pressburg held by the rebels in May 1621. A terrible fight for the town started and both parties were aware that it was the decisive moment for the success or failure of the rebellion. The Imperial Army led by an experienced commander count Henri Duval de Dampier first tried to destroy the log bridge over the Danube using burning boats floated down the river. Bethlen's people though, succeeded in putting them out. The battle lasted nine hours. Dampier with two hundred soldiers tried repeatedly to conquer the town walls. He was taken prisoner at the third attempt and executed. The victorious flag of the Imperials appeared above the town on May 7th, 1621. However, Bethlen was not giving up, and he tried to win the town back. He might have been successful thanks to efficient artillery, which fired from Suché

mýto, if not for the enemy's reinforcement of five thousand infantry soldiers and one thousand cavalrymen led by the general Albrecht of Waldstein. The Coronation jewels returned back to the Coronation Tower of the castle after the Mikulov peace was signed in 1622.

The ink of the signatures put under the Mikulov peace was hardly dry when the Habsburgs had to face another rebellion of the protesting Hungarian estates. Nevertheless, the Bethlen's second and third expeditions relying on assistance from the Turkish Sultan and German Protestant movement also failed. It terminated in the peace signed in Pressburg on December 20th 1626. The only and catastrophic result of the series of rebellions was devastated land and suffering of the population of severely destroyed Pressburg. Plague epidemic in November 1632 added to the overall destruction.

Left: Baštová ulica street
Right: Cardinal's hat

At the beginning the persecution related to Counter-Reformation in Pressburg was not as ruthless as, for instance, in Bohemia after the Biela hora event. The municipal council was long tolerant to the domestic and newly arrived Protestants and did not recourse to any harsh measures. The Protestants of Pressburg were even granted the permission to build two churches, and the larger one of them was constructed right next to the Town Hall. In spite of adverse times a Evangelical gymnasium or grammar school was also established in 1607. The Archbishop **Peter Pázmanyi**, who also invited Jesuits to the town to help him with the task, brought the first comparatively intense re-Catholicizing efforts to historical Bratislava. However, Pazmanyi's actions in Pressburg were still not as severe as those of the Catholic ruler, who fostered his religion with substantially more repressive means. The Archbishop rather preferred education. He contributed to establishment of the Jesuit grammar school, which was a follow-up to the Catholic grammar school founded in 1577. He also initiated construction of numerous Church buildings built in the Late Renaissance style. Catholic literature was published and printed by the printing plant in the Archbishop's palace. Another printing house of Pressburg also published the works of Protestant authors, such as the prayer book of Jan Amos Comenius under the title *Everyday Christian Prayers from the Holy Scriptures*.

Vesselényi's unsuccessful rebellion in 1667 had a sad conclusion in Pressburg. Emperor Leopold I responded to another rebellion of the Hungarian estates by depriving Hungary of many of its rights. Moreover, the majority of the privileges left belonged to the Emperor's loyal servant and despotic **governor Ján Gašpar Ampringen**. He had his seat in Pressburg Castle. Ampringen established the institute of an extraordinary court of justice in 1671, also called "the Pressburg court". This court was very similar to the courts of Spanish inquisition. All persons suspected of conspiracy were prosecuted and if convicted cruelly punished. The extraordinary court of justice convicted about two hundred noblemen to execution or many years of prison. The leaders of Vesselenyi's revolt were judged and executed in Vienna. The public was also well informed about the trial of Mikuláš Drábik a priest of the Czech Brothers (→ 108). Ampringen's repression was aimed not only against the ever-discontented Hungarian estates, but also against the Reformed Churches. The governor became the executing hand of the Emperor's effort to suppress the Reformation. He ordered the closure of the two Evangelical churches, which were later given to the Jesuits and Ursulines. The Ampringen's terror in Pressburg was terminated by **plague**, which burst out in 1677. The hated governor fled and never returned to the town.

The last act of the **Turkish wars** that took place in the area of historic Bratislava started in 1683. One could say that this was also the most dangerous one of all. The town prepared itself for the attack although it was expected that the Turkish Sultan Mehmet IV would be more interested in neighbouring Vienna. **Imrich Thököly** and his Anti-Habsburg revolt aggravated the complicated situation. Twenty thousand men soon occupied almost the whole of territory of Slovakia, and so instead of the expected Turkish troops the suburbs of Pressburg were full of Thököly's soldiers. At first Pressburg refused to follow the example of other towns, which surrendered to the rebels without fight. However, after they started to bombard the town from what is today Krížna street, the citizens preferred to open the town gates to the invading army. The castle with its garrison loyal to the Emperor did not surrender and resisted the siege. In the meantime the decisive **battle of Vienna** took place, which was saved from miserable defeat by the troops of the King Ján III Sobieski of Poland. His help offered at the last minute contributed to the famous victory of the Anti-Turk coalition

over the army of Grand Vizier Kara Mustafa on September 12th, 1683. The Imperial troops led by Charles of Lorraine were then free then to help Pressburg. The rebels supported by the Turks were chased as far as beyond the Váh river. The last episode of the series of Anti-Habsburg rebellions of estates was the revolt of the Hungarian Catholic nobleman **Francis II Rákoczi**.

It opened the calmer 18th century though it did not bring any changes on the throne. The rebels got as far as the gates of Pressburg but did not try to conquer the town. They were contented with 1,500 guldens of contribution. The period of wars and rebellions was terminated by the Szatmár peace treaty signed on April 30th 1711.

The Turkish threat, rebellions of estates and epidemics slowed down the economic development of historical Bratislava for almost the whole of the 17th century. Adverse circumstances did not allow the full Renaissance reconstruction of the town. The suburbs were the parts of town

that suffered most, because they were regularly sacked and burnt. The outer fortifications did not provide as good protection as the inner. In this time only several curias were built in the town. Rich burghers owned them. One of them belonged to the Primate of the Catholic Church in Hungary. The seat of the Royal Chamber on Michalská street and the building of Parliament on Laurinská were representative. The Evangelicals of Pressburg built several churches and Archbishop Peter Pázmány cared for the construction of Catholic churches. The first half of the tumultuous century was also characterized by the presence of **Count Mikuláš Pálffy** in Pressburg. Count Mikuláš, nominated palatine and comes (governor) of the county Pressburg for his merits in fighting against the Turks, concentrated his efforts on the **reconstruction of Pressburg Castle**, which was very damaged in time of Bethlen's revolt. An extensive reconstruction of the castle area started in 1635 and took fourteen years. Pálffy also started a grandiose summer residence at the northern foothill of the castle hill with an admirable garden. The famous Archbishop's Garden in the place where the seat of the Government is situated today was started at this time.

The 18th century can undoubtedly be describe as the best period in the long history of Pressburg, although it did not look so at the beginning. A terrible **plague** swept the town in the years 1710-1713 and caused the death of about one tenth of its population. During the reign of Charles VI the **Hungarian Governmental Council** started to function. Its opening session was held on March 21st 1724. The fact that this executive body of the inner administration was seated in Pressburg meant that the town partially maintained its metropolitan position. The session of the Hungarian Parliament held in Pressburg on June 20th 1722 was historic. It decided the destiny of the Habsburg dynasty on the Hungarian throne. The Parliament adopted a resolution called the **Pragmatic sanction** and it meant that the Habsburg House obtained succession right in the female line, as the current ruler Charles VI did not have a male heir. Later developments showed that it was a good decision as the country got a competent queen in Maria Theresia.

The period of greatest prosperity and expansion is connected with the forty-year rule of **Maria Theresia** on the Hungarian throne. Her indeed unusually positive relation to Pressburg may have originated on the day of her pompous coronation on

Left: Queen Maria Theresia
Right: The angel in St. Martin's Minster

June 25th 1741. After this she used every occasion to visit the beloved town. Thanks to the queen's favour the life of the town became more varied and refreshed by various attractive events and feasts. The ceremonial oath of 129 members of the Hungarian noble guard, which was held in Pressburg on September 27th 1760, was one of them. The men led by the commander field marshal Leopold Štefan Pálffy served as the personal guard to the queen. Maria Theresia with her balanced policy and enlightened reforms was able to reach what none of the Habsburg predecessors did. She attracted and obtained the support of the majority of Hungarian estates. Every ambitious nobleman in Hungary was longing to get as close to his queen and her court as possible. They visited her in Pressburg during her frequent stays in this town. For the sake of comfort, many aristocrats decided to own residences or fashionable **palaces in Pressburg**.

The life of the nobility of Pressburg was full of varied cultural and social events. The aristocrats invited the most important musicians of the time to the town. So it happened that the music of Mozart, Haydn or Beethoven interpreted by the composers themselves could be listened to. Pressburg also contributed to the artistic enthusiasm that seized Europe in the 18th century. The town was the native place of important composer **Johann Nepomuk Hummel** (1779-1837). The queen also wanted to make her stays in Pressburg more pleasant and decided to **reconstruct the castle**. The Renaissance palace of Pálffy was adjusted and the style adapted to the most recent trends of fashion. New buildings in castle area and a big Baroque garden of French type were added to it. The castle almost entirely lost is defensive function and its residential and prestige functions were emphasised. In 1766 a Rococo palace called the **Theresianum** next to the eastern wing of the castle was constructed for the governor. This important office was given to **Prince Albert**, the queen's son-in-low, and spouse of her daughter

Christina, which has added glamour and social prestige to the town.

Maria Theresia's wars with Prussia luckily did not affect Pressburg at all. A long period of peace similar to that in the 14th century was repeated. All areas of human activity throve in such a favourable: Trade, crafts, learning, education, arts, and spiritual life. The spirit of **enlightenment and tolerance** entered Pressburg. Number of its population increased more than three-fold. The town sheltered 33 thousand inhabitants and it meant that Pressburg was the largest city in Hungary. Pressburg was larger than Buda, Pest or Debrecen. The town was expanding and new suburbs were originating outside the inner walls. The municipal fortifications again became the principal obstacle to the further urbanistic development of Pressburg. It was obvious that the town had to be liberated from its **restraining ring of the town walls**. Maria Theresia had the inner walls pulled down and entrusted the builder F. A. Hillebrandt with the preparation of the plan, which would

link the inner town with its suburbs. It also meant filling the moat to obtain space for construction of new outer squares. The *Promenade* (today's Hviezdoslavovo námestie square) fulfilled the function of the main square and became the place, where all social and cultural life concentrated. The Estates Theatre was built in the middle of the new square with a promenade and rows of trees in front of it. It became a favourite place for walks. Increased interest in nature stimulated foundation of the Sternallee, the oldest public park in Europe in today's Petržalka. In 1801 the private Palffy's garden was opened to the public. In an effort to make local transport more efficient the outer town walls were also pulled down. Incoming traders were passing through newly established toll stations at the transition point called the *Šance*. The stations were an important element of the new urbanization at the dawning of the industrial era.

Left: Gate of Mirbach Palace
Right: Grassalkovich Palace

The new city of Pressburg

What is called now Nové mesto or the New Town spread on a plain east from the Old Town already in the 1770's. It consisted of several suburbs, the total area of which amounted to about two square kilometres. In the east it bordered on today's crossroads of Špitálska and Lazaretská streets. A little bit further south it reached Ondrejský cintorín cemetery and the Hungarian grammar school in Dunajská street. The forked bed of the Danube restricted expansion of the town to the south. Today's Bratislava on the other bank of the Danube did not exist then and apart from the above mentioned park it remained for long a wild landscape of alluvial forests, gardens, and fields. West of the city were the villages of Schlossberg, Vydrica, and Zuckermandel, which were administered by the castle. The settlement under the castle was still an independent administrative unit. The hills in the north were covered by vineyards and scattered little houses and wine cellars. Beyond the outer town walls there stood the village of Blumental with its own church and numerous farms along the roads heading to the gates of the city. Pressburg's nobility continued building summer residences with wonderful gardens. In front of the Archbishop's palace rows of trees were planted on a large area, which later delimited the area called Fursten Allee (colloquially Firšnál) or the future Námestie slobody, Freedom Square.

Son of Maria Theresia, Emperor **Joseph II** was much less interested in Pressburg than his mother. The governor Albert left Pressburg for Brussels and afterwards also the Hungarian coronation jewels were moved to Vienna and deposited as useless antiquities. As the Emperor refused the Hungarian royal crown he won the nickname of "the hatted king". The departure of Prince Albert and removal of the royal insignia were the prelude to further decay of Pressburg Castle in 1811, which culminated in fire. But before that its buildings were used as military barracks and even a school.

Joseph II finished the religious reforms started by Charles VI by his famous **Toleration Patent** in 1781. This gave origin to a mighty Evangelical community settled around today's Panenská street. When the despotic governor Ampringen deprived the Evangelical of their churches they had to construct new ones and they did so in their quarter adding to them **Evangelical Lyceé**, which was to become one of the principal centres of learning in Hungary. Names of personalities such as the historian and geographer Matej Bel (1684-1749), the cartographer and mathematician Samuel Mikovíni (1686-1750), and the physicist and physician Ján Andrej Segner (1704-1777) are linked to the Lyceé. To the scholarly Evangelical elite living in the city we have to add the Catholic Johann Wolfgang Kempelen (1743-1804), a famous inventor and architect.

In the period of enlightenment the national consciousness of the Slovak part of population also started to awaken. The Evangelical community joined the process in the first half of the 19th century as manifested by the whole generation around Ľudovít Štúr. The group around this key personality continued in the work done before by the followers of the enlightenment movement, which in turn was in Catholic circles of the **General Seminar** at the castle of Pressburg. The leading personalities were the Cardinal and Primate of Hungary Alexander Ruddnay (1760-1831), Anton Bernolák, author of the first codification of the Slovak language and of its first book of grammar (1762-1813), Jozef Ignác Bajza, the author of the first Slovak novel, and the writer Juraj Fándly (1750-1811).

The political position of Pressburg weakened during the reign of Joseph II although the city still had good conditions for economic growth. It was not the capital anymore but it thrived due to its advantageous geographical position and emancipated population. The **first factories** appeared in the last quarter of the 18th century. In 1728 Viliam Berger founded a small plant producing the steel char-

acters for printing. Hundreds of Pressburg women and children made yarn in their homes for a big factory in the village of Čeklis (today Bernolákovo). Businessmen Wachtler and Hiberger owned it. The first genuine factory situated in the town was a wool cloth producing plant of Ernest Strasser in operation from 1764. Small factories producing pencils, mirrors, gloves, aluminium foil, and spirits followed it. By the way, the famous inventor Johann Wolfgang Kempelen was also a businessman and in 1760 he started a small plant producing wool cloth in Pressburg. Other more or less famous personalities who were involved in industrial sphere of the city included, for instance, Count Leopold de Pauli, owner of a palace on Ventúrska street, who founded a saltpetre plant. The first machines used in production of yarn were introduced in the factory of count Rubini von Walterstein, when 50 spinning and 6 combing machines operated by as many as 200 workers in 1780's were installed. An enormous asset of the starting industrial activities in the city was the proximity of the Danube. The products were comparatively easily **shipped to foreign markets**, namely those of Vienna and Germany, but also to the Balkans or the East. The trade of river navigation was one of the traditional occupations of the local population and typical for people from the settlement under the castle. The best-selling article was the famous wine of Pressburg.

The economic growth of Pressburg was slowed down by the **Napoleonic Wars** at the beginning of the 19th century. French troops came close to Pressburg twice. The first time was in 1805, when they easily took the town. A squad of thirty cavalrymen occupied the shuttle bridge over the Danube and opened the way to three hundred cavalrymen and 9,000 infantry soldiers. Shortly after the Battle of Austerlitz (today Slavkov) took place. The peace treaty that entered history as the Peace of Pressburg confirmed Napoleon's famous victory. The documents were signed on December 26th 1805 in the Hall of Mirrors of the Primatial Palace (→ 112). The treaty brought about great losses of territory for the defeated kingdom. Moreover, Francis II lost his title of German Emperor. Formally it also meant the end of the thousand year old Holy Roman Empire of the German nation.

The inhabitants of Pressburg had to face the French army again in 1809. This time it was not so simple for the French to enter the city. They ran into tough resistance, and they did not really conquer the city. The artillery firing from the other bank of the Danube caused damage equalling to one million guldens. Enemy soldiers entered the city only after the conclusion of armistice. Some have it that Napoleon Bonaparte himself among them.

In the first half of the 19th century the second generation of emancipated Slovak intellectuals became active. The beginnings of their public life are linked with

Left: Statue of a Frenchman
Right: Janko Kráľ, the poet of Štúr's circle

the **Evangelical Lycée** then situated in what is now Konventná street, where a group of Slovak students and teachers expressed their revolutionary ideas concerning the Slovak nationality and its language. As it was led by **Ľudovít Štúr** (1815-1856), the generation was called *štúrovci*.

Ľudovít Štúr and Pressburg

By departure of Bernolák and his followers to Trnava the Slovak emancipation movement in Pressburg became inactive. The students and teachers of the Pressburg Evangelical Lycée restored it. Štúr entered the college at the age of fourteen and was strongly attracted by the ideas of the classic Slovak poet Ján Kollár, who was an ardent advocate of Slavic solidarity. Nevertheless, Štúr later, and contradicting his great idol, arrived at the conclusion that the Slovaks needed a language of their own as the basic and indispensable attribute of a modern European nation. During his stay in Pressburg in Štúr published his most important linguistic works Nárečia slovenskuo *(The Slovak Dialect),* Nauka reči slovenskej *(Studies in Slovak Language) in 1843. Štúr also edited the Slovenskje Národnje Novini (Slovak National Newspaper) with its literary supplement Orol Tatránski issued in Pressburg in the years 1845-1848. Pressburg printing houses also printed the first literary works written in Slovak as codified by Štúr. Last but not least we have to mention also his passionate speech which he, in the function of deputy for the town of Zvolen, presented at the memorable session of the Hungarian Parliament held on Michalská street on November 17th of 1847. Štúr pronounced the revolutionary words: "Finally, also the holy fact of being human compels us to utter once for all the principle of freedom for the people", in support of the abolition of serfdom in Hungary.*

The **1848-1849 Revolution** was very dramatic in Pressburg. In its first phase the city was the venue of passionate de-

bates in the Hungarian Parliament. Kossuth's radical Liberal Party provoked an open conflict with the Austrian Chancellor Metternich. There were Imperial troops gathering around the city as they expected the attack of rebelling peasants led by the Hungarian poet Sándor Petöfi. In its session of March 18th 1848 in Pressburg, the Parliament adopted a series of social acts that are remembered as the **March Laws**. Emperor Ferdinand V confirmed them with his signature on April 11th again in Pressburg. Immediately after the Emperor dissolved the Parliament. The following revolutionary actions moved to Budapest. In summer the **Slovak voluntary corps** joined the revolution in defence of the Emperor and the citizens of Pressburg responded by founding an association which sent the municipal guard to intervene against the Slovak volunteers. The chief commander of the Hungarian revolutionary troops Artur Görgey, who placed his headquarters in Pressburg, occupied the city as was to become the main salient point of the attack

Lefto: Danubius Factory
Right:: Suché Mýto at the beginning of the 20th century

against Vienna. However, Hungarian troops were defeated at Schwechat in Austria and the Imperial army occupied Pressburg in December and Budapest in January. The repression that followed also affected Pressburg. After the definite suppression of the revolt its followers were imprisoned in the Vodné kasárne of Pressburg and Primatial Palace was the building, where the military court of justice pronounced the sentences against the rebels. Thirteen of them were executed. By the end of May the allied army of the Tsar's Russia with its chief commander General Paskievič settled in the city and its environs. This was how Pressburg changed into a gigantic barrack for 94 thousand soldiers and 20 thousand horses in October 1849. A month later the Slovak revolt officially ended with a ceremonious military parade: 1,200 Slovak volunteers marched in front of the Austrian generals. The day after handing in the arms, the chief commander Lewartovski dissolved the corps at Pressburg Castle.

The second half of the 19th century is characterized by the onset of the **industrial revolution**. In 1830 the brothers Kissling founded the first chemical plant in the city. It produced dyes, vinegar, and starch. The Kisslings were later successful in sugar processing. A year on Vysoká street later Bavarian businessman Johan Sebastian Feitzelmayer opened the first factory producing tools and equipment used in viticulture. The Austrian gas company founded the first gas plant in Hungary in 1856 in historical Bratislava. The number of industrial plants working in the city jumped up to forty-one in the sixties. In 1869 there were 2,392 firms employing 5,293 workers. And before the end of the 19th century another 19 factories giving jobs to additional 1,700 people were founded. The biggest factories of Pressburg originated in the years 1873 to 1911. Dynamit-Nobel (1873), Stein Brewery (1873) Apolo Refinery (1895), Cvernovka (textile factory) (1900) and Gumonka (rubber factory) (1911) are worth mentioning. The first power plant in Pressburg was put into operation in 1895. The first bulb was put on eleven years later. Energy was supplied by dynamo in Ludvig's mill at today's Krížna street. Traditional viticulture was also modernized. In 1825 the company J. E. Hubert, the first large-scale producer of wine was established. It was the first one outside France, which was able to master the production of sparkling wines. The pioneer company in the area of finances was the **First Pressburg Savings Bank** opened in 1842 on Laurinská street. It was followed by several branches of the Budapest banks and in 1907 by the **Slovak Bank**.

The development of industry was accompanied by that of modern transport. The introduction of **steam engine in river navigation** in 1818 meant a revolutionary progress in the industry. Travelling to the right bank of the Danube by the **Press-**

burg "propeller" was a favourite pastime of the citizens. The following year they even could walk to the Petržalka park via the first fixed bridge over the Danube, later called after the Emperor Franz Joseph. In 1840 the **first train on the horse railway** left Pressburg for Svätý Jur. Pressburg did not lag too much behind the rest of the world in the sphere of steam engines. **The first steam locomotive** entered its railway station on August 30th 1848. The railway track of the trains going to Marcheg was later extended to Vienna, and this track is linked with the oldest railway bridge and tunnel in the former territory of Hungary. When in 1895 the **first tram** set out on a journey across the city, it meant the beginnings of the modern municipal transport. **Trolley buses** were introduced in 1911.

The calmer latter half of the 19th century favoured the development of culture and education in the town. After a long time university education was restored in 1858. The **Imperial and Royal Law Academy** moved from Trnava to Kapitulská street. The theatre building (today the Slovak National Theatre), which opened in 1888, became the pride of the Promenade. Various associations were developing; among of which the **Municipal Beauty Association** founded in 1868 carried out significant activity beneficial for the town. In the same year the still existing **Municipal Museum** was established. **Musical life** also revived and was cared for by the municipal archivist Ján Nepomuk Batka, who invited such figures of world music as Franz Liszt or Anton Grigorievich Rubinstein to Pressburg. Ernest Dohnány and Béla Bartók started their successful careers here. **The trio of excellent sculptors**, Viktor Tilgner (1844), Johann Fadrusz (1858), and Alojz Rigele (1879) were born in Pressburg.

The economic development of the city in the 19th century was accompanied by rather **chaotic urbanization**. The municipal council in an effort to gain control over the construction of suburbs entrusted the architect Haláczi with preparing a regulating plan. However, it was not ac-

complished and a new one was ready as late as 1907. Pressburg entered into the second half of the 19th century with a population of about 42 thousand, which rose to 78,000 by the First World War. This almost double population was due to in-migration intensified by the decree abolishing serfdom issued in 1848. The new inhabitants were mostly settling in the expanding suburbs of Pressburg. New quarters were springing along with new factories, which too, were constructed outside the town's core and prevailingly on the north-eastern edge of the city. Many worker colonies originated comparatively far from the official administrative border of the city. The suburbs were mostly poor and lacked the basic amenities. Urban fabric of better quality was originating around today's Štefánikova and Šancová streets. By the end of the 19th century it had progressed toward the vineyards below the hill of Slavín.

Pressburg was spared the direct impact of the **First World War**. The population suffered from the war only indirectly. Nevertheless, the war lasted longer for the citizens of Pressburg. When the arms stopped firing on all the fronts, the battle for Pressburg only began. When the Czechoslovak Republic was declared on the ruins of the Monarchy on October 28th 1918 and two days later was confirmed in Martin by the Slovak National Council, the destiny of Pressburg was unclear. Members of each of the three nationalities living in the city claimed the city for themselves. The battle for the city was going on in the framework of the Paris negotiations, but the moods in the city were no less militant. At the beginning it seemed that the Hungarian Republic established on October 31st 1918 was the going to win because the Hungarian army controlled Pressburg and its environs. Moreover, the German population also adhered to the idea. They founded jointly a National Council defending German and Hungarian interests. The Slovak population was prepared to protest and to rebel as represented by the Slovak National Council. A dramatic change came at the beginning of November when the Czechoslovak army entered Slovakia from Moravia. The Czechoslovak units consisting of experienced legionaries started to march to Pressburg on December 30th. They occupied the main railway station on New Year's Eve and the next morning they controlled the whole town. The 1st of January 1919 became the day of annexation of Bratislava to the Czechoslovak Republic. The victorious powers supporting the origin of the new states in Central Europe approved the step.

On February 2nd 1919 the Slovak Government led by Vavro Šrobár moved from Žilina to Pressburg, which became the capital of Slovakia. Pressburg lasted only for another month, because on March 6th 1919 its **name was changed to Bratislava**. The first years of Bratislava in inter-war Czechoslovakia were the ones of establishment of numerous national institutions, such as the Slovak National Theatre, Comenius University, etc. The population increased from 83,000 in 1919 to 124,000 in 1938. Bratislava remained a city of three nationalities also after the disintegration of Monarchy, only in different ratios. The share of Slovaks (and Czechs) increased from 33% in 1919 to 59% in 1938 (Czechs were represented by 17%). The share of Germans dropped in the same period from 36 to 22%, and in case of Hungarians it was from 29 to 13%. The Jewish community in the city amounted to 14,454 in 1938.

Left: The building of the Parliament of the SR
Right: The monument of Slavín

When on March 14th 1939 the independent Slovak State was declared, **Bratislava became its capital**. President Jozef Tiso had his seat in Grassalkowich's Palace. The state created under the pressure of the Nazi Germany did not last long. It practically disappeared in April 1945 with the entry of the Red Army accompanied by the Romanian troops. Bratislava was also expanding during the Second World War, when in 1943 it absorbed the village of Karlova Ves and in 1946 those of Devín, Dúbravka, Lamač, Petržalka, Prievoz, Rača, and Vajnory. The area of the city increased to 193.6 square kilometres. Bratislava's population number increased from 143,000 to 190,000. Post war Bratislava experienced development to an extent unparalleled in its history. In four decades the population of the city quadrupled. **The extreme population increase** was attributed to in-migration from the whole of Slovakia. People were coming in search of jobs and possibility to obtain flats. The post-war city was experiencing an unusual boom. But it has to be said that the development was extensive. Mass construction of housing estates started. Flats were built but the basic amenities lagged behind. In pursuit of space additional villages around Bratislava were agglomerated: Devínska Nová Ves, Záhorská Bystrica, Vrakuňa, Podunajské Biskupice, Rusovce, Jarovce, and Čunovo in 1972. This was how Greater Bratislava was created with an area of 367.5 square kilometres. In 1978 construction of flads continued on the right bank of the Danube, in Petržalka. Petržalka with its 120,000 inhabitants became in ten years the biggest housing estate in Czechoslovakia. This extensive growth stopped after the November 1989 revolution and the population stabilized for the whole following decade at about 450,000. **Bratislava became again the capital of the independent Slovak Republic** after the division of the Czech and Slovak Federal Republic on January 1st 1993.

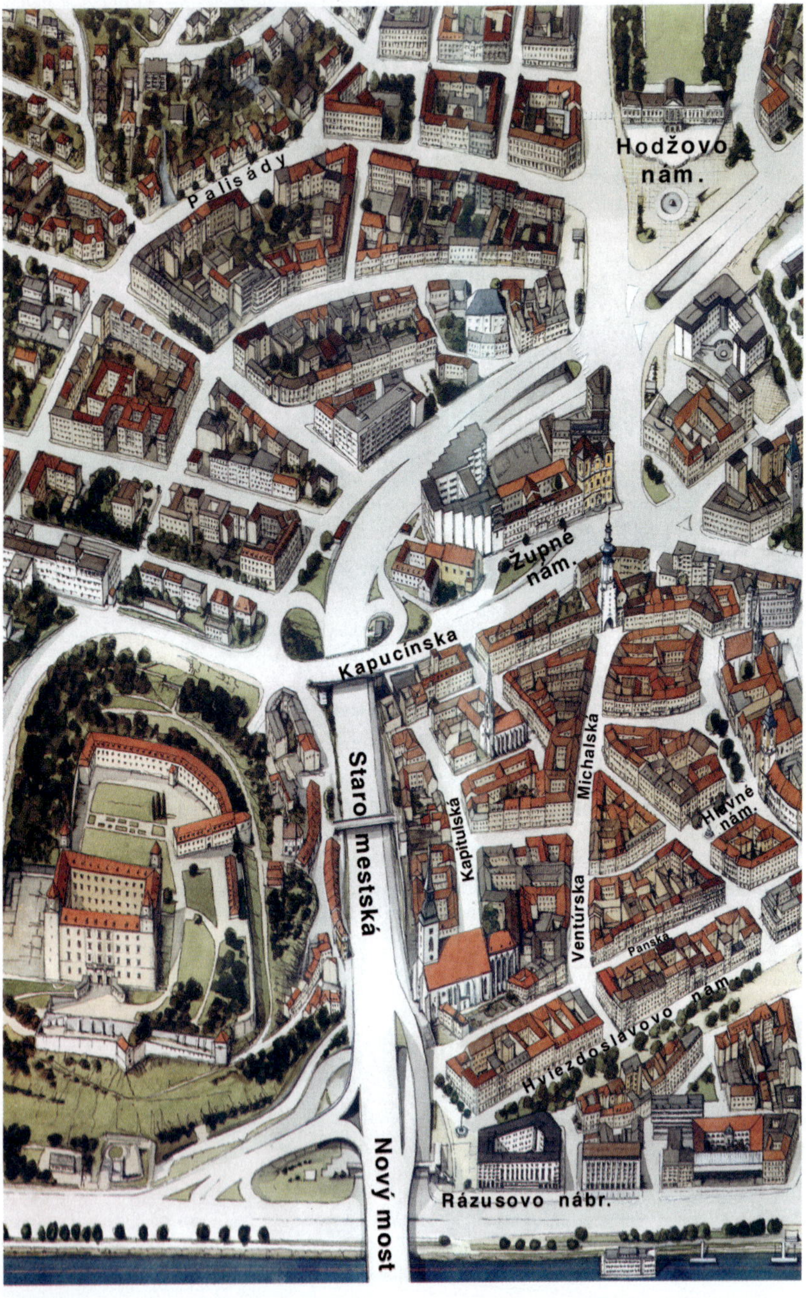
Palisády
Hodžovo nám.
Župné nám.
Kapucínska
Staromestská
Michalská
Kapitulská
Hlavné nám.
Ventúrska
Panská
Hviezdoslavovo nám.
Nový most
Rázusovo nábr.

Kollárovo nám.
Obchodná
Špitálska
Nám. SNP
Dunajská
Laurinská
Štúrova
Vajanského nábr.

The Staré Mesto

The centre of Bratislava is also referred to as the Staré Mesto or Old Town (134 m above sea level, population 46,550). It became the district of Bratislava I in 1996 and its area 9.6 square kilometres makes it the smallest one of Slovakia. It is simultaneously the most densely populated district (4,790 inhabitants per square km). The Old Town includes the historic core of the city and adjacent quarters, originally medieval suburbs. The eastern part of the Old Town is flat and covered by dense urban fabric. The western part lies on the hills with greater part of urban greenery compared to the rest of the city. The southern limit of the Old Town coincides with the channel of the Danube.

Michalská and Ventúrska streets

A walk up the Michalská and Ventúrska streets offers precious cultural and historic monuments, a pleasant break with coffee, and good shopping in luxurious shops. The route runs through the pedestrian zone in a north-south direction from Hurbanovo to Hviezdoslavovo námestie squares.

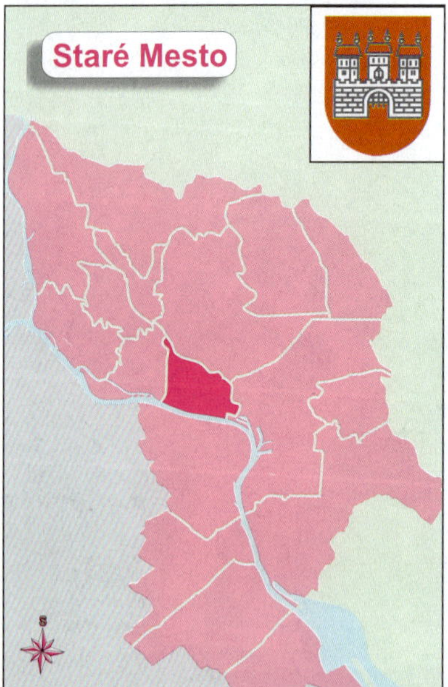

You should start at Hviezdoslavovo námestie square with a wonderful view of the slender silhouette of Michalská veža tower with its typical onion-shaped roof. The view of this traditional landmark is framed on the left by the modern building of the **Dom obuvi** (House of Shoes) colloquially called by the natives *Veľký Baťa*. The building of the first large-capacity shoe shop was built in 1930 following the design of the architect V. Krafík. It was soon found that the planned building would cover the original view of the historic parts around Michalská tower so the plan was changed and the right part of the building lowered. Opposite the shoe shop there is a functionalist building of the **Café Regina** from the 1930's. There use to be café house in the building before but the art gallery **Galéria Cypriána Majerníka** replaced it. The café was opened again in the building after many years, but only in its ground floor.

The beginning of Michalská street runs along the old stone **bridge of St. Michael** ❶ over the former water moat. It was built in the first half of the 18th century and replaced the original wooden drawbridge. The pair of statues on this oldest surviving bridge in Bratislava matches the Baroque style its environs. On the southern side there is a stone statue of St. John Nepomuk, from 1727. This Czech saint and traditional patron saint of bridges and rivers was a favourite in 18th century Hungary. Opposite on a plinth with Rococo ornaments is the statue of St. Michael the Archangel. Its presumed author is Ľudovít Gode. On the left side of the bridge the passers-by get a nice view of the rest of the former **town moat** ❷. Huge moat, which used to be 8 metres deep and 20 meters wide, must have certainly provoked the respect of any potential conqueror of the city. Originally it ran around the walls, which protected the inner town and was filled with water. The lower parts of the moat lying on a plain near the river were supplied by water directly from the Danube in a natural way. The builders of the fortifications had to solve the problem of how to get water to the long reaches of the moat in undulating terrain. They partially used a brook flowing down from the vineyards. As it dried up occasionally, water had to be pumped into a tank, which stood somewhere near the Capuchin monastery. However, experts admit that the higher situated parts of the water moat were dry the same as its short reach near Michalská veža tower today, which was known under the name Strelecká priekopa (Shooter's Moat). There used to be a theatre building of logs in the moat in the 18th century. The view of the rear sides of the houses over the moat on Zámočnícka street provides an idea of what the town walls, which surrounded medieval Pressburg for almost five centuries once looked like. Left from the Michalská veža tower the parts of the double **town walls** ❸ have been preserved. The preserved and visible part of the walls consists of higher and lower parts. The lower part was added to the original higher part in the time of Turkish wars, approximately in the mid-16th century. It stands on the foundations of older medieval fortifications. If you bend a little over the railing of the bridge at the extreme left, the half-circle of the **Prašná bašta bastion** ❹ appears. It was preserved in the back part of house No. 11 standing at the bend of Zámočnícka ulica street. It was first referred to in 1520. The

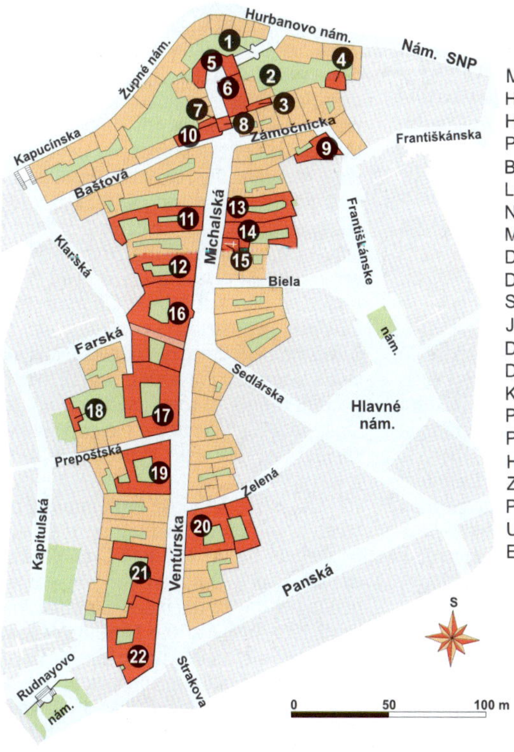

Most sv. Michala ❶
Hradbová priekopa ❷
Hradbový múr ❸
Prašná bašta ❹
Barbakán ❺
Lekáreň U červeného raka ❻
Najužší dom ❼
Michalská veža ❽
Dom na Zámočníckej 10 ❾
Dom na Baštovej 2 ❿
Segnerova kúria ⓫
Jeszenákov palác ⓬
Dom na Michalskej 14-16 ⓭
Dom na Michalskej 10 ⓮
Kaplnka sv. Kataríny ⓯
Palác Uhorskej komory ⓰
Palác Leopolda de Pauliho ⓱
Hudobný pavilón ⓲
Zichyho palác ⓳
Pálffyho palác ⓴
Univerzita Istropolitana ㉑
Erdődyho palác ㉒

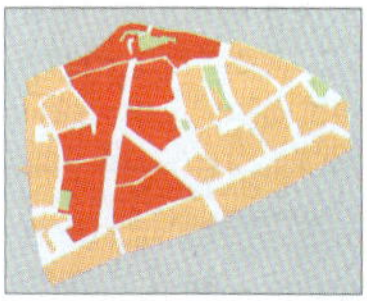

upper section of Michalská ulica passes through the preserved remains of **barbican** ❺, which protected the entry into the inner town from 15th century. The curve of the street was intentional as it prevented the direct artillery attacks on the actual Michalská brána gate.

The Do-not-fear fort and superstitions

Construction of the fortified space in front of the gate of Michalská veža tower, which became a little fort or in local dialect "polberich" *is referred to by the records in the chamber book several times. There is also a 1443 list of arms stored in the tower and its fortifications. Medieval cannon shooting stone balls and a howitzer, the biggest ever possessed by the city were intended for protection of the fort. Many a reference from that time denotes the fort by the German expression* "polberich forich dir nicht" *or "do not fear". The passage over the bridge continued with the double passage of the barbican. A more poetic interpretation of the purpose of double passage has that the narrower passage was built for the executioner, who used it to go out to suburb where he executed. More rational explanation is that the wide passage, usually very muddy, served to carriages and horsemen and the narrow one was for pedestrians, possibly also the headsman of the city. Superstitious students never use the narrow part of the passage and girls, if they use it, do not talk while walking because if they do not keep silence they will never marry.*

The Baroque house built into the barbican in the second half of the 18th century shelters the **At the Red Crab pharmacy** ❻ which contains the original furnishing of one of the oldest pharmacies in Bratislava and also the Museum of Pharmacy. Before passing under the Michalská brána gate do not forget to look at the narrow house on its right side. It is **house** ❼ with the narrowest facade in the city

Left: Michalská ulica street
Right: Bellow Michalská veža tower

(1.6 m), which documents the skills of Bratislava's medieval builders when they had to come on terms with the limited space inside the town walls. The width of this extremely narrow house corresponds to that of the moat and its peripheral walls coincide with those of the fortifications.

The **Michalská veža** ❽ tower constitutes one of the symbols of the city. It is the only one preserved out of four providing for the entry into the fortified medieval town. It provided for the passage into the town from the north, coming from the Záhorie or Moravian regions. In the night it was closed. Its name derives from the village that existed in early Middle Ages beyond the gate and around the long before demolished church of St. Michael. The tower has seven floors now. One can identify several architectural styles from Gothic to Baroque. The lowest part is the passage with a brick cross vault and five floors of a massive four-sided tower. The part from the second floor down to the ground is the oldest. It originated as a Gothic fortified gate sometime in the first half of the 14th century. The rest of the prism with another three floors was added in the first third of the 16th century when Turkish attacks were expected and the city was more thoroughly fortified. A precious **stone slab** above the northern portal with three coats of arms is linked to the period of the first reconstruction of the tower. There is the coat of arms of the old Kingdom of Hungary, the one of Bratislava and the third belongs to the royal House of Jagelonski. Kings Vladislav II and Louis II were the Jagelonians on the Hungarian throne. Some older literary sources attribute the third coat of arms to the King Sigismund from the House of Luxembourg. It is believed that the slab was originally placed above the gate of the moat. The prismoid tower has an outer gallery open to the public. In 1679 another and bigger bell was put in the tower while the older bell from 1589 was also left there. Both of them are there up till now. The purpose of the reconstruction in the Baroque style in the years 1753-1758 was to adapt it to the

new fashionable style. The **lead cartouche** in the southern portal bears an inscription expressing the gratitude of the inhabitants of Pressburg to their queen Maria Theresia for her affection. By reconstruction the tower acquired a smart high onion-shaped copper roof where a statue of Archangel Michael was also placed. It was made of copper plates by the kettle-smith Master Peter Eller in 1758. Under the tower is the **zero kilometre**, from which the distances of the individual Slovak settlements are calculated.

The clock of the dodgers

When the long expected new clock was finally put in the top of Michalská veža tower, the people of Pressburg were surprised to see that there were dials on three sides of the tower only, the fourth was missing. A legend explains why it was so. Thrifty aldermen decided that every citizen of the town should contribute to the new clock, as it was useful for everybody's comfort. All of them contributed except for the people living in the Jewish quarter,

who argued that they lived outside the town walls and hence were not the proper inhabitants of the town. They were subject to the lord of the castle and had to obey no one else. Yet they were secretly amused by the idea that they would have the clock without having to pay a penny for it. But the angry aldermen decided otherwise. They agreed that on the western part of the tower there would be no clock dial and the only thing the Jews living under the castle could see was the plain wall of the tower. Today there are four dials on the Michalská veža tower. Ján Matej Korabinský, the enlightened scholar, confirmed the authenticity of the legend in his description of the town from 1786, where he asserted that the western dial of the clock was missing.

Ascent to the gallery of Michalská tower is worthwhile as you can also see an **exhibition of historic arms** from the Town Museum deposited in the tower. The panoramic view from the top of the tower is superb. It encompasses the castle, St. Martin's Minster, the New Bridge and many old and new landmarks of the city. The view of the near Zámočnícka and Baštová streets deserves special attention. These two streets originated as narrow castle lanes in the immediate vicinity of the town walls. On the left there is **Zámočnícka ulica street**. Its name (Smith's street) reveals that there were workshops of craftsmen here in the past. The fire of 1590 destroyed its original Gothic buildings. **House No. 10** ❾ used to belong to an interesting native of Pressburg. It was **Franz Rómer**, a scientist and one of the founders of the modern Hungarian archaeology.

On the right of the tower is **Baštová ulica street.** Its name derives from the bastions, which used to be part of the defensive system north of the street. The headsman used to live in this street and that is why the name of the street before 1879 was Katova or Headsman's street. People rather avoided the street whenever possible. They feared the headsman's sword hanging on the wall opposite the door. When somebody entered the house and the sword moved without any obvious reason, it was an omen suggesting that the person would die on the scaffold. The bad fate could not be avoided even by moving out or fleeing to the forests.

At the site of the headsman's house a Classicist burgher house was built in the 18th century. In an originally Renaissance **house at No. 2** ❿ **Ján Nepomuk Batka** was born in 1845. This educated man, the municipal archivist was one of the founders of the Municipal Museum and later he donated to the Museum his personal correspondence with the personalities of Russian music – P. I. Tchaikovsky, A. G. Rubinstein, and N.R. Korsakov.

Standing at Michalská tower one gets a view of the whole of **Michalská ulica street,** which is one of the oldest in the city. Its lower part existed as early as the Romanesque period of Pressburg. Later it

Left: Upper part of Michalská street
Right: Michalská veža tower
At the Red Crab pharmacy

was widened by the addition of more houses along the road used by merchants on their way from the north to Bratislava's ford over the Danube. The builders of the inner town walls set its present length sometime in the 14th century. The modern urban fabric of Michalská street is varied in styles with preserved or restored Renaissance houses prevailing.

Let us stop first at **Segner's curia** ⓫ (house No. 7) in the western row of houses, which attracts attention with its two two-storied oriels. A well-to-do Pressburg's burgher and rich merchant with an aristocratic title, Andreas Segner had the curia built in 1648. He bought the land with an old house from the indebted Johann Gattitsch from Sopron for 3,300 guldens. The curia built for an Evangelical family is typical for the northern variation of the Renaissance style. The front of the house is lavishly ornamented with stone ornamentation. Above its **portal** the family coat of arms of the Segner family can be seen. The founders of the family were brothers Baltazár and Michal Segner who moved to Pressburg from Italian town of Rimini before 1589. They were persecuted in their homeland for their Evangelical confession. The successful and rich brothers received aristocratic tittles in 1596. They fought for the rights of the persecuted Evangelical Churches for their whole lives. It was mostly their effort that resulted in the

building of two Evangelical Churches in Pressburg by the early 17th century. Baltazar Segner was also distinguished for his merits in fighting against the Turkish invaders. Later he settled in the village of Svätý Jur, but his only son Andreas, who got rich from the wine trade, moved again to Pressburg and had another curia built on Michalská street. It is also the house where his grand-grandson **Johann Andreas Segner** (1704-1777), a scientist of European rank was born.

Johann Andreas Segner

In 1704 Johann Andreas Segner was born into a respectable family of Pressburg burgher family of Segner living at Michalská street. He studied at the Lycée of Pressburg tutored by the world famous scientist and the chancellor of the Lycée Matej Bel. Then he studied medicine, mathematics and philosophy in Debrecen and Jena. Afterwards he worked as a physician in his native Pressburg and it was also where he started experiments in physics, which initiated his creative career as famous sci-

entist. In a mill built on the river Vydrica near today's Zoo he experimented with the first prototype of the water wheel which was later named after him. Segner's wheel was a revolutionary discovery in the field of hydraulics. Segner improved the basic principle of the wheel to make a reactive water engine that was later universally used as, for instance, the driving unit of the press in an oil pressing plant in Nörten, Germany. Then Johann Andreas Segner moved from Pressburg to Germany. He practically abandoned his profession of physician and assumed employment as professor of nature sciences and mathematics in Halle, Göttingen, and Jena. His hobby was astronomy. In fact, it was more than a hobby, because one of the craters on the Moon was also named after him. He also observed an eclipse of the sun. He died at Halle in 1777.

Left: Baštová ulica street
Windows of Segner's curia
Right: The palace of the Hungarian Chamber

The Segners' owned the curia until the second half of the 18th century. Luckily the new owners did not make any major changes in the house. All the following building activities concentrated into the yard where flats and one of the Bratislava's oldest cinemas Apollo-Bio were built. The first films were projected in this cinema as early as 1908. Left of the curia is house No. 5. This shorter Renaissance building from the 16th century has a wide bay typical of the houses of the Danubian countries. It stands next to **Jeszenák Palace** ⓬ (house No. 3), built in 1730 as a city palace, the second oldest of Bratislava. Only Esterházy's palace in Kapitulská street is older. The royal counsellor Pavol Jeszenák built it in the 17th century. It is similar to Hillebrandt's palace of Daun-Kinsky in Vienna. Its pilasters are similar to those produced by the workshop of this famous Viennese architect. Two houses on the opposite side of the street were reconstructed in an attractive Renaissance style. In the yard of the **house No. 14-16** ⓭ now housing the Fisher travel agency, one can see the Late Renaissance loggias once typical of Bratislava. **House No. 10** ⓮ is also built in Renaissance style. While restoring it, some remarkable paintings from the Biedermayer period were found in its interior. It is the native house of the Baroque painter **Fridrich Oeser** (1717-1799), who became the director of the Academy of

Fine Arts in Leipzig. One of his paintings is installed in the Evangelical church on Panenská street. A comparatively modest building with simple Neo Classical facade standing on the eastern side of Michalská street hides one a pleasant surprise: the wonderful Gothic interior of the **Chapel of St. Catharine** ⓯. The charm of the remote past breathes from the white walls with tender arches. The chapel is one of the oldest surviving buildings of Bratislava. The Cistercian Francis de Columba, the chaplain of the Pope's ambassador Cardinal Gentile, built it. The chapel was consecrated in 1325. The Cistercian monastery in Heiligenkreuz in Austria owned the plot where it stands until the early 16th century. In 1522 the ownership of the chapel was passed over to the city of Pressburg. In 1676 the city preferred the Capuchins to the Ursuline order and entrusted the administration of the chapel to them.

The most magnificent building of Michalská street is at its lower end. It is **Palác Uhorskej kráľovskej dvorskej komory** ⓰ (the palace of the Hungarian Royal Court Chamber), today the University Library. The Chamber was placed in two burgher houses at Michalská street rented from the burgher Krištof Meixner in 1531. Later the Chamber occupied three additional houses. The Chamber did not have its own building for a long time, as it was believed that its stay in Bratislava would be only temporary. Paradoxically though, finally in the 18th century the new building was built in time when the whole of Hungary was liberated from the Turks, and there was no reason for the top administrative bodies to stay in Pressburg. However, it seems that the court was happy with the proximity of Pressburg to Vienna and that it was another of Maria Theresia's many brilliantly accomplished political moves. The new and smart seat of the Royal Chamber in Pressburg offered the Hungarian nobility a certain feeling of independence and formal separation of this office from Vienna. Another aspect of this move was that the Queen herself won extra affection and fidelity from the Hungarian Estates. The palace of the Royal Court Chamber was built in the years 1753-1756 as a public building with features of a city palace. It is the work of the chief architect of the building company and the architect of the Viennese imperial court Giovanni Battista Martinelli from Italy and the co-operating Austrian architect J. B. Fischer, who applied the combined Baroque Neo Classical style to this building. The street facade of the four-wing building with irregular ground plan and inner courtyard has a monumental form. Besides the Chamber, the building was the seat of various judicial bodies. This was the reason why the allegoric statues of Justice and Jurisdiction were placed on the **tympanum** made by an unknown artist presumably from the circle around the sculptor Donner. After 1780 the palace became the seat of the **Hungarian Parliament**. In its central hall the lower council of the Hungarian Parliament formed by the county deputies, free royal borough, and chap-

ters, had its sessions in the years 1802-1848. This is the place, where the manifests of the followers of the radical wing of the Hungarian nobility against the obsolete social system in the country were read and where the passionate speeches of Juraj Palkovič and Ľudovít Štúr (→ 39) concerning national and social rights were heard. This body adopted social laws, including the one on abolition of serfdom in 1848. The building was adapted to the needs of the **University Library**, its present purpose, in the years 1951-1953.

Ventúrska ulica street, continuing Michalská, bears the name of the family Ventura from Italy. Their original name was Bonaventura de Salto and the first members of this family appeared in Pressburg in the 13th century.

Ventúrska street is connected with Michalská by a short tapered section caused by close proximity of the facing houses. One of the buildings forming this bottle neck is the **Palace of Leopold de Pauli** ⓱ (house No. 13). It was built in the years 1777-1776 for the main administrator of the royal property on the former royal plot. Gothic houses probably occupied the site before this. The chamber architect F. K. Römisch, who probably followed the design of Hillebrandt, built it. De Pauli's city palace is a nice sample of the new trend in the architecture of Pressburg's city palaces applied in the last quarter of the 18th century. The fashionable Neo Classical architecture is obvious in various elements of its facade including the portal. Rococo bars adorn the courtyard with galleries. The interior of the palace was rather insensitively adapted to the University Library, which expanded here from the neighbouring building. This palace has got all that is absent in other palaces. In its interior there is a garden with a graceful Rococo **music pavilion** ⓲. Some sources assert that in 1820 **Franz Liszt** gave a concert there. The famous composer did give a concert in Pressburg at the time, but not in this pavilion. He performed inside the palace, in a lounge on the first floor.

The cult of Liszt in Pressburg

On 28 November of 1820 wonderful music spread from the Pressburg residence of Prince Michal Esterházy on Ventúrska street. The city elite was listening to the concert of the then nine year old piano virtuoso Franz Liszt. The Princess was so charmed by the miraculous child that she gave him the precious diary of Haydn. Moreover, the thrilled patrons of Pressburg offered Liszt a grant for six years of music studies. The local newspaper Pressburger Zeitung *informed about the concert in Esterházy's palace. The article written by Professor Heinrich Klein made the young artist so famous, that many European cities started to invite the little genius. Franz Liszt returned once more to Pressburg as a nineteen year old artist known all over the world. During his second stay in the town that triggered his career he de-*

Left: Michalská ulica street
Right: Gate of Pálffy Palace
Bust of Franz Liszt

veloped close contacts with the local Association of Church Music and it became the main reason for his frequent visits to Pressburg. After an especially successful concert in 1840 what is now called the cult of F. Liszt started in Pressburg. The Maestro accepted invitations from many respectable burghers, for instance, one of the director of the post office or the spiritual father of the Pressburg's musical life, Ján Nepomuk Batka. The musical event of the year 1873 was the ceremonious presentation of Liszt's Esztergom Mass at St. Martin's Minster. Franz Liszt personally directed his Coronation Mass in the same church in 1884. The acoustics of the church was tried a year before at the occasion of the first presentation of Liszt's oratorio The Legend of St. Elisabeth.

The corner of Ventúrska and Prepoštská streets is occupied by **Zichy Palace** ⓳ (house No. 11) with its smart and strictly Neo Classical facade. Its builder was F. Feline. It was built on the site of three older medieval houses as a four-wing building with inner gallery-rimmed courtyard. Count Franz Zichy had it build in 1775. The palace was restored for the purpose of ceremonies and feasts in the 1980's. **Pálffy Palace** ⓴ (No 10) which was reconstructed in 1747 stands on corner of Ventúrska and Zelená streets. The portal of its main entrance reveals something about the occupation of its first owner marshal Leopold Pálffy, commander of the Old Hungarian Noble Council. It is ornamented with military symbols. More military motifs carved into the wood of the gate do not match the mastery of the ones of the portal carved in stone. The motif of rocaille appears for the first time on the gate and stairway of the palace announcing the arrival of Rococo to Pressburg in the mid-18th century. The building now has five wings arranged so that the fifth wing separates the two internal courtyards from each other. Originally there was also a third courtyard on the site of today's Perugia Hotel on Zelená street. The tablet on the facade of Pálffy's palace facing Ventúrska street announces that it was presumably the venue of the concert of the then six year old child known by the whole world as **Wolfgang Amadeus Mozart** (1756-1791). Nevertheless, the historians say that it was not so. The young genius indeed visited Pressburg accompanied by his father in December 1762. He played compositions of his own in the palaces of other noble families.

In the agitated time of the Velvet Revolution immediately after November 1989, the headquarters of the Public against Violence, the principal political current of opposition was seated in Pálffy's palace. In the early 1990's the "men of Ventúrska street", as the revolutionaries of the PAV were called, were replaced by Mozart's compatriots. This beautiful Baroque building now shelters the Embassy of the Austrian Republic.

In two venerable looking **houses** ㉑ opposite Pálffy's palace the history of university education in Pressburg started more than 500 years ago. It includes the thirty-year lasting activity of the first humanistic university in Hungary known as the Academia Istropolitana. Today historians point to the incorrect reference to this institution as the founding act says **Universitas Istropolitana** and not Academia Istropolitana. In the first year of the King Matthias Corvinus' reign the older universities in Buda and Pécs did not exist anymore and the students of different parts of Hungary had to travel to pursue studies to Prague, Vienna or Krakow. Under the influence of the Italian humanism, the ruler decided to have a proper *alma mater* also in his country. He sent a message to Rome carried by Ján Pannonios, the Bishop of Pécs applying for permission to establish a university in his country in 1465. The Pope agreed and entrusted the foundation of the new Hungarian University to the Ján of Sredny, Archbishop of Esztergom. The University's first chancellor and spiritual father was **Juraj Schomberg**, the provost of Pressburg. After Rome consented, only an adequate seat for the university had to be found. There are a lot of doubts and confusion around the actual decision to seat the University in Pressburg. Some versions are almost legends. One of them alleges that the surprising decision of the King Matthias was caused by the death of the mayor of Pressburg, Štefan Gmaitl. As he had no progeny his property accrued to the king. Part of this heritage included two Gothic burger houses from the mid-15th century apparently suitable for educational purpose. It was decided that the university would be established in Pressburg. Preparation took two years. The Archbishop consulted the details with Leonard Huntpichler, the professor of theology at Vienna University and he also let himself be inspired by the experience of those in Bologna, Paris or Heidelberg. Universitas Istropolitana was ceremoniously opened on July 20th 1467. Lectures started in autumn of the same year. The new university with four faculties chose its teachers well, as several personalities came to lecture here. At the Faculty of Free Arts there was Martin Bylica from Poland, the Faculty of Theology such personalities as the widely recognized expert on the Old Testament, Vavrinec Koch of Krompachy or the librarian Mikuláš Schricker of Hüttendorf.

The professors also lived in Gmaitl's houses. The main building of the Univer-

Left: Ventúrska ulica street
Right: Universitas Istropolitana
Erdődy Palace

sity was presumably situated behind these two houses. Judging from accountancy records from 1491 and 1507 the University was seated in a luxurious **royal curia** standing in the middle of a garden donated by King Matthias. The detailed research of the buildings between Ventúrska and Kapitulská street confirmed that once there was a big medieval building standing on the site of today's provost's palace. If one looks at it from Kapitulská street this palace looks like single building, but if one looks from behind it is suddenly obvious that it consists of two independent buildings, later connected into one. Apparently the northern part of these attached houses was the presumed main royal curia and the building of Universitas Istropolitana. The curia was rebuilt, but not finished before the end of University's existence. The University thrived until 1471, when Archbishop Ján of Sredny fell into disgrace with the king Matthias who accused him of conspiracy and imprisoned him. The humiliated man was not able to bear the injustice and died in prison. Many indignant professors left the University, which led to its decay. As the city was supporting the institution its end was prolonged. Finally it was closed when king Matthias died in 1490. The building was then given to the Pressburg provost and the chapter. Today the Gmaitl's houses are again busy and full of students, as the Faculty of Performing Arts uses them.

Gmaitl's original houses were built in the Late Gothic style sometime in the 15th century. They were reconstructed in the Renaissance and Baroque styles. The medieval appearance of the street facade is the result of Romantic adjustments made in the course of the 19th century in the area of the former Universitas Istropolitana although the remains of older architectures were found. Research revealed foundations of an older stone house from the 12th-13th century and also proved local settlement of a Slav population in the 9th century. The lowest horizon is from the turn of the Neolithic and Bronze Ages. Remains of a ground-level stone building and a log house with a well were discovered in the yard. The well contained some remarkable objects: a couple of knives with holders made of beef bone. The lowest horizon contains the traces of people of the Volut Culture from the Neolithic.

Ventúrska street slightly widens in its lower part. The narrow triangle is very probably the remnant of an old market place from the beginnings of the medieval settlement below the castle. Its western part is occupied by **Erdődy's palace** ㉒ (house No. 1) The former private seat of the state judge Count Juraj Erdődy is the last palace built in Pressburg from the second generation of the city palaces. The local architect Matej Walch finished it in 1770. It is in the Rococo style but fully enriched by Hillebrandt's Neo Classical interpretation of architecture. It has a Rococo portal with a balcony, which looks too small in the wide facade. Originally there were two floors and in the first half of the 20th century a third floor was built on top of them.

St. Martin's Minster and Kapitulská street

The pride of every Christian city is its parish church. This is undoubtedly the case with **St. Martin's Minster** ❶, Bratislava's biggest, oldest and most spectacular church. First the Pope's approval was needed to move the provost's church dedicated to the Most Holy Saviour from the castle into the settlement below the castle Pope Innocent III approved the request of the King Emerich of Hungary. The oldest act issued by the **Pressburg chapter** says that this Church institution possessed archives, a library and a deposit room where valuable liturgical objects were kept. The oldest seal of the Pressburg provostship is from 1288.

We know nothing about the oldest form of the Romanesque **church of the Most Holy Saviour** from the 13th century. Only fragments secondarily put into the masonry of the pointed window next to the southern anteroom survived. Originally they were part of another window destroyed by the Gothic reconstruction of the Romanesque church. Indications exist that some of the fragments were originally tombstones in the disappeared cemetery which was next to the church in the settlement below the castle. The remains of a circular building found under the chapel of St. Anna near the northern wall of the church are also very old. It was most probably a Late Romanesque two-storied chapel. Its ground floor was used as an ossuary, for the remnants of skeletons from the graves, which that had to give up the ground later in favour of the bigger Gothic church.

When Pressburg became a free royal borough in 1291, the town privileges of King Andrew did not tackle the question of division of powers between the mayor, provost and the members of chapter and it was a frequent cause of arguments between the representatives of ecclesiastical and secular power. Nevertheless, the Church maintained its autonomous position. Only the 1311 act of the Pope's legate Gentilis established the formal inclusion of the Most Holy Saviour church into the free royal borough. The settlement below the castle had its own church of St. Nicolas. The Most Holy Saviour church was built in the course of the 13th century and it occupied the central position in the settlement below the castle. In the meantime, the urbanism of the town expanding to the east shifted the church to the western edge of the town. This was used by the builders of the town fortifications who included the western wall of the church into the town wall protecting the town on the side of the castle. The new Gothic tower to be used as a bastion was built in the moat.

Reconstruction, which was carried out since the 14th century under the pa-

Left: St. Martin's Minster

tronage of the ruler and the town council, was in the Gothic taste. The indulgence act of the Archbishop of Esztergom from 1318 asks the believers to contribute to construction of **St. Martin's church**. This means that the parish and its new Gothic church were given the name of the patron saint it bears now. However, some historians prefer to connect the change of patronage with the famous Pressburg's mayor Jacob II and his family. This burgher is often considered the initiator of the reconstruction of parish church, which took place in time, when Jacob's career was culminating. His brother Martin was a priest and as a canon he was also member of the chapter and an administrator of Pressburg. However, recent findings prove that the patronage of St. Martin existed even before 1204.

The builders of the Gothic church consecrated to St. Martin first built the presbytery and a new tower. The original Early Gothic **presbytery** was pulled down and replaced by another bigger one in the Late Gothic style. The original presbytery was only half as tall as the new one. Both of them slightly deflected from the central axis towards the north.

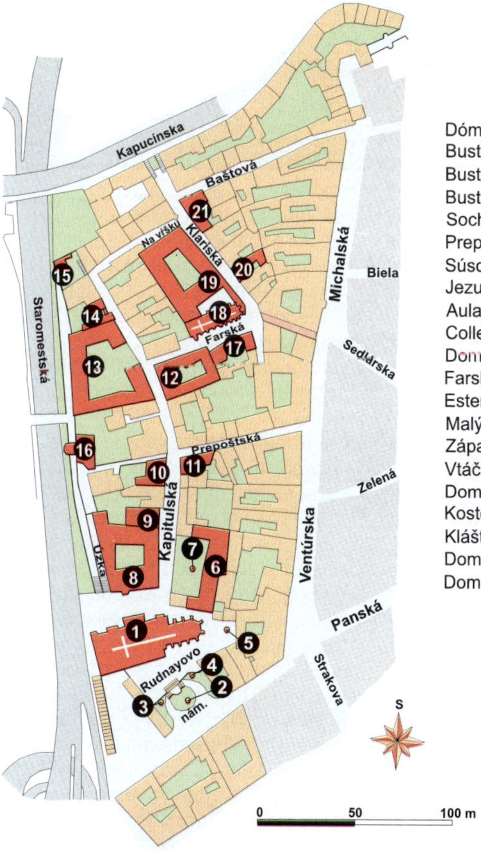

Dóm sv. Martina 1
Busta Antona Bernoláka 2
Busta Georga Rafaela Donnera 3
Busta Franza Liszta 4
Socha Jána Hollého 5
Prepoštský palác 6
Súsošie sv. Alžbety 7
Jezuitské kolégium 8
Aula 9
Collegium Emericanum 10
Dom na Kapitulskej 15 11
Farský úrad 12
Esterházyho palác 13
Malý Prepoštský dom 14
Západné mestské opevnenie 15
Vtáčia bašta 16
Dom U dežmára 17
Kostol klarisiek 18
Kláštor klarisiek 19
Dom na Klariskej 8 20
Dom na Klariskej 14 21

This almost invisible asymmetry may have been intentional to imitate the Gothic churches in southern Germany. It is explained by symbolism linked to the original patron saint of the church, the Most Holy Saviour. The nave of the church imitated Christ's body on the cross and the presbytery possibly represented the bowed head of our Saviour. A new Gothic tower replaced the older Romanesque four-sided tower. Its core can be seen in the lower part of the existing tower of the Minster approximately as tall as the roofs of the lateral chapels. The situations of the tower and presbytery determined the basic dimension of the main part of the church and delimited its length. Originally a three-aisled basilica was planned, but the builders changed their intention and united all naves at the same level of the ceiling, giving origin to what we call a **three-aisled hall church** similar to churches built in Swabia.

As usual in all big European churches, construction of **St. Martin's Minster** also took several decades. Apart from the demanding architectural intention the necessary funds were also the problem of such a huge building. The work was naturally interrupted at the time of the Hussite wars. The roof of the church was eventually made as late as 1452. The architectural design of the building reveals participation of several principal builders from the building workshop of St. Stephen's Cathedral in Vienna. There are several similar Gothic churches around Vienna. But elements influencing the development of Central European architecture such as segmented arches in the tower appeared for the first time in this building. The author of the special **Gothic ribs on the vaults** of the three-aisled hall is Hans Puschpaum. They represent the beginning of grandiose compositions of the Late Gothic vaults in many European cities. The church was ceremoniously consecrated in 1452. As it became

Left: St. Martin's Minster
Right: The relief of the Most Holy Trinity

part of the town walls, the main entrance had to be situated in the western part of the northern lateral wall of the nave and not into the western facade under the tower, as usual. Only fragments have been preserved included in the existing northern Neo Gothic portal. The portal of the entrance on the southern side was destroyed in the 19th century reconstruction. A smaller and older entrance in the middle of the northern part of the three-nave hall later became the entrance into the added chapel of St. Anna. The inner pointed portal of this entrance with preserved precious tympanum is indeed magnificent. The **tympanum** bears a remarkable **relief of the Most Holy Trinity**. This artistic works is one of the most valuable architectural details of the St. Martin's Minster. The most compact preserved architecture of the Minster is the western part with tower, the three-nave hall with an impressive net vault and the oldest chapels. In the tower the vaulted two-storied space and also two little corner towers with spindle stairway, as well as the numerous fine details such as windows, masks, gargoyles, canopies or consoles, are original. The majority of these Gothic details are in the Gothic chapels.

After 1401 two western chapels were added to the church. In the northern part of the tower is the **chapel of**

canons. It has preserved its original ribbed vault with a protruding boss. On the opposite side is a two-storied chapel of Sofia of Bavaria, which was later consecrated to St. Joseph.

The search for the lost grave of Queen Sofia

The chapel on the southern side of the tower is connected with the stay of the Queen Sofia of Bohemia of Bavarian origin, the widow of Václav IV in Pressburg. She left Bohemia because of the Hussite wars. She lived in the town under the partially imposed protection of her brother-in-law King Sigismund of Luxembourg. His interest in his brother's wife was very pragmatic and motivated by her wealth and also the possibility of her lucrative marriage with King Vladislav II of Poland. Queen Sofia came to Pressburg in 1423 and stayed until her death in 1428. During her five-year stay she cared for the construction of the chapel. However, after her death she was soon forgotten. It was King Sigismund´s fault because he had not fitted her grave with a tombstone corresponding to her position. Consequently it was never really identified. It is mentioned in several acts of the period but nobody knew where it was. At the beginning of the 16th century the existence of two empty graves on the ground floor of what is today St. Joseph's chapel was mentioned. They were actually found in the 19th century. One of them used to belong to the Pressburg provost Juraj Schomberg and the other was probably destined for Queen Sofia.

The third **chapel** is the one of **St. Anna**, which was added to the Minster in the latter half of the 15th century, and it has the similar net vault like the hall of the church. In the southern wall of the church hall with the tympanum of the Most Holy Trinity, the **southern portal** was made and due to its complicated shape it was one of the most original items of the Bratislava Gothic. Only

the pointed bow survived. The **relief of Veraicon** in the upper part of the tympanum of the southern field has been well conserved. It depicts the Christ's face print on Veronica's scarf. By the beginning of the 20th century a relief of the Mount Olives was put in the rest of the pointed bow. The final stage of the medieval construction of St. Martin's Minster was the addition of the **southern porch** in 1510. Its artistic form with rich ornamentation hints that its author was Anton Pilgram (about 1460-1515), the last great figure that took part in construction of the Cathedral of Vienna.

St. Martin's Minster was a **coronation church** in the years 1563-1830. The first ruler to be crowned here was Maximillian II. The coronation ceremony took place on September 8th 1563. It was followed by eighteen other coronations including that of Maria Theresia on June 25th 1741. The last king who received St. Stephen's royal crown below the lead statue of St. Martin was Ferdinand V on September 28th 1830. An incomplete **list of eleven kings and eight royal spouses** crowned in Pressburg's Minster is on the board placed on the inside northern wall.

The golden age of the 18th century Pressburg is reflected also in the Minster. Reconstruction started and it and gradually gave the Minster a new Baroque face. The works speeded up especially after the Minster was stricken by fire in 1760. The tower suffered most damage. Construction of the new Baroque tower was supervised by Franz Karl Römisch and designed by the chamber architect Franz Anton Hillebrandt. The new tower lasted only until 1833 when it burnt down again. The Baroque metamorphosis of the church notably affected its interior. All 16 Gothic altars were destroyed by fire. In 1732 also the legendary **Corvin's altar** bearing the coats of arms of King Matthias Corvinus and his wife Beatrix of Naples was removed as well. It was moved to Vásárút (today Trhová Hradská) where it was destroyed by fire in the 19th century. Parts of other altars went to Alistál (today Hroboňovo). The precious Madonna of Alistál from 1510 of the former Minster altar is one of the exhibits of the Museum of Christianity at Esztergom in Hungary.

Reconstruction in the Baroque taste first concentrated on the interior and later on the construction of the fourth chapel. In the years 1732-1734 the ground plan of the church was

Left: E. Esterházy's statue by Donner
Donner's Carrying of the Cross

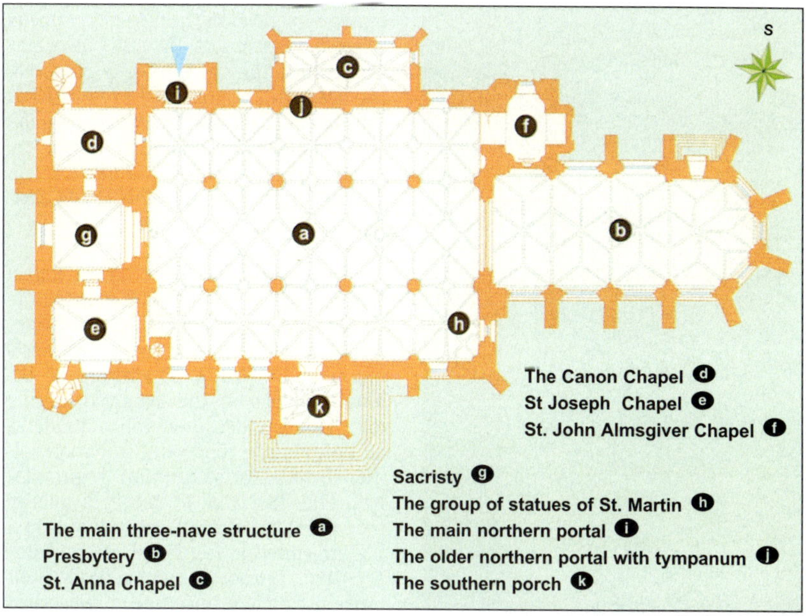

widened by thc **chapel of St. John the Almsgiver** one of the most valuable artistic monuments of Bratislava. It was built in the period when **Archbishop Emerich Esterházy** who was often called the Hungarian "Medici" for his addiction to arts and support of artists was in the office of the Hungarian Primate with the seat in Pressburg. He invested seventy thousand guldens, which was considered an extreme amount then, only in the chapel. The Baroque chapel was probably built according to the **George Raphael Donner's** design (1693-1741). This outstanding Austrian Baroque sculptor also created the interior ornamentation of the chapel. The chapel is built on the ground plan imitating the shape of Greek cross and it has two functions. It is a mausoleum for the remains of St. John the Almsgiver deposited in a coffin on an untraditional altar and its second function is that of the tomb of Emerich Esterházy situated in the crypt of the chapel. The relics of the saint were given indeed a special place in the chapel. The ceiling part of the interior ornamented in red marble is decorated with figural frescoes painted by Daniel Gran. Along with marble angels and archangels the golden and glass coffin with the relics of St. John the Almsgiver looks as if hovering in the air.

Archbishop Emerich Esterházy had his grave placed near the famous saint in token of continuation in his charity. The kneeling statue representing the Archbishop himself expresses the utmost humbleness. The chapel is full of outstanding works by Donner, such as marble statues of two mourning ephebes, seven lead relief of the Passion cycle and the already mentioned statue of Emerich Esterházy.

The fate of the remains of the St. John Almsgiver

The Baroque chapel of the St. John Almsgiver enshrines the relics of an important saint of the Eastern Church who was born in the 6th century on the island

of Cyprus. In spite of the fact that his father was the ruler of the island, he preferred the career of a priest and became the Bishop of Alexandria. King Matthias Corvinus of Hungary received the relics of the saint as a present from the Turkish sultan, which complied with the wish of the Christians to hand over the bones of the Patriarch of Alexandria to Christian Hungary. They were moved from Constantinople to Buda. After the defeat of the Hungarian troops at Mohács the castellan of Buda castle Ján Bornemisza packed the relics and moved them along with other valuables out of the town, which was soon after conquered by the Turks. The boxes travelled by boat to Pressburg in company of Queen Mary, King Louis II's widow. When Archbishop Emerich Lósy visited the chapter of Pressburg, he found that the precious relics were not as respectfully deposited, as they deserved. Archbishop Peter Pázmany provided for moving the famous relics to a new crypt. The relics were carried around the city in time of plague in the years 1678-1679 and 1712-1713 in the hope that they would drive away the black death. Most of the valuables returned to Buda in 1721, but the relics remained in St. Martin's Minster of Pressburg up to the present time.

Left: The chapel of St. John the Almsgiver
Right: Rudnayovo námestie square

The recognized artist Georg Rafael Donner was entrusted with more works in the interior of the church. The new bulky Baroque altar with Donner's monumental **group of statues of St. Martin** replaced the removed Gothic one. This wonderful sculpture made in 1744 from lead represents a Roman soldier from Transdanubian Pannonia, who cuts his cape in two in a mighty movement of sabre to give half of it to a beggar suffering from cold. It is an impressive Baroque composition with inner dynamism and a deep allegorical meaning. The Roman soldier riding a horse wears the uniform of a Hungarian soldier and his face resembles the Archbishop Esterházy's face. The scene symbolizes the Archbishop's character as a generous patron of artists. The beggar, looking happy and healthy, is an allegory of the arts. Donner's group of statues as seen on pictures of the coronations stood in the middle of the main altar, which was ceremoniously consecrated by the Archbishop himself on November 5th 1735. The altar was in the presbytery only until 1865, when it was dismantled and removed. Today the statue of St. Martin is at the east end of the south aisle.

The Baroque **tower** was destroyed by fire caused by lightning in 1833. It was only three years after the last coronation was held in the Minster. Reconstruction was entrusted to an important Pressburg Classicist architect Ignác Feigler senior. He chose the fashionable **romanticizing style**. The tower was given the Neo Gothic face, which has survived until today. The tower of the Minster is

85 metres tall. At its top is a gilded 2x2 m cushion bearing the **copy of the Hungarian royal crown**. The imitation is one metre tall and weighs 300 kilograms.

The visitors of Bratislava Minster's monumental interior of 70x23 metres can admire there many remarkable works of art, and others are deposited in the parts of the church closed to the public. There is a valuable one metre tall **Late Gothic monstrance** from 1517. The **chalices** made in the 15th and 16th centuries are also of high artistic value. The **chalice-shaped Gothic font** made in 1402 of bronze is worthy of attention. In the lateral Neo-Gothic altar is the **Renaissance relief of Pieta** from 1642. The most valuable **grave monument** is that **of Juraj Schomberg** made of sandstone. The vice-chancellor of Universitas Istropolitana had it made before he died in 1470 and it bears his portrait. On the wall of presbytery there is the **epitaph of Mikuláš Pálffy** from 1601 made of red marble. The modern tombstone of the author of the first Slovak novel and the canon of Pressburg chapter **Jozef Ignác Bajza** is placed in the chapel of St. Anna. His body is deposited in the crypt of the Minster. The marble board bearing the portray of the writer was made by Jozef Pospíšil in 1933. The Minster had an **organ** as early as 1452, as is evident from the request of Ján Hunyady addressed to the Viennese workshop in which he insists they sell him the organ just finished, for Pressburg. He wanted to compensate the city with another bigger and more beautiful organ. The city ordered another organ from Leopold Suderspitz from Vienna in 1582. The Pressburg painter Hans Fink ornamented this organ.

South of the St. Martin's Minster is the rectangular **Rudnayovo námestie square**. Its position in the neighbourhood of the Minster predestined the older names of this square: *Domplatz* in German or Dómske námestie in Slovak. There was a cemetery with numerous

chapels on the site of today's Rudnayovo námestie square until the 18th century. The name of the square used since 1939 commemorates **Alexander Rudnay** (1760-1831), the first Slovak who achieved the title of Cardinal. In spite of reaching the top office of the Hungarian Primate, he never forgot his Slovak origin and on the occasion of his nomination to Cardinal, he said to Pope Leo XII: "I am Slovak and will always remain Slovak, even if they promote me to the St. Peter's chair." Rudnay helped the new Slovak intelligentsia emerging by the end of the 18th century, particularly the group of emancipators studying at the General Seminar in Pressburg Castle, who gathered around another important Slovak **figure** and writer **Anton Bernolák** ❷ (1762-1813). The monument to this leading personality of the group, the first codifier of the Slovak orthography (1787) and author of the oldest book of Slovak grammar, stands in the centre of the square. Jozef Pospíšil made the sculpture in 1937. Amidst the

greenery of the park, which divides the square into two terraces are another two interesting works of sculpture. Left of the stairway is the **bust** of an important Baroque sculptor **Georg Rafael Donner** ❸ (1693-1741) who lived eleven years in Pressburg. His finest works can be seen in the interior of the Minster. On the right side is the **bust of Franz Liszt** ❹ (1811-1886) by the Pressburg native sculptor Viktor Tilgner. The metal banisters around the statue remind of the musical event in 1884. Their shape is that of a stave with a passage from the Liszts's Coronation Mass directed by the composer himself in St. Martin's Minster. On the upper terrace is the **statue** of the Slovak poet **Ján Hollý** ❺ (1785-1849) made by the sculptor Ervín Staník.

The street leading northward from presbytery of the Minster is called **Kapitulská**. Its length was determined by the town fortifications at its northern end. This is one of the oldest streets of the town and the Church dignitaries, who were moved from the castle to the settlement below the castle by the beginning of the 13th century, created it. The houses of provost, canons and priests formed the street. It used to be the main street of the Romanesque Pressburg. It ran further to Zámocká ulica and the castle. Expansion of the town in the 14th century pushed the street to the western edge of the town. The Chapter of Pressburg merged with town as early as in Middle Ages, but the buildings of the Church institutions and houses of canons remained privileged objects with rights of noble residences and Church asylum. The German version of the temporary street *Capitel-Gasse* appeared for the first time in 1750. Before the names *Pfarergasse* (1443) and *Kirchgasse* (1636) and their variations also closely connected with Church function of this part of old

Left: Coronation of Carolina Augusta
Right: Kapitulská ulica street

Bratislava were mentioned. The old prevalence of the population groups connected in some or other way with the Church survived in this quarter until today.

There was a cemetery next to the St. Martin's Minster for several centuries. By early 18th century it became "overcrowded", so the town council prohibited its further use in 1747. It was abolished only by the end of the 18th century and several buildings were erected on its site. When a school building and two Gothic chapels were pulled down in the 19th century, the vacant place was changed into a small square. In the right corner, at the end of the eastern row of houses of Kapitulská ulica street stands a big building with a comparatively large forecourt. It originated in 1632 by reconstruction of an older house as ordered by the then provost Juraj Draškovič. The provost used it and this is the reason why it is called **Prepoštský palác** ❻ or the Provost's Palace. The oldest building of provostship stood presumably next to the church of the Most Holy Saviour on the eastern terrace of Pressburg Castle. However, the office moved down along with the church and chapter into the settlement below the castle to today's Kapitulská ulica in 1221. This was where the Gothic predecessor of the present palace stood. It is referred to for the first time in official acts from 1311. The royal curia probably stood next to it. Research on the buildings between Kapitulská and Ventúrska streets associate the part of the present Provost's building with Universitas Istropolitana (→ 56). Well-conserved architecture of this developmental stage of the Provost's Palace dated into the 15th century is in form of Gothic barrel vaults and stone portals. The present Provost's Palace though, is a two-storied Renaissance building with short lateral wings, which close the mentioned forecourt or rather a garden. This arrangement of the plot suggests an older reversed orientation of the building from before the Renais-

sance reconstruction into the yard of the Gmaitl-owned houses on Ventúrska street. Such an orientation also suggests the connection of the building with the University. The provost's palace was again adapted in 1776, this time in the Baroque taste. The representative interior of the main hall with wonderful cassette ceiling is especially impressive. The exterior of the building is rather sober, lacking any ornamentation. However, the **Late Renaissance portal** in the wall of the courtyard of honour of the Palace from 1632 is quite different from the simple facade. It is a unique architectural element in Slovakia. It is a part of the wall added to the palace in the 19th century. The coat of arms with the Bishop's insignia points to the initiator of reconstruction Juraj Draškovič. The **statue of St. Elisabeth of Hungary** ❼ by sculptor Alojz Rigele from 1907 standing in the courtyard represents the Saint allegedly born in Pressburg Castle in 1207. The Provost's Palace is today the seminary for priests.

Left: The Jesuit College
Coat of arms of Emerich Lósy
Right: Kapitulská ulica street

St. Elisabeth of Hungary

In 1207 Elisabeth, the daughter of the Hungarian King Andrew II was allegedly born on Pressburg Castle. As a four-year-old girl she was engaged to Ludwig, son of Count Herman of Thüringen. She passed her childhood at the castle of Wartburg. She was an unfortunate girl. When she was six years old the Hungarian aristocrats assassinated her mother Queen Gertrude. Moreover, young Elisabeth lost her husband, and her brother-in-law ousted her from her home. As a widow with children she found a new home in the German town of Marburg where she dedicated herself to the life-long vocation in charity. She founded the female order of the Elizabethans, whose mission was work in hospitals and asylums. Elisabeth died very young, at 24 years of age. Four years after her death she was declared a saint. St. Elisabeth is the patron saint of the poor and sick. The Elizabethan order founded monasteries all over Europe in the vicinity of hospitals and asylums. Archbishop Emerich Esterházy gave them a church and monastery in Pressburg. St. Elisabeth is the patron saint of another church in Bratislava known under the name Modrý kostolík or Blue Church (→ 161).

Kapitulská street not only possesses a long Church history, but it also represents an inseparable part of the development of medieval schools. One of the oldest school buildings in Hungary stood in this street in the 14th century. It was replaced by a new and modern building with two classrooms in 1550. The **Jesuit College** ❽ built opposite the Provost's Palace continued this educational tradition. It was erected on a plot with three older houses, which the Archbishop of Esztergom and Cardinal Peter Pázmány donated to Jesuits in 1626. The medieval school was in one of these houses. The college building built in the years 1628-1635 is a wonderful example of the Late Renaissance style of the second quarter of the 17th century. Court architects of Vienna, the Jesuits Jakub Rava and his son Giovanni designed it. The design prepared in Rome brought to Pressburg the Roman type of architecture typical of the time. The

three-storied building of the college has survived in its original form. The Rococo stone portal in the corridor on the ground floor is from the mid-18th century. The portal bears Pázmány's coat of arms, and in the courtyard are the remains of a Late Renaissance arcade. In the corner room of the ground floor was the Salvator Pharmacy. Its original furnishing was moved to the ground floor of the building on Panská street No. 35. After abolition of the Jesuit order by King Joseph II in 1782 first the town school and later the censor's office got the building of the Jesuit college. Finally it was restored for the Imperial and Royal Law Academy. One of its famous students was the Slovak writer, dramatist, and journalist **Svetozár Hurban Vajanský** (1847-1916). The Law Academy became part of the newly founded **Hungarian Royal University of St. Elisabeth**. After the First World War two faculties of **Comenius University** seated in the building – the Faculty of Philosophy moved there in 1918 and Faculty of Medicine in 1919. In 1926 a modern **aula** ❾ (great hall) with a statue of Roman orator and philosopher Cicero on the facade was added next to the right flank of the building. It was given back to the Church after the Second World War and the still existing **Faculty of Roman-Catholic Theology** was established in it.

The next building in the western row of houses in Kapitulská street is **Collegium Emericanum** ❿. The Italian architect Jakub and Giovanni Rava erected this building in the years 1641-1642. Archbishop Emerich Lósy, who decided to establish a seminary for secular priests of the Esztergom Archdiocese, funded it. The name of this school institution derives from the Latin name of the Christian name of its founder. The only ornament of the otherwise sober facade of the college is the bulky portal with an inscription and Lósy's coat of arms. Heavy metal bars protect the windows at the ground floor. Several Slovak intellectuals active in the

emancipation movement of the 18th century, such as Alexander Rudnay, Ján Hollý, Ján Palárik were the students of the college. The college moved temporarily to Buda in the years 1783-1801.

The house ⓫ (No. 15) on the corner of Kapitulská and Prepoštská streets is from the early 14th century. It was one of the houses of the disappeared settlement below the castle. Parts of portals and windows can be seen on its western facade. The stairway with loggia were added to the house in the 16th century. The Baroque saddle portal is from the 18th century. Not long ago remains of a **wall fresco** depicting Adoration of the Blessed Sacrament were discovered under the younger plaster. There is also the Art Nouveau stucco ornamentation. On the corner of Farská ulica in house No. 9 is **Farský úrad** ⓬ (the Parish Office). The Parish Office on Kapitulská was mentioned as early as 1396. It was mentioned as the *domus honorifica lapidea* or noble stone house. The oldest northern wing of today's Parish Office with a passage and oriel oriented to Farská street is from the same time. The house belonged to the counsellor Martin Protesser who sold it to the priest of St. Martin's Minster.

The Parish Office burnt down after an artillery shell of Napoleon's troops hit it in 1809. The house has a reconstructed medieval facade in the Gothic taste. **Jozef Ignác Bajza** (1755-1836), the author of the first Slovak novel, lived the last ten years of his fruitful life in this house. He was the member of the Pressburg chapter and is buried in the crypt of St. Martin's Minster.

The **Esterházy Palace** ⓭ (house Nos. 6-10) is the only secular building on Kapitulská street. It is one of the oldest palaces in the city, as it was built almost a century before the city was seized by building frenzy in time of Maria Theresia, which gave origin to plenty of wonderful Baroque, Rococo, and Neo Classical palaces. It was built in the mid-17th century and restored in the Baroque style in the following century. The Liszt family owned the original house. Later Count Esterházy bought it. The governor Albert, son-in-law of Queen Maria Theresia also lived in the house for some time.

The venerable looking **Gothic house No. 4** ⓮ in the northern part of Kapitulská street called **Malý prepoštský dom** or the Small Provost's House will certainly attract the visitor's attention. As a matter of fact, it consists of two Gothic houses from the 15th century, as the gap in the middle of the plot, now bridged by the arch of the gate, suggests. Some of the inner spaces have barrel vaults. Behind the eastern row of the houses of Kapitulská ulica are the **western town fortifications** ⓯, which were subject to extensive reconstruction,

Left: The view of castle from Prepoštská street
Right: Farská ulica street
The towers of the Old Town

when the New Bridge over the Danube was constructed in the early 1970's. Remains of fortifications were disclosed after demolition of the lower streets of the former settlement below the castle. Conservation of the preserved and completion of the missing parts of fortifications eventually created a compact system of castle walls with bastions, an upper wall, central gallery and the lower wall. The massive **Vtáčia bašta** ⓰ (Bird's Bastion), which was the defensive counterpart of the Luginsland bastion at the opposite slope of the castle hill, stands outside of the fortifications. Busy Staromestská ulica street connecting with the New Bridge and Petržalka on the other side of the river, runs along the bottom of the former moat. The terraces on the northern bend of the town walls offer interesting views of the Kapitulská street and the former lane inside the walls now called **Na vŕšku**. The remains of a Gothic castle tower from the second half of the 13th century were found here. The access to the walls from the north is via a flight of stairs and the gallery ends in the south at the entrance to St. Martin's Minster.

Prepoštská ulica connects Kapitulská and Ventúrska. It has always been the connecting lane between the inner town and the walls of the western part of fortifications. The oldest reference to this street is from 1420 and it is mentioned as an access road to St. Martin's Minster. Its name in 1754 was *Kleine Capitel Gasse* or Small Kapitulská street. A new name *Pázmanygasse* in honour of Archbishop Pázmány was mentioned in 1879. Today's name relates to the top Church dignitary of Provost who has influenced the life of the town for centuries. It has been used since 1950. The members of the Pressburg chapter had their houses in Prepoštská ulica in the past. Today there are several Renaissance houses built on older medieval plots. In one of them was the Patz's printing house, which published the first newspaper in the Hungarian language in 1780. In the Renaissance **house No. 10** is now the Spanish Embassy.

A bit further to the north is the short **Farská ulica street** parallel to Prepoštská. Farská connects Kapitulská and Klariská streets and also Michalská street through the passage in the building of the University Library. This street originated when the monastery of the female Cistercian order was built here in the first half of the 13th century. In the upper part of the street the house of the priest of St. Martin's Minster has stood since the end of the 14th century. The

present name of the street has been used since 1921. It is the Slovak version of the original German name *Pfarergasse.* Farská street is especially picturesque. The entrances to the buildings standing on Farská are from the neighbouring Klariská street.

Klariská ulica street is longer and richer in monuments than Farská. Both streets have the same origin. This street also originated with the construction of the Cistercian monastery. The street ran from the monastery to the town walls on the northern side of the fortifications. It was a continuation of the wall lanes and connected with Baštová on the right and with the Na vŕšku street on the left. Very old records mentioning this street are available. The finding of three Roman bronze hairpins also evidences the settlement of the area. An act from 1232 mentions Klariská as *Nonnengasse* or the Street of Nuns. The names that followed derived from this oldest one. However, the name of the Cistercian order does not appear in the names given to this street over the centuries. Right opposite the passage to Michalská ulica is the **house** called **U dežmára** ⓱. Originally it was a Gothic house with passage, rebuilt in Renaissance style in the latter half of the 16th century. It attracts the passers-by with its original facade ornamented by graffito. Careful restoration brought additional discoveries of original Gothic windows and a preserved remnant of the Gothic plaster. The name of the house and restaurant on its ground floor is connected with the person who collected the taxes – the tenths.

The dominating building of Klariská street is the **St. Clara church** ⓲ and monastery. Monastic building have stood here since the 13th century. They were originally Cistercian nuns, who along with Franciscan monks, were the first to come to Pressburg. In that time

Left: The western town walls
Right: The tower of St. Clara church

the monastery was outside the settlement, which existed below the castle. As it was insufficiently protected it suffered a lot from the raids undertaken by King Přemysl Otakar II of Bohemia in 1270. The monastery with church was later settled by another female order, that of St. Clara (klarisky). With the consent of King Andrew III they started its restoration in 1302. By the end of the 13th century the **Gothic nave of the church** was started and it was finished in 1375. The vault of the church had to be restored again after fire in 1515. **Presbytery** was added to the nave and both are vaulted with ribbed cross vaults. The width and length of both parts are identical. An arch of triumph divides them. Supporting pillars reinforce its peripheral walls. The nuns had the interior of the church rearranged in line with the emerging Rococo taste by the end of the 18th century. Altars with statues by Ľudovít Gode and paintings of F. X. Palko enriched the interior. The Rococo pulpit with a canopy by Sartory belongs to the valuables of the church. In the early 15th century a five-sided **Gothic tower** lavishly adorned by pinnacles, gargoyles and little statues in what is called the Beautiful Style was added on the side of Farská ulica street. Today there are true copies of four statues on the tower. The original statues are kept inside the church. This Bratislava's landmark is impressive not only for its beauty, but also for its bold architectural solution. The builder decided for an unconventional approach when he did not build the tower on the foundations buried in earth. He rather built it on the lateral wall of the church nave. An earthquake in 1700 slightly damaged the tower and this was the reason why the original Gothic prism was replaced by the Baroque onion helmet. The tower was secured by supporting pillars in the 20th century. Part of the adjustments of the end of the 19th century was the removal of the Baroque elements of the church tower, which then regained its

original Gothic form. The Church of St. Clara was used until 1913. Old sources mention that the Jesuits read their sermons in this church in Slovak language in 1622. The church served as a gallery where the jewels of the Gothic fine arts were concentrated. The excellent acoustics of the church motivated the town councillors to organize concerts of chamber music and choral singing there.

The original Gothic **monastery of St. Clara** ⓳ became dilapidated, when the nuns left Pressburg fleeing from the Turks in 1526. The order moved to Trnava. Later they came back only to face ownership problems with the city and the consequences of another fire. Finally it was Archbishop Peter Pázmány who decided for a deep change of architecture of the monastery. He supported all Catholic institutions within the framework of the Re-Catholicizing program of the Church and also helped to the nuns of St. Clara's order. The **new monastery** was built on the foundations of the old.

A bulky building in the taste corresponding to the end of the Renaissance period sprang up in Klariská ulica street. Their authors were again the traditional builders of monastic buildings of the mid-17th century, Jakub Rava and his son Giovanni Batista from Rome. Inside the four-winged building on an irregular ground plan a space shaped into a form of what is called the cloister with an arcaded corridor was created. The abolition of some orders by Joseph II in 1782 concerned also the order of St. Clara. The nuns had to abandon their monastery. Collections and library were sold out and the interior of the church did not survive either. In the years 1783-1784 the monastery was adapted for use by the Law Academy and the Catholic grammar school. Among the pupils of the grammar school were **Béla Bartók** (1881-1945), an outstanding Hungarian composer and **Jozef Murgaš** (1864-1929), the Slovak inventor and pioneer of radiotelegraphy (1864-1929). The former monastery was reconstructed in the years 1957-1961 and it became the seat of the Slovak Pedagogic Library. The monastery now shelters the **Office of the European Council**.

On the opposite side of Klariská ulica street are several houses built on medieval plots. Most of them are built in the Late Baroque or Neo Classical style. **House No. 8** ⓴ used to be the home of the composer, piano player and native of Pressburg, **Ernest Dohnány** (1877-1960). He studied at the Catholic grammar school in the former monastery. His father Fridrich taught mathematics and physics there. Young Ernest was a classmate of the famous Béla Bartók and played with him in the school orchestra. Both of them liked to play the organ in St. Clara's church. Even after he was famous all over the world he always liked to perform in his native Bratislava. He passed the last years of his life in New York where he also died. The **house No. 14** ㉑ on the corner with Baštová street was recently restored and the new facade displays some architectural details of an older Renaissance house. Since the 19th century the house was owned by the Jewish community, which opened a Jewish school in the new building behind this house.

Left: The upper end of Kapitulská street
Right: Under the Michalská brána gate

Panská and Laurinská streets

Panská and Laurinská form together the longest long street line in the historical centre of Bratislava with total length of 700 m. In the past they bore the common name of Dlhá or Long street. The more easterly-situated Laurinská is busier with more shops and less luxurious houses. Panská (or Lordly) street is what its name suggests, as there are many city palaces, which used to belong to the nobility and rich burgers. There are also numerous embassies and travel agencies. Panská and Laurinská are the oldest of Bratislava streets. They have seen the oldest times of the city including that of the primeval settlement below the castle. They originated in the same way as Michalská and Ventúrska along the old trade route called the Danube road, which headed to the Bratislava ford, bringing the merchants from the east: from Nitra and Trnava.

Left: Panská ulica street

Panská ulica street is the one more westerly situated of the inseparable twin street. It starts at the former Vydrická brána gate and ends at the crossroads with Rybná brána. If you want to gain an idea of the development of building styles used in Bratislava in the 18th century you only have to walk down Panská ulica from Csáky's palace to Esterházy's palace. In this 200 metres long stretch one finds six wonderful buildings to contemplate. In the 15th and 16th century there were several inns in Panská street such as the *Golden Eagle, Sun, White Swan* or *Blue Pike.* Before Vodné Kasárne barraks was built in the southern suburb, the inns accommodated soldiers. In the 19th century there was as also a casino in Panská street, a favourite place for officers.

As said before, Panská ulica was formerly part of Dlhá. It is referred to for the first time in 1467 as *Langern Gasse* in German. Before it was called *Fleischprukke* or the Butcher's street, as there were slaughter houses. These moved beyond the limits of the inner town to what is today Šafárikovo námestie square in the 18th century. In the same century the wonderful palaces inhabited by the Pressburg nobles were built in Panská. The name of the street in its German form *Herren Gassen* was mentioned for the first time in the official acts from 1783. The street preserved its name up till now except for several decades after the Second World War, when it was called Nálepkova after a partisan commander, who fought in the territory of the Soviet Union.

The corner of Panská street and Rybné námestie square is occupied by the house No. 41 which is known under its common name **Bibiana** ❶ as it is the venue of Biennial of illustration of children books. The Bibiana house originated from two houses, which were the first ones built in the moat running around the whole medieval town. One of them was built in 1746 that is about three decades before the town walls were pulled down. Both houses were burgher houses and the reconstruction in the Neo Classical style gave them both a common facade. They connected the place with the now disappeared Vydrická brána gate, the remains of which were covered by pavement and the arches of the bridge were used as the top of the basement of the new house.

The immediate vicinity of the Bibiana totally changed when the New Bridge was built. The rather awkward situation of the bridge reduced the former Rybné námestie square to two small areas. The upper one originated on the site of the disappeared main synagogue of Bratislava built in a typical historicizing style. Unfortunately, the pair of its nice towers reminiscent of Oriental architecture can now be seen only on photographs or in the drawing on the **Wall of Memories,** which closes the square from the side of the New Bridge. **The Holocaust Memorial** ❷ stands on the very site of the disappeared synagogue, in the middle of the small square in front of the Bibiana. It is a four metre tall bronze sculpture on a marble plinth bearing an inscription in Hebrew: ZACHOR (Remember!).

At the southern end of the house built in the former moat parts of old stone architecture can be seen. It is a small part of the former **Vydrická brána gate** ❸ in the town walls. A part of wall with disclosed face of ashlaring can be

seen. Experts regard the Vydrická brána gate as the most important of the gates of Pressburg because it was on the trade route leading to Vienna. It led to the ford next to Vodná veža tower. It was allegedly long and dark and its sides were fortified by bastions. There were two bastions on the sides of the Vydrická brána gate: *Himmerleich* and *Leonfelderturm*. The first mentioned was also a chapel where the valuables from the royal chapel were hidden in time when the Turks occupied the town of Buda in the 16th and 17th centuries. The gate had a drawbridge, which was later replaced by a stone bridge mentioned in connection with the Bibiana.

The ground floor of a narrow **house No. 35** with a nice facade in the Viennese eclectic style was **The Salvator Pharmacy** ❹ until not long ago. The pharmacist Rudolf Adler had the house built in 1904. The precious Baroque interior furniture of the pharmacy from 1727 was some of the oldest in Bratislava. It was moved there from the pharmacy, which existed in the building of the Jesuit college on today's Kapitulská street. When the college was closed, the furniture was moved to the ground floor of Csaky's palace and remained there in the years 1883-1904. The Baroque pharmacy had original glass and ceramic pharmaceutical pots from the 17th and 18th century brought here in 1847 from Brno, as well as some younger interior details from the19th century. The Jewish owner was taken to concentration camp during the Second World War and never came back. Several years after the war a treasure of family valuables was found, when the building was under repair. The unfortunate pharmacist had probably hidden them before he was taken away. The furniture of the pharmacy was bought and moved to Trenčianske Teplice in 1996.

Left: The original Rybné námestie square
Right: The former Salvator pharmacy

The Neo Classical **Csáky Palace** ❺ stands at the point, where Panská ulica

street opens to the rectangular area of Rudnay's square. The domestic builder Matúš Walch built it for Count Juraj Csáky in 1775. Csáky financed the construction of the first Theatre of the Hungarian Estates, which used to stand in front of Rybná brána gate on the site of today's Slovak National Theatre.

Let us stop at the house No. 29, and particularly in front of the stone sculpture placed in the niche on the left side of the street facade. The figure is called **Posmieváčik** or Joker ❺ for the malicious grin on his face.

Who is the Joker laughing at?

Nobody knows who or what the Joker is laughing at. The legend has that two young Pressburg gentlemen fell in love with one beauty. The girl could not decide which one of them to marry so she put them on a trial: The one who built a house would get her hand. Both rivals started their houses near each other competing for the hand of the girl. The owner of the house with the Joker on its facade eventually won the race. The Joker grins mockingly at the house of the defeated competitor, which stands opposite.

The Keglevich Palace ❼ stands on the corner of Panská and Strakova street. Side by side the proud Erdödy Palace it looks like a country mansion of some yeoman from the north of Slovakia. The short facade of the single floor house compensated by the tall red roof typical of old village mansions causes this rustic impression. The Baroque palace originated by rebuilding an older burgher house. The family of Keglevich, members of the old Croatian aristocracy had it rebuilt as a family residence. Their ancestors had been the lords of the Devín Castle. In 1616 they faced the rebellion of their serfs in the little town of Devín. The Keglevich family living at Panská street had a daughter Babetta, who was at first the pupil and later a good friend of composer **Ludwig van Beethoven**. The young countess was a good piano player and Beethoven dedi-

cated his Sonata for piano and some other compositions to her. The famous artist visited Pressburg in November 1796 and spent at least nine days there.

The eastern wing of the Keglevich Palace faces Strakova ulica street. The urban fabric on the southern side of Panská ulica was compact by the end of the 18th century. At the point where a linking passage to today's Hviezdoslavovo námestie square was opened, the Župný dom or the County Office used to stand. The office moved to the building of the former monastery of the Trinitarians on Župné námestie Square after 1844.

The **Pálffy Palace** ❽ at Panská No. 19-21 revealed some pleasant surprises to the historians and archaeologists in recent years. Even before the detailed research was started it was known that its rather austere facade covers traces of the remote past. And indeed, during the thorough reconstruction of 1981-1988 unknown fragments of medieval architecture were found under the thick layers of plaster and archaeological probes discovered precious objects from the oldest periods of the settlement of this territory The lowest layer with traces of Celtic settlement proved to be especially valuable. The Celtic finds under the Pálffy Palace were more than interesting. Apart from skeletons, numerous crucibles from the local **Celtic mint** were also found here. Maybe it was right here that the famous *biatecs*, the old Celtic coins were struck. Among the younger finds, graves from the Great Moravian period, for instance, the one of a Slav warrior with an axe are worth mentioning. Unique medieval architectural elements and in unusually good conditions were discovered in the actual structure of the building. The past building adjustments had luckily not damaged them. Experts also investigated the original structure of the neighbouring house (Panská No. 17) during reconstruction and recognized some remarkable remains of a **tower** with a defensive wall dated at least to the beginning of the 13th century. They admitted that there might have been even older walls, perhaps of Roman origin. The builders of the house used the remains of some Roman building for construction. Remains of a rectangular **urban Gothic palace** with dimensions of 28x8.5 m were dated to the 14th century. Many details such as windows, portals, pieces of finishing plaster, remnants of paving, arcades, etc. have been preserved. The restored part of a star-shaped ribbed dome is interesting. The finds of Gothic architecture prove the luxury and pompousness of this palace. there used to be a Tower with battlement in the eastern part, with all its body standing on the neighbouring plot of the house No. 17. It was 15 metres tall. The oldest written documents relating to this palace on today's Panská street are from 1415 to 1516. It is re-

Left: Keglevich Palace
Right: Inside the Pálffy Palace

ferred to as *domus comitis Karl* (the house of Count Charles). Somewhat younger records from the years 1430 and 1439 denote this house as the *domus regia* or the king's house, the royal house. It was presumably the royal curia, where the ruler with his suite lived during his visits to the free royal borough of Pressburg. The Pálffy family bought the house in 1715. Count Pálffy was later nominated palatine and state judge. He paid thirty thousand guldens for the house. In the first half of the 19th century the Pálffys unified the original building in the Neo Classical style with the facade preserved up to now. In 1885 the rear parts of the palace were pulled down and a new palace was built facing the Promenade (Hviezdoslavovo námestie square).

Extensive reconstruction of the interior of the palace carried out in the 1980's adjusted the palace for the purpose **of Art Gallery of the city of Bratislava**. At the ground floor there are standing expositions of Slovak paintings and sculpture from the turn of the 19th and 20th centuries including our classic painters such as D. Skutecký, L. Mednyánszky, etc. The first floor is dedicated to the founders of Slovak modernism: G. Mallý, M. Benka, M. Galanda, and Ľ. Fulla. At the second floor a display of artistic works of the European artists can be seen, including representatives of Italian, Dutch or Flemish painting. The gallery occasionally organises other exhibitions showing works of such geniuses as P. Picasso, S. Dalí or A. Warholl.

A defensive tower occupied the site of **house No. 17** ❾, now used by the *British Council*, in the 13th century. A century later it became part of another luxurious medieval palace already mentioned in connection with Pálffy Palace. Discovery and study of the remains of old architecture was facilitated by the restoration of the neighbouring Pálffy Palace. It was discovered that this building used to have an inner yard

reaching as far as the wall of the city's southern fortification. At its western side, the remains of walls with battlements as tall as the ledge of the existing house were found. At the stairway a Romanesque window and a Gothic stone arch of the inner portal were discovered. The Gothic house from the 15th century belonged to palatine Rozgoň, the protagonist of the civil war between the castle and the town. The owners of the house alternated until the Pauline monks from Marianka bought it. The Paulines wore typical white gowns and that is why the house was called **The House of the White Monks.** In the second half of the 17th century the Paulines changed the back part of the house into a **chapel of the Most Holy Trinity**. The later owners of the house pulled down the chapel of which only the Early Baroque portal with the year 1671 carved in it has survived. In the 18th century the house sheltered a popular inn called At the Snake's. The present Empire style of the street facade is from the mid-19th century.

House No. 16 ❿ in the northern row of houses of Panská street is the seat of the British Embassy. Recent restoration of this original burgher house from the second half of the 17th century carried out in 1965 enhanced the beauty and charms of its former Late Renaissance appearance. The street facade was cleared of the Baroque alterations made in 1754 and the original graffito ornamentation was restored. The dominating element of the facade is now a two-axis oriel with stone consoles

passing over two floors. The iron gate of the garage is also impressing.

Let us go back to the southern part of Panská. In its middle there are two palaces. It is good they are standing side by side because we can compare the heavy, majestic Baroque building with the light and graceful Rococo house. **Esterházy Palace** ⓫ (No. 13) on the left was built in 1746 for Count Ján Esterházy, a member of one of the richest noble families in Hungary. The palace was one of the most luxurious in the city, though its exterior does not confirm it. The facade of the three-storied house is comparatively simple. The Baroque portal with massive atlantes is more lavishly ornamented. The of atlantes were made by an unknown Viennese craftsman. The Rococo **Balassa Palace** ⓬ standing on the right (No. 15) is quite different from its neighbour. The three-storied house is lower, less massive and the ornamentation of the facade is considerably finer and more elaborate. The Rococo sculptured ornamentation of the facade is full of symbols and allegories of the Classical deities. On the attic above the ledge there are decorative vases and allegorical statues of Deliberation and Wisdom. Above the portal with decorative rocaille ornaments two sculptures expressing additional human virtues of the owner of the palace were placed. They are Constancy and Modesty. Only the street wing survives from the four-wing building built in the years 1754-1762. The other parts were pulled down and replaced by modern buildings.

Apart from churches the medieval town also contained several chapels. One of the surviving examples is **Dom bratstva Kristovho tela** ⓭ or the House of the Brotherhood of Christ's Body (house No. 11) at the eastern end of Panská ulica street. The old chapel of Corpus Christi was originally part of the rear wing of the house. When Pressburg was occupied by Gabriel Bethlen's troops in 1620 it was severely damaged. Bishop Telegdy had it restored in the Renaissance style in 1827 as the tablet on the gate leading to the courtyard reads. The Brotherhood of Christ's Body ordered the reconstruction of the house with the local builder Matúš Walch while the chapel had to be moved from the rear wing to the street wing, where it is now. It is accessible by the street door. The house with its Neo Classical facade does not look like a Church building at all. The symbol on the tympanum of the portal and the above mentioned board from the old chapel are the only reminders of its religious purpose.

The crossroads of Rybárska brána, Panská and Laurinská street is certainly the liveliest spot of the city. People like to stop here to listen to the street musicians and the tourists love to have a snap made with **Čumil** ⓮ in background.

Left: The Brittish Embassy
Right: Schöner Nazi
Čumil

Čumil or the gazing man

The small bronze statue placed next to café on the corner is a comparatively new attraction of what is colloquially called Bratislava's Corso. News about Čumil quickly spread about. One of the regional Canadian newspapers published the photograph of the statue with a short commentary, which evokes smile. The photographer visited Bratislava as a tourist, and asserted that the statue wearing a helmet represented a member of a paramilitary organisation fighting against the Russian tanks in August 1968 (Russian invasion of Czechoslovakia). A close look at the statue reveals that instead of a helmet, a cap with strap covers the gazing man's head. Čumil is a common man observing beautiful girls passing by, as Bratislava is also famous also for an unusually high rate of beautiful girls per square kilometre.

Rybárska brána street is a short street in the historic centre of Bratislava and part of the already mentioned *Corso*. It is a pedestrian zone between Hlavné námestie and Hviezdoslavovo námestie squares, and one of older transversal streets, which in 1403 was referred to as *Pey den Vischer Turml* (Next to Fisher's Gate). The name suggests that this street crosses the site of the fourth gate in the town wall, which was used by fishermen and boatsmen for an access to the arms of the Danube. The passage continued from the gate by a bridge over the moat. The gate was bricked up in times of threat. Ján Pavol Royer founded a printing plant next to Rybárska brána gate in 1715. The printing plant was later in 1750 bought and modernized by rather notable printer Johann Michael Landerer. **Landerer's printing house** was located next to Rybárska brána until the 1780's and afterwards it moved to today's Šafárikovo námestie square. Rybárska brána gate disappeared along with the town walls in 1775 and the street that has taken its place has also assumed its name. The southern end of the street ends in the Promenáda or today's Hviezdoslavovo námestie square. Two triumphal arches were erected at the vacancy left here after the gate was pulled down on the occasion when the Tsar Alexander I of Russia visited Pressburg. Today there are no traces left of Rybárska brána gate and the architecture of the street is varied with prevailing buildings from the 19th and 20th centuries.

Next to house No 1 stands a life-size statue with a top hat in his hand and a welcoming gesture. In contrast to the statue of Čumil this one painted in

gleaming silver paint represents a real person, a native of Bratislava nicknamed **Schöner Nazi** ⓯ (Fair Nazi). His real name was Ignác Lamar, and he was born on August 12th, 1897 into the family of a shoemaker in Petržalka. He was lucky to escape the post-war displacement of the Germans living in Bratislava to Germany. Schöner Nazi frequented Bratislava's pubs and coffee houses and became an inseparable part of the city's folklore. He spent the last twenty-one years of his life in an asylum for the retired at Radlinská street. He is buried in Lehnice as he died in the local TB sanatorium on October 21st 1967.

Nazi is coming

Every city has its special attraction or figure known by all. Schöner Nazi was such a figure for Bratislava. This peculiar man was always moving around the coffee-houses or sweetshops from 1930's to the 1960's. He looked like an English gentleman who has just stepped out from some aristocratic club. Short and slim Schöner Nazi was very meticulous about his clothes and insisted on a black-and-white colour combination. He was always wearing tails, although a little bit scruffy. The top hat made him look a little bit taller. He wore polished patent-leather shoes and white gloves. Walking down the street Nazi swung a cane in one hand and usually carried a little parcel in the other. Normally it was a present from one of the Bratislava's sweetshops, which used Schöner Nazi as a walking advertisement for their goods. He also often carried flowers and gave them away to ladies passing by. He was very polite and courtly. Groups of children used to accompany this picturesque figure and if in good mood he would sing them one or another of the Bratislava hits. He regularly stopped in one of his favourite coffeehouses. On Thursdays, for instance, he was sitting in the Bláha Hotel, today the Krym, taking a cup of coffee with cake.

Left: The passage on Laurinská street
Right: Carneval in the Old Town

Laurinská ulica street is the prolongation of Panská. It starts at Rybárska brána and ends in Štúrová. It has lost most of its historical buildings. Modern buildings, more or less happily included in this inner town environment, have replaced them. Shops, restaurants or coffee-houses compensate for the absenting history in Laurinská. It is also a bit more animated than other streets of Bratislava. Its present name derives from the suburb of St. Laurence that was the predecessor of this street. Its older name *Lange Gasse* or Long Street occurring in old acts from 1421 referred also to Panská street. The Latin version of its present name was mentioned for the first time in 1667. The middle generation of Bratislava's population knows the street as Leningradská, the name of which was used for forty years after the Second World War.

Laurinská originated in the early Middle Ages when houses on both side of the Danube trade road heading to the ford next to the Vodná veža tower were built. Archaeological research in the middle part of the street also identified older buildings and constructions. There were remains of a road from the Roman era coming from what is today Dunajská street. Several important institutions seated at Laurinská in the past, such as the building of the Hungarian parliament or the a tax office.

The first (No. 1) in the northern row of houses on Laurinská is a four-storied house with a Neo Classical facade. It was built after design of Ignác Feigler Senior in 1846. First of all it was the seat of the **Prvá prešporská sporiteľňa** ⓰ or the First Pressburg Saving Bank founded in 1842 as the oldest bank institution in the city. More banks, mostly branches of the Budapest banks, followed it only by the end of the sixties of the 19th century. Prvá prešporská positively influenced the development of the city as it supported many social and artistic activities. For instance financial injections helped to two famous sculptors, who originated from Pressburg, Johann Fadrusz (1858-1903) and Viktor Tilgner (1844-1896).

Resources provided by the First Pressburg Bank were also used to finance the beautiful Ganymede fountain standing in front of the Slovak National Theatre on Hviezdoslavovo námestie square. Opposite the First Pressburg Savings Bank is a modern corner building, **Dom slovenských spisovateľov** ⓱ (House of the Slovak Writers). There is a bookshop in its ground floor. On the corner of Laurinská and Radničná the Neo Classical **house of Baron Walterskirchen** ⓲ (No. 3) was built in the 19th century and in the second half of the same century two tenement houses were built in neighbourhood of the rear wing of the Primatial palace on the square of the same name. They face Laurinská street. **The house No. 5** ⓳, which shelters the Municipal library, is

connected with the courtyard of the Primatial Palace. Part of a group of sculptures of St. John Nepomuk stands in its courtyard.

Motešicky's house ⑳ (No.10) belongs to the generation of houses built on Laurinská street in the second half of the 19th century. It was built on foundations of an older house, which used to be the inn of *The Wild Man*. The inn was considered a better one, where the deputies were accommodated in the time when the Hungarian Parliament had its sessions in Pressburg. Nowadays two restaurants occupy the ground floors of the front wing of Motešický's house. In the first half of the 18th century famous cartographer **Samuel Mikovíni** (1686-1750) had an observatory in the back part of the plot next to the town walls. Mikovíni was also a mining engineer, expert in hydro-energy, builder, graphic artist and a copper plate engraver. His versatile talents won him the attribute of the "Slovak Leonardo da Vinci." He closely collaborated with another brilliant Slovak scientist, Matej Bel. He prepared numerous maps and engravings of the provinces and towns for the Bel's most important scientific work *Notitia Hungariae Novae Historico-Geographica*. He produced the first scientific map of the Austro-Hungarian Empire. Mikovíni lived ten years of his indeed fruitful life in Pressburg. He came to the city in 1725 to assume the office of the county engineer and later left for Banská Štiavnica. He founded and managed the first mining school in Europe. He died in 1750 in Trenčín.

Left: Divadlo P. O. Hviezdoslava theatre
Right: Laurinská ulica street

The Parliament building used to stand on the plot of what is now **house No. 12** ㉑. Before it was built the Parliament held its sessions in various places. The two-storied building of the Parliament had two entrance gates wide enough for coaches which could pass across the yard of the building. When the Hungarian Royal Chamber moved to Buda in 1780, the Parliament moved to its vacant building. The old seat of the Parliament was pulled down in 1924 and replaced by the building, which is there today.

House No. 9 ㉒ standing in the northern row of the street originally consisted of two Renaissance buildings. They were attached to each other by adjustment of their facades into one. The facade is Neo Classical from the first half of the 19th century. On the corner of Laurinská and Uršulínska streets a Renaissance oriel sticks out. Some assert that the famous physician and alchemist **Philippus Theophrastus Aureolus Bombastus de Hohenheim Paracelsus** (1493-1541) lived in one of the two original Renaissance houses.

The tricks of the famous alchemist

Philippus Paracelsus showed some remarkable tricks to the astonished in-

habitants of Pressburg. Much applauded was the one of reviving a burnt rose. The alchemist first burnt down a red rose in a copper bowl. He put the ashes into a glass flask and heated it on fire, adding thyme herbs into it. After a while a fresh rose appeared in the flask in front of the astounded public. Paracelsus also demonstrated a classic trick of all alchemists, conversion of wood dust, iron or copper into pure gold. Treasure seekers believe that there are golden bricks hidden in the house on Laurinská.

At the eastern end of Laurinská street stands the **theatre building of Divadlo P.O. Hviezdoslava ㉓. A copy of bars ㉔** hangs across the street and above the heads of passers by just to remind us that it is the place where **Laurinská brána gate** used to stand. The first reference to the gate is from 1412, and it even quotes the salary of the gatekeeper. Contemporary drawings show that the two towers, Michalská and Laurinská were very similar. Both were protected by barbicans, and the curve of the upper part of the streets was the same. The tower of the gate had a shingle roof ending in a ball with a banner. For some time it was used as a jail. Laurinská brána was pulled down in 1778.

The Hlavné Námestie or The Main Square

Out of the three central areas in the historic centre of Bratislava the Main Square with its squarish ground plan is the most impressive one. Through the history it was the stage and witness to practically every important event, which took place in the town. It used to be the main market place, stage for the Passion plays, gatherings, and the place, where the rulers were greeted and welcomed, but also where executions or public punishments were carried out. The splendid coronation trail headed by a new King of Hungary always attracted the crowds to Hlavné námestie. The affection of Bratislava's citizens toward their square survived. They still like to go to traditional Christmas fair, performances of musical bands, tower concerts of trumpeters and other events or simply to relax next to the Renaissance fountain or under the sunshades of cafés.

The name of **Hlavné námestie square** has undergone a complicated development. The oldest known name *Forum* (Market) is from 1373. Variations and modifications followed. In 1404 it was referred to as *Marchte*, thirty years later there was the name *Ring*. The German version of its modern name *Hauptplatz* appeared in historical acts in 1783. In 1850 its name was changed to *Franz Joseph Platz*. Later it was *Masaryk's* and even *Hitler's Square*. In 1953 it was called the Square of the 4th of April to commemorate the date when the Second World War finished in Bratislava. In 1989 it was decided that the central area in front of the Old Town Hall would be again called Hlavné námestie. Let us hope that this historical and, as a matter of fact, original name of the square will last, as it has nothing to do with politics.

People often meet next to **Maximilian's fountain** ❶ in the western part of the square perhaps the same as Londoners meet at Piccadilly Circus under Cupid's statue. The square lacked a public water source until the second half of the 16th century. Only in 1572 the financial contribution of King Maximilian II made it possible to finish the fountain, which now bears his name and portrait. The stonemason Andreas Lutringer from the Austrian town of Deutsch Altenburg portrayed the ruler as a knight in armour carrying the Hungarian coat of arms on top of the pillar plinth and an eulogistic poem carved into the block under the statue. The fountain was changed in the 18th century. The central pillar was made taller by adding a stone bowl to it, taken from the fountain in Lippay's garden. Then the burghers called for another modification. Part of the pillar with figures of four urinating little boys had to be replaced by a less provocative segment – the boys holding a fish. And as the lower basin of the fountain was also completely changed we have to admit that today's fountain has

Left: The Old Town Hall

almost nothing in common with the original one. Moreover, after 1919 a rumour, lacking any historical justification, spread that the knight standing on top of the fountain is not the Emperor Maximilian but the brave knight Roland, patron saint and protector of the medieval towns. The public believed it and accepted Roland instead of Maximilian.

The unconfirmed miraculous capacity of the knight Roland

People also believe that Maximilian, or as you like, Roland's fountain moves. They say that once a year, at the New Year's Eve at the moment when the clock strikes twelve the statue turns around its axis. However, this remarkable and unexplained phenomenon was not seen by anybody for a long time, because only a virgin could see it and virgins do not occur at such a time in Hlavné námestie. It must be admitted though, that some merry citizen of Bratislava invented this version of the legend. Better said he modified a considerably older legend, which has that the knight indeed moves. He is turning to the house No. 6, where the municipal council once held its sessions to greet the councillors, who died while defending the town in the past. But Roland also moved the last night of 1999, and was eyewitnesses by the people celebrating the coming year 2000. The organisers of the festival arranged it. Miracles have to be helped to occur sometimes.

Every building at Hlavné námestie deserves attention. The most important of them is the **Stará radnica** ❷ or the Old Town Hall. Its appearance is owed to a complicated architectural development marked by numerous changes of style and reconstruction. The history of this wonderful building started in the remote past, when the city was founded. If we leave out the Celtic, Roman or Slav settlement of this locality, we can say that the oldest predecessor of the Old Town Hall was **Mayor Jacob's fortified house** built on the north-eastern side of the new central square. The house was walled by high stone fortification with battlements. A tower protected the entrance. The upper floors were presumably destined for living. Stairway in the inner yard led to the elevated ground floor of the house. In the back part there was a small farmyard with a low stone fence and a well. Behind the house there was a large plot (on the site of today's Primatial square) used as the meat and bread market. Jacob's house was reconstructed in the course of the 14th centu-

ry. A two-storied **northern yard wing** with a big hall on the first floor replaced the northern wall and the rear farm building. Remnants of its Early Gothic architecture have survived until today and it is the oldest of the four wings enclosing the courtyard of the Old Town Hall.

Two sons, Pavol and Štefan, inherited the property of Mayor Jacob II. They were not as good administrators of their property as their father. They lost a great deal of it by exchange and sales. The Jew Izák acquired the Pavol's share in 1387. But then the municipal council intervened. The prosperous town of Pressburg needed a building to shelter the town hall. The council met at various places, most frequently at what was called the Burg on the opposite side of the square. The municipal council compelled the new owner to sell a part of Jacob's house to the town. The bought out part cost the town 447 florins. This unusually high price corresponded to the fact that Jacob's house was the most luxurious building in the town. The council bought only the Pavol's share. The former Jacob's house was divided in two by a wall until 1451, when Štefan's part was bought out as well at 50 florins. This purchase helped the expansion of the town hall. It also facilitated the later attachment of the neighbouring **Unger's house** (end of the 16th century) built right next to the fortified courtyard of the Archbishop of Esztergom. To the houses facing the square the building of the influential burgher Hans Pawer was added. It was squeezed between the older part of the Town Hall and Unger's house. It is first mentioned in the tax lists from 1422. Its unusually varied and dissected facade has undoubtedly enriched the overall appearance of the square. It is also possible that there was a stone **statue of St. Ladislav**, which is to be seen today on the facade of Unger's house. Pawer's house soon after it was

Left: The Hlavné námestie square
Right: Maxmilian's fountaine

finished was bought by the city and included among the buildings of the Town Hall.

Pressburg was the first town in the Upper Hungary to acquire the building of Town Hall of its own. The municipal council had its sessions in Jacob's house even before the town bought it. The rebuilt Pressburg Town Hall on Hlavné námestie was fully used only after 1434. Before the bought houses could serve their purpose they had to be reconstructed. The reconstruction lasted the whole of the 14th century. It was slowed down by the war of the town with castle in the years 1440-1444. The fights damaged the tower of the Town Hall and it had to be repaired. A new **passage** opening the entry into the Town Hall from the square was made before 1442. This remarkable architectural element has been preserved in its full beauty up till now. The original segmental quadripartite vault has five bosses with figural-heraldic ornamentation. The five **relieves** depict the apotheosis of Queen Elisabeth, King Albrecht of Habsburg's widow and mother of King Ladislav the Posthumous. The first relief, looking from the square, which depicts a head of swan with a fish in beak, is probably the coat of arms of Ján Rozgoň, regional judge and personal adviser to Queen Elisabeth, donated by Ladislav the Posthumous in 1453. The second boss bears the portrait of Queen Elisabeth. The relief of the middle boss portrays the young King Ladislav the Posthumous. The coat of arms on the fourth boss is attributed to Rozgoň's brother-in-law Mikuláš of Uljak from the younger branch of Csáky's family. The last keystone carries the portrait of the Church administrator, Dionýz Széchy, who owned the house next to the Town Hall. Queen Elisabeth made him the head of the Church Hungary.

Several Gothic elements seen on the front facade, such as the oriel over the portal of the passage, the dissected front of Pawer's former house or the windows

of the safe deposit room, were made during the Late Gothic reconstruction of the Town Hall. The trio of **dormer windows** is from 1498 and was probably made by the stonemason Pavol Plüemel. Ceramic tiles covered the roof of the Town Hall. The Gothic tower originated from alterations to the Jacob's former house. Today it is in the Baroque style, but old engravings offer an idea of what it looked like in the past. The resemblance of the tower to that of the Town Hall in Prague is obvious from the woodcut of F. Hogenberg from 1593 and the engraving of M. Merian from 1638.

The eastern wing of the courtyard also displays many original Late Gothic elements from the 15th century reconstruction. The careful reconstruction of the wing preserved several Gothic window and portals overlooking the courtyard.

The ground floor of the Gothic Town Hall contained the municipal tavern, a mint, and a foundry. The **mint** was working thanks to the King Sigismond's

privilege granted to the town in 1430. There was also a jail in the town hall. At first it was a little cellar guarded by the headsman himself, as the acts from 1444 confirm. An important part of the courtyard was the arsenal built immediately behind the tower. The first floor of the front wing contained the hall, chapel, treasury, archives and the hall of elected citizens. A big kitchen and another large hall were placed in the eastern wing of the compound. **The hall** was used for the sessions of the municipal council. The Late Gothic reconstruction gave it more windows and decoration of the walls by figural paintings, some of which are preserved until now. The most complete sample of the Late Gothic reconstruction is the **chapel of St. Ladislav**. One enters from the passage. The interior of the chapel is decorated with unique medieval **wall paintings** preserved in comparatively large fragments. They originated in the 15th century. The paintings show the episodes of Christ's life: Annunciation and five pictures of the Christological cycle with the Crucifixion and Resurrection.

The Town Hall of Pressburg entered the 16th century in a new Late Gothic shell and became the dominant building of the square and an important part of the city's silhouette. In the second half of the 16th century the tower of the Town Hall was slightly adjusted to the principles of the Renaissance style. Three earthquakes, which struck the city in the last decade of the 16th century, required more interventions. Six identical **Renaissance windows** were put into the facade facing the square; Unger's house had another two from 1581. **Renaissance arcades** on pillars, preserved up to now, and made by the stonemason Bartolomej from Wolfstahl were added in 1581. The 17th century Renaissance modifications were concentrated in the interior of the Town Hall. The hall itself was divided into two smaller halls, which were given new ceilings. But the most beautiful thing that happened to the Town Hall came at the end of the 17th century when Bastiano Corati Orsati made the lavish stucco ornamentation of the rooms: rims of the vaults and frames in which the painter Johann Jonas Drentwett from Augsburg placed beautiful **wall paintings**. He followed in style the Italian and Flemish patterns of the 17th century. The painting placed in the middle of the vault represents the theme of the Last Judgement.

Description of Pressburg from the first half of the 18th century written by Matej Bel contains information about the Baroque reconstruction of the Town Hall. Bel mentions the archives on the first floor, the hall with portraits of Kings Leopold I and Charles VI with flattering inscriptions, court room and office room (today's Pompeii hall). He also mentions

Left: Inside the Old Town Hall
Right: Passage in the Old Town Hall
Ceiling of St. Ladislav chapel

the Renaissance jails in the wing turned to Obilné (today's Primatial) Square. As the space of this square, due to the presence of the luxurious Renaissance curia of the Archbishop of Esztergom was gaining in importance, the rear wing of the Town Hall with the jail had to be made more impressive. Its facade was ornamented by a monumental **illusive fresco** by a Venetian painter David Antonio Fossati in 1728. The painter imitated his compatriot Galli-Bibiena, who painted the similar illusive fresco on the ceiling of the church of the Trinitarians. The painting on the wall represented a view of a symmetrical Baroque palace. It was an irony that behind this illusive splendour were the dark cellars of the jail and a torture chamber in the basement of the house. The square was later adorned with the statue of St. John Nepomuk. Construction of the new Primatial palace in 1778 first called for covering the fresco with a wall containing a large niche for the statue of this saint. From of the original interior furnishing of the Baroque Old Town Hall **the requisites of the municipal jurisdiction** are the ones best preserved. It is the whipping post, stocks, and other "utensils" prompting the confessions of the prisoners. Now they are exhibited in the municipal museum. The Old Town Hall acquired its Baroque appearance after the fire of 1733 and paintings from the 19th century represent the Town Hall, as we know it now.

In the 19th century the Town Hall became too small and the municipal authorities of Pressburg were compelled

to solve the problem of space for the ever-expanding office. They bought the neighbouring Apponyi Palace, but it lacked a hall big enough for the purposes of the Town hall. The solution was a new building on the courtyard of the Town Hall after the design of Ignác Feigler Senior in 1876. We only know what it looked like from historical photographs, as the building has not survived. When the municipal offices moved out in 1868, the **Municipal Museum** moved into the vacant building. Henrich Justi (1804-1878) and his friends from the Pressburg Beauty Association founded the Museum. The first collections, then exhibited in three rooms of the Old Town Hall, were the basis of today's Museum of Bratislava which now has ten exhibitions all over the town. It is the oldest museum in Slovakia.

When it became obvious that not even the Aponyi Palace would satisfy the needs of the Pressburg municipal authorities, the councillors proposed the purchase of the Primatial Palace. It was

eventually bought in 1903. Then there was the necessity to connect the older building with the Primatial palace and an architectural tender was announced. The jury, which met in 1907, chose the project of architects J. Hübner and S. Mészner from Budapest. They respected the historicizing principles with special regard for the Neo Gothic style. They tried to keep to the style of the existing buildings and imitated the architectural elements applied in the Middle Ages. The project was completed in 1912 and it involved construction of the eastern and southern wings of the Town Hall. All later interventions were mere repairs and reconstruction of some hidden valuable architectural details. Such was the reconstruction of the disappeared Gothic chapel, restoration of the statue of the Virgin Mary on the corner of the tower, etc. While restoring the facade the **cannon ball** stuck in the facade, which commemorates the attacks of Napoleon's army in 1809 was also preserved. There is also a **board with a line** marking the water level of the Danube at the time of the disastrous floods on February 5th 1850. On the left side of the Gothic portal there are **control measures** serving the merchants and their clients for verification of the ones used in the market place. The thin iron rod with lines represents the Pressburg ell (1.286 ell = 0.783 m) used to **measure cloth**.

Left: The courtyard of the Old Town Hall
Right: On Hlavné námestie square

The Apponyi Palace ❸ next to Unger's house is out of the Hlavné námestie square in a short **Radničná ulica street**. By the end of the 18th century and the beginning of the 19th the name *Apponyi Gässel* was also used because the palace of Count Juraj Apponyi is the dominating building in this street. The smart Rococo palace filled in the comparatively small plot in the neighbourhood of the Town Hall. Originally there were several old burgher houses. The architect of the palace was probably F. A.

Hillebrandt. It was build in the years 1761-1762 for count Juraj Apponyi, a member of a rich Hungarian noble family from Oponice near Topoľčany. The Apponyi family entered higher politics in the second half of the 18th century. They held top military and governmental offices in Hungary. Apponyi's laws from 1907 are especially well known. They negatively affected other the non-Magyar nationalities in Kingdom of Hungary. Count Juraj, the owner of the palace at Radničná street was the first important politician in this family. He was a chamber counsellor to the governor of Hungary. The municipal authorities bought the palace in 1876 with the intention of expanding the Town Hall. Pulling down two courtyard wings in order to connect the interior of the palace with Town Hall and Primatial palace reduced the original four-wing building. At present the Apponyi Palace shelters the **Viticultural Museum** and regional library. The collections displayed on the ground floor and basement of the palace document the rich history of wine growing in the traditional viticultural region of the Little Carpathians. An original press used in wine production is placed in the courtyard.

The house ❹ (No. 2) standing opposite the Apponyi Palace with its main entrance from the Hlavné námestie square is one of the oldest in the city. Due to remarkable discoveries of very old architectural elements from the last third of the 13th century the citizens of Pressburg know it as a **house with a tower**. Extensive renovation of the building in the 1980's century led to discovery of the remains of an original burgher house with tower which was, like the predecessor of the Old Town Hall, made for living. The facade of the restored building preserves the contours of the disappeared medieval tower with battlements. However, the final restoration of the exterior of the house covered them again. Inside the house several fragments of medieval architectural elements of the oldest stage of its develop-

ment were found. There are remnants of the Gothic phase of the house, for instance, the corner pillar supporting the tower and decorated with masks from the 15th century or the Gothic segmented portal. Renaissance left there the remains of graffito from the 16th century found during the repair of the facade in 1962. The present rather bulky appearance of the house is caused by the superstructure of the third floor and a new roof both made in the 19th century. The last of the trio of houses at the southern part of Hlavné námestie is the **Jeszenák Palace** ❺. The Baroque building on the corner of Hlavné námestie and Rybárska brána was built in the 18th century at the site of an older house. The stone cartouche on corner bears the coat of arms of the original owner of the palace, Baron Ján Jeszenák. Recently the stylish and in the past very popular **café and sweet shop Café Mayer** returned to the ground floor of the palace. The basement contains an old well discovered during the restoration of the building. Torsos of Romanesque-Gothic pillars from the first half of the 14th century were found within the supporting walls of the palace.

The western row of houses at Hlavné námestie is the youngest one. **House No. 5** ❻ is especially interesting. It was built in 1906 on the site of an older medieval house of the Auer family from the 15th century. Queen Mary, the widow of King Louis II lived in it for some time. The architect N. Körösy applied several historicizing architectural forms of what is called the Hungarian national style combined with elements of Viennese eclecticism. Today it is the seat of bank, but it has also the **café U Rolanda** on its ground floor. The interior of the café was refreshed by a true imitation of Kempelen's chess automate (→ 160). The **Palugyay Palace** ❼ (No.6) standing on the corner of Hlavné námestie and Zelená Ulica street acquired its Neo Baroque appearance in 1880. The style is based on the traditions of the French Baroque. It was built for an important businessman trading in wine, František Palugyay. The architect was the Pressburg native Viktor Rumpelmayer. The house called Burg formerly stood on the site and it sheltered the municipal authorities before they moved to the Old Town Hall at the opposite side of the square. The noble family of Mednyánszky also lived there for some time and as it had four floors it was also the tallest house in the city in the 18'h century.

The opposite corner of **Zelená street** is occupied by the **Zelený dom** ❽ or the Green House (Sedlárska street No. 12). The name derives from the green painted facade and in its ground floor was a popular tavern and restaurant. In fact, the name is a corrupted translation of the older German name of the house *Grünstüblhaus* or the house with a green room. The interior of the house was or-

Left: The Green House
Right: The house of the Royal Governing Council

namented with green paintings. Green rooms with vegetal motifs and figural compositions were quite common in noble houses built in time of the Late Gothic. They were also found in other Bratislava houses. Its basis is the Gothic house mentioned in the act from 1419. It was a tavern, where wine from the municipal vineyards was tapped. However, it had also extensive halls where various social events and celebrations were held. In the 16th century the representatives of the Hungarian Estates met here for parliamentary sessions. In time of coronation of the kings and queens of Hungary, the Green House hosted noble guests taking part in the pompous celebration. The Green House also has a theatrical past. In 1761 in its rear part a theatre hall was built, where the citizens of Pressburg had the opportunity to watch for the first time the plays of famous dramatists such as Shakespeare or Moliére. The actors also performed for the Queen Maria Theresia and her court. By the end of the 18th century the city sold the house to a private owner, who rebuilt it in the Baroque style. Its present outer appearance is Neo Classical. The gable of the house from 1755 bearing an older **stone relief** is the one deserving attention. It depicts a scene from the Old Testament in which Joshua and Caleb bear a grape of wine from Canaan. The Green House is now a bank.

Eponymous **Zelená ulica street** or the former Obuvnícka (the Shoemaker's street) connects the Main Square with Ventúrska ulica street. In its middle is the functionalist modern building of **Perugia Hotel** ❾ from 1929. It is an example of appropriate inclusion of a modern building in historic surroundings. The name of the hotel symbolizes the friendly relations of the city of Bratislava with Perugia in Italy. A curiosity of its bar is that in the period of political thaw in Czechoslovakia 1960's it offered the first ever strip-tease show to the citizens of Bratislava. The front wing of the Zelený dom overlooks the **Sedlárska ulica**

street. This medieval street, along with Rybárska brána, connects Michalská and Laurinská streets. Its name (The Saddler's street) suggests that in the past it was inhabited above all by saddlers. The oldest known name in German *Sattlergassen* is first mentioned 1617. It bore the name of the Hungarian politician Ferenc Deák for some time before the fall of the monarchy. Then its original name was assumed and remained untouched even by the Communist regime, which was especially particular about the names of places. The houses on it mostly have Neo Classical facades, but these cover older Gothic and Renaissance cores of houses, the oldest dating from the 15th century. Today this street is the favourite route of walks of the citizens and a most lively part of what is called the **Bratislava Corso**. In the sixties the avant-garde theatre of *Divadlo na korze* (now the building of the Hungarian embassy) attracted the young audience, while today it is rather the Irish pub **The Dubliner** that has won popularity among both the younger and older generations.

The Bratislava Corso

An important part of life of Bratislava's youth was walking up and down the Corso. Every day at dusk the youth met in the streets of the old town. They walked along Michalská, and Sedlárska, Hlavné námestie down to Rybárska brána, Hviezdoslavovo námestie square, Mostová ulica street, Námestie Ľudovíta Štúra square and the embankment of the Danube around the port of propeller and back. It was the best occasion to meet friends, to show up in new clothes or to have a cup of coffee, tea or lemonade with cake in one of the sweet shops on the route. The best time of the Corso was the inter-war years when the streets of the old town were full of tiny shops, cafés, and bars. But in the 1970's the Corso started to lose its charm. The cause was the gradual depopulation of the city centre. Flats were turned into offices and shops disappeared. When the ones that remained closed at six in the afternoon, the streets were empty. The majority of people went to sleep in their houses in the outskirts and one could meet only several drunkards returning from the bars. But the bad times of Corso are over and now it offers a choice of attractions for the young and old. Restaurants and sweet shops were reopened and the pedestrian zone is again attractive for walks.

Let us go back to the Hlavné námestie square along the western wing of the **Kutscherfeld Palace** ❿ turned to Sedlárska street. The windows of the palace (No. 7) overlook Maximilian's fountain. The corner two-storied palace is one of the most beautiful Rococo buildings in the city. It was built in 1762 on the site of several medieval plots. The unknown architects of the palace chose an untypical facade without pilasters

Left: Christmas market
Right: The tower of the Old Town Hall

and with lavish stucco ornamentation of the ledge above the windows. The portal too, was untraditionally designed with a two-wing wooden gate and a light looking balcony with metal bars over it. In the interior of the palace the original Rococo stucco ornamentation has survived. The first owner of the palace was Ludwig von Kutscherfeld, administrator of property at Magyarovár in Hungary. He sold the palace to Count Esterházy, member of the Čeklís branch of a top Hungarian noble family in 1800. In 1847 the Esterházy's hosted an oustanding Russian pianist and composer **Anton Grigorievich Rubinstein** (1829-1894). The eighteen-year-old artist spent the summer in Pressburg. He won the popularity of the Pressburg audience due to three successful performances in the Theatre of Estates. He even composed three compositions here; one of them was the well-known Concerto for piano and orchestra in d-minor. Rubinstein returned to Pressburg as a world famous artist on another two occasions. Today the Kutscherfeld Palace houses the **French embassy** and the **French Institute**. The presence of the French on Hlavné námestie square is suggested also by a recently installed bronze **statue of an Frenchman** ⓫ of a man in uniform wearing a typical three-horn Napoleon hat. The soldier looking like Napoleon himself leans on a bench, a favourite spot of the tourists making snapshots.

When in 1723 **Palác miestodržiteľskej rady** ⓬ (the Palace of royal governing council) was established, Pressburg was chosen as its seat. It was placed in the house in the north-eastern corner of Hlavné námestie. The city obtained this top office which represented the ruler in Hungary seated in Vienna. It

was not entitled to take final decisions as it had to have them approved by the ruler represented by the Hungarian Office in Vienna. In 1762 the office also bought the neighbouring house. The two buildings were connected and rebuilt as the palace of the royal governing council. The eastern facade of the palace faces Františkánske námestie square and its southern side overlooks the Hlavné námestie square. The two-storied building with interior courtyard was reconstructed in Rococo style. The carriages entered the yard from the Hlavné námestie square and left it by the exit to Františkánske námestie square or vice versa. There is again a top governmental body seated in the palace: the **Office of the Government of the Slovak Republic.**

The Františkánske námestie square

Františkánske námestie square is a kind of counterpart to busy Hlavné námestie or the Main square. It offers a much quieter, almost chamber ambience amidst antique historic houses. Františkánske námestie originated some time in the 13th century, hence it is one of the oldest in the town. Its present name is linked to the presence of the church and monastery of the Franciscan order. The medieval archive documents mention also other names such as *Chlebový* or *Rybný trh* (Bread or Fish Market). Both markets were moved to the lower part of today's Square of the Slovak National Uprising. Františkánske námestie bore a common name with Hlavné námestie for a comparatively long time. Then it was called *Jesuiten Platz* (the Jesuit Square) for a while. In 1764 the name used at present appeared in the historic documents. In recent history Františkánske námestie was again renamed in 1954. Until the velvet revolution it bore the name of the Russian partisan commander I. D. Dibrov.

At the point where Biela ulica (The White Street) joins Františkánske námestie square there used to be a drinking water fountain with water brought here from the Little Carpathian springs. The water was also used for extinguishing fires. A Renaissance **fountain** ❶ equipped first by wooden then by leaden pipes was placed there in 1549. The fountain got a new basin made of pink marble in 1592. In the middle of the basin a pillar with a stone lion bearing the municipal coat of arms was fitted. On the plinth in turn the Austrian two-headed eagle with coat of arms of Hungary on its chest was put. In 1804 a **statue of woman** wearing a helmet and pouring water from a jug replaced the worn out central pillar. The statue came from stonemason Feiglers' workshop a centre, which was, so to say, the nursery of important Neo Classical architects. The fountain was dismantled by the end of the 19th century and its parts were distributed all over the city. The stone lion was displayed in several squares. It used to stand in front of the Avion building in the American square; today it is to be seen in the front yard of Stará tržnica on the SNP square. The statue of woman with jug in turn was standing for a long time in front of the Stará tržnica. On the occasion of the general restoration of Františkánske námestie square the statue was returned to its original place and in the form of 1804.

Biela ulica or White Street is a short connecting street between Františkánske námestie square and Michalská ulica street. It originated in the 15th century. Its name derives from the fact that the facades of houses were painted in white to make the narrow and dark lane look lighter. The white facades were eventual-

Left: Františkánske námestie ssquare

ly ornamented by different patterns. In 1528 this street was referred to as *Schneeweis Gassel* (Snow-white Street). By the end of the 19th and the early 20th century it was called Corvinus' street in honour King Matthias Corvinus of Hungary. After the Second World War it was given the name of the Czech poet Jiří Wolker (1900-1924) and it was called Wolkrova until the beginning of the 1990's, when its name was changed again to Biela. There are two houses in Biela ulica street which deserve attention. The first of the two is standing right on the corner in the southern row. It is called **U čierneho havrana** ❷ or At the Black Raven (No. 6). Maybe it is related to the above-mentioned king, better said to the Latin version of his name derived from *Corvus* or raven. The core of this house is very old, from the 13th century. Originally it was a fortified residential tower. A precious Renaissance **painting** on its facade attracts the attention of passers by. One can discern in this figural painting viticultural theme depicting St. Christopher, St. Florian and workers at a vineyard. In the yard of the house is a preserved Renaissance **arcade** bore by stone Tuscany pillars. The house shelters a stylish restaurant and a small musical theatre. In its historical basement theatrical shows, concerts of folk and jazz music are held. The citizens of Bratislava especially love the shows of an amateur **theatre** group called **GUnaGU**. Another interesting building of Biela ulica stands on the northern side closer to Michalská ulica street. It is the **Habermayer's house** ❸ (No. 3). It was originally a Renaissance house with a hall on the ground floor street wing. Its present appearance is owed to a Neo Classical reconstruction made for a rich merchant in tobacco. The hall on the ground floor was divided in two rooms and a passage through the house was made. Nice stucco ornamentation was preserved on the Neo Classical facade.

The northern row of houses of Biela ulica street continues with a block of medieval buildings, which taper along the upper part of Františkánske námestie square. It is the space where probably another house of the mayor Jakub used to stand in the early Middle Ages. Historians believe it was on Jacob's plot, which originally stretched

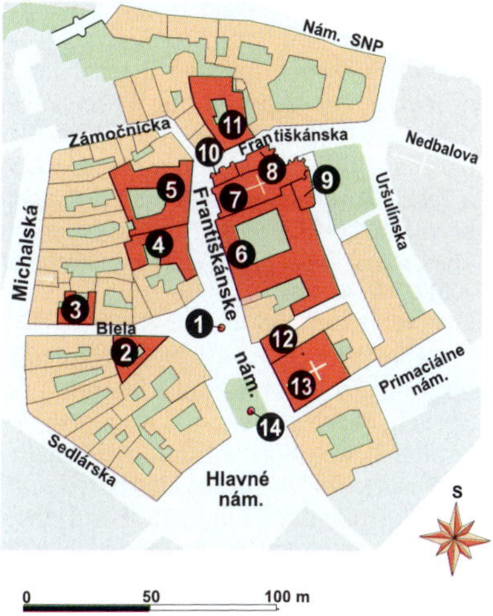

Fontána s plastikou ženy ❶
Dom U čierneho havrana ❷
Habermayerov dom ❸
Vinohradnícky dom ❹
Mirbachov palác ❺
Kláštor františkánov ❻
Kostol františkánov ❼
Kaplnka sv. Jána Evanjelistu ❽
Kaplnka sv. Rozálie ❾
Loretánska kaplnka ❿
Husitský dom ⓫
Dom na Františkánskom nám. 4 ⓬
Jezuitský kostol ⓭
Stĺp Panny Márie Víťaznej ⓮

from Hlavné námestie square up to Michalská street. There exists a reference to Jacob's house at Fish Market (now Františkánske námestie square) in connection with the sale of the property inherited by Jacob's two sons. Pavol sold it along with the plot to pharmacist Prandi and his wife in 1368. Part of this block is what is called **Vinohradnícky dom** (the Vintner's house) ❹ (No. 10), the best preserved burgher house in the city with original medieval inner division. Some fragments such as the main segmented portal, the original truss of the roof and medieval basements have been preserved from the Late Gothic form of the house. In the upper floor of the house a valuable Late Gothic painting from late 15th century was discovered. In the 16th century Evangelical school used the house. This is also the period of arcades in the courtyard. The name Viticultural house suggests that it was the seat of the vintners association. The tradition is maintained by the popular **tavern Veľkí františkáni** in the basement stretching as far as the neighbouring Mirbach Palace.

The **Mirbach Palace** ❺ is the architectural gem of the upper part of Františkánske námestie square. It is rightly admired along with the Primatial Palace as one of the most beautiful sights offered by Bratislava. This Rococo building was built by Matej Hörlligl in years 1768-1770 on the site of the former Weitenhof house (Wide Yard House). It was a city property bought from the Franciscans.

Theatre in the Weitenhof

In the Weitenhof, or today's Františkánske square there was a theatre hall in which theatre shows were given as early as the beginning of the 17th century. It is referred to for the first time in 1609 in relation to a session of the Diet in Pressburg. Travelling German theatre groups that usually performed in inns used to stop in Pressburg and give shows on this oldest theatre stage in the city. It was here that the citizens of Pressburg accustomed to Passion plays saw the first secular dramas. The municipal accountancy books mention performances of wandering actors in the Weitenhof in the years 1649 and 1696. The city issued permissions for performances for two weeks. The actors paid the rent to the city because the hall was a public property. The house was burnt down in October 1733.

The Mirbach Palace was presumably built for a rich brewer of Pressburg, M. Speech. However, he sold it immediately after it was finished to Imrich Csáky. The owners of the palace alternated until Count Emil Mirbach bought it and eventually donated to the city in his last will, with the conditions that it would become an art gallery. The city fulfilled the principal condition of the testament. The **Art**

Left: The staircase of Mirbach Palace
Right: Exterior of Mirbach Palace
Interior of Mirbach Palace

Gallery of Bratislava is located in the palace and offers valuable occasional fine art expositions along with standing collections of the Baroque artists whose work or life was connected with Bratislava. There are, for instance the famous heads by František Xaver Messerschmidt and canvasses by František Xaver Palko.

The Mirbach Palace preserved its original Rococo form. It represents the supreme sample of this style, and even its branch bearing a separate denomination - the **Rococo of Bratislava**. It had to be squeezed onto a rather irregular corner plot and the builder excellently accomplished the job. There are two notable portals in its Rococo facade boasting stucco ornaments. The left portal is real, the right one is fictitious. They were both passable in the past. The ornaments include rocailles and picturesque plant motives and images of musical instruments. Fortunately, also the original interior lavishly ornamented by rocailles has survived. The ornamentation is in the stairways, corridors and in individual rooms. Two halls are covered with cases containing a valuable **collection of the French reproduced Rococo graphics** from the 18th century. A series of reproductions of what is called the Medici cycle by Peter Paul Rubens depicting important life events of Queen Mary Medici is among them. The collection of graphics was brought to the Mirbach Palace in the period when it was owned by the family of Nyáry.

In the middle of the four-wing building is a courtyard skirted by galleries

and with a fountain. The **fountain** with a circular basin includes a bronze cast of the group called **Triton with nymphs**. Its artist is Viktor Tilgner, native of Pressburg (1844-1896) who was active in Vienna as the professor at the Academy of Fine Arts. He made the representation of a mythological subject while on a study journey in Italy in 1873. Later the above-life-size model of a group of statues aroused great interest among the demanding Vienna art lovers. The Emperor Francis Joseph bought the model and had it cast in bronze. The cast was placed in Volksgarten Park near the Emperor's residence. In 1883 the sculptor exhibited his works in his native Pressburg and donated twenty-one exhibits to the city including the successful bronze cast of Triton with nymphs. After the Second World War another two casts were made, one of them is in the courtyard of the Slovak National Gallery and the other is adorning the courtyard of the Mirbach Palace. The original has not been preserved.

Opposite to the Mirbach Palace is the Franciscan church. Let us stop first at the neighbouring building of the monastery, the history of which is closely connected with this church. It used to belong to the monks, who were among the first to come to Pressburg. The mendicant order with the official name *Ordo Fratrum Minorum* (Order of Minor Brothers), though much better known after the name of its founder, St. Francis of Assisi, settled in the town in 1238. Franciscans helped the poorest layers of population and tried to palliate the hard fate of the urban poor by charity. They built their monastery at the eastern end of Podhradie, the townlet existing below the castle. The first Franciscan monastery was considerably damaged during the siege of the town by Přemysl Otakar II in 1270. It is this event to which also the first reference to monastery is linked and mentions that the monks provided shelter to people living nearby when the troops of the Czech king attacked the town. The restored **Franciscan monastery** ❻ was later included among the buildings of the town. It was built next to the southern wall of the somewhat older Franciscan church. The monastery was originally a complex of several Gothic buildings with an inner courtyard. The architecture was later changed, as the repeated natural disasters called for general reconstruction. It was damaged by an intense earthquake in 1850, and fire did not avoid it either. The worst fire, which damaged the monastery happened in 1439.

More rebuilding followed in the course of the 17th century and ended in the following century. The complicated architectural development produced a hybrid complex of buildings with two courtyards and a garden. Inside the monastic complex the original **arcade stations of cross-corridor** built around the squarish cloister has survived. The

Left: Promotion to the Knight of the Golden Spur
Right: Interior of the Franciscian church

present **facade** of the main monastic building facing Františkánske námestie dates from the latter half of the 19th century. Part of monastery was a granary and hospital for the monks. One of few Gothic parts of the monastery that survived the reconstruction was the hexagonal **Gothic tower** built in 15th century. But earthquakes partially damaged its stability. In 1897 it was carefully dismantled and moved to the Sad Janka Kráľa park in Petržalka. The monastery got a new **Neo Gothic copy of the tower**.

The monastery also became the venue for events of a secular nature, such as elections of the Pressburg mayor (every year on April 24th the feast of St. George) and immediately before the Christmas 1526 the memorable session of the Hungarian Diet, which approved the election of Ferdinand as the King of Hungary was also held there. This was the place, where the almost four hundred year history of the House of Habsburg on the throne of Hungary started.

The **Franciscan church** ❼ consecrated to the **Annunciation of the Virgin Mary** is very old. It is the oldest preserved sacral building in Bratislava. Unconfirmed sources have that it was built by the King of Hungary Ladislav IV Kumánsky in honour of the victory over the King Přemysl Otakar II of Bohemia in the famous battle on the Marchfeld in 1278. The interest of crowned heads in this church was confirmed by the personal presence of King Andrew III at its ceremonial consecration on March 25th 1297. It was built in Gothic taste as a simple single-naved church. The earthquake of 1590 caused the fall of the Gothic cross vault. It was replaced by a new **Renaissance vault**. The original Gothic **presbytery** and the **lateral walls** of the nave were preserved and today are the oldest part of the church. The precious sandstone **statue of Pieta** standing on the left lateral altar is also from that period. It was probably made for the chapel of the Jacob's family. It is from

the early 15th century, the time when style called beautiful was very popular. The monument to V. Drughet from 1609 placed on the northern wall of the nave is from the Renaissance period. The last extensive intervention into the building was the Baroque adjustment of the **facade** of the rear part of the building. On a tall gable above the entrance portal there is the **statue of Immaculate Conception**. Originally there was a big fresco of the Assumption of the Virgin Mary. The Baroque style penetrated also into the interior of the Franciscan church. The **main altar** is from the mid-18th century and bears the painting of glass of the Assumption of the Virgin Mary from the end of the 19th century made according to the original painting from the 18th century. The **side altars** are also in the Baroque style, all of them are from the mid-18th century. The pulpit from 1756 is in the Rococo style and it is adorned with several notable reliefs. One of traditional ceremonies of the Pressburg coronations took place in the Franciscan

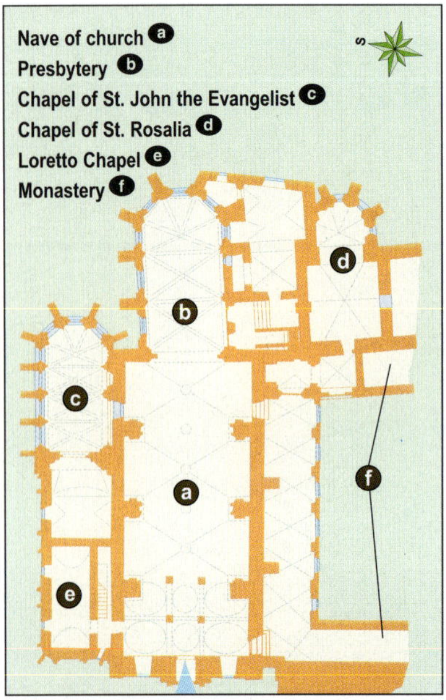

church. It was the promotion of selected aristocrats to the **Knights of the Golden Spur**.

The night worship of the dead monks

Every year on Christmas Eve strange things occur in the Franciscan church: a thousand candles on the altar and the Christmas tree light the crypts in the basement. The long dead monks get up from their graves and gather in the chapel of St. John. The eldest brother serves the mass and the monks sing. Precisely at midnight this special worship finishes and the church suddenly remains still for the whole of the next year. However, only a good Christian and one born in Pressburg, can observe this extraordinary show.

There are three chapels around the Franciscan church. Two of them are next to the northern side of the nave and the third is near the sacristy. The oldest Gothic church from the end of the 13th century had its chapel which was consecrated a year before the church was. It was probably pulled down on the orders of the mayor Jakub II, who wanted to build a new one: the still existing **chapel of St. John the Evangelist** ❽. It was built in the second half of the 14th century and it is referred to in connection with the fact that mayor Jakub II was decided to donate 150 denars to it. The interest of the most powerful man in the town in a new elegant building, attached to the wall of the Franciscan church, was comprehensible; it was to be his family's burial place. The Gothic building is a very pure and balanced example of a two storied burial chapel. The famous Sainte Chapelle of Paris inspired its creators. They were indeed successful. Pressburg acquired one of its most beautiful Gothic buildings. It contains the relics of the priest and martyr **St. Reparatus** tortured to death in Nola near Naples in 533. They were deposited in the church of St. Lorenzo in Rome until the latter half of the 18th century, when they were brought to Pressburg by the Franciscan priest Eugen Kós (1714-1783). The day of the ecclesiastical remembrance of St. Reparatus is October 21st.

The **chapel of St. Rozália** ❾ originated afterwards. It was built in the 15th century and consecrated to St. Sebastián. It was placed on the opposite side of the church and it can be seen from the open plot in front of the Ursuline church in Uršulínska ulica street. The third chapel is the youngest and adjoins the first chapel. It dates from 1708. Like additions to some other churches, its interior tries to imitate the legendary dwelling of the Virgin Mary in Loretto. For this reason it is called the **Loretánska kaplnka** ❿ that is the Loretto Chapel.

The best view of the couple of very different chapels next to the northern wall of the Franciscan church is from the short Franciscan street. It was origi-

Right: Chapel of St. John the Evangelist

nally a lane inside the wall of the northern fortifications of the medieval town. It was first mentioned in 1457. Besides the above-mentioned chapels there is another interesting building on Františkánska street. The House of Hussites or **Husitský dom** ⓫ at No. 3 stands right in front of them.

The legend of the Hussite House

The Hussite troops led by the commander of the Trnava garrison Blažek of Borotín came back to the gates of Pressburg and tried to conquer the town again in 1432. A group of conspirators met in the house in Františkánska ulica where they were preparing plans to let the Hussites into the town. But the legend has that the monks of the Franciscan monastery revealed the conspiracy before it started. The monks made use of a secret corridor leading from the monastery underground directly into the centre of the plot in the opposite house. The monk spies naturally spread the information and the conspirators were imprisoned. Blažek waited in vain for the opening of one of the four town gates. The leader of conspiracy, the knight Peter was beheaded and his confiscated property was used for drilling a well in the castle premises.

Let us go back to Františkánske square and look at the landmarks in its eastern row of houses. Below the Franciscan monastery is the only **modern building** of the square (No. 3). It was built in the years 1934-1936 on the site of pulled down service building of the monastery. The neighbouring **No. 4** ⓬ was built in the 18th century in the Baroque style and it was given its present Neo Classical facade by the beginning of the 19th century. The **commemorative plaque** reads that the first Slovak music school was established there in 1919. The recognized composer and excellent teacher **Miloš Ruppeldt** (1881-1943) taught gifted youth in this school. Ruppeldt also founded other music in-

stitutions in the city such as the Slovak Philharmonic Orchestra.

The **Jesuit Church** ⓭ in the lower part of the square was not always owned by the Jesuits. It was built and used for the first decades of its existence by other congregation, against which the radical counter-reformers of the Society of Jesus came to fight. The German Evangelicals of Pressburg built the church following the royal consent in 1636. As there were many rich burghers among them, they could afford to build the temple in close vicinity of the Town Hall. However, an Evangelical temple had to comply with several limiting conditions. It could not have a tower and the entrance on its front side. The Evangelicals of Pressburg fulfilled only the first condition and ignored the second. The architects designed what was called the **German Evangelical Church** as a very simple structure, in line with the ideas of the reformed Church concerning the temple free of luxury and pompousness. The Cisalpine variation of the Renaissance

style had abundant means to realise such an intention. Spacious hall church had emporiums, applied in the Protestant architecture in Slovakia even today, along its three walls. The re-Catholicizing pressure became stronger during the reign of King Leopold I and Archbishop Szelepcsényi took away the temple of the Evangelicals. The German church was given to the **Jesuits** who dedicated it to **the Most Holy Saviour**. The new administrators of the church started its reconstruction. The facade remained almost intact, except for the original Renaissance **portal**. Jesuits installed a lavishly ornamented and **multi-coloured symbol of their order** on it. It was presumably made by the stucco master Johan Wüngler. Substantial changes were made in the interior of the church. The interior is essentially in the Baroque taste enriched by the Rococo details. For instance, the **pulpit** from 1753 is in the Rococo style. It was made by one of the best Donner's pupils, Ludwig Gode. Allegorical statues and images of the lead reliefs depict the missionary activity of the patron, the Most Holy Saviour. **The main altar** from the 19th century bears the picture of Christ on the Mountain of Tábor by S. Majsch.

Sightseeing of the square ends under the **pillar of the Virgin Mary the Victorious** ⓮ which the oldest of the kind in the Kingdom of Hungary. It belongs to the group of pillars built by the Habsburg's all over the country in honour of their military successes. The one of Františkánske námestie stands here since 1675. The foundation stone was laid down on 25th April and on 7th December (a day before the feast of the Immaculate Conception of the Virgin Mary) of the same year it was consecrated by Archbishop Juraj Szelepcsényi personally. The pillar celebrates the victory of the Emperor Ladislav I of Habsburg over the Turks at St. Gotthard in 1664 and subsequent rebellions of the Hungarian Estates (those of Vesselényi and Rákoczi in the years 1667-1671). At the same time it symbolizes the successful fight of the Catholic Church against Reformation in Pressburg. This precisely was the reason why was the pillar erected in front of the entrance to the church taken away from the Evangelicals and passed over to the Jesuits. Moreover, the preacher Mikuláš Drábik of the Czech Brethren was executed at this place for predicting disappearance of the House of Habsburg his book *Lux in tenebris*. The ideological message of the pillar is completed by two sculptures: that of Madonna and Adoration of the Blessed Sacrament.

Left: The pulpit of the Jesuit church

The Primaciálne Námestie Square

Comparatively young buildings surround **Primatial square**, with the oldest house counting not more than four hundred years. But that does not mean that the square is young. Archaeological finds prove that Celts, Romans and old Slavs inhabited this territory. The open space behind the Town Hall existed long ago. But in contrast the Hlavné and Františkánske squares, the ground plan of which had stabilized very early and did not change afterwards, it took several centuries for Primatial square to acquire its present form. It gained its rectangular shape in the mid-18th century. The older urban fabric disappeared under a new one, which did not always respect the original medieval plotting. The oldest historical source from 1370 mentions that the meat market was moved from the central square in front of the Town Hall to another open space behind it. It is fairly possible that the market drew closer to butchers who lived next to Butcher's bastion. The bastion used to stand at the northern part of the municipal fortification, next to Jacob's lands and today's Klobúčnícka ulica. Some bastions bore the names of the guilds, which were responsible for their defence. Shoemakers defended the Shoemakers' bastion, and the butchers cared for the prismatic Butchers' bastion. In order to be able to intervene in its defence they had to reside nearby. The grain market occupied the Primatial square in the 16th century, after moving here from Františkánske námestie square. The first reference to it as a square dates from the 18th century. The name *Jesuiten Platz* (the Jesuit Square) is from 1754, and the name *Platz vor dem cardinal*

Studňa 1
Súsošie sv. Jána Nepomuckého 2
Primaciálny palác 3
Fontána sv. Juraja 4
Nová radnica 5
Dom na Kostolnej 1 6
Stará radnica 7
Hummelov dom 8
Hudobná expozícia Mestského múzea 9
Mestské hradby 10
Stará tržnica 11
Pamätná tabuľa Paracelsa 12
Dom na Uršulínskej 6 13
Kostol uršulínok 14
Kláštor uršulínok 15

Palee (the Square next to Cardinal' Palace) in turn is from 1783. The present name denoting the square has been used since 1920.

Today's appearance of the Primatial square is the result of recent reconstruction finished in 1976. The new pavement is cherished especially by young roller skaters. Archaeologists used the occasion and at the time of reconstruction discovered an **old well ❶**, which has been included in the renovated area of the square. The face of the square had been changing over history. Historical photographs show that a **group of statues of St. John Nepomuk ❷** used to stand here. It was placed there in 1725 to underline the presence of the Church institutions (Archbishop's palace and two monasteries). The actual statue of the saint carved from stone was placed on a tall pillar. A group of angels seemed to be carrying the saint.

Left: The Primatial square
Right: The Primatial Palace

The **Primatial Palace ❸**, which with his bulky building occupies the whole southern side of the Primatial square, is considered the most beautiful in Bratislava. It was built in the years 1778-1781 on the site of an older Archbishop's palace. A mansion of the Archbishop of Esztergom stood here long before, this highest Church dignitary in Hungary had to abandon Esztergom on its capture by the Turks, and move his office and seat to Pressburg and Trnava. The reference to the construction of the palace supervised by mayor Jacob is from 1369. Historians assume that it was rather a reconstruction of an older palace building to which a chapel was added in 1454. The Archbishop's palace had to be reconstructed again after the fire of 1590. An arcade was added at the eastern end and the chapel acquired an arcade stairway and a corridor leading to the upper floor of the palace. In the years 1610 to 1662 there was a printing house working within the palace and its role was to propagate Catholic literature. Presumably the predecessor of the Primatial palace was a splendid and luxurious building corresponding to the position of its owner. In spite of this, the Cardinal and Primate **Jozef Batthyány** (1720-1799) decided to build a new and even more pompous residence. In the 1770's almost every noble of Pressburg owned some kind of palace or at least a better-off burgher house. The seat of the head of the Church in Hungary then had to match and outclass them. Nevertheless, the old palace although pompous was also obsolete. It was the medieval type of building with an evident defensive purpose. Adding of new space to the palace was out of question. The unwillingness of Count Alexander Károlyi to sell part of the plot at the eastern corner of the land was the main obstacle. This was the reason why the construction in a comparatively cramped space started in 1778.

In the time of the fading Baroque era in Pressburg a palace in pure Neo Classical style originated. There was no other way, as its creator Melchior Hefele was one of a group of Vienna architects with uncompromising Neo Classical orientation. The purely Neo Classical Primatial palace became the most grandiose expression of the principles of the new style, different from the Baroque or Rococo styles. Unusually successful outcome of the style applied in the construction of the new palace provoked a response. It opened the way of Neo Classicism in Hungary. The domestic architects and builders obtained an ideal example and source of inspiration. Hefele applied with utmost sensitivity the rational aspects of the Neo Classical style. The irregularity of inner space corresponds to the irregular ground plan. The facade and a symmetrical courtyard though, ingeniously hide this asymmetry. The central hall is placed in lateral wing and the chapel is in the rear wing of the palace. The front wing overlooking the Primatial square is strictly Neo Classical.

The virtues and distinctions of Cardinal Batthyányi

The ornamentation of the facade of the Primatial palace was selected in a way, which represented its first owner, Cardinal Jozef Batthyányi. The gable of the palace is ornamented by a row of allegorical statues expressing the Cardinal's virtues and distinctions. The first of the pair couple of statues at the left edge is Minerva, protector of science and arts. *The statue holds the measure, number and a scale in one hand, and an open book with an inscription reading: "All comes from unity and returns to unity" in the other. The second figure with a lance in its hand is a token of active virtue and a reward for virtue adorned by a laurel wreath. The following isolated statue symbolizes* Love to Homeland. *It is represented by a figure of a young man trampling on an enemy's arms and ready to offer any sacrifice for the homeland's glory. He holds a grass wreath in one hand and an oak branch in the other. In the middle at the top of the pediment is the Batthyányi family's coat of arms. Two geniuses adorned by worldly and spiritual distinctions carry it. A black Cardinal's hat with a diameter of 1.80 m and weighing 150 kilograms at the top finishes the top of the palace. The purpose of this representation of the traditional hat of a Cardinal made of iron is to remind the citizens that the master of this palace is a top Church dignitary. Two statues at the right side of the gable above the pediment represent the symbols of the coat of arms. The figure standing immediately next to the coat of arms is the allegory of* Virtue in Service. *The statue with the ribbon of an order and a laurel wreath holds a sealed letter on its chest. There is sword in its left hand prepared to protect the secrets and defend the homeland. The second figure holds a heart in both hands and expresses the* Purity of Heart, *the obligatory condition of all virtues. The last group of statues is an allegory of* Constancy, *the principal spiritual virtue of Cardinal Batthyányi. The female figure symbolizes Piety. She is sitting on a ball and touches the wheel on her left side. It means that the priest should have a minimum contact with the wheel and the heavenly ball. The other figure of the group of statues leaning on a*

broken pillar represents constancy in devotion to God. In the middle of the facade there is an inscription on red marble: Curia Arciepiscopalis Peculio Cardinalis Josephi de Bathian Excitata *(Archbishop's curia built for Cardinal Joseph Batthyányi). Above it are two* putti *carrying the initials C and I, which symbolize the Batthyányi's personal motto:* Iustitia et Clementia *(Justice and Kindness).*

One enters the Primatial palace through a three-axial vestibule where a wide flight of stairs leads to the main halls on the first floor or Piano nobile. It overlooks the square and is directly connected with the main representative hall of the palace in its eastern wing. The huge hall looks even bigger because of the numerous mirrors on its walls. It is called the **Zrkadlová sieň** or the Hall of Mirrors. The role of the mirrors was to make the hall look bigger but above all to improve the lighting. The buildings surrounding the Primatial palace shade it and reduce its lighting. The 1805 Christmas season was a time celebrated by the French as one of their historic moments. After the battle at Austerlitz representatives of the countries which took part in it met in the Primatial palace. The victorious Napoleon Bonaparte was represented by his Minister of Foreign Affairs Maurice Talleyrand and Prince John of Liechtenstein represented the defeated Emperor Francis. The treaty, later called the **Peace of Pressburg** was signed on December 26th 1805 in the Hall of Mirrors. Austria lost the territories of Tyrol, Istria, Dalmatia, and Venice and her access to the sea. France gained self-assurance and greed. The memory of the Peace of Pressburg was expressed by giving the name of the city to one of the Paris streets: *Rue de Presbourg* still existing near the Arc de Triomphe. After the castle burnt down in 1811 the impressive halls of the Primatial Palace became especially convenient. Activity was aroused around the palace on the occasion of another historical event in 1848. The Emperor Ferdinand V signed there the act of abolition of serfdom in Hungary. The city bought the palace in 1903 with the intention to expand the Town Hall. During reconstruction of the palace some folded pieces of cloth were found. When they were spread on the floor of the corridor, the astounded custodian of the Municipal Museum August Heimar found out that it was a series of precious tapestries now known as the **Bratislava tapestries**. The Archbishop as owner of the palace gave up the precious find in favour of the city with the particular that they would be displayed in public. But first they had to be restored in the artistic workshops of Belmonte in Hungarian town of Gödölö. The German expert and connoisseur of tapestries W. Zisch from Berlin estimated that the tapestries of Bratislava were made at the royal weaving workshop at Mortlake near London.

Left: The ceiling of St. Ladislav chapel
Right: The Bratislava tapestries
The group of statues of
St. John Nepomuk

The trade mark woven into the edge used by this particular workshop in the years 1616-1688 is the proof. The series of tapestries was made after the cartoons painted by Francis Cleyn from Rozstock. Tapestries were woven on wool and silk and the style of this true work of art is called mannerism. If one weaver made them it would take him twenty years to finish six big tapestries. How and when they got to the palace is still not known. Reliable data are missing. One of the hypotheses is that they were made for the English King Charles I who ended on the scaffold and that was why they remained in ownership of Francis Crane, the proprietor of the weaving workshop. After his death they probably passed to the collections of the French Cardinal Mazarin. Then a short notice appeared that the London merchant Rolf Grafen bought the series *Hero and Leander* in a sale of royal property for 180 pounds. It is supposed that other identical series of tapestries were made, at least three, in Mortlake. We know about one series donated by Count Axel Osenstiern to the Swedish king Karol Gustav X as a wedding gift. Today, though not complete, it is at the Drottningholm Castle in Sweden. They differ in some details from those of Bratislava and they are incomplete. How the tapestries were brought to the Pressburg's Primatial palace is a mystery. Perhaps they were hidden there during the Napoleon's siege of Pressburg in 1809, when also the Emperor Francis found refuge in the palace. Maybe nobody was interested then in tapestries because their price dramatically dropped in the 19th century.

The story of Hero and Leandros

The sad story of the couple of immortal lovers has been the subject of many artistic works of different genres. It originated in the fifth century before Christ in verses of the mythological poet Músai, an alleged pupil of the divine Orpheus. Four centuries later it was refreshed by the great Ovidius, who brought the lyrical love poetry to the very peak of perfection. The Mortlake weavers used this story and transformed it into the woven beauty in six big tapestries creating one complete series. The story took place on the coast of the antique Helespont strait (today's Dardanelles). The Greek Leandros fell in love with beautiful Hero, who lived on the opposite shore of the strait. The first of the series of Bratislava tapestries called The Meeting of Hero with Leandros *depicts the first encounter of the lovers at a ceremony, where they fell in love with each other. Since then Leandros undertook every night the troublesome and exhausting journey of swimming across the strait to see his beloved Hero* (Leandros swimming to Hero). *The light of the lamp at the window of Hero's house showed him the way. The third tapestry called* Janthe announces Leandros' arrival to Hero *represents the moment when the tired, though happy Leandro overcomes the last stretch of the journey. The fourth tapestry is called* Hermiona tries to discourage Leandros from the passage over the strait. *The overall mood of the scene depicted on the tapestry is distressing, Leandros did not obey the warning of his sister and entered the turbulent waters of Helespont. When the wind put out the flame in Hero's lamp, Leandros lost his way in the dark and got drowned in the sea. Eventually a wave threw his dead body out on the shore, where the desperate Hero found it. The tragic end of the story is depicted on the fifth tapestry called* Hero mourns dead Leandros. *Hero responded in the same way as Juliet from Romeo and Juliet' story: She jumped from a steep cliff into the waves of the Helespont to meet her beloved on the way to immortality. The last tapestry* The mourning Eros *is the epilogue to the story. The little god of love is contemplating the water of Helespont and thinking about the unfortunate lovers Leandros and Hero.*

Left: St. George fountain
Right: Kostolná ulica street

In the vestibule there is also a passage to the inner square courtyard. In its centre is the **fountain of St. George** ❹. The group of statues made of sandstone represents the legendary knight fighting against a dragon. It was brought here from the famous Archbishop's garden founded by Archbishop František Forgách in 1614, though the person who promoted the garden to perfection was his successor, Archbishop Juraj Lippay. This is why the garden is called Lippay's. Some assert that the figure of knight George should represent Archbishop Juraj (George) and his fight against the dragon, a symbol of the efforts of the Catholic Church to defeat the Reformation. The garden disappeared by the end of the 19th century and the group of statues of St. George ended up in one of the private burgher gardens. Later it was donated to the city and in 1930 put in the courtyard of the Primatial palace.

In the back and on the right there is the **chapel of St. Ladislav**. Its interior with oval ground plan contains a couple of fairly precious artistic works. The dome of the chapel is adorned by remarkable **illusionist fresco** called *The Miracle of St. Ladislav*. The presumed artist is A. F. Maulbertsch. The wall painting represents a scene from the life of St. Ladislav, King of Hungarian from the Arpad dynasty who, as a legend says, opened a rock cliff by a single stroke of his lance and the rock released a spring of water for his thirsty soldiers. The theme obviously also conveyed a political message. It was a challenge for the Primate to lead the Church out of the chaos into which was Hungary tossed after Joseph II's reforms. Three figures dressed in national costumes from the 18th century also suggest it. A remarkable fact about the chapel is that it is not visible from outside within the silhouette of the palace, as one would expect.

Opposite the Primatial palace is **Nová radnica** ❺ (the New Town Hall). This modern building replaced the 17th century Jesuit monastery demolished in 1948. Its modern form fits historic square comparatively well. The noted Slovak architect Emil Belluš designed it. Left of the New Town Hall stands a three-storied house with tall roof. It is the only **building** ❻ (No. 1), which has an entrance from the narrow **Kostolná ulica street** and to the passage to the Main Square between the walls of the Old Town Hall and the Jesuit church. It was built as a single-floor building in the first half of the 17th century and attached to what used to be the German Evangelical Church. Another three floors were added in 1656 and the building was destined to shelter the grammar school or "gymnasium" for German speaking children of the Pressburg Evangelical families. Evangelicals lost their church and Jesuits took over also

their gymnasium in 1673. Its original purpose was preserved, only this time it was a Catholic grammar school, and it outlived even the abolition of the Jesuit order in 1673. It was the seat of the Hungarian royal school almost until the end of the 19th century, when it had to be moved to a new building in today's Zochova street. It was attended, besides other, also by **Filip Lenard** (1862-1947) a scientist, which received the Nobel Prize for physics in 1905.

The eastern side of today's Primatial palace is closed by the buildings, which have their entrances from Uršulínska and Klobúčnícka streets. **Klobúčnícka ulica street** as we see it now, is a comparatively young street. It was built in the 18th century, though there must have been some street before, in the Middle Ages. Perhaps the one called today Nedbalova. When the town walls were pulled down in 1775, the eastern part of the inner town was rearranged. New buildings covered the narrow and winding lanes of the medieval quarter of merchants and craftsmen. The dominating building of

Klobučnícka street is the Neo Baroque tenement house No. 2 from 1910. In the yard of the smart four-storied house with attic roof is what is called **Hummel's house** ❽. It is a small and picturesque Renaissance house often denoted as the native house of **Johann Nepomuk Hummel** (1778-1837). This world famous composer and pianist though, was born in the house, which existed there before. Hummel's house contains now part of the **musical exhibition** of the Municipal Museum ❾, which documents the life and work of the composer, and the musical history of Bratislava.

The most famous native of Pressburg

Johann Nepomuk Hummel was born in a family of an active musician and teacher of music. His father, a member of the private orchestra of Prince Anton Grassalkovich and also director of the Municipal Theatre orchestra endowed Hummel with an excellent musical education. Hummel moved with his parents to Vienna when he was a little boy and became a pupil of Wofgang Amadeus Mozart. On one occasion Mozart allegedly said that one day his pupil would be a better pianist than his teacher. As a twelve year old "prodigy" child Hummel toured Germany, Denmark, England, Scotland and Holland. He was guest of several European royal courts. During his studies in Eisenstadt he was a deputy to Joseph Haydn. He was successful not only as an interpreter but also as a composer. He wrote various compositions for piano solo, operas, ballets and masses. Thanks to Hummel the piano composition progressed from Classicism to Romanticism. He gave three concerts in his native Pressburg. During his third visit to this city in 1834 connected with concerts his whole family accompanied him. Johann Nepomuk Hummel died three years after at Weimar in Germany. He is buried side by side with such geniuses as J. W. Goethe and F. Schiller.

Around today's **Nedbalova ulica street**, perpendicular to Klobučnícka, was the **Jewish ghetto** with a synagogue. It occupied the eastern part of the town between the Franciscan monastery and Vydrická brána gate. Presence of the Jewish community in Pressburg is referred to in the text of the privilege granted to the town by King Andrew II from 1291. However, the Jews were presumably living here even before. Andrew's privileges guaranteed them rights identical with those of the citizens of the free royal borough. The Jewish ghetto originated before 1335 on Jacob's extensive lands. It was also the year when the Cistercians living at the Archbishop's court demanded destruction of the local synagogue because it allegedly interfered with their religious rituals. The Jews of Pressburg had their own mayor in 1375. A written reference from 1434 mentions the existence of a Jewish school in Pressburg.

Left: Hummel's house
Right: The Old Market Hall
Primaciálne Námestie Square

It is very probable that a long wall fenced the Jewish quarter. Remains of it were found on the edge of the Primatial square. It probably ran toward today's Uršulínska street. All economic activities connected with money lending were concentrated in the Jewish quarter. Citizens came to borrow money from the Jews because this activity was prohibited for other burghers. Jews got rich on high interests. They built luxurious houses or they bought them out from rich debtors. The transactions, which preceded the founding of the Town Hall, prove it. Jews lent money also to the king Sigismund of Luxembourg.

In the 15th century the Jewish community became the object of anger of the poor of the town who assaulted and sacked the synagogue in 1446. Several Jewish houses also did not escape the *pogrom*. A historical turn in the life of the Pressburg's Jewish community came after 1526. The Mohács tragedy and the Turkish threat frightened the Jews so much that they left the city, and the strict laws of Queen Mary prevented them from coming back. The property of the Jews who had fled was confiscated in favour of the city and they were never permitted to return. Even those who did not leave were moved out of their houses. This is how the more than three hundred-year history of the Jewish ghetto in the eastern part of Pressburg was suddenly interrupted. Only in 1599 were the Jews allowed to settle here, though it was not on the actual territory of the free royal borough of Pressburg. Palatine Pálffy allowed them to settle in his part of the settlement under the castle.

Nedbalova ulica, as we know it now, originated as the street skirting the town walls of the medieval town. It followed the eastern section of the fortifications. Opposite the school standing near the crossroads with Klobučnícka street there is a preserved **section of the town walls** ❿ from the 15th century. The inner part of the stone wall reaching the height of the neighbouring two-storied house is visible here. When it was called *Juden Gassen* or the Jewish Lane it was closed at both ends by iron gates at night. The members of hatter guild had their shops there and that is why it was called Klobučnícka or Hatter street in the 16th to 18th centuries. In the years 1879 to 1945 it was called Hummelova after Bratislava's famous native composer. Its present name Nedbalova is also a tribute to a musician, the Czech director and composer Oskar Nedbal (→ 170), one of the first directors of the Slovak National Theatre. The houses in Nedbalova ulica are comparatively modern. The northern row of houses originated on the site of the demolished walls and the filled-in moat. The most important building here is the recently restored **Stará tržnica** ⓫ that is Old Market, from 1910 standing on the corner with Klobučnícka street.

Left: The interior of the Ursuline church
Right: Uršulínska ulica street

Uršulínska ulica street connects Laurinská street with Primatial square and the square of the SNP. It is not one of the oldest in the city though. Originally it was only a pathway between the gardens of the Franciscan monastery and the medieval Jewish ghetto. The northern extreme of the path, later street, ended at the town walls. Next to today's Ursulines church it joined the system of streets inside the walls around Nedbalova and Františkánska streets. It was connected with today's square of the Slovak National Uprising only in 1775. Uršulínska ulica was never fully built with houses and remained so. There is still a free plot behind the Franciscan monastery, as a matter of fact, the only one in old town. Archaeological research carried out during construction of underground garages at this place discovered traces of Celtic settlement. The name of the street used now appeared for the first time in its German version *Klein Ursulinner Gasse* (Lesser Ursuline Street) in 1676 and it denoted the section between Laurinská and Primatial square and Františkánska street and the rest of it called *Gross Ursulinner Gasse* (Greater Ursuline Street) was the section from the Primatial palace up to Františkánska ulica street. It is related to the arrival of the Ursuline order at Pressburg in 1672.

In the western row there is the eastern wing of the Primatial palace with a **commemorative board** ⓬ referring to the visit of the physician and alchemist Paracelsus to Pressburg in 1537. Renovation of the neighbouring **house No. 6** ⓭ gave it its original Renaissance appearance. In the arcade yard there is an interesting sundial painted on a wall. The eastern row consists of a group of picturesque Renaissance houses from the latter half of

the 16th century. The former Greater Usuline Street is an example of unfinished urban development. The western row of houses is incomplete. The only building here is the lateral wing of the New Town Hall built a bit retired from the street. Further north is the above mentioned vacant plot, which givea a fine view of the Franciscan monastery with a typical Neo Gothic tower. The site was the Franciscan garden until 1950. The **Ursuline church** ⓮ and **monastery** ⓯ at its western corner unifies the eastern row of the Ursuline Street. Before the nuns came, the Evangelicals occupied the western edge of Bratislava's former Jewish ghetto. The Evangelicals built the church in 1640 for their Slovak and Hungarian believers, thanks to the prominent Pressburg citizen and counsellor Andreas Segner. The church complied with the ruler's request not to be similar to the Catholic churches. So it is a single-nave building with a long rectangular ground plan and a symbolically hinted presbytery. The Evangelicals eventually lost the building in 1676 and it was adjudicated to the Ursuline order, which added a monastery and school to it. The Ursulines consecrated the church to the **Virgin Mary of Loretto**. The outer appearance was not changed at the beginning and the simplicity of style was preserved until 1745 when a wooden church tower with onion shaped roof was built next to it. Extensive adjustments were made in the interior of the church. Shortly after the arrival of children, the Ursulines built a new **main altar** with a **statue of the Black Madonna**, a copy of the Virgin Mary of Loretto. The painting of St. Augustín and St. Anna on the lateral altars were painted by M. Speer. The Ursuline monastery was started on the site of the former Jewish ghetto in 1676 and its construction took ten years. Due to the support of Archbishop Emerich Esterházy the monastery was enlarged in 1731. In 1809 it was partially damaged by the cannons of the Napoleon's troops and consequently a large reconstruction was needed.

The Bratislava Castle

The monumental building of **Bratislava Castle** that cannot be confused with any other building in the city is visible from a great distance. Certainly every visitor of Bratislava notices the pronounced silhouette similar to an overturned table. The majestic impression is enhanced by the hill it stands on some eighty-five metres above the water level of the Danube.

The inhabitants of the height settlement left the oldest traces here from the end of the **Younger Stone Age**. They were the people using what the experts call volute pottery. The castle hill above the Danube was not deserted in the Iron Age either. People who left us heaps of objects evidencing their skills in crafts and cultural progress settled it. Pottery, jewellery and Celtic coins made several decades BC were found on the castle hill as well as down in the city. Immediately after the Celts left, the Germanic tribes and Romans came. Only indications consisting of bricks marked by the XIVth legion of *Gemina Antoniniana* based at Carnuntum exist about the existence of an advanced **Roman camp** or at least a guarding station. The bricks from the period of Emperor Caracalla might have formed a part of walls of the military watch tower providing wide view of the then Germanic country. The tower was ideal for sending signals to Gerulata and over Hainburg also to Carnuntum. The important ford over the river near the Vodná veža tower under the castle hill on the left bank of the river certainly needed protection. However, later moving of the Roman bricks from Carnuntum to be used for the construction of the medieval castle cannot be excluded.

The castle hill had a special function within the system of **Great Moravian fortified settlements**. It was an important fortified settlement in the

Left: The Bratislava Castle

last third of the 9th century as it is mentioned in the Salzburg annals in relation to a bloody battle between the Bavarians and early Magyars (→ 16). On the western side of the hill where a medieval castle was later built there was a seat of some noble. The Church with a three-nave **stone basilica** ❽ and a cemetery occupied the eastern part of the hill top. The whole settlement was skirted by a defensive wall made of thick oak logs connected into chambers filled with earth and stones. Fortification enclosed an area equalling in size to six football grounds.

The Great Moravian Basilica

Discovery of the stone basilica on the eastern terrace of the castle hill is another proof that wood was not the only construction material used in construction of the Great Moravian fortified settlements. A certain idea of the size of the Bratislava's Great Moravian Christian church was gained due to the fact that its rests were preserved. Brown quarry stones outline the ground plan of the basilica from the 9th century and white stones represent somewhat younger buildings from the post-Great Moravian period. Six pillars of the main nave and a part of the walls of the southern nave are identifiable. They suggest the width of the basilica, which was thirteen metres.

Building activity documented by archaeology took place on the castle hill of Bratislava as early as the 10th century. But another three centuries were needed before at the site of the old settlement a Romanesque castle was built, attributed to the period of the Arpád dynasty. Its resulting form, which it acquired in the 13th century, was preceded by a comparatively complicated development. First there was a pre-Romanesque **stone palace** in the 11th and 12th centuries. The fortification of the castle hill made use of the defensive system of the previous fortified settle-

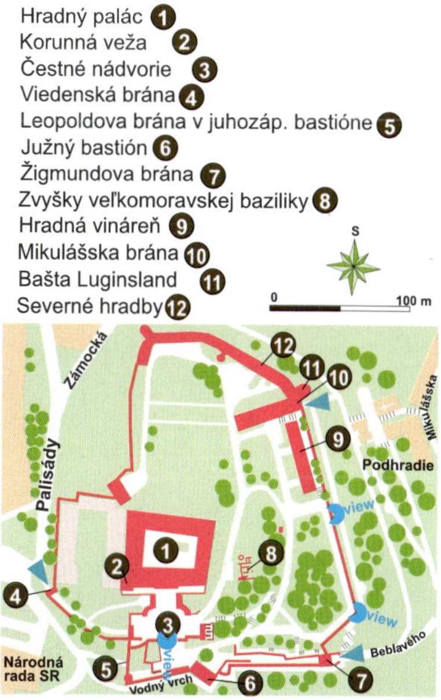

ment. The original earth-wooden walls were reinforced by stone towers. The fortifications also included **religious buildings** within the castle area until they were moved by the early 13th century out to the settlement below the castle complying with the decision of the Pope. There was the pre-Romanesque church of the Most Holy Saviour, provost's house, and the like. The rests of these sacred buildings from the 10th to 12th centuries are visible as well at the eastern terrace immediately next to the Great Moravian basilica. Their ground plans are marked by light-coloured stone ashlars. The strengthened post-Great Moravian fortification system must have been sufficiently strong as it resisted the attack of the German Emperor Henrich V's army. In the second half of the 13th century the castle progressively gained the shape of the Romanesque **Arpád period castle,** which it kept until the Gothic reconstruction carried out in time of King Sigismund in the first half of the 15th

century. Solid stone castle walls with a high prismatoid tower were built around it. The plan of the Arpád period castle can be seen on the pavement of the courtyard of the existing castle palace. They are discernible by different colour of the paving stones. The residential tower had a square ground plan with one side 22 metres long. Such dimensions were unusual for the time. The adjacent tower was added on the most vulnerable western side of the hill. The tower is the only building element of the Romanesque castle that was preserved until now. After numerous building adjustments it became the core of the biggest of the castle towers later called **Korunná veža** ❷ (Crown Tower). It is the only one, which does not stand on the castle wall, but it has its foundation in the ground and stands outside the ground plan. Nobility, in contrast to other castles, never owned Pressburg castle. As a strategic building it remained in the ownership of the crown. It was the seat of the *comes* (governor of the county). Changes of property occurred only in the settlement below the castle where two different individual settlement forms developed: there was the castle with the comes', which kept the settlement of St. Mikuláš along with several other settlements. The second municipal settlement was granted the privileges of a free royal borough from King Andrew III. The castle and its settlement were an independent unit connected with Pressburg only by name. By the end of the 13th century the castle twice failed to resist the enemy's attack. In 1273 it was conquered by the King Přemysl Otakar II of Bohemia and it fell to the hands of the Duke Albrecht of Austria in 1287. Generous reconstruction of the castle started in 1423 during the rule of Sigismund of Luxembourg, but it was not finished in time of his death in 1437. The result of this reconstruction was a Gothic castle referred to in literature as a **Sigismund's castle**. The principal royal builder master Conrad of Erling managed extensive building activity on the castle hill. The work initially concentrated on strengthening of the defensive system. It concerned above all the northern and western fortifications, which from the topographic point of view seemed the most urgent. Two semicircular cannon **bastions** reinforced the castle walls. The northern bastion was called **Luginsland** ⓫. Even today it is the dominant architectural element of Bratislava's castle well visible from the Hodžovo or Župné squares. A new entrance to the castle via **Žigmundova brána** ❼ (Sigismund's Gate) was built on the steep slope of the castle hill above the Danube. The gate is often incorrectly referred to as Corvinus' Gate. This wonderful Gothic building with rich stone ornamentation is on the eastern side of

Lefto: The tower of Sigismund's gate
Right: Leopold's gate
Bratislava Castle seen from the north

the castle. It shortened the way to the ford next to the Vodná veža tower. The fortifications also included the moat. It was a technically demanding job because although it was on the top of the hill the builders were able to fill it with water in case of necessity.

The former Arpád period castle underwent substantial changes. The reconstruction followed the style of Italian castles. The palace acquired the form of a bulky fort. Only the **tower** at the south-western corner was left while the older architecture was pulled down. An impressive four-wing palace with a square courtyard was added to the tower. The furnishing of the palace was matching the position of the German Emperor, as this was his only residence outside the Empire. The castle chapel occupied the south-eastern corner and at the opposite end of the wing was the above mentioned tower with a separate stairway. Due to its inassailability it could also be used as the last refuge. Almost the whole eastern wing was an extensive hall with a cross vault. The cellars of the eastern and western wings were used for economic purposes. The western wing fulfilled another important role, that of defence because it was on the most vulnerable side of the castle hill. This was the reason why the thickness of its wall was doubled. The seven meter thick walls were indeed unique in Europe. Sigismund's reconstruction endowed the castle with a ground plant, which was later maintained by all builders that followed. The castle did not yet have the typical four

corner towers. Its Gothic details were covered by younger layers. Many of them were identified only during the last extensive restoration of the castle area. Some of them are easily visible, such as the fragments of the **Gothic window** on the southern facade; others require more attention from the visitors. These include the remains of the southern **portal** with lavish Gothic stone ornamentation.

There was never enough water on the castle hill. It had to be carried on donkeys, so the question of digging a **castle well** was more than urgent. The ruler had to borrow money from the Pressburg town hall and the counsellors provided the amount of two thousand gulden asked for by the wellsinker Wolfgang. But there was still not enough water in his well. Additional money was needed for its deepening. The castle well from 1434 is accessible by a stairway in the north-western corner of the courtyard. It had to be deepened to 84.75 meters to reach the level

of the Danube. The big reservoir next to the well is much younger. It was built in the 18th century during the reign of Maria Theresia.

When Sigismund died only the rough structure of Pressburg Castle was finished. The ruler did not live to see the finishing of some spaces inside the palace. Further work without the careful supervision and corresponding support of his successors slowed down to stop later altogether. Sigismund's castle then existed in this form and without substantial changes for another century. It also became the seat of Sigismund's grandson Ladislav the Posthumous for a short spell. Matthias Corvinus visited it sporadically and when the rule of the Jagelonsky's finished it was almost uninhabitable and abandoned. The conflict of the castle garrison led by Rozgoň in 1440-1444 contributed to its dilapidation. The parties of this small war often used cannons, which caused a lot of damage on both sides. Only the arrival of Emperor Fedinand of Habsburg brought about a positive change in the history of Pressburg Castle. The castle became an important strategic point in country's defence after the Mohács tragedy and fall of Buda in 1526.

When the Emperor's intention to modernize the Pressburg Castle was approved by the Diet in 1552, the **Renaissance restoration of the castle area** could start. The result of the 1552-1562 reconstruction was a well-fortified and simultaneously luxurious Renaissance seat of one of the most powerful rulers in Europe at that time. Its appearance is reflected on the engravings from the latter half of the 16th century. The reconstruction led by the Emperor's court architect of Italian origin, Pietro Ferrabosco, united the height of all four palace wings, and the palace became more similar to its present form. In its silhouette were only two corner towers. The bulkier south-western tower became shelter of the **Hungarian crown jewels** in 1608. Since then it has been called the Crown Tower. Gothic windows of various forms were replaced by new ones in Renaissance taste. Thus, the facade acquired a sober almost military appearance similar to that of the Hofburg, the royal palace of Vienna. The lavish ornamentation and luxury of its interior compensated the austere exterior of the castle palace in the second half of the 16th century. Italian artists authored artistically valuable decoration of the state halls of the palace, stucco master Giulio Licino from Venice and the painter Ulisseo Romano da Voltera from Rome. They used different means such as stucco, wall painting and gilding. Luxurious wooden panelling and tapestries contributed to the resulting impression of luxury. However, the Renaissance decoration was severely damaged during Bethlen's rebellion in

Left: Castle in 1760
Right: Rococo stairs of the castle

the first half of the 17th century, and except for isolated cases it was not restored. Remains of **fresco decoration** with plant and figural motifs were found in the fragment of the Renaissance oriel from 1562 discovered in the space of the south-eastern corner on the first floor of the palace, which was presumably part of the Emperor's apartment.

The Palatine Mikuláš Pálffy inherited the serious consequences of the siege of Pressburg Castle by Gabriel Bethlen's troops. The hero of the Turkish wars obtained the castle from the Emperor Rudolf, who did not need it as he moved to Prague. A new reconstruction of the palace was approved by the Hungarian Parliament in 1623. Pálffy's ideas for the restored palace were realised by architect Giovanni Albertali and the Imperial court builder Giovanni Battista Carlone supervised it. The demanding reconstruction included construction of Pálffy's summer residence with garden on the northern foothill of the castle hill. Another floor was added to the castle palace and two additional towers were built on the corners of the castle compound giving the castle its typical square and four-tower form. Changes in interior comprised the building of a new chapel placed in the north-western corner. The state rooms in the southern wing were adorned with big canvases celebrating the virtues of Emperor Ferdinand III. The German painter P. Juvenel of Nürnberg decorated the residential part occupied by the Imperial family with paintings. The scientist Matej Bel gave a true description of their beauty.

Reconstruction of the castle generally referred to as **Pálffy's** was carried out in the period of the fading Renaissance style. Pálffy's luxurious castle palace was a part of ambitious plan for reconstruction of the whole castle hill, with the settlement below it included in a massive fort with a complicated system of bastions and ramparts arranged

in an irregular seven-pointed star. Out of this extensive project led by the Italian builder Jozef Priami only a tiny part was made reality. Only two cannon bastions were added to the castle. A long tunnel was drilled under the south-western one. The tunnel was used as an entrance gate and its name was **Leopoldova brána** ❺ (Leopold's Gate). However, it proved to be an error as it was not conveniently situated and moreover it was rather unattractive from the architectural point of view. A new and more pompous entrance gate was started. Since it was situated on the western edge of the castle hill and as it was on the road from Vienna it acquired the name **Viedenská brána** ❹ (Vienna gate). This gate similar to Antique triumphal arches was ceremoniously opened on the occasion of Charles III's coronation in 1712. It has remained the main entrance to the area of Bratislava Castle until today.

The last stage of big building adjustments of the Pressburg Castle was

accomplished under the orders of Queen Maria Theresia. The ruler tried to rid the castle of any outdated functions of the former military fort as the political climate of the 18th century was that of relative peace. She had all fortifying elements removed and simultaneously improved or widened its residential function complying with the criteria of what was considered the utmost luxury. The works pursuing the project of reconstruction as presented by the imperial architects Jean Nicolas Jadot, Giovanni Batista Martinelli and Nicolas Pacassi started in 1755. The castle now called **Theresian** was prepared to serve the royal court in 1765. The obvious and intentional disproportion between the dreary exterior and impressive interior was again applied. Money not spent on the outer appearance was invested in the interior of the castle. The simplicity of the outer facades complied with the canons of Classicising Baroque. In front of the southern facade a couple of Baroque guard houses were built and on the southern terrace a kind of **čestné nádvorie** ❸ (courtyard of honour) was created. Various constructions and buildings were erected on the three remaining facades of the castle palace. The Riding Hall and Sally tereny building with winter garden were built on the northern side of the castle. The western terrace had an open riding space and service buildings. The most interesting building though was that of the **Theresianum** built next to the eastern side of the palace in 1768. This lovely Rococo palace was the seat of the Governor, Prince Albert, who acquired the office after he married Archduchess Maria Christina, daughter of Queen Maria Theresia. But the palace burned down in 1811.

The rococo taste was also applied in the decoration of the state rooms of the old palace. The prettiest sample of the

Left: Fire in 1811
Right: Castle seen from the south

style was the **stairway** that originated by partial demolition of the massive peripheral wall of the western wing of the palace from the times of King Sigismund. Its beauty was enhanced by the most recent restoration. The remarkable and ingenious **castle water main** circuit designed by Johann Wolfgang Kempelen (→ 160) is worthy of attention. Steam or electricity were not available then so the water was pumped by means of horse power from the level of the Danube up to the castle basement where it accumulated in a newly built reservoir.

The departure of the Governor Albert in 1780 meant the end of the good times for Pressburg Castle. It lost its noble lord and artistic collections, and the crown jewels were moved to Vienna. Joseph II' intentions for the abandoned castle were quite different. He had it adapted for a newly established **General Seminary**. The royal residence was changed into study rooms, libraries and dormitories for students and their professors. As it was used for education of Catholic clerics it did not need any ornamentation in its interior. The new educational institution at Pressburg Castle was managed by state and it was opened on June 1, 1784, when 459 students of various abolished Church seminaries initiated their studies there. The number of students increased to 555 the following year. A great part of them were Slovaks who were allowed to study in their mother tongue. The study of national languages was part of the tuition imparted in the General Seminary in line with the principle, that only a priest who understands the local language of the believers can propagate the Catholic religion. The atmosphere was tolerant and enlightened, which fostered the formation of the first generation active in emancipation of the Slovaks. The main protagonist of this new wave was Anton Bernolák. When Joseph II died in 1790 the seminary was again acquired by the Church and

cared after by the individual Old Hungarian bishoprics. The castle was in hands of the Church until 1802 when it was passed over to the army. But the army did not stay long. In May 1811, a devastating fire burst out in the castle and soon spread to the Podhradie or the settlement below the castle.

Castle in flames

The Pressburg people woken by the toll of the church bells on the morning of May 28th 1811 certainly remembered the date for the whole of their lives. The castle was in flames. Allegedly an imprudent soldier set the fire, though it was never confirmed. It is also uncertain whether it was a member of the Italian or Waloon troops returning from Galicia. The only thing certain is that the summer riding hall used then as a store burst in the flames. Windy weather helped the propagation of the fire and when the roof of the neighbouring central palace caught fire, the flames were several tens of meters high. Soon the

whole population was participating in extinction but the fire was too fierce and the weather was adverse. The sparks and embers were carried by the northwesterly wind to the settlement below the castle and soon the fire jumped from one roof to another. The merciless element was raging for three days. The results were disastrous. The palace burnt down to bare walls and Podhradie, the settlement below castle, lost 77 houses, 5 breweries and the local Town Hall. Nine people died in the flames and smoke.

For the next hundred and fifty years the people had to tolerate the sad picture of the destroyed castle on top of the hill, a vanishing symbol of the city's past glory. The army used the place, dismantled parts of the preserved walls and sold them around as construction material. In 1847 the castle cellars were changed into a prison where the Hungarian revolutionaries were imprisoned, among them also children of Lajos Kossuth held as hostages. The army partially used some preserved buildings in the castle area. The newly established military barracks later became the scene of the rebellion of Slovak soldiers of the 72nd infantry regiment who refused to fight in the service of Monarchy. The call for restoration of Pressburg Castle started by the beginning of the 20th century. The municipal chronicler Ján Nepomuk Batka and counsellor Theodor Bolly were the first enthusiasts in this matter. Unfortunately, the Government was not in favour. Discussions concerning the future destiny of the otherwise dangerous ruins became more intense after the First World War. In the thirties the recognised Slovak architect Dušan Jurkovič presented his ideas for renovation of the castle to the public. But his plans, as well as the extreme proposal to remove all that remained of the palace, were not listened to. The extremists wanted to preserve the Crown Tower and to clear the rest of the castle hill for building some top governmental offices or buildings for Comenius University. Even an international architectural tender was published calling for proposed designs for a student complex on the castle hill and the neighbouring Vodný vrch hill. But the castle of Bratislava was **renewed** after the Second World War as a result of the efforts of an outstanding Slovak

Left: Falconers in front of the castle
The courtyard
Right: The Danube seen from the Crown Tower

painter **Janko Alexy** (1894-1970). Research of the ruins led by Professor Alfred Piffl started in 1953. The actual building activity though started only after July 5th 1955 when his proposal of reconstruction was approved. Piffl´s design did not aspire to reconstruct the castle in a way imitating one of its historical forms. As a matter of fact, it was not possible, because documentation either from the time of King Sigismund, that of Ferdinand or Maria Theresia did not exist anymore. The principle to preserve everything valuable and to create a harmonious whole was preferred. Hundreds of builders, archaeologists, historians and craftsmen were invited to participate in the project. Especially the archaeological team accomplished its feat with remarkable success as they discovered numerous significant remains from the castle's history. The most important phase of the castle's reconstruction was finished in 1968. The palace was prepared for ceremonious opening on October 28th and signature of the Act on the Czech-Slovak Federation. **Three lime trees** planted next to the Great Moravian basilica at the southern corner of the eastern terrace commemorate the event. Renovation of the Bratislava castle though has not finished. Several historical buildings including the above mentioned Theresianum palace should be reconstructed in the future.

Some parts of the castle are open to the public. They contain permanent exhibitions of the **Slovak National Museum**. There is an exhibition of **historical furniture** in the main palace and a remarkable collection of exhibits called the **Jewels of Slovakia's Remote Past**. Exhibits documenting the **history of musical instruments** are displayed in Luginsland bastion.

The Western part of the Staré Mesto

The western part of the Old Town is quite different from the other parts. It spreads over the foothills of the Little Carpathians and its urban fabric consists predominantly of family houses. The **Bratislavské vŕšky hills** are sharply limited in its southern side by a steep slope descending to the Danube. Their western limit coinciding with Dolná Mlynská dolina valley is also pronounced. The northern limit of the hills runs along the transport corridor through Lamačská brána, a transversal depression of the southern part of the Little Carpathians. Its eastern part, the most comfortable for living, ends in Štefánikova ulica street, Palisády and historic centre of Bratislava. On a flat hill at its south-eastern edge is the **Bratislava Castle** ❶ and on its eastern and southern slopes is Podhradie, the historic settlement below the castle.

The medieval Podhradie originated in the 12th and 13th centuries. The settlement below the castle with market lying near important ford over the Danube quickly grew into a busy little town. In 1221 the church of the Holiest Saviour and all Church institutions were moved from castle to this settlement giving its growth an additional stimulus. In 1291 when the major part of the town became a separate royal borough called Pressburg only several little settlements on the slope and foothill of the castle hill belonged to the province. In the lower part squeezed between the castle hill and the Danube were the villages of **Vydrica** (→ 175) and **Zuckermandel** (→ 177). The settlements had a church consecrated to the patron saint of traders and sailors, St. Nicolas. The settlement bore the same name, and it is referred to in the 14th century as the **Settlement of St. Nico-**

Left: The Bratislavské vŕšky hills in the 19. century.

1. Bratislavský hrad
2. Dom U dobrého pastiera
3. Zsigrayova kúria
4. Kostol sv. Mikuláša
5. Penzión a reštaurácia Chez David
6. Dom na Beblavého 1
7. Reštaurácia Arkádia
8. Budova Národnej rady SR
9. Reštaurácia Parlamentka
10. Hotel Bôrik
11. Pomník padlých hrdinov v 1. sv. vojne
12. Ekoiuventa
13. Pamätník Slavín
14. Kostol Panny Márie Snežnej
15. Kríž na Kalvárii
16. Lurdská jaskyňa
17. Ministerstvo zahr. vecí SR
18. Sonnenfeldova vila
19. Jurkovičova vila
20. Bellušova vila
21. Pomník Henricha Justiho
22. Pomník Johanna Andreasa Bäumlera
23. Študentský domov Horský park
24. Prírodný amfiteáter
25. Slovenský národný archív

las. The Gothic church was pulled down in 1531 but the settlement stayed though under the new name of **Schlossberg** (German for Castle Hill).

By the end of the 16th century Palatine Mikuláš Pálffy became the administrator of the settlement below the castle. His name is connected with arrival of the **Jews**. First they fled in panic from Pressburg fearing the Turks and later when they were not allowed to return, they settled in the environs - in Stupava, Kopčany and other villages - and waited for the opportunity to move back to their old houses in the ghetto of Pressburg. As it was not possible, under Pálffy s protection they did draw closer to their confiscated property and settled in Schlossberg and a new settlement on the site of today's Zámocká ulica street. The Jewish colony was rapidly growing. In 1714 it acquired permission for self-administration led by a rabbi. The 1736 census of Pálffy's property mentions the presence o 123 Jewish families accounting for 800 people. Thanks to them Podhradie became the principal centre of trade and finances, with the Jewish craftsmen and traders becoming serious rivals of the Pressburg guilds. The municipal council was trying to defend the non-Jewish population by strict limitations, such as punishment of the storage of Jewish goods by the loss of municipal rights.

Podhradie was annexed to Pressburg in 1851 as its fourth district. The upper part of what was called the Theresian quarter was inhabited mostly by Jews up to the Second World War. The quarter consisted of poorly equipped burgher houses, two synagogues, a famous yeshiva, and the Jewish girl's school, all standing in a dense network of narrow streets and lanes. Few of its inhabitants returned to their homes after the war. The majority of Bratislava's 6,000 Jews deported in 1942 perished in the Nazi concentration camps. Only some luckier ones emigrated abroad before the Holocaust.

Several buildings in Beblavá, Židovská, Mikulášska streets and at the stairway called Zámocké schody deserve attention. Let us look at them and start with the house at the lower end of **Židovská ulica street**, which is rightly, considered one of the most beautiful in Bratislava. It is the impressive **Dom u dobrého pastiera** ❷ (House of the Good Shepherd) (Židovská ulica street No 1) and its conspicuously slender construction makes it the best specimen of small-scale Rococo architecture in Bratislava. Its name derives from a tiny statue of Christ - Good Shepherd - standing on its corner. It was built in 1760. Each floor of the former burgher house had only one room, as its ground plan did not allow for more. The architecture emphasizes the narrow facade of the house adorned by Rococo ornamentation. Since 1975 the House of the

Left: The house of the Good Shepherd
Right: Exposition of crafts
Exposition of the Jewish culture

Good Shepherd has sheltered the **exposition of historic clocks** of the Municipal Museum. Also the collection of portable sun dials from the 16th-18th centuries is interesting. **Zsigray's curia** ❸ standing at the opposite end of Židovská street (No 7) offers the opportunity to see the exhibits of the **Museum of Jewish Culture in Slovakia** explaining the history of the Jewish community of Bratislava and Slovakia. On the slope of the castle hill above **Mikulášska ulica street** there stands the **St. Nicholas'** (Sv. Mikuláš) **church** ❹. Originally there was rotunda later replaced by Gothic church from the 14th century. The church standing there now is a Baroque building from 1661.Count Pálffy's widow had it built. The church has belonged to the followers of the Eastern Orthodox Church since 1950. The most frequently used access road to the castle since the Early Middle Ages was **Zámocká ulica street**. The Jews inhabited it from the 17th century. The orthodox part of the Jewish community built a synagogue there in 1863. On the outer side of the street was the big Pálffy's garden (→ 140). In the lower part of the street, the **pension and restaurant Chez David** ❺ provides excellent Jewish cuisine.

Beblavého ulica street climbs the castle hill from the corner of the House of the Good Shepherd. It was the shortest possible connection between the castle and St. Martin's Minster. As the famous Hungarian poet Sándor Petőfi lived in its upper part the street bore his name for some time. Today it offers

an opportunity to sit and chat in pleasant stylish little cafés and restaurants in venerable houses from the 18th century. At the lower end of Beblavého street stands the Late Baroque **house No 1** from the late 18th century. It contains the **Museum of crafts** ❻ exhibiting works of artisans made of glass, porcelain, various types of jewels, toys and liturgical objects. In the upper part of **Zámocké schody stairs** are two Renaissance houses from the beginning of the 17th century. The house on the corner of Beblavého was once the **Town Hall of Podhradie**. After Podhradie obtained municipal privileges in 1713 the magistrate consisting of six aldermen and a notary used to have sessions in the house. The former Town Hall is now the **Arkadia restaurant** ❼, a smart place, the name of which derives from its main architectural feature – an open pillar arcade passing through two of its wings.

The round hills of Bratislava spreading from Štefánikova ulica street

up to Dolná Mlynská dolina valley were for centuries a viticultural landscape with scattered little huts. This attractive locality acquired a new function only in the first half of the 20th century. The footpaths between the plots changed to streets built up with elegant villas; the property of the Bratislava's privileged class and social elite. The locality is the most expensive and most luxurious quarter of the city. It main street is **Mudroňova ulica street**, originally called *Kaiserweg* or the Emperor's Road. Next to the castle on the Vodný vrch hill is the modern **building of the National Council of the Slovak Republic** ❽. It was opened in May 1994 and the Slovak Parliament moved here from its old seat in Župné námestie. The new buildings of Parliament also include the popular **Parlamentka restaurant** ❾ with a terrace above the Danube offering a wide view of the city.

The street network on the western side of the Mudroňova ulica is somewhat thinner and with younger buildings. Last remnants of vineyards and orchards are preserved on the southern slopes of the hills, around Radvanská street and Fialkové údolie valley. On the hill of **Machnáč** (248 m) on the south-western edge of the Bratislava hills remains of Celtic settlement were found. Machnáč is covered by a little wood of tall pine trees (in Slovak *borovice*) and this is why it is called **Bôrik** ❿. Next to the wood is the building belonging to the Government of the Slovak Republic used for occasional accommodation of important guests, negotiations and celebrations. Again the terrace above the entrance to this modern building (from 1974) provides a wonderful view of Devín Gate, the passage of Danube between the hills, and if the weather is fine even of the villages on the Austrian side of the

Left: View of castle from Slavín
Right: Lourdes cave

Danube. At the upper end of Mudroňova in the north-east is **Murmannova výšina** hill with the **House of Ekoiuventa** ⓬ built in 1952, colloquially called "Michurin" (surname of Soviet scientist known for bold experimentation with plants). The building is a perfect sample of what is called Stalinist architecture. It is still serving its original purpose - it provides space for children's leisure activities. Stará vinárska ulica street starting nearby leads to the neighbouring height (252 m) with the **monument Slavín** ⓭ and military cemetery where 6,845 Soviet soldiers who died while liberating Bratislava by the end of April of 1945 are buried. When the war was over all soldiers who died in the are of western Slovakia were concentrated to this cemetery. Architect J. Svetlík designed the project of the monument and it was finished in 1960. It stands in a park boasting various wood species brought here from different areas of the former Soviet Union. The eastern terrace of the hill provides a panoramic view of the city.

Slavín

The access to the area is by a wide stairway with a relief by Ladislav Snopek called The Oath on the wall between a pair of flight of stairs. It symbolizes the long and toilsome way of the Red Army towards victory over fascism. The stairs climbs to the cemetery with six collective and 278 individual graves. The central and dominating part of the monument is the ceremonial hall skirted by a stately colonnade. The dates carved on the walls under the colonnade report on the progress of the Red Army in the territory of Slovakia. Two groups of statues in front of the entrance to the ceremonial hall symbolize the famous battles. A bronze relief by Rudolf Pribiš that commemorated the sufferings of the Second World War adorns the entrance door to the ceremonial hall. The monumental pylon of granite standing above the ceremonial hall is 39.5 metres tall and bears on its top an 11 metre tall statue of Victory by Alexander Trizuliak. It represents a soldier raising the banner above the liberated country.

At the north-eastern tip of the Bratislava hills is a round height called **Kalvária** (257 m), and in the saddle below Kalvária is the Roman-Catholic **church of the Virgin Mary of Snow** ⓮ built in 1943. The Calvary of Bratislava was the first of the kind in Slovakia. It was started in 1694. It led to the place where in 1683 Turkish banner was placed announcing the invasion of the Turkish and Thököly's troops to the town. The builders fitted the Calvary into the dissected terrain. Parts of the upper section with serpentines running in a little wood on the slope inclined toward the upper part of Pražská street are preserved. The Way of the Cross ended at the top of the hill where the Jesuits of Bratislava had a chapel of **Holy Cross** ⓯ with exterior pulpit built. The site of the Turkish flag

is still marked by a cross with an original bronze body by an unknown craftsman. The original cross did not resist time and the weather and was replaced by a new one.

Romantic and deeply cut **Hlboká cesta street** passing by Kalvária leads down to the city. It originally led to a quarry, which was mentioned as early as 1493. The old quarry was converted in **Lurdská jaskyňa** ⓰ (Lourdes Cave) with tablets of gratitude. Two springs of drinking water on Hlboká cesta were channelled into the municipal water main. In the lower part of the street is the building of the former **Corn Stock Exchange** ⓱ (No 2) from 1941 designed by architect Juraj Tvarožek. Before 1989 it belonged to the central bodies of the Communist Party. Colloquially it was called "The White House" as the people associated it with the centre of power. The recently restored building is now seat of the Ministry of Foreign Affairs of the Slovak Republic.

The continuation of Mudroňova ulica towards the north-west is Búdkova cesta road, which connects the quarters of Bratislava hills, Patrónka and Mlynská dolina. Búdková cesta is one of the roads leading to **Horský park** (The Landscape Park) – the favourite Bratislava's citizens. It is a natural park or rather a large forested area, the founders of which were trying to imitate the English gardening style avoiding the artificial geometry so typical of French parks. The original natural forest with oaks, firs, pines, beeches, etc. extended as far as today's Slavín. The designers of Horský park inserted amidst the original wood species also foreign species such as exotic species of pine or yew. In the immediate neighbourhood of the park are **halls of residence of the Economics University** ㉓. On the opposite slope above Horský park is and **open air theatre** ㉔ and on the top of hill is the building of the **Slovak National Archives** ㉕.

Left: Game-keeper's lodge in Horský park

The Northern part of the Staré Mesto

The quarters in the north of the historic centre of Bratislava are full of contrasts. There are busy wide streets and romantic narrow alleys. One can walk in wide squares and pleasant parks. Venerable buildings breathing with history stand side by side with modern buildings. In the northern part of the centre are the buildings of the government, ministries, the Presidential Palace and the seats of many other central administrative bodies and institutions. The main railway station in the northern centre is the place of the first contact with the city for visitors to Bratislava.

Several squares originated around the disappeared town walls. One of them is **Župné námestie square** connected with the contiguous Hurbanovo square in the east. In the Middle Ages it was the site of the settlement of St. Michael, which later developed into a suburb. In time of Turkish wars the aldermen themselves decided to demolish the suburbs for the sake of better control over the immediate space beyond the town walls. Such was the destiny of the St. Michael suburb including its Gothic church bearing the name of the same patron saint. It was pulled down in 1529. The **Trinitarian order** later built one of the most beautiful Baroque **churches** ❶ in the town on its ruins. The historic literature often incorrectly denotes

this church as that of the Most Holy Trinity. This church is in fact dedicated to the founders of the Trinitary order, that is **St. John of Matha and St. Felix of Valois**. The foundation stone of the church was laid in 1717. But the works proceeded very slowly and it was consecrated in 1727 in spite of the fact that the dome was not ready yet. The works in its interior were not finished before the 1750's. Its interior arrangement is very similar to that of St. Peter's in Vienna. This is the reason for the speculations that both churches were designed by the same architect, either by J. L. Hillebrandt or F. Jänggle. The dome of the church with an oval ground plan is adorned with an **illusionist painting** by the Baroque painter A. Galli-Bibiena from 1740's. A. G. Bussi probably constructed the **main altar** of the church consecrated in 1752. Its main work of art is an unusually big **altar picture** by F. X. Palko depicting the founders of the Trinity order, St. Felix of Valois and St. John of Matha buying slaves out of Islamic slavery. The sculptures of the main altar are also valuable. They consist of the monumental **statues** of St. Agnes and St. Catherine standing on the side of the altar. They are attributed to the Bavarian sculptor J. B. Straub. The **lateral altar** of the Virgin Mary carries a **picture of the Madonna**, which is a copy of the Regensburg Virgin Mary. Count Zichy had it painted in 1736. A remarkable work of art on the exterior of the Trinitarian church is the lavishly ornamented main Rococo portal celebrating the Most Holy Trinity. Above the portal is the slogan of the Trinitarians: *Tres unum sunt* (Three are one).

In the time when this church was consecrated, construction of the **Trinitarian monastery** on the neighbouring plot of the disappeared cemetery was going on. The main mission of this order was to buy

Left: Grassalkovich palace in the 19th century
Right: Interior of the Trinitarian church

Christian captives out of Turkish slavery as did the founders of the order already at the turn of the 12th and 13th centuries. The Archbishop of Esztergom, Leopold Kollonich, invited the order to the Kingdom of Hungary in 1696. He wanted to make use of their good contact with Oriental countries, which could help the peace negotiations with the Turks. Protests of the Franciscans delayed their arrival in Pressburg until 1715. The Trinitarians hardly enjoyed the newly constructed monastery as Joseph II abolished their order in 1782. When the Trinitarians left, the building was given to the county administration. But it was not suitable for the offices. It was pulled down and in its place a new **Župný dom** (County House) ❷ for the Pressburg county administration office was built in 1844. Some remains of the monastic building survive in its southern courtyard. The design of the Neo Classic building on the northern side of Župné námestie square (house No. 12) is by J. Hild and adapted by I. Feigler senior. In the great lounge of the Župný dom concerts of several important interpreters were held. Franz Liszt, Johannes Brahms and A. G. Rubinstein gave concerts here. In 1921 President T. G. Masaryk was lodged here during his first official visit in Bratislava. In the years 1939-1994 the Slovak legislative bodies held their sessions in the Župný dom and after 1945 it became the seat of the Slovak National Council (in 1992 renamed to the National Council of the Slovak Republic). Since 1994 the sessions of the Slovak Parliament are held in a new building on the Vodný vrch hill. In the course of its fifty-year existence the old building of the original County House has seen numerous important political event. Tiso's government declared the independent Slovak State here on March 14th 1939. In 1992 a political decision with similar result was made here when on 17th July the Parliament adopted the declaration on the sovereignty of Slovakia.

The shortest western side of the triangular Župné námestie coincides with the facade of the **Capuchin church** ❸ conse-

crated to **St. Stephen of Hungary**. The Capuchins came to Pressburg in 1676. First they were given St. Catherine's chapel on Michalská street which the aldermen took as an interference with their rights. The monks then preferred to build a church and monastery of their own in 1708. They bought plots situated beyond the north-eastern corner of the town walls, which were previously considered inadequate for building because of clayey ground. The Capuchin church was consecrated by Bishop L. A. Erdödy of Nitra in 1717. Part of the church was pulled down and rebuilt in 1735. The Capuchin church and monastery of Pressburg are in a sharp contrast with other sacred structures in the town built in the Baroque period. Their architectural conception fully expresses the austere and simple nature of this order. Capuchin churches built in the Central Europe are very similar to the simple churches of the Protestants. They usually lack a tower, the nave is single and outer or inner ornamentation is almost missing. This basic characteristic also ap-

plies to the Capuchin church of Pressburg. The only ornamentation of its exterior is the **statue of St. Stephen of Hungary** placed above the main portal. The saint's statue is the work of A. Brandl. The interior of the church is also comparatively simple yet a bit more ornamented. The **main altar** along with two lateral ones was made in 1737. A **big altar picture** was painted by Brother Udalricus. It depicts the patron saint of the church, St. Stephen of Hungary putting Hungary under the protection of the Virgin Mary. Pressburg with its castle is depicted in the lower part of the picture. The artist of the **paintings on the lateral altars** of St. Francis of Assisi and St. Anthony of Padua was A. Rosier, the local artist and a disciple of Donner. The altar and some other parts of the church interior are made of dark stained wood, which is a typical characteristic of the Capuchin churches of the Western Slovakia.

Left: The gate of former Pálffy Palace
Right: The Capuchin church
The Immaculate of the plaque pillar

The space in front of the Capuchin church is adorned by the **Morový stĺp** (Plaque pillar) ❹. The pillar was erected in 1723 to commemorate the terrible plague which ravaged Pressburg ten years before (→ 176). The central work of art is the true copy of the original stone sculpture of the Madonna with child, which is now conserved and deposited in the Gallery of Bratislava to protect it from further deterioration. The texts on the pillar are quotations of the New Testament relating to the Immaculate Conception of the Virgin Mary.

The wonderful, but unfortunately disappeared, **Palffy's Garden** originated in early 17th century on the northern slope of the castle hill. It stretched from today's Zámocká street over Svoradova and Zochova streets up to Palisády. Pálffy's Garden was made for the county administrator and palatine Pálffy, who was then engaged in reconstruction of the royal palace of Pressburg Castle. The moderate slope inclined toward the city was changed into terraces with regularly planted vegetation. It was irrigated by water brought here from vineyards by piping. In 1630's a **garden palace** was built here. It used to stretch approximately over the site of today's student dormitories of Mirko Nešpor on Svoradova street. Pálffy's Garden was opened to the public in 1801. It became the place where popular feasts of the burghers were held, but it was not properly maintained and the precious vegetation was gradually deteriorating. In the 1890's the houses in Zochova, Svoradova and Podjavorínska streets were built in the garden. All that survived of Pálffy's Garden were isolated trees in the yards of the newly built houses. Pálffy's Palace was not spared either. It was almost completely demolished in the 1920's. Only the **main gate** ❺ survived and it was moved to the stairway between Svoradova and Zámocká ulica streets. A **pavilion** was made from part of one of the palace rooms. Its dome has the original Baroque stucco ornamentation from the second half of the 17th century.

Palffy's Garden, like the long vacant

plots stretching further to the east, lay on the inner side of the second town fortifications. These consisted of an earthen rampart, stones, and logs - palisades. Today the **street of Palisády** coincides with the disappeared fortifications and is the main access route to the villa quarter spreading on Bratislava hills. The gate of Suché mýto, which was the entrance made through the outer fortifications, is documented in the early 14th century. Sigismund of Luxembourg tried to strengthen this fortification system when the attack of Hussites was feared. The Turkish threat was another reason speaking in favour of improvement of the fortifications. Kozia brána gate as documented by archive material existed already in the 15th century. It stood on the medieval road amidst gardens and was the predecessor of the present **Kozia ulica street**. Beyond the Kozia brána gate is the **cemetery of Pressburg Evangelicals** ❻. Several figures of Slovak culture and social life, such as composer Ján Levoslav Bella, music teacher Miloš Ruppeldt and inventor Ján Bahýľ are buried here.

The environs of **Panenská ulica street** belonged to the Pressburg Evangelicals or Lutherans since the late 17th century. They lost their two churches in the town centre in 1672 and a special imperial commission prohibited the Evangelical service in the inner town. They were ordered out to the

northern suburb, a scarcely built area between the Suché mýto and Kozia gates. The services were held out of doors before a wooden articled church on the corner of the present Panenská and Lýcejná streets was built in 1682. The church soon became too small for the big Evangelical community of all three nationalities. Consequently, the German congregation obtained permission to build a church of their own. Construction of the **Large Evangelical Church** ❼ on Panenská ulica took place in years 1774-1777. The architect M. Walch tried to imitate the original German Evangelical Church, which used to stand near the Old Town Hall. It is built in the Neo-Classical style. The building is divided into three naves by prismoid pillars. The interior has got excellent acoustics, an asset appreciated by music lovers, who attend concerts held in this church. The **altar** from 1776 forms a whole with the **pulpit**. The artist who created the altar is P. Brandenthal. A. F. Oeser, a Pressburg native, painted the **painting of the altar**: *Christ in Emaus.*

A year after opening of the Large Evangelical Church the Slovak and Hungarian Evangelicals also built theirs. The **small Evangelical Church** ❽ on Panenská stands on the site of the former wooden articled church from 1682. It is again Walch's design and it is equally simple. The interior of the church on an irregular ground plan was modernized in the 1970's. The original furniture from the 18th century with the exception of the altar and pulpit was not preserved.

Konventná ulica street is closely associated with Evangelical schooling in Pressburg, the beginnings of which date to 1606. The Evangelical community of Pressburg was one of the largest in Hungary in the early 18th century. It associated about seven thousand believers of the three nationalities. The community invited to its Lycée in Pressburg **Matej Bell** (1684-1749), the former student of this institution in 1714, immediately after the retreat of the plague epidemic.

It soon became obvious that it was a good move. Matej Bel was not only a scientist of world importance, but also a good teacher and educator. He wrote and published text books, adapted the Latin grammar and initiated the publishing of the newspaper *Nova Posoniensia* (Pressburg Newspaper) in Latin. He became the first priest of the German Evangelical Church and the chancellor of the Lycée. For his scientific achievements he was referred to as *Magnum Decu Hungariae* (The Great Ornament of Hungary). During his stay at the Evangelical Lycée in Pressburg, Bel worked on his monumental work *Notitia Hungariae novae historico-geographica* (Historical-geographical knowledge of the New Hungary). In total he wrote seven volumes, five of which were published in book form. Numerous colleagues and correspondents, known as good connoisseurs of the particular described counties, helped him to collect the large amount of facts and information needed. Samuel Mikovíni, who also stayed in Pressburg for some time, contributed with maps to Bel's work (→ 86).

Pressburg as seen by Matej Bel

The knowledge on Pressburg and Pressburg county were included in the first two volumes of the famous Bel's Notitia. *The* Notitia *brings interesting facts about face of Pressburg shortly before the Maria Theresia's accession to the Hungarian throne. Matej Bel describes the town where he lived in a very positive light. He acquired quite a warm relation to the town over the years he spent there. He referred to it as the Paradise of Hungary for its numerous parks and gardens. He describes the natural setting, hills, rivers, minerals and the living parts of nature. He characterizes the population structure, state institutions existing in the town, the noble families and their residences. He did not avoid the question of nationalities, paid attention to fashion and folk usage. The* Notitia *contains the names of the streets, squares, monasteries and the*

Left: Lýcejná ulica street
Right: The new building of the Evangelical Lycée

local landmarks spiced with the personal attitudes of the author. For example, Matej Bel wrote about the shuttle bridge, Pressburg ale, the inns on Panenská street and the theatre in the Shooter's moat. He describes the famous Archbishop's garden with its fascinating fountains, sculptures, artificial caves and other attractions.

In 1783 the still existing building of what is called the **old Evangelical Lycée** ❾ (No. 15) on Konventná street was built. Although the Pressburg Lycée was a German school above all with tuition in Latin, numerous students of Slav nationalities attended it. Slovaks, Czechs, Serbs and Croatians were among them. This is why the Lycée gradually became a place where the idea of Pan-Slavic solidarity spread. The **Chair of the Czechoslovak Speech and Literature** was founded on the premises of the school in 1803 and led by Professor Juraj Palkovič. The aim of the new department was to educate priests in Biblical Czech, the language used in services of the Slovak Evangelicals. Numerous personalities of the Slovak and Czech culture and science such as František Palacký, Ján Kollár and Pavol Jozef Šafárik met in the Lycée. In 1828 they founded the Společnost učencú československú (Association of Czech-Slav Scholars), a student association directed towards a deeper study of the Czechoslovak language and literature. **Ľudovít Štúr**, then fourteen, came to study to Pressburg Evangelical Lycée the following year. Soon a new generation of emancipated students formed around him (→ 39). The main opponents of Štúr's ideas were the Hungarian speaking Evangelicals enforcing Magyarization of the member nations of the Kingdom of Hungary. They relied on the support of the General Inspector of the Evangelical Church Count Karl Zay. Commission of the General Convent of the Evangelical District prohibited Štúr from lecturing at the Lycée. It was the reason for the departure of the Slovak students from the Lycée. Their demonstrative departure with Štúr to Levoča in 1844 practically finished the important role of this institution in the formation of the national history of the Slovak nation in the first half of the 19th century.

The Evangelical community of Pressburg started to plan construction of a new building for the Lycée after the revolutionary years 1848 and 1849 were over. This was realized in the years 1854-1855 in the neighbourhood of the old building. The **new building of the Evangelical Lycée** ❿ (No. 13) is the work of the architect Gottfried Bendl who built it in the Neo Classical style. On the corner of this building, which is now a national cultural monument, is a travertine tablet bearing the list of 67 personalities of the Slovak national history of the 18th and 19th centuries, who studied or were active in both buildings of Pressburg Evangelical Lycée on Konventná ulica street. The building served as the Evangelical Faculty of Theology until the early 1950's. After its renovation was finished in 1968, it became the seat of the Institute of Slovak Literature of the Slovak Academy of Sciences.

Suché mýto square appeared in the historic documents in 1375 under the name *Dauermauth*. It was the medieval toll entrance into the inner suburbs through the gate and bridge over the moat. The place in front of the gate where several inns and an area of weekly markets existed, was normally used by military camps. Luxurious quarter with summer residences of nobles, gardens and parks originated on the plots of Suché mýto in the 18th century. They are depicted on the engraving of Samuel Mikovíni from 1735. The modern Suché mýto is completely different in comparison with the past. Demolition of old houses and reconstruction of the transport system connected Suché mýto with what is now **Hodžovo námestie square** into one big open space framed by modern buildings. One of them is the **Forum Hotel** ⓫ on the south-eastern side of the square. The hotel built according to design of the architect J. Hauskrecht has a capacity of 450 beds and was opened in 1988.

The dominant building of Hodžovo námestie square is the **Presidential Palace** ⓬ built after 1760 as the **garden palace of Anton Grassalkovich**. The building of this wonderful Rococo palace was outside the town and it was placed between the garden of the summer Archbishop's Palace and the town. The Chairman of the Hungarian Royal Court Chamber, the guard of the crown, comes of the Novohrad County, Anton Grassalkovich had it built. The central architectural element of the palace is the **pavilion** in its middle from which **two palace wings** spread. In front of the palace is a **courtyard** skirted by an impressive fence with a pair of gilded metal gates. On the ground floor of the central pavilion was the entrance to the **garden hall** and further to the French garden behind the palace building. The staircase with marble balustrade and decorated with vases leads to the ceremonial rooms on the first floor. **Allegorical statues** of the year seasons personified by the Classical deities of

Left: Presidential palace
Right: Grassalkovich's garden

Flora, Ceres, Bacchus, and Volcano stand in the corner niches. They are rightly regarded as the best Rococo sculptures in Bratislava. Two of them (Ceres and Bacchus) are attributed to sculptor Fridrich Wilhelm Bayer. The other two may have been made by someone from his circle. The dominant room of the central pavilion is the **principal hall** with preserved original Rococo ornamentation. The next room is the small musical hall adorned by music emblems and figural scenes on a musical theme. **Grassalkovich's garden** ⓭ originated simultaneously with the palace. Originally there were vases and baskets with flowers, cypresses and oleanders. It was partially opened to the public in the late 19th century. It was repeatedly modified. The last modification was made in 1999. The Grassalkovich Palace became the seat of the President in 1939. In the years of the Second World War it served the President of the Slovak State, Jozef Tiso. The top representative of the state returned to the palace when the Slovak Republic achieved its independence in 1993. It was adapted as the presidential residence of President Michal Kováč. The Palace, in contrast to the garden, is not accessible to the public except for occasional "open door days ". The space in front of the palace got the **fountain** called **the Earth, Planet of Peace** ⓮ made by Tibor Bártfay in 1982.

Štefánikova ulica street was once a field road between vineyards and gardens denoted in archive material as *Märtzgasse*. From the early 17th century it passed by the Archbishop's garden which was on its eastern side. On the opposite side of the road, on the place of today's Lermontovova, Tolstého, and Kuzmányho streets was Erdödy's garden with a big pavilion. When the steam railway connected Pressburg with Vienna, the area of what is now Šefánikova ulica became very attractive because it found itself between the town and the railway station. Massive construction on this street began in the 1880's. It soon became the most luxurious and spectacular street of the city. It was called *Stefánia utca* in Hungarian after the Crown

Princess Stephanie, wife of the Crown Prince Rudolf. The existing name is phonetically similar, but it is linked with the name of **Milan Rastislav Štefánik** (1880-1919), the personality of the modern Slovak history who invested great efforts in the origin of the First Czechoslovak Republic. His bust is placed on the **building of the Slovak Academy of Sciences** ⓯ .

The buildings on Štefánikova ulica and the contiguous streets are mainly smart residential houses, which document the wide range of architectural styles, used in the city. Members of the new class thriving on trade and industry had the opportunity to show off their wealth and prosperity and precisely this is reflected in luxury and spaciousness of the palaces or at least comfortable burgher houses standing on Štefánikova ulica street. **Swetlik's house** ⓰ (No. 3-5) is one example. This building in Romantic style in the latter half of the 19th century was built by a Pressburg craftsman, the glover Swetlik. He won his big property in a Viennese lottery. In the central part of the western row of Štefánikova is **Pistori Palace** (⓱ house No. 15). The pharmacist Pistori had the Neo Rococo building erected in 1899. The author of the project was architect J. Hubert. Abundant stucco ornamentation, wall paintings and coffer ceilings survived in the interior of the palace. After the Second World War Pistori Palace became the Museum of V.I. Lenin for a long time. Now it is museum again, but this time it is **Krajinské múzeum Matice slovenskej**. The former **department store** (No. 17, today a bank) was built in 1928-1929. In its time this building represented an avant-garde architectural work based on the principles of *Bauhaus*. Architect J. Víšek applied in its structure a modern construction with concrete and steel skeleton, which facilitated a more spacious inner division suitable for the purpose it was built for. On the eastern side of the street and neighbouring with Grassalkovich's garden is **Karácsony Palace** ⓲ (house No. 2) with the Neo Baroque facade. It was built by the end of the 19th century and later rebuilt into an administrative building. Between Spojná and Leškova streets on the eastern side of Štefánikova ulica are several **luxurious family villas**, which sprang up in the 19th century on the western edge of the former Archbishop's garden. One of the most beautiful was built for the physician B. Tauscher in 1891. **Tauscher's villa** ⓳ on the corner of Spojná and Štefánikova is a nice example of Pseudo Rococo architecture.

Villas cover the view of an extensive **park** ⓴, which is closed to the public. It belongs **to the area of The Office of the Government** of the Slovak Republic. The park occupies the site of the former Archbishop's garden, which stretched from today's Štefánikova up to Námestie slobody square. In the north it extended beyond Leškova and Štefaničova streets. Its origin dates back to the Renaissance period. Archbishop František Forgách founded

Left: Štefánikova ulica street
Right: Summer Archbishop's Palace

it in the early 17th century. In this garden tulips appeared for the first time in the Kingdom of Hungary. Forgách's nephew, Archbishop Juraj Lippay contributed most to the beauty the garden was famed for. This is the reason why it is often referred to as **Lippay's garden**.

The **letný arcibiskupský palác** ㉑ (summer Archbishop's Palace) on the upper part of Námestie slobody square lived through the good and bad times together with the garden. The first Archbishop's residence stood on this place from 1614. It was a Renaissance country-seat built by Archbishop František Forgách. Another Archbishop Emerich Esterházy rebuilt it into a palace. The **palace chapel** was adapted in 1740. Decorative **frescoes** were painted by A. Galli-Bibiena. The **altar** is the work of A. Hüter and K. Wiederkehr. The basis of its present form was given to the palace in the years 1761-1765 in the time of Archbishop František Barkóczy. F. A. Hillebrandt created the design of this luxurious palace. The bulky **central pavilion** of the palace with a shelter for carriages on one side of the **courtyard of honour**, resembles older Baroque buildings, but the ornamentation reveals Rococo influence. Two lateral wings skirt the courtyard of honour. When the Archbishop's office was moved from Pressburg to Esztergom there was not enough money for the maintenance of the palace and it started to deteriorate. In the revolutionary years of 1849 it served as a hospital, which stayed there until 1938. Then it was completely restored and adapted for administrative purposes. The renovation was planned by the architect Emil Belluš. Today it is the seat of the **Office of the Government of the Slovak Republic**.

In front of it is the largest square of Bratislava. Its area is five hectares. Its present name is **Námestie slobody square**, but for older Bratislavians it is still *Firšnál*, corruption of German *Fürstenalle* (The Prince's Row of Trees). This big space was empty and lacked any definite purpose for a long time. It was occasionally used for the military exercises and marches or circus shows.

Construction of the building of the Austrian **gas company** Österreichische Gasbeleuchtung AG started on the south-eastern edge of the square in 1855. It was put into operation on March 19th 1856 and to the existing 209 street gas lamps another 167 were added. The evening lighting and the morning putting off the gas lamps was the daily routine that existed in Bratislava until the 1960's. Today's Námestie slobody square is modern, as a matter of fact, the only older building out of those that frame the square is the Archbishop's Palace. On the northern side is the former **Post Office Palace** (No. 6) now the Ministry of Transport, Post and Telecommunications of the SR. It was built in the years 1946-1951 following a design by E. Kramár and Š. Lukačovič. On the opposite side stands the pavilion of Theoretical Institutes and the Faculty of Architecture of the **Slovak Technical University** (No. 19). On the eastern side of Námestie Slobody stands Faculty of Machine Engineering of the **Slovak Technical University** ㉒ built in 1963. The building complemented the area concentrating five faculties of the Slovak Technical University. The tall building of the Faculty of Construction has its entrance from **Radlinského ulica street**. Before the buildings of the STU were constructed, a plant producing sparkling wines with trademark **J. E. Hubert** used to stand in Radlinského street. Production of the champagne of top quality started already in 1825, using the original French recipe. Sparkling wines are today made in Sereď. The area of Námestie Slobody is now a park framing the biggest Bratislava **fountain** called **Družba** ㉓. It was built according to a design by J. Hovorka, K. Lacko, V. Droppa, and J. Hlavica. In the middle of the fountain is a monumental metal sculpture in shape of an opening lime tree flower with 9 m diameter and weighing 12 metric tons.

Two unusual buildings enhance the modern face of the quarter around Ná-

Left: Námestie slobody square
Right: The station of the first steam railway

mestie Slobody. The one of **Slovenský rozhlas** ㉔ or the Slovak Radio (Mýtna ulica street No. 1) is in the form of an overturned pyramid. It was designed by Š. Svetko, Š. Ďurkovič, and B. Kissling. The radio moved to this new building in 1984. Its concert hall contains one of the biggest organs existing in Slovakia.

Passing by the complex of administrative buildings of the Ministry of Finances of the SR on **Štefaničova ulica street**, one gets to the quarter around the main railway station of the city. The space around the station is the junction of six Bratislava streets. Three of them (Pražská, Štefánikova and Šancová) are the busiest of the city. No. 1 of Pražská is a nice building of former **Vinársky podnik** (Viticultural Company) with large wine cellars from the end of the 1870's. The complex originally belonged to the Pressburg businessman **Jakub Palugyay** (1819-1886). A member of an old yeoman family from the Liptov village of Palúdzka, Palugyay founded a successful company producing the top quality wine in 1863. He exported its products to 43 countries. Especially the sparkling wine Chateau Palugyay catered in transoceanic steam ships was famous. The first trolley bus line going to the Red Bridge in the Bratislava quarter of Patrónka was established in 1912 and its first stop was just in front of Palugyay Palace in Pražská ulica street.

Another interesting building the former **steem railway station** is connected with the beginnings of steam railways in the Kingdom of Hungary. This building painted in conspicuous yellow (Šancova street No. 1) is the oldest railway station where the first train pulled by a steam engine came from Vienna on Sunday 20th August 1848. The engine of this train was made in England and its name was *Bihar*. The railway track leading through Lamač, Devínska Nová Ves, and Marcheg, ending in Vienna, was a part of what was called the Emperor Ferdinand Northern Railway.

The **railway tunnel** under the quarter of Kramáre is also unique, for it is the oldest in the Kingdom of Hungary. Its length is 703 metres and it was built in the years 1846-1848. The trackage of the old railway station of terminal type and the platforms survived and have become part of the **Museum of the Road and Railway Traffic** ㉕. The existing Hlavná stanica or the **Main Railway Station** ㉖ is nearby, on Predstaničné námestie square. The shape of the platforms of this railway station serving the public since 1882 is oval because they trace the foothill of the mountain above the station. The station building was repeatedly adapted and the tracks passing through Bratislava station were electrified in 1967. The last train pulled by a steam engine departed from the Main Station on 17th October 1980 at 7:30 am. All other occasional departures of steam engines from the station are just nostalgic memories of their past glory.

The Eastern part of the Staré Mesto

This part of the centre attracts the shoppers and visitors of Bratislava, because it has the majority of shops, shopping centres, and department stores. The busiest spot is the **Námestie Slovenského národného povstania** (SNP) or Square of the Slovak National Uprising. The vacant space beyond the town walls was here before 1379 and it fulfilled the role of efficient defence of the fortifications. It was a **market place** above all, the place reserved for in-coming merchants in order to eliminate competition with the domestic merchants and craftsmen settled in the inner town. It was referred to as *Brot Markt* (Bread Market) in 1461. Later other food articles were also sold here. By early the 18th century the corn market moved here from the Main Square and soon the offered assortment became more varied: corn, groceries, meat, vegetable merchants were standing side by side with workshops of smiths, black-smiths, stonemasons or traders in spirits and wines. Several inns also moved to the proximity of the market place. There was, for instance, the Golden Goose, Golden deer or Black Eagle there including one with the unusual name *Flucht nach Ägypten* (The Flight to Egypt). When town walls were pulled down in 1778 the area was included into the expanding town as its biggest square with a triangle shaped ground plan. The south-western row of houses originated on the filled-in moat. Constructions on the outer, north-eastern side of the square connected the suburb of St. Laurence in the south with Schöndorf suburb in the north.

Left: The SNP square at the beginning of the 20th century

The square beyond the wall was

long referred to as a market (Bread, Corn or Green Market). Later the names linked to cultural or political figures also appeared. Such was the name of the Emperor Wilhelm II of Germany during the First World War. In 1921 the square acquired the name Námestie republiky, later Hlinkovo námestie or Stalinovo námestie in 1949. Its current name SNP has been used since 1962. It commemorates one of the biggest national anti-Nazi uprisings in Europe which burst out in Central Slovakia at the end of August 1944. **The monument to the SNP** ❶ with a trio of big bronze statues by Ján Kulich is associated with this significant event of the modern Slovak history. The Partisan's statue and those of women are 4.6 and 3 metres tall respectively. The monument was ceremoniously introduced to the public in 1974 on the occasion of the 30th anniversary of the Slovak National Uprising.

The dominating landmark of the upper part of the square in the past

was the **fountain of Carolina Augusta**, the fourth wife of the Emperor Francis I. The fountain was fed with water brought there by pipes from the Little Carpathians and the same water was supplied to some surrounding burgher houses including the monastery with a hospital standing nearby. The water of the fountain was the source of refreshment for the marketers. It is linked with the following legend:

The Lions of Pressburg

Once upon a time when the area of today's SNP square was only a meadow, a big battle was prepared. The king's soldiers faced the troops of a foreign conqueror. However, the rulers agreed that only two of their strongest warriors selected by each party should fight. The domestic party won both of the two encounters. The defeated ruler accepted the result and drew away with his army. The winning ruler had a well dug out to commemorate his victory. After many years the well was changed into a fountain with an obelisk and four lions which spouted out water filling the fountain. It was the favourite place of one old man who was nicknamed the Beggar of the Lions. A rumour spread that the beggar was in fact a wealthy man pretending poverty. One night thieves assaulted the beggar in his house and killed him for the money they believed he possessed. But when the poor old man died, four big lions appeared and tore the thieves in pieces. Then they returned to the obelisk, sat down in their places and went on spouting water just like before.

In the upper part of the square is the spacious building of the **Old** or **Main Post Office** ❷ (houses No. 34-36). The first post office ever was probably in the Old Town Hall. It was moved to the building on the corner of Ventúrska and Prepoštská ulica streets in 1725. The office moved after eight years to the inn on Schöndorfská (today's Obchodná). Predecessor of what we now know as the Old Post Office at the SNP Square was **Wachtler's palace** built in 1778 on the filled in moat. Its appearance is known only from photographs. The city bought the palace from its owners, Counts Szápary and Pallavicini to move there the management of the post office, while the post office itself stayed at Schöndorfská. It moved only after Wachtler's palace was pulled down in 1908 to give way to the building that is now the Old Post Office. Its construction was finished in 1912 and the designer was the architect G. Pártos from Budapest. The building won its attribute "Old", when a new post office, now the seat of the Ministry of Transport, Post Office and Telecommunications of the SR, was built.

A bit lower, on the corner of Uršulínska street, is the building of the

Left: The SNP square
Right: The Fountain with lion
The SNP monument

Tatrabanka (No. 33) built in the years 1922-1925. Milan Michal Harminc was its designer. When it was under construction the workers found at the site a unique treasure of 399 Celtic coins. The building was used by the Slovak Television and now it is the seat of the Ministry of Culture. Left form Tatrabanka is the **Dom odievania** (House of Clothing) (No. 31) built in the years 1978-1985 following the design of the architects Peter Minarovič and Ján Bahna. The left neighbour of this building is an interesting construction **Obchodný dom Dunaj** ❸, No. 30. It is one of the oldest of Bratislava's department stores, dating from 1936 and originally called Brouk a Babka after its owners. Construction of this, for the time very modern building, was accomplished with revolutionary innovations following the design of Christian Ludwig. The building was finished in a record time of 90 days.

The square widens in its lower part. The paved space in front of the building of the Old Market Hall (Stará tržnica) used to be a market place (Green Market), which originated on the site of the former cemetery next to the St. Laurence's church. The Gothic church of the eponymous suburb was demolished in 1529. Remnants of the foundations of the disappeared church survived under the pavement of the square. When the area was reconstructed, archaeologists discovered another disappeared sacral building. It is the Romanesque **chapel of St. Jakub** (St. James) from the 11th century, from

the time of the above mentioned cemetery. At the place where Klobučnícka ulica ends is a **fountain with one lion**. It was put together from the remains of various fountains. Remarkable part of it is a copy of sculpture representing a lion holding the municipal coat of arms from 1592. The pillar the lion sits on is from the 17th century. **Stará tržnica** ❹ (The Old Market Hall) has stood here since 1910. F. Neshyba designed it as the first in-door market in the city and it held this primacy for a long time. It served its purpose until the 1960's and afterwards Slovak Television converted it into studios. The recent thorough reconstruction changed it again into a market hall. The last building of the SNP square on the lower end of the side bordering with historical part of the city is the building known under the name **Manderla** ❺ (No. 23). This eleven-storied house is the first of Bratislava's "skyscrapers", and for long the tallest building in the city. It was built in 1935 for the rich businessman

trading in meat Rudolf Manderla. It was designed by Christián Ludwig and Ernest Spitzer. There are 64 flats, a café and a butcher's shop in the building.

The dominating building of the north-western side of the triangle-shaped SNP square is the Neo Romanesque **Calvinist church** ❻ with a tall tower. It was designed by the architect F. Wimmer and built in 1913. The biggest building of the square though is the **church and monastery of the Merciful Brothers** (Milosrdných bratov) ❼ in the north-east. The order, which owned it came to Pressburg in 1672 following the invitation of Archbishop Juraj Szelepchényi. The builder of this monastic complex was inspired by the facade of the principal monastery of this charitable order in Vienna. Its construction took a comparatively long time. It was started in the late 17th century and finished by the beginning of the following century. The complex of buildings is an example of the Early Baroque style. The church consecrated to the **Visitation of the Virgin Mary** by Martin Speer has an elegant Baroque **tower** and vertical architecture, which matches the facade of the monastery facing the square. The Soviet soldiers shot at the tower when the troops of the Warsaw Pact invaded Czechoslovakia in August 1968. In the interior of the church, **main altar** with pillar architecture dates from 1735-1737. In its middle is a monumental **painting** of the *Visitation of the Virgin Mary* by Martin Speer. The church possesses a valuable Baroque **pulpit** with reliefs of saints. The former monastery is now a **hospital**. In the lower part of the square is a block of modern 20th century buildings. The trio of buildings, colloquially called **družstevné domy** (the co-operative houses Nos. 13-15) ❽, is older. They were built in the years 1934-1939. The appearance of this multifunctional

Left: Obchodná ulica street
Right: Blumentál church

complex bears the features of an important Slovak architect Emil Beluš's style. On the left is the **House of Culture** (Dom kultúry) finished in 1965. It was a popular building for Bratislava's youth as it sheltered the famous **V-klub**, the club of university students. Now it is the seat of the Czech Cultural Centre.

Obchodná ulica street starts at Hurbanovo námestie square and runs in north-eastern direction. It is one of the oldest streets that existed outside the medieval fortifications. Its north-eastern end was the site of the community called *Széplak* (Beautiful Village) in the 13th century. It is referred to for the first time in a historic document from 1279. Pursuing the decree of King Andrew III from 1297 the village inhabited by Hungarian guests was abolished. Its church of St. Gotthard was demolished in 1311. However, settlement of this area must have continued or it was renewed because the 14th and 15th century sources mention the **Schöndorf** (German for Beautiful Village) **suburb**. A precious information source is the tax list from 1379 mentioning that 126 tax payers lived in the village. The land register from 1439 contains an entry saying that there were 52 houses and one large farm in the Schöndorf suburb. The suburb was included in the urbanisation of the left side of outer town walls with palisades in the course of the 15th century. The Main Street, which was the predecessor of today's Obchodná started at Michalská brána gate and headed to **Schöndorfská brána gate** in the outer walls (today the north-eastern end of Obchodná). The suburb, like other quarters outside the medieval town, suffered a lot in wars. Fires of the end of the 17th century and in 1883 destroyed older buildings. This is the reason, why there are only younger buildings, all of which were built between the 18th and 20th century. The older houses that are there now are mostly one- or two-storied buildings with long

yards, which were owned by vine cultivators or craftsmen. All the bigger buildings sprang up in Obchodná during the 20th century. They include the former **Palace Hotel** (Poštová No. 1) from 1928 designed by architect František Krupka or the neighbouring **house No. 22** with **Royko Passage** from 1924 designed by architect E. Steiner. One of the most recent buildings of Obchodná is the **Forum Hotel** ❾. It was built on the spot called Jama (The Hole) which existed here after the removal of ruins caused by an air-raid of the American air force in 1944. Parallel to Obchodná is Heydukova with the only **synagogue** ❿ in the city. Vysoká ulica is a short street starting near the Forum Hotel and ending in Obchodná with its famous **taverns** ⓫.

If you continue from Obchodná to Radlinská ulica street you enter the area where there was the **Blumentál suburb** in the past. It developed from a medieval settlement. Its original German name *Blumenthal* (Flower Valley)

appears in the historic sources from the 17th century. On the farther side of the suburb the outer earthen dikes were built. The striking feature of this quarter of the eastern city centre is the Roman-Catholic **church** of the **Ascension of the Virgin Mary**, better known by the public as **blumentálsky kostol** ⓬ (the Blumentál church). It is the parish church of the quarter Nové Mesto established in 1770 for the believers in the suburbs. The existing parish church was built in the years 1885-1888. This monumental building was designed by the Viennese architect Fridrich Rumpelmayer; the engineer in charge was Ignác Feigler junior. The three-nave Neo Romanesque basilica with transept is 57 metres long and 18 metres wide. The church **tower** is 76 metres tall. The interior of the church of the Marian type is from the time when it was built. Some of its parts were moved here from other sacred buildings. For instance, the pews were formerly in St. Martin's Minster. The porch contains the **bust of the priest Joseph Poeck** who invested great efforts in promoting construction of this church. It was made by the Pressburg born sculptor Viktor Tilgner. The most valuable work of art inside the church is the cast of the famous **statue** of the *Crucified* from 1892 by another native of Pressburg, **Johann Fadrusz** (1858-1903).

On the Floriánske námestie square in front of the church is the Baroque **pillar of St. Florián** ⓭. It was moved here in 1938. Originally it stood near the disappeared Laurinská brána in the bottom part of the SNP square. The saint was supposed to protect the city against natural disasters. The south-eastern side of **Floriánske námestie square** is skirted by the massive block of tenement houses called **Avion** ⓮. This is the area, where Esterházy's garden existed. The buildings of Avion were built in 1930-1932, to designs by the architect J. Marek.

Not far from Avion and opposite the hospital is the **Aspremont Palace** ⓯. It was built in 1769 for Count Gobert Ján of Aspremont in front of the Špitálska brána gate, an opening in the palisades, and on the site of Count Erdödy's garden. Aspremont's palace built by J. J. Thaller represents the youngest, as far as the architectural style is concerned, palace of the preserved summer residences of aristocracy built outside the city. It is built in the Baroque taste. There is a **central pavilion** with two **lateral wings**. The shapes of windows with ledges, the bleak balcony on Tuscany pillars and the pediment of the central pavilion, reveal Classicizing tendency. The Esterházy's bought the palace by the end of 18th century and it was they who had here an orchestra directed by composer Joseph Haydn on one occasion. The As-

Left: Statue of Martin Kukučín
Right: The Medical Garden
The cemetery Ondrejský cintorím

premont Palace is now the seat of the **Dean's Office of the Medical Faculty of the Comenius University**. There was still enough room on the lands bought by Count Aspremont from Erdödy for a spacious garden. This originally wonderful garden in French style is now known to the public as the **Medická záhrada** ⓰ (The Medical Garden) because of its proximity to the mentioned Faculty of Medicine. The garden was originally divided into four separated parts. Its later owners modified its style. The last adjustments made in years 1984-1987 suggest renovation of the original French garden. Now it is the public park. The park is adorned by sculptures. One of them is a modern fountain called **Labutia fontána** or Swan Fountain by Pavol Mišík. The **statue** of an important Slovak writer **Martin Kukučín** (1860-1928) by the Croatian sculptor Ivan Meštrovič was placed in the park in 1984.

Beyond **Poľná ulica** street with a small market place is the **cemetery Ondrejský cintorín** ⓱. It is the oldest of the surviving historic cemeteries of Bratislava. It was founded in 1784 when Emperor Joseph II decided to prohibit burials in the old cemetery of St. Andrew next to the Elizabethan monastery. It had been used for more than 150 years. In the 1970's and 1980's the Ondrejský cemetery was changed into municipal park. The entrance to the cemetery is from **Ulica 29. augusta street**. It is its only entrance just beside the **chapel of St. Andrew** ⓲ built in 1861 as designed by Ignác Feigler junior. Ondrejský cintorín is not only a quiet and refreshing place in this busy part of the city. One can also admire valuable works of the Pressburg stonemasons. Many of them come from the workshop of famous stonemason Alojz Rigele, who is also buried here. Ondrejský cintorín cemetery is also a particular chronicle of the city's history in the time between the late 18th and early 20th centuries. **Cintorínska ulica street** leads from the cemetery to the city centre. On its corner is the biggest beer restaurant of Bratislava **Stará Sladovňa** ⓳ (The Old Malt House). As a matter of fact, with its 1,800 places it is one of the biggest in Europe and for its unusual dimensions it is colloquially called *Mamut* (The Mammoth). The restaurant originated by reconstruction of an old malt house from 1872.

The **Špitálska ulica street** starts in the SNP square and heads to the northeast. Its name is linked to the fact it has been the site of several hospitals since

the Middle Ages. As early as 1307 the municipal council agreed with the Antonite Order about administration of the hospital built on plots east of the town. The municipal **hospital of St. Anton** stood opposite today's St. Ladislav's church. The hospital was demolished along with the Špitálska brána gate standing near in fear from the Turkish attacks in 1529. It was restored at the order of Ferdinand I in 1543 when the Turkish raids finished. Next to the **hospital of St. Ladislav** was a cemetery with a chapel. The hospital was decaying and it had to be closed in the early 19th century. A new one had to be built. The design of Ignác Feigler senior, which offered a purposefully arranged disposition with the church placed on the middle axis won the competition. Emperor Ferdinand V laid the foundation stone of the construction in presence of Archbishop of Esztergom Alexander Rudnay in 1830. The church with municipal workhouse was built in two years thanks to the charitable gifts of the local Catholics. The central architecture of the complex is **St. Ladislav's church** ⑳. The street facade of the church with adjacent four-wing building of workhouse is strictly symmetrical. The central axis is represented by rectangular church tower built somewhat later. St. Ladislav's church was slightly modified in 1891. The originally white painted interior acquired figural **wall paintings** by painter Johann Grünwidl. This step has neutralized its original Classicist nature. Part of the interior is a big wall painting of Apotheosis of St. Ladislav from 1830. It was painted by Ferdinand Lütgendorf. The **altar painting** by the Viennese artists Joseph Kliegl from 1830 is a part of the **lateral altar** of St. Anna.

Some metres away from St. Ladislav's church are the **Elizabethan church and monastery** ㉑. The female Elizabethan order came to Pressburg thanks to Archbishop Emerich Esterházy who had a four-wing monastery building with a hospital and church built for them in the years 1739-1743. This Baroque monastic complex reveals a strong influence of the Viennese atmosphere. It was designed by the architect A. Pilgram. The Elizabethan church is consecrated to the founder of the order of St. Elizabeth of Hungary. It is a single-nave sacred building and the street facade of the church is a typical example of what is called the radical Baroque. In the facade niches are Baroque sculptures. The sculptural decoration of the church facade suggests Donner's workshop. It was most probably created by Ľ. Gode. The church interior contains also a wonderful **painting** *Celebration of St. Elizabeth* by Paul Troger placed in the dome, which creates an impression of endless heights of heaven. Under the dome are

Left: The main altar of St. Elisabeth church
Right: Tesco department store
Špitálska ulica street

allegorical figures of four virtues of the sponsor of the order, Archbishop Emerich Esterházy: Wisdom, Justice, Courage, and Temperance. Wall paintings and altar pictures are united around the central motif of Jesus Christ and his imperative of love. The basic stone of the main altar of the Elizabethan church was laid down in 1739. Paul Troger painted the monumental **altar picture** of *The Vision of St. Elizabeth* for this altar in 1743. At the sides of the altar with pillar architecture are **statues** of St. Francis of Assisi and St. Antony of Padua.

West from the church is the building of former Elizabethan monastery with a **hospital**. The Elizabethan order bearing the name of its founder St. Elizabeth of Hungary (→ 68) originated in Germany in the 13th century. Its members obey the regulations of St. Francis of Assisi and their own statues. Their main mission is care for the sick in hospitals, including the women's hospitals. Every Elizabethan monastery has its hospital. The one in Pressburg had 22 beds and a pharmacy with notable interior furniture. Next to the hospital was a big garden.

The **Kyjev Hotel** (22) standing opposite the hospital has its entrance in Rajská ulica. This 18 storied building forms a joint architectural whole with the **Tesco department store** (23). The older part of the store with triangle ground plan was opened in 1968 and the more recent buildings were opened ten years later. Until recently this store with its 11,000 square metres was the biggest in Slovakia. Today's **Kamenné námestie square** neighbouring the lower part of the SNP square gained vacant space by demolition of several Classicist houses from the 19th century. Among the modern building perhaps that of the **Slovenská Sporiteľňa** (24) (SNP square No. 18) deserves attention. Experts regard it as one of the most progressive architectural works in Slovakia from the inter-war period. It was designed by the architect Juraj Tvarožek in the years 1927-1931. It has an iron-concrete skeleton and it bears a steel mantle of the facade, which was a revolutionary architectural solution for its time.

Dunajská ulica street starts in the lower part of the SNP square and heads eastward. It originated from what used to be the Danube trade road running from Pressburg over the ford near Prievoz outside the town. In the 15th century Dunajská brána gate was built near where Rajská ulica street starts. This gate was the easternmost passage

through the palisade fortifications. The first reference to the gate is from 1493 and it was pulled down in 1825. The now disappeared arm of the Danube called Novozámocké flowed along the medieval trade road and by the Dunajská brána gate. The road crossed it by a bridge, which led to an often flooded area of today's Mlynské Nivy. A house called Spindlerovský dom used to stand on the site of the **Maďarské gymnázium** (Hungarian grammar school) ㉕ at No. 13 of Dunajská street formerly. In this house the famous inventor **Johann Wolfgang Kempelen** (1734-1804) lived and worked. Kempelen won his nickname the "Edison of Pressburg" for his experiments and successful, sometimes revolutionary, discoveries. For instance, he was the one who solved the problem of the water supply to Pressburg castle by an ingenious pump, he allegedly constructed a speaking machine functioning on the principle of the modern gramophone for the blind or machines pumping water out of salt mines and constructed weaving machines working in his own factory. Though he died in Vienna on March 26th 1804 during an occasional visit, he lived a great part of his fruitful life in Pressburg.

Left: Kempelen's chess machine
Right: The Blue Church

But what won Kempelen perhaps the greatest fame and admiration was his miraculous **chess-playing machine**. There was a figure of a Turk with pipe on Kempelen's chess machine and as it was shown all over the Europe it defeated all its counter-partners, among them also some of the European rulers. The machine was taken away to America after Kempelen's death and destroyed during a fire.

The quarter south of Dunajská ulica street originated only at the beginning of the 20th century. The citizens of Pressburg called this area of alluvial forests, wet meadows and gardens *Grössling*, the name perhaps derived from the German word for the Danube fish *kressling*. Before the later half of the 19th century only several bold fellows built houses in this land flooded only too often. The track of a horse railway crossed the area in 1845 approximately coinciding with today's Dostojevský rad street. Only after the Danube arms were filled and the main river channel regulated, did the lands become more attractive for builders. By the end of the 19th and beginning of the 20th centuries modern blocks of flats were built here creating a rectangular street network. Two areas in this network remained vacant and they progressively became squares with regular ground plans and greenery (Jakubovo and Šafárikovo squares). In that period Pressburg was admiring the new end-of-the-century style coming from Vienna and Budapest. It was used with a creative approach in architecture of many buildings of this new quarter.

The new quarter lying next to Starý

most bridge also got a new church in 1913 thanks to Countess G. M. Szapáryová. It was a beautiful one, still to be seen on **Bezručova ulica street**, and known by the natives as **Modrý kostolík** ㉖ or the Blue Church. It is a wonderful example of the Art Noveau style in sacred architecture. Architect Edmund Lechner's design was realized by the Pittel and Braunswetter building company. Its cross was ceremoniously erected on June 26th 1910, and on May 14th of the next year the Bishop Medard Kohl consecrated the installed church bells. The ever active Countess Szapáry with the assistance of Cardinal F. Nagl in the meantime provided for transportation of the relics of St. Elizabeth from Vienna. Along with the relics of St. Climent of Rome, St. Vicentia and St. Theodora they were deposited inside the main altar. The Blue Church is a single nave one with cylindrical tower 36.8 metres tall. Romanesque pillars and Baroque domes and its layout demonstrate inspiration from historic styles. The facades bear ornamentation with oriental or Hungarian flair. The exterior of the church is covered by conspicuous blue majolica and the glazed roof shingles are of the same colour. Above the entrance is an Italian **mosaics** with a motif from the well-known *legend about St. Elizabeth with roses*. The motif of rose is the basic element of ornamentation used in the church interior. A big **painting** of St. Elizabeth is placed above the main altar depicting the saint as she gives out charitable gifts in front of the Wartburg castle. It was painted by the Budapest painter J. Tury. Architect E. Lechner also designed the neighbouring building of **gymnázium** ㉗ (the grammar school) on Grösslingová ulica street. It was built in 1908.

Šafárikovo námestie square originated after 1891, when the first fixed bridge was built over the Danube. The square was built up as its rectangular ground required, though it became

larger after June 1944 when a bomb launched by an American bombing aircraft fell on the **Landerer Palace** which was then temporarily used by army. The building erected in 1770 for the renown Pressburg printer and publisher Landerer was completely destroyed. Once the plot was cleared it became a park. In 1958 the **fountain** called **Poézia** ㉘ (Poetry) with a bronze statue by T. Bárfay was put in the park. However, there also is another **fountain called Kačacia** ㉙ (Duck Fountain) hidden under the tall trees in the southern part of the Šafárikovo námestie square. It is one of the Bratislava's most beautiful fountains and R. Kühmayer made it in 1914. The group of statues is linked with a legend about three boys and their ducks.

The Legend about the Duck Fountain

Once upon a time three boys were playing on the green meadows of Mlynské rameno, an arm of the Danube. The

old water sprite living in a hollow tree on the bank heard their shouting and they quickly became friends. Once the water sprite even allowed the boys to dive and see the underwater realm of fish and crabs. The little shepherds liked it so much that they tried to visit it again only this time without the water sprite's company. Their curiosity became fatal for them, as the boys and their ducks turned into stone and stayed there in the same posture the sculptor endowed them.

Varied buildings frame Šafárikovo námestie square. One of the most recent is the **Comenius University** ㉚ (house No. 5). Architect F. Krupka built it in 1930 for the stock exchange following the winning design. Today it is the seat of the vice chancellor's office, Faculty of Law and part of Faculty of Philosophy of Comenius University.

Left: The Duck Fountain
Right: University of Comenius

History of the oldest of the existing universities in Slovakia started in 1919. It was founded as Czechoslovak University of Bratislava and renamed the same year as Comenius University. Its first vice chancellor was Professor of medicine Kristián Hynek. The first Slovak university started with three faculties: medicine, law, and philosophy. The Faculty of Nature Sciences was added only in 1940 and after the Second World War another four originated. The University was struggling with lack of space from the very beginning. Single departments and theoretical institutes were distributed in different buildings all over the city. This was the reason for the decision that the new building of stock exchange on Šafárikovo námestie square would be given to the university. The law and philosophy faculties moved there after indispensable adjustments in 1936. Later part of philosophical faculty moved to another building in Gondová street nearby. On the premises of the university the **Šafárik's Scholarly Association** was founded in 1926. The Association that existed until 1939 bore the name of an important Slovak scholar **Pavol Jozef Šafárik** (1795-1861) who besides other, is the author of today's name of our city.

Let us go via **Štúrová ulica street** back to Námestie SNP square where we start our trip around the eastern centre. Today's Štúrova ulica was only a narrow alley heading across Grössling to the main bed of the Danube until the latter half of the 19th century. One of few big buildings, which used to stand here, was Landerer's palace. When in 1891 the **bridge of Francis Joseph** (the existing Old Bridge) was opened, the narrow street gained importance and it changed to one of the most beautiful and elegant Pressburg streets. Tenement houses in the Art Noveau style that provided luxurious housing for the better-off social classes built it up. Former Landererova, Borosova, and Šrobárova street is bearing the name of

the most important figure of the Slovak national emancipation and codifier of the Slovak languages, **Ľudovít Štúr** (1815-1856). The mentioned architectural style was applied on several buildings of Štúrova ulica street. One of the **houses** bearing the features of this style is on the corner of Štúrová and Tallerova streets (**No. 10**). It is called Tulipán (Tulip). Also the second corner building of Tallerova (**No. 12**) is built in the Art Noveau style. It is the work of Budapest architects M. Komor and D. Jakab. Older buildings of the street nearer to today's SNP square were replaced by new ones after the First World War. The former **printing house of Pravda** (No. 4) is one example. It replaced older buildings including the inn called *Red Bull* in 1955. Part of the new structures of the northern end of Štúrova ulica street are the architecturally attractive bank buildings.

The oldest one of them is the former Austro-Hungarian bank on the corner of Štúrová and Medená streets. It was designed by J. Hubert and built in 1902. Today it is the seat of our best professional folk dance ensemble **Lúčnica**. The **building of the National Bank of Slovakia** ㉛ panelled with travertine boards stands between the streets Gorkého and Jesenského giving on the Kamenné námestie square and it was built in 1936-1939 to design of the architect E. Belluš.

Bratislava's embankment

The mighty Danube ruled the territory south of the medieval town. The river branched into uncountable arms and flooded the surrounding territory every year. The land around the river was completely inadequate for settlement or for farming. The reverse side of this disadvantage was that it was also a perfect natural defence. The attacks of the enemies coming from the south were doomed to fail.

However, in the 18th century the citizens of Pressburg started to adapt the previously barren land and built a water-management system which regulated the Danube's riverbed. The banks of the Danube became firmer and the city also expanded towards the south. An attractive space originated there. The entire space beyond the southern town hall was called *Neuschift* (The New Settlement).

Left: Námestie Ľ. Štúra square in the early 20th century

Starý most 1
Slovenské národné múzeum 2
Pomník československej štátnosti 3
Osobné prístavisko Danubius 4
Pomník Ľudovíta Štúra 5
Lanfranconiho palác 6
Dessewffyho palác 7
Café Propeler 8
Reduta 9

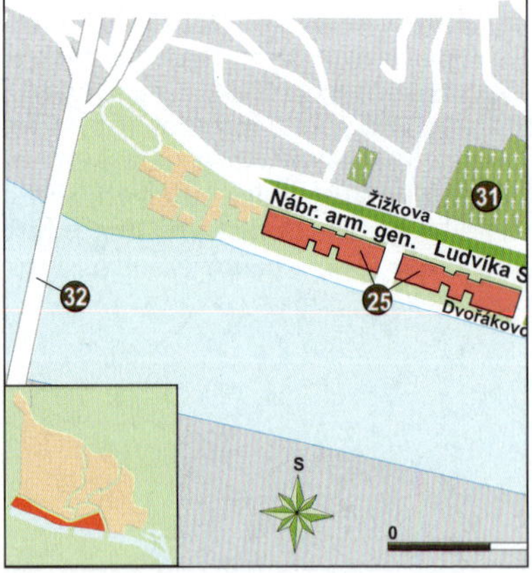

Today the area around the embankment of the city between the historic centre and the left bank of the Danube are the favourite routes of walks, occasional visits to a museum or gallery or meetings in one of the boat hotel restaurants on the river. The route starting at the Old Town and heading up stream toward the Botanical Garden is perhaps the most popular one for a Sunday afternoon walk.

The first part of the route runs along **Fajnorovo nábrežie embankment** bearing the name of the Evangelical bishop and writer **Dušan Fajnor** (1876-1933). Even before the origin of embankment the oldest of the existing four Bratislava bridges over the Danube, now called the **Starý most** ❶ (Old Bridge), was built. Construction of a fixed bridge of the Danube was an insoluble problem for many centuries. Only after the first extensive adaptations over the Danube's bed by the end of the 19th century could Bratislava finally acquire its first fixed bridge. It was built in two years and it was given the name of the Emperor Francis Joseph. The bridge opened a day before the New Year's Eve of 1890 and remained the only over the Danube in Bratislava for another 83 years. It has lived through the worst of its days at the end of the Second World War, when the Germans trying to slow down the advancing Red Army destroyed it. On August 6th 1945 six hundred Soviet soldiers and four hundred and fifty German prisoners of war repaired the destroyed bridge. It was then called The Bridge of the Red Army. The repairs took only five months and seventeen days. When a 50 ton tank crossed it and did not end up in the water of Danube, the traffic over the bridge was restored.

Construction of Fajnorovo embankments started in the first half of the 20th century only after the bank of the river was reinforced and heightened. In the northern part of the embankment there are three blocks of buildings. The eastern one is a bulky **building** often denoted **Governmental** (Gondova street No. 2) al-

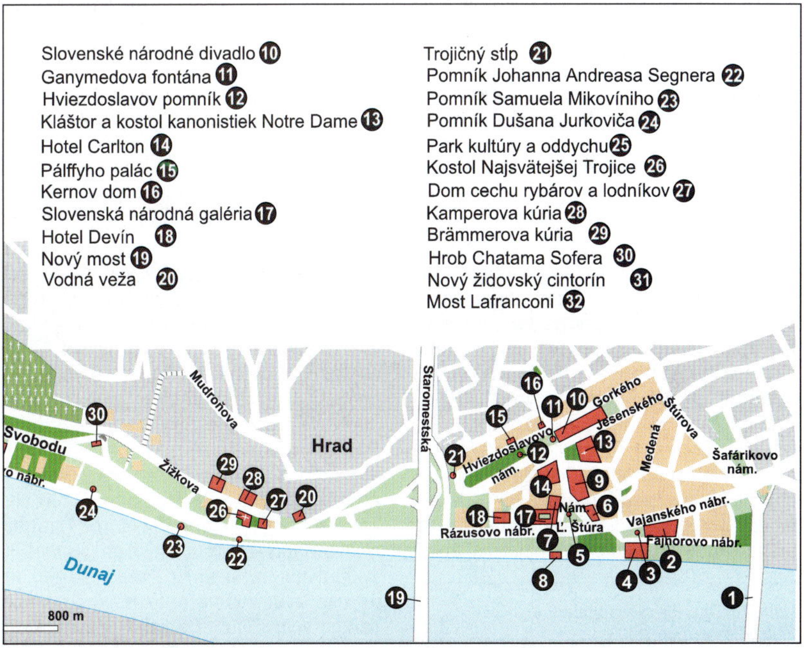

though no governmental institution is seated there. The name is linked to the period between the two world wars when it sheltered the **Ministry of the Czechoslovak Republic with full powers for administration of Slovakia** led by Minister **Vavro Šrobár** (1867-1950). The building was designed by J. Ritter and built for the Austro-Hungarian army in the years 1911-1912. The Ministry moved to it in the spring of 1919. The Governmental building built in the Viennese Art Noveau style is now the seat of the **Faculty of Philosophy of Comenius University**. In the space between Fajnorovo and Vajanského nábrežie embankments is the **building of the Slovak National Museum** ❷ built in the years 1924-1928 for the branch of the Czech *Zemědělské museum* or Museum of Agriculture. The architect M. M. Harminc designed it. It remotely resembles a Classic temple with pillars and conspicuous triangle shaped tympanum with statues. But the building did not survive the war events taking place at the end of the Second World War. Only the stone reliefs at sides of the main facade by the Prague sculptor F. Úprka were preserved. Now the Museum contains exhibitions of natural history. The monument to the Czech and Slovak statehood adorns the space in front of the Museum. It was ceremoniously introduced to the public on October 28th of 1988. A bronze **statue of lion** ❸ leaning on the state symbol of the former Czechoslovakia stands on almost fifteen metres tall pylon.

The passenger port Danubius ❹ is at the eastern end of Fajnorovo embankment. It operated sightseeing navigation on the Danube. The boat transport on the Danube has a long tradition. The **first steamer** called *Carolina* appeared in the port of Pressburg on September 2nd 1818. The regular boat transport on the Danube was ceremoniously opened on June 17th 1830 when the steamer *Franz I* started on its trip from Vienna to Pressburg. In the same year The **Danube Steamship**

Left: The Danube embankment
Right: Coronation Hill

Company was founded. They had an agency in Pressburg and two steamers called *Nándor* and *Arpád*. By 1878 the company owned as much as 193 steamers. The history of the Danube steamers ended in 1967 when the last steamer Devín was condemned.

Vajanského nábrežie embankment bears the name of the Slovak politician, journalist, and writer, **Svetozár Hurban Vajanský** (1847-1916). The most interesting building on Vajanského embankment from the architectural point of view is **Jurenák Palace** (house No. 4). In this Neo Classical house of burgher K. Jurenák, composer **Johannes Brahms** (1833-1897) stayed during his visit to Pressburg. Next to the building of the Slovak Philharmonic Orchestra the embankment opens onto **Námestie Ľudovíta Štúra square** skirted by elegant buildings. Until 1938 it bore the name *Coronation square* as it used to be the setting of the final ceremony of coronations.

Coronation hill

All recently crowned Kings of Hungary closed the pompous coronation feast by ascending a low coronation hill. They waved with what was believed to be St. Stephen's sword in the direction of the four cardinal points, which symbolized the determination to defend the country against enemies coming from the north, east, south or west. The hill called in Latin monticulus regia *(Coronation hill) was made by piling earth brought from all counties of the kingdom before each coronation. The hill was originally made in front of Rybárska brána gate, progressively it moved towards the south. In 1773 during the reign of Maria Theresia the vacant space in front of the municipal granary was chosen and it was the place where the Coronation square later originated. The new Coronation hill was not a mere heap of earth. It gained the form of a slightly elevated Baroque construction with octagonal terrace rimed by stone balustrade. It also bore the coat of arms of the Kingdom of Hungary and a stone relief representing the Hungarian royal crown. The designer of the structure was the architect F. A. Hillebrandt. The hill was used only twice, when Kings Leopold II and Ferdinand V were crowned. The municipal council entrusted J. Fadrusz to build a monument celebrating the Coronation City of Pressburg, which should occupy the place instead of the coronation hill. The monument consisted of the statue of Maria Theresia mounted on a horse accompanied by the royal guard, made of white Carara marble. The monument was introduced to the public on May 16th 1897 but it did not last long. In 1919 the authorities of the new state decided to remove the Theresian group of statues as a reminder of the hated monarchy.*

Then in 1938 the vacant place in the middle of the Coronation square got a new monument. This time it was dedicated to the memory of Milan Rastislav Štefánik But it soon followed its predecessor because the cult of Štefánik was not in line with the prevailing political ideology. Now there is the **monument of Ľudovít**

Štúr ❺, made by T. Bártfay and J. Salay and erected in 1972.

On the eastern side of the square is **Lanfranconi Palace ❻** (No. 1). It was built in the later half of the 19th century on the site of the former salt office. Successful Pressburg businessman E. Lanfranconi ordered construction of the Neo Renaissance house designed by Ignác Feigler junior. What is interesting about the building is its roof construction, which was moved here from the Viennese World Exhibition. The building now belongs to the Ministry of the Environment of the Slovak Republic. Opposite is the **Dessewffy Palace ❼** (No. 2). It was built in the latter half of the 19th century and the name derives from its owner Count Dessewffy. It used to be one of the most elegant and luxurious palaces in the city. Original ornamentation and antique furnishing from the 17th and 18th centuries in its interior partially survived.

Left: The Reduta
Right: The Slovak National Theatre

Café Propeler ❽ on the Danube embankment offers an opportunity to take refreshment and contemplate the river. This nice functionalist building was built in 1931 following the design of E. Belluš. It was, as a mater of fact, the platform for the passengers of **Bratislava's propellers**. The history of the company colloquially called "propeler" started in 1890. Businessman H. Hornes founded it. He bought three steamers to provide service to the citizens of Pressburg, who enjoyed the dancing parties, held regularly on their decks. The transport of passengers to the left bank of the river became the principal task of the steamers only later.

The short **Mostová** (The Bridge) **ulica street** connects Námestie Ľudovíta Štúra with Hviezdoslavovo námestie squares. The street originated after the regulation of the river. Originally it headed to the pontoon bridge of Carolina Augusta over the Danube what explains the name of the street. Historic documents quote that there used to be the *Zum König von Ungarn Hotel* (King of Hungary Hotel) on this street. Now the principal landmark of this street is the **Reduta ❾** building. It was built in 1911-1915 as designed by the Budapest architects M. Komor and D. Jakab. The monumental silhouette of this elegant building tries to copy the basic shape of the older building of the **provincial granary** which was built here in the years 1773-1774. The city did not have any appropriate building for the ceremonious political or social events and assemblies, so it was decided to buy out the decaying granary in 1901. The site was cleared in 1911 and construction of the Reduta finished in 1915. The only thing preserved from the old granary is the **portal** built in the courtyard. The grandiose building of Reduta standing close to the river is an excellent example of the Eclectic style. The skeleton of the building was made from iron-concrete construction. Historicizing architectural decoration covers the modern building technology used for the construction of Reduta. Numerous artists took part in the process of ornamentation.

The concert hall is the work of the local sculptor A. Messner. The Reduta is now the seat of the **Slovak Philharmonic Orchestra**. Occasionally it hosts the top domestic and foreign musical ensembles and outstanding soloists of classic music. The concert season culminates in the **Bratislava Music Festival** organized in Autumn every year.

Hviezdoslavovo námestie square is a wonderful and lively place. It was formed in the 18th century. Until then only houses of fishermen and the river port built on the Danube's arm existed here. This port belonged to the town as the castle had another, an upper port next to the ford near Vodná veža tower. After demolition of the town halls, filling of the moat and of the Danube arm a better exploitation of the space immediately bordering on the historic city centre was considered. The square was paved, lines of tree were planted and the first smart buildings were built here. Its popularity was growing and as the citizens liked to walk here, it was called the *Promenade*. Among its other names was also *Theaterplatz* (The Theatre square) of 1840. The square bears the name used at present, Hviezdoslavovo námestie, since 1932. It derives from the name of the best Slovak poet and playwright **Pavol Országh Hviezdoslav** (1849-1921).

The most impressive building on Hviezdoslavovo námestie square is the **Slovak National Theatre** ❿. The elegant eclectic theatre building has adorned the city since 1886. It was not the first theatre building on this site. The first was a provisional theatre built of wood for the occasion of the coronation of Maria Theresia in 1741. It existed only for several years and then it was dismantled. The citizens of Pressburg had to wait for a brick theatre until 1776. The local architect M. Walch designed the theatre building standing in front of Rybárska brána gate and a great theatre fan Count Juraj Csáky financed a great part of it. The new municipal theatre opened with the play *The Medici's* written by a less known author J. Ch. Brandis. In 1793 the rear tract with a dance hall

called the old Reduta was added to the theatre building. The old theatre definitely closed on June 26th 1884 and immediately after its demolition the pompous building of the new municipal theatre was started. The investments amounted to 340,600 guldens following the plans of the recognized Viennese architects F. Fellner and H. Helmer. The interior of the theatre was in pure Baroque taste while the outer part can be classified as Baroque-Renaissance in style. The paintings in the foyer (partially destroyed) are by K. Spányi of Budapest. The artist-aristocrat Baron Leo Lütgendor-Leinburg from Munich painted auditorium. The exterior of the building was also lavishly ornamented. The stone group of statues of the Muse Thalia by the sculptor T. Friedl from Vienna above the main portal and the figures symbolising tragedy and comedy from the studio of V. Tilgner of Pressburg are the only survivors from the original sculptures. The new municipal theatre was opened on September 22nd 1886 with the opera *Bán Bank* of F. Erkle, the founder of the Hungarian national opera and the author of the Hungarian anthem. German and Hungarian spoken plays alternated in this theatre while the Hungarian prevailed. After the First World War in 1920 the Co-operative of the Slovak National Theatre or SND was founded and it engaged actors from the East Czech Theatre of B. Jeřábek. The first opera show prepared with Czech actors was B. Smetana's *Kiss*. Its opening night took place on March 1st 1920. The SND reached a high professional level under the management of the recognized Czech composer and director **Oskar Nedbal** (1874-1930) who provided sufficient space for the emerging Slovak ballet and opera. The SND put on dramas and operas until 1955 when the drama ensemble moved to a separate new building on Laurinská street leaving the stage of the SND to ballet and opera only. The SND hosted some important figures of world opera and ballet. It was also here where several opera stars of Slovak origin started their careers: Peter Dvorský, Edita Grúberová, and Lucia Poppová.

The space in front of the SND building is adorned by **Ganymedes' fountain ⓫**. The fountain is the present of the First Pressburg Savings Bank. The sculptor V. Tilgner of Pressburg made it in 1888. The figures of the fountain were cast in bronze.

Left: Detail of Ganymedes' fountain
Right: The Carlton Hotel on an old post card
The church of Notre Dame

Ganymedes' flight to Olympus

Ganymedes' fountain is rightly considered the most beautiful in Bratislava. It is based on the classical legend about the beautiful boy Ganymedes. The legend has that Zeus found Ganymedes so attractive that he converted to a rapacious bird and carried Ganymedes on his wings to the top of the mountain Olympus. Ganymedes was supposed to wait on the Gods living on top of the mountain. The statue at the very top of the fountain represents precisely the moment of the kidnapping. The child

figures at the middle part of the fountain are holding in their hands the four most typical fish species living in the Danube: carp, sheat-fish, pike, and walleye. On the edge of the basin are three pairs of water animals sitting. Crabs, frogs and turtles symbolize the close vicinity of the Danube.

Ganymedes' fountain is not the only artistic work on the rectangular area of Hviezdoslavovo námestie square. There is also the **monument to the poet P. O. Hviezdoslav with its fountain** ⓬ standing here since 1937. The authors of the statue are J. Pospíšil and V. Ihriský.

The south-eastern part of Hviezdoslavovo námestie square widens into a small squarish area with a park. This was the plot originally reserved for the **church of the St. Augustín of Notre Dame female order** ⓭. Only the chancel with a little porch added in the 19th century was built. In the interior of the **presbytery** a ceiling **fresco** by the Baroque painter P. Troger survived. In front of the unfinished building stands a little wooden tower. The former **monastery** of the Notre Dame order built in 1754 as the front wing of the building is now the **Church school of Mother Alexia**. Its entrance is from **Palackého ulica street**. The name of this street derives from the one of the Czech historian and politician **František Palacký** (1798-1876) who taught at the Evangelical lyceé of Pressburg. North of the former monastery is **Jesenského ulica street**. It bears the name of **Janko Jesenský** (1874-1845), the Slovak writer, poet, and politician. On the corner of Jesenského street and Hviezdoslavovo námestie square stands a **building** (No. 2)

with wonderful Art Noveau facade ornamentation. It is a copy of the original building known to the Bratislava public as **Mindszenty's photo-study**. The building from the latter half of the 19th century was rented and rebuilt by Béla Mindszenty. The sculptor A. Messner placed an Art Noveau **relief of an Allegory of the Photographic Art** on its western side. The relief was the symbol of the oldest photo-study of Bratislava, which disappeared by the end of the Second World War. In the little park in front of the unfinished church of the Notre Dame order is the **Victory Monument** by J. Kostka to commemorating the victory over Nazism. The park with the adjacent area of Hviezdoslavovo námestie square was the place where the "**candle demonstration**" took place on March 25th 1988. The security units using water cannons cruelly attacked the calmly protesting and praying believers with lit candles.

Left: The Slovak National Gallery
Right: Bratislava's embankment

The dominant building of the southern row of the Hviezdoslavovo námestie square is the **Carlton Hotel** ⓮. There were some inns on the site of the hotel as early as late 18th century. They later became hotels. The best known one of them was *The Green Tree*. The family of Palugyay rented the hotel in 1848 and had it rebuilt by I. Feigler junior. Feigler built another hotel *Savoy* (also referred to as hotel *National*) in 1860. In the years 1908-1912 H. Prüger bought both hotels and connected them with the house standing in between. The *Green Tree Hotel* is also linked to the history of Bratislava cinematography as in one of its halls on December 15th 1896 the first movie show ever was held. K. Palugyay converted the hotel hall to the **first cinema in the city** called *Elektrobioskop* in 1905 Its capacity was 200 seats. The great pioneer in the field of cinematography, T. A. Edison, visited one of the movie shows here while he stayed in Palugyay's hotel. The Prüger's heirs radically reconstructed the hotel complex according to design of the archi-

tect M. M. Harminc in 1925. The common facade united three houses into one and another three floors were added. This was how the biggest Bratislava hotel now called the Carlton with a capacity of 400 beds originated. The hotel needs general repair again and it was a long time before someone decided to take on this gigantic task. Nevertheless, it seems that the Carlton Hotel will be again the pride of the city as the reconstruction works have already started.

The corner of Hviezdoslavovo námestie square and Pauliniho ulica street is occupied by an elegant building known as **Kozics's house** (No. 3). It was built in the latter half of the 19th century. There used to be the photo-study in the house, which belonged to the first professional photographer **Edward Kozics** (1829-1874), a remarkable figure for his experiments with the transfer of photographs onto other materials than paper. He took photographs of many sights of old Pressburg providing us with valuable documentation. Kozics' s house is now the **US Embassy**. The United States has owned the building since 1948 and it has always been American property after the Embassy was closed in 1950. **Csom's house** (No. 6) is one of the oldest on the square. It was built in 1778 following a design by J. Zillacko. The style of this building is a mixture of Baroque and Classicism. **Albert Einstein** visited this house in 1923, when he was trying to find there the writings of the passed on Pressburg native František Zach (1764-1832), an astronomer and physicist. The southern row of houses includes the Neo Classical **Nestor Palace** (No. 10). I. Feigler junior built it in 1856 for the Hungarian Governor Josef Nestor. A. Brandl's **reliefs** under the windows are allegories of the twelve months of the year. It now houses the **German Embassy**.

The almost uninterrupted row of houses framing the square in the north stands on the former southern town walls and the filled moat. Only Strakova ulica street interrupts it. On the western corner stands Neo Classical **house No. 22**. It was

built around 1800. Today it is the oldest cinema of the city. In the middle part of the northern row is **Pálffy Palace** ⓯ (No. 18) built in the years 1884-1885 in the Neo Baroque taste. The palace was owned by one of the wealthiest people of Hungary, Count Ján Pálffy (1829-1908). He had his luxurious residence built in the back part of the palace of his ancestors facing Panská ulica street. Its architect V. Rumpelmayer was a great admirer of the French and Viennese Baroque. On the attic are six stone statues representing Classic deities. Count Pálffy was a passionate collector of artistic works and objects. Today the building shelters the School of Fine Arts. Sightseeing of the square ends next to Rybárska brána gate, or better said, the spot where it used to stand, the **Kern's house** ⓰ (No. 26). This elegant Neo Classical building from 1845 was the place of memorable meeting of the Slovak leftist politician Vladimír Clementis with the future Prime Ministers of India Nehrú and his daughter Indira Ghándhí in the local café in Summer 1938.

Rázusovo nábrežie embankment running from Námestie Ľudovíta Štúra to the New Bridge was created in the 18th century in the place where there was a fishermen's village before. Building in this space started in the mid-19th century and the embankment was called Dunajské. Now it bears the mane of the Slovak poet, writer and politician **Martin Rázus** (1888-1937).

The oldest building on Rázusovo embankment is the compound of former barracks called **Vodné kasárne**. They were built in the years 1759-1763 as ordered by the municipal council to relieve the citizens of the nuisance of having to billet soldiers in their houses. It was originally a four-wing building with a large arcaded yard. In 1939 the time arrived to pull the barracks down. But two years later only the southern wing was demolished and the yard was opened to Rázusovo nábrežie embankment. The building was adapted

Left: Shuttle bridge in the 18th century
Right: The New Bridge

in the years 1949-1951 for the **Slovak National Gallery** (SNG) ⓱. As it became gradually too small, a new administrative building was added to the north-eastern corner and the front wing facing the embankment were constructed. The steel construction and metallic mantle used for the new buildings are often criticized, as the result does not fit the architecture of the older 18th century buildings. The collections of the SNG include the most important works of the Slovak fine arts since the 13th century until the present time and examples of European arts from the 15th to 18th centuries. Beside the permanent collections, interesting temporary exhibitions are sometimes held. West of the SNG complex is the **Devin Hotel** ⓲ (entrance is from Riečna ulica street). It originated in 1954 according to the plans of an outstanding Slovak architect E. Belluš.

The western part of the Rázusovo embankment has undergone dramatic changes since the end of the 1960's. In 1973 the second bridge over the Danube was built in this place. A great part of old Bratislava was pulled down. The bridge's original name *Most SNP* (The Bridge of the Slovak National Uprising) was recently changed to **Nový most** ⓳ or The New Bridge. The bridge is 432 metres long and its steel constructions weighs 7,537 metric tons. The structure of the bridge is hung on two massive pylons by thick steel cables. Inside the pylon on the left hand side is the lift to sightseeing **café Bystrica** and in the right one is the emergency stairway consisting of 430 stairs. The café offers a wonderful view of Bratislava from its height of 80 metres.

Close to the New Bridge is the area of the historic settlement below the castle or **Podhradie**, which existed for several centuries as an independent settlement. As a matter of fact, there were two of them on what is now the embankment: Vydrica and Zuckermandel. The people living by the river drew closer to the city in the 13th century when the Tartars destroyed their village. The inhabitants of **Vydrica** sustained themselves with fishing, shipping

and transit over the ford. There were also famous mills in Vydrica. Vydrica and Podhradie were added to Pressburg in the mid-19th century as the *Theresian quarter*. It was always the poorest city quarter and later also full of brothels. By the end of the 1960's Vydrica was completely demolished. When everything was pulled down, the remains of **Vodná Veža** ⓴ or the Water Tower were found. Historians expected it because it appeared on numerous historic pictures of the town and it was also frequently referred to in historic documents. The Water Tower was strategically very important. It protected the ford, controlled the access to the town from the west and it was a toll point as well. The tower was mentioned for the first time in the document of Belo IV from 1254. The tower was gradually rebuilt as a strategically important fort, which disappeared in 1620 when soldiers of the Imperial general H. D. Dampier destroyed it. The remains of it got lost under the houses of Vydrica for a long time before it was discovered after the demolition of the

quarter. Archaeological research around this **oldest building in the city** identified settlement in the area of the tower from as early time as the Celtic era. Remains of Celtic building (probably a hut), a fire place, La Téne pottery, amber and a glass ring from about the 1st century BC were discovered there. A short metal dagger was also a unique find. Also a regular stone pavement and fragments of walls from the Roman period were disclosed and finds from the Great Moravian period were not missing either. The ruins standing there here are from the 11th and 12th centuries. Pillars carrying a stone vault of an Early Medieval fort with the remains of four meter thick walls were preserved. In the south-western part of the fort remnants of two towers dated to the early 13th century were found.

Vydrica was separated from medieval Pressburg by **Rybné námestie square**. It originated in the second half of the 18th century on the vacant space in front of Vydrická brána gate. The dominant feature of today's Rybné námestie square is **trojičný stĺp** ㉑ (the Holy Trinity pillar) erected in 1713 immediately after the plague swept the town. Three statues of the traditional patron saints protecting people from the plague adorn the pillar: St. Roc, St. Andrew, and St. Charles Bartholomew. The pillar was adapted in the Baroque taste and reliefs by the Pressburg sculptor J. Sartory were added to in 1780.They depict the events of the plague: St. Rosalia, the Extreme Unction, and Carrying of the Dead. Also a group of statues of St. Stephen the King donating the Hungarian crown to the Immaculate Conception of the Virgin Mary, the patron saint of Hungary, was added to it.

Plague in Pressburg

Celebration of King Charles VI's coronation and simultaneously the Parliament session were the notable events that took place in Pressburg in April 1712. Some servants accompanying the participants of the Parliamentary session fell sick and showed the symptoms of the plague, known to everybody as the black death. The session was immediately closed and quarantine was imposed. Nevertheless, infection was spreading with the most dramatic deterioration of situation coming in Autumn of the same year. The number of houses of the affected marked by the white cross was increasing. The epidemic struck 680 houses sparing only 218. The plague was gaining monstrous dimensions. The carriers of the dead called trógeri *were*

Left: The Water Tower
The Trinity Pillar
Right: The Most Holy Trinity church

busy. They drove the dead out of the city on open carts and when the town became short of space they buried them in collective graves. Panic burst out, and culminated in a revolt on 30th April of 1713. The mob consisting mostly of women gathered at Laurinská brána gate and came close to the sanitary line, which was the limit nobody was supposed to trespass. The people robbed, sacked, attacked the sanitarians and threatened the plague physician. Only the mayor's promises calmed them down. The retreat of the epidemic came only a year later in October 1713. Its end was declared in January 1714. The report prepared by the principal Viennese physician Ján Jakub Zebriak says that the black death killed 358 persons in the Old Town and there were 2,535 victims in the suburbs. The sad balance was even higher when 529 dead from the Castle and Podhradie were included.

The busy traffic in the western part of Bratislava embankment can be avoided in two ways. The first option is to walk on the pathway leading along the left bank of the Danube. In the narrow strip of the park greenery are the **monuments** dedicated to three important figures, natives of Bratislava: inventor and physicist **Johann Andreas Segner** ㉒, the cartographer **Samuel Mikovíni** ㉓, and architect **Dušan Jurkovič** ㉔. The path continues to the **Park kultúry a oddychu** ㉕ (The Park of Culture and Rest) or PKO. This polyfunctional complex of buildings was built in 1940's for the **Danube Fair**. International Fair of Chemistry **Incheba** was held here repeatedly for many years and the **international fairs of flowers** held alternatively in Bratislava and in Olomouc were also very popular. The fairs and exhibitions have moved now to the new centre built on the right bank of the Danube.

The second route avoiding busy embankment communications leads from Vodná veža on **Žižkova ulica street**. In contrast to Vydrica several most valuable cultural and historical monuments of the former settlement **Zuckermandel** have

survived here. The name of this settlement, which was subject to the castle, appeared for the first time in 1565. There used to be a quarry beyond the village. The village had an unusually high number of inns in the 18th century and in the 19th century there were several factories as well. In 1803 a factory producing muslin and in 1841 one making hats were working here. The group of the surviving buildings includes only the church, two Renaissance curias and one Rococo house. The Baroque Roman-Catholic **church of the Most Holy Trinity** ㉖ was built and consecrated in 1783 on the site of an older wooden chapel. On the pillars of the gate stand stone sculptures of St. John and St. Florian from the 19th century. Archaeologists found remains of a Romanesque rotund from the 11th century next to the church. In the neighbourhood is the Rococo **Dom cechu rybárov a lodníkov** ㉗ (house of fishermen's and boatsmen's guild) with a stylish restaurant called Rybársky cech. It was built in 1759-1760 after N. Danko's design.

The two preserved curias on Žižkova ulica street are examples of the Renaissance style in Podhradie or the settlement below the castle. Nearer to the centre is **Kamper's curia** ㉘ (house No. 12). It was built in the second half of the 16th century for the castle official F. Kamper. It stood outside the town fortifications and that is why it is a small fort. Apart from thick walls it was also protected by a moat and drawbridge. The Evangelicals or Lutherans of Pressburg allegedly used to have their services celebrated by the priest Andreas Reus in this house at the beginning of the 17th century. At present the house serves as the **Museum of Archaeology** of the Slovak National Museum. **Brämmer's curia** ㉙ (house No. 18) is remarkable for two bulky cylindrical risalites on its corners. The official of castle garrison F. Brämmer had the house built in the early 17th century.

Left: The Lafranconi Bridge

The **Old Jewish Cemetery** of the rather numerous Jewish community which used to live in Podhradie was founded by the end of the 17th century on Pálffy's lands lying on the southern slopes of the castle hill. It became full after a hundred-year use. As the Jewish religion does not permit moving the dead, the old graves were covered by a thick layer of earth and the cemetery could be used again. Also the body of the famous Pressburg rabbi **Chatam Sofer** ㉚ (1762-1839) was deposited here in 1839. The Orthodox rabbi whose real name was Moshe Schreiber came to Pressburg in 1806 at the invitation of the local Jewish community. He was chosen as a recognized expert on the Talmud and it was hoped that he would prevent propagation of the ideas reforming the Jewish religion. Chatam Sofer raised hundreds of rabbis who spread his learning all over Europe. He was a highly respected authority. He wrote and published books including a collection of religion songs. The Jewish cemetery on the Danube embankment was used until

1846. Then again it was covered by earth and the stones excavated from the tunnel, which was under construction then.

The burial place of famous Chatam Sofer still exists in front of the tunnel on the Danube embankment. The entrance to the tomb is right beside the tram stop. Hundreds of people from all over the world visit it. Jewish people do not bring flowers to the graves of their dead; instead they bring a stone and a little folded paper with a supplication written on it.

The Western Suburbs

Six urban districts are situated west of the Bratislava centre: Karlova Ves, Lamač, Dúbravka, Záhorská Bystrica, Devínska Nová Ves, and Devín. The last five of them are also denoted by a collective name Záhorská Bratislava (trans-mountain Bratislava), because viewed from the centre of the city these urban districts lie beyond the mountains, on the other side of the Little Carpathians. They are set in a pleasant environment of mountain meadows, alluvial forests; there are two wonderful great rivers, vineyards, gardens and conserved rural settlements with surviving folklore. The western suburbs together create the district of Bratislava IV, which is the largest of the five Bratislava districts.

Karlova Ves

Altitude:	140 m
Area:	10.9 km^2
Population:	32,950

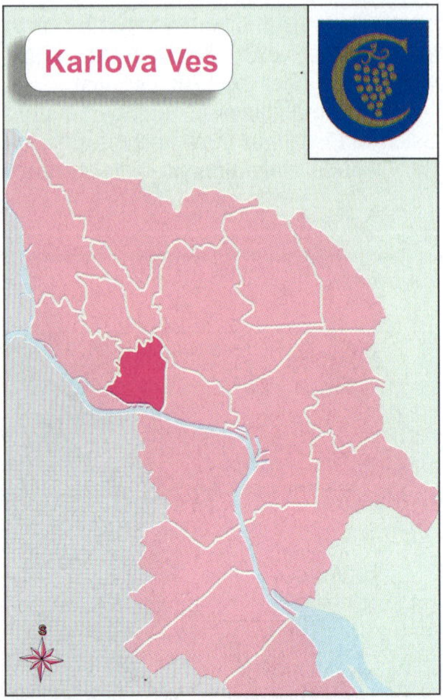

Closest to the centre is the urban district **Karlova Ves**. It is the only western suburb not included in Záhorská Bratislava. Its core is situated in a small valley ending next to the lower part of the Danube gorge. The valley was called Suchá Vydrica in the past, its present name is Líščie údolie. The north-western limit of Karlova Ves is Devínska Kobyla Mountain and its southern limit is the Danube. In the eastern part of its administrative territory is the slightly elevated locality of Staré grunty ending in the east in the Dolná Mlynská dolina valley. In the north borders Karlova Ves on its quarters Krčace, Sitina, the Zoo and Patrónka on Lamačská brána.

The territory of Karlova Ves was already settled in the Younger Stone Age. It is documented by the finds from the Mlynská dolina valley. The oldest medieval community in Karlova Ves was Vydrica. Historians denoted it Devínska Vydrica to distinguish it from the village, which existed below Bratislava Castle. This original settlement probably disappeared at the time of the Tartar invasion. Its inhabitants moved next to castle and founded a new Vydrica. The departure of people from the territory of the original Vydrica did not mean its complete depopulation in the second half of the 13th century, because the donation act of King Ladislav IV to the Pressburg mayor Jakub I from 1388 mentions the settlement *Widriche*. Jakub developed the donated land founding settlements, mills, and vineyards. In 1360 King Louis I the Great of Hungary granted Vydrica the same privileges and freedoms as Pressburg. Vydrica became part of the Devín estate in the 15th century. Its population worked in vineyards and cleared the woods owned by the Devín landlord. In 1635 the Pálffy family became the owners of the Devín estate and retained it until 1932. Karlova Ves is referred to as independent village in close vicinity to Bratislava in the second half of the 19th century. It

Right: Karlova Ves
Mlynská dolina valley

became part of the city in 1944. Its old core was progressively pulled down and new housing estates built: Kútiky (1967-1975) and Dlhé diely (after 1984).

The Roman-Catholic church of **St. Michael Archangel** in Karlova Ves was built in the 1940's. It incorporates an originally Baroque chapel from the last third of the 18th century. It is a single-nave building with its front wall decorated by the **ceramic relief of St. Michael Archangel** by I. Bizmayer. The adjacent cemetery with a small **chapel** was founded in Karlova Ves in the 1920's.

The most visited places of Karlova Ves are the Botanical garden and the Zoo. The **Botanical garden** on Botanická ulica street is owned and administered by the Faculty of Nature History of Comenius University. It lies close to the Danube, west from the Lafranconi bridge. It was founded in the years 1942-1943 on an area 50.7 hectares. Its core was the part of the now disappeared Lanfranconi villa, the rest of the area was used as agricultural land at the beginning of its existence. The idea to found a Botanical garden came from the scientists of the Botanical Institute of Comenius University and the garden became the research ground immediately after the war. When the green house was constructed the garden acquired many tropical plant species. The pride of the green house is a little lake with precious water plants and numerous collections of cactuses. Today there are about 5,000 foreign plant species including 650 wood species. The botanical garden is interesting in every season, but it is most beautiful in the spring when the flowers are in full bloom.

In Mlynská dolina valley in the neighbourhood of the Slovak Television is the **Zoo** of Bratislava. It was opened to the public in 1960. Its original area was 9 hectares. Later it was enlarged to the present 90 hectares and contains more than 200 animal species. The area of the **Slovak Television** is 1.9 hectares and its dominant 107.5 metres tall building was the tallest building in Bratislava, even in Slovakia until recently. The adjacent valley, which is erroneously referred to as **Slávičie údolie valley** contains a **cemetery** with the same name. Many public figures and famous personalities of the Slovak cultural and social spheres are buried in Slávičie údolie. There is also the grave of the leading personality of recent Slovak history **Alexander Dubček** (1921-1992). Student buildings surround the cemetery with **student dormitories** built in the years 1970-1998 to the northwest. In the south are the buildings of the Faculty of Nature History, Faculty of Mathematics and Physics and the Faculty of Management of **Comenius University**, and Electromechanical Faculty of the **Slovak**

Technical University. The fertile vineyards in Staré grunty changed into the largest student campus in Slovakia.

In the south-west of the territory of Karlova Ves is the **island of Sihoť** covered by thick woods. It is one of the biggest river islands on the Slovak section of the Danube. It used to belong to the Devín estate and the landlords used it as a hunting ground. In the second half of the 19th century *Käsmacherinsel*, the original name of Sihoť, became an interesting area for hydrologists. The first experimental well was dug out here in 1882 and it was decided that the island would be the drinking water resource for the city of Bratislava. The first litres of a top quality drinking water from the municipal water plant in Sihoť flowed to the city in February 1886. Today there are 46 wells 9-15 metres deep in the island of Sihoť.

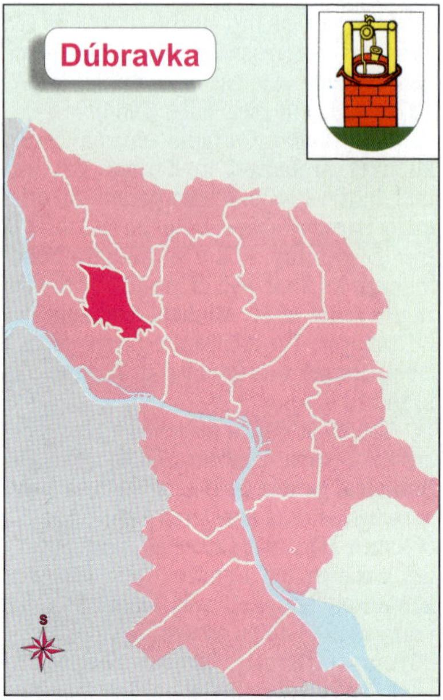

Dúbravka

Altitude:	265 m
Area:	8.6 km^2
Population:	38,400

North of Karlova Ves is the village of **Dúbravka**. Its western part enters into the area of the Devínska Kobyla massif. The old part of the village lies on the eastern foot of the Dúbravská Hlavica hill (360 m a.s.l.) and the new housing estate was built on the plateau of the edge of Lamačská brána.

Historic sources refer to it as *Hidegkút*, in German *Kaltenbrunn*, later *Dubrawka*. The opinion on the origin of the village differs. Acts from the years 1288, 1439 and 1447 exist but the most reliable one is the document from 1574. It mentions Dúbravka as the village inhabited by Croatian colonists. They came from Lamač, their original settlement as they often moved further to the surrounding estates, those of Devín, Svätý Jur, and Pajštún and even to the Austrian boundary villages such as Marchegg and Markthof. After 1574 the people of Dúbravka were mentioned in the acts of the Devín estate, which owned the village. The village grew bigger after arrival of immigrants from Hungary occupied by the Turks in the 17th century. The population lived on wine growing. They sold some wine in the village and hauled the surplus production to Pressburg or the Austrian markets. The 19th century was not favourable for Dúbravka. First the Napoleonic troops on their way to Vienna burnt Dúbravka down. Plague burst out in 1831 and again in 1866 after the Austrian and Prussian soldiers sacked it. Moreover, a great part of the village was burnt down again at the same time. Dúbravka as a small agricultural village was joined to Bratislava after the Second World War. After 1970 a big housing estate and modern communications were built in its territory, which changed its rural character.

The Baroque Roman Catholic **Church of St. Cosma and Damian** built in 1723 on the foundations of an older building is Dúbravka's most important cultural and

Right: Church of St. Cosma and Damian
Villa rustica

historic monument. The Late Baroque altar of this church is from the last third of the 18th century. The lateral altar of the Virgin Mary made in the work shop of G. R. Donner was moved to its original place, the summer Archbishop's Palace, now the Office of the Government of the SR. The Early Renaissance **chapel** from the late 16th century in the local cemetery was built on the Gothic foundations. The last of the sacred buildings of Dúbravka is the Baroque **chapel** near the parish office from the latter half of the 18th century.

The glass factory **Slovenské závody technického skla** has stood in the northwest of Dúbravka since the 1960's. Behind the factory and in the middle of a field are the foundations of a **Roman building** of the *villa rustica* type. It was the historian Oskar Čepan who predicted the possible existence of Roman structure on the territory of Dúbravka after he found remains of old pottery and fragments of Roman bricks in a ploughed field. The invited archaeologists eventually found it in 1982. According to a silver coin of Emperor Alexander Severius found here, the structure was dated to the 3rd century. The villa rustica of Dúbravka was a well equipped farming and craft homestead building with living and servicing rooms, a bath and maybe a sanctuary. The dimensions of the known ground plan are 11.20x13.20 m. Outside the basic, almost square ground plan were four apsides. It is supposed that it was not inhabited by a Roman, but rather by some German noble influenced by Roman culture. Maybe he was a pensioned soldier of Quadian origin. The homestead was situated between the Roman camps in Devín and in Stupava. Not far from this structure

and in the middle of the gardens remains of an Early Slavic settlement from the 6th century were found. The settlement originated at the beginning of the settling of this territory by the Old Slavs.

Villa rustica and bath

A classical Roman bath consisted of three parts. The first was a small room heated by hot air and a hot water basin. This first room communicated with a room with a lukewarm water basin and lower temperature of air and in the last room was a cold water basin. Archaeologists found only the remains of the system of water supply and the sewage. No traces of the heating system were found. It is presumed that the building had only a cold water bath or the bath remained unfinished.

Lamač

Altitude:	140 m
Area:	6.5 km^2
Population:	7,050

In the east Dúbravka borders on the urban district **Lamač**. In the east it reaches the plateaux of the Little Carpathians, where it borders on the urban districts lying on the other side of the mountains. In the north it borders on urban district Záhorská Bystrica.

Historic documents refer to four villages in this territory. The first of them of unknown name disappeared during the Tartar invasion. The royal donation documents from the years 1279 and 1288 reveal that this territory belonged to Jakub I, the mayor of the settlement below Pressburg, who founded here two villages: *Blumenau* and *Sellendorf*. Sellendorf disappeared in the 15th century while Blumenau existed until the 19th century. The fourth village of *Krabatendorf* was a serf village of Pressburg. It originated in the 16th and 17th century, when Croatians moved to this area. The disappeared *Sellendorf* became the subject of one old legend.

Sellendorf

Sellendorf existed in the Mlynská dolina valley in the Middle Ages. Its inhabitants were well-off thanks to fertile vineyards, inns and mills. They were rich, but also proud, cruel and thrifty. One old man experienced their vicious characters when he went to one of the Sellendorf mills to have a bag of wheat ground. As he walked through the village framed by smart stone houses the rich villagers mocked and insulted him and eventually they stole his money purse. The old man complained to the mayor. But the mayor too defied and ridiculed him. The old man cursed the village. He wished that the village would disappear to the dark entrails of the earth and his curse worked immediately. Sellendorf disappeared from the surface at once.

The oldest preserved documents on the village *Lamocz* or *Lamas* are from the years 1540 to 1549. Its founder was probably the

Right: St. Rosalia church
The monument at Kamzík mountain
Lamač

Croatian stone-breaker Ján Skerlič, who worked in a quarry near the place and built the first houses on the site of today's Lamač in 1506. More Croatians fleeing from the Turks came after the battle at Mohács in 1526 and built their houses here. The fire of 1561 destroyed the chapel of St. Margaret and a great part of the village. Sustenance of the anti-Turkish troops represented a great burden for Lamač. Moreover, the soldiers eventually sacked the village in 1624. The ordeal was repeated when the Imperial troops sacked it again in the years 1703 and 1711. This sequence of blows was topped by the progress of the French troops and several epidemics. Lamač entered history in July 1866 with the last battle of the **Prussian-Austrian war**. Immediately after the war finished an epidemic broke out causing death of 77 people. Lamač developed into a rural agricultural village, with its people working in the factories of Bratislava and in the local quarry. It was annexed to Bratislava in 1946 and acquired its present urban character when the housing estates were built.

The sacred buildings of Lamač are its main historic monuments. The Roman Catholic **St. Rosalia Church** is the oldest of them. It was built in the years 1568-1569 outside the village and on a hill presumably on the foundations of an older church. Great part of it fell down and the building had to be reconstructed. It was accomplished in the years 1667-1673 when the new tower was built and the church got a Baroque vault. The much younger Roman Catholic **Church of St. Margaret** was built in the years 1947-1949 following the design of M. M. Harminc.

Záhorská Bystrica

Altitude:	175 m
Area:	32.3 km^2
Population:	1,999

Záhorská Bystrica is the northernmost urban district of Bratislava. It spreads on a comparatively large area, a great part of which lies in the Little Carpathian woods. The village spreads on the western foothills of the mountains, only two kilometres from the famous pilgrim locality of Marianka. The western part of the administrative territory of Záhorská Bystrica consists mostly of fields on the plains of the Záhorská nížina lowland.

The village was mentioned for the first time in 1314 in a donation charter of King Charles I Robert of Hungary. Its names in the past were *Pistrich, Byzthrycza*, in Hungrian *Besztercze*, in German *Bissternitz* or *Wisternitz*. The village belonged to the Stupava estate. King Louis I the Great of Hungary donated the settlement to the Pauline order of Marianka in 1377. By the beginning of the 16th century part of the village was owned by the Stupava estate and part by the Paulines of Marianka. When Gašpar Serédy acquired the Stupava estate from King Ferdinand I of Hungary, Záhorská Bystrica definitely became part of the Stupava estate. It was among the first villages settled by the Croatians and peasants from Moravia, Austria and the neighbouring estates. The tax list from the 16th century refers to Záhorská Bystrica as *Bystricz*, a village of Slovaks and Croatians. The parish of Záhorská Bystrica also included the people from Lamač in the years 1624-1752 although the two villages had different landlords. Záhorská Bystrica had the reputation of the wealthiest village in the area in the 18th century. It was not only big (population 1,503) but it also produced most of all. The soil in its territory was very fertile and suitable for horticulture, namely growing of cabbage. People of Záhorská Bystrica traded their cabbage in Pressburg and Vienna. The last battle of the Prussian-Austrian war partially also took place in the territory of Záhorská Bystrica. The village kept its rural character after it was annexed to Bratislava in 1972.

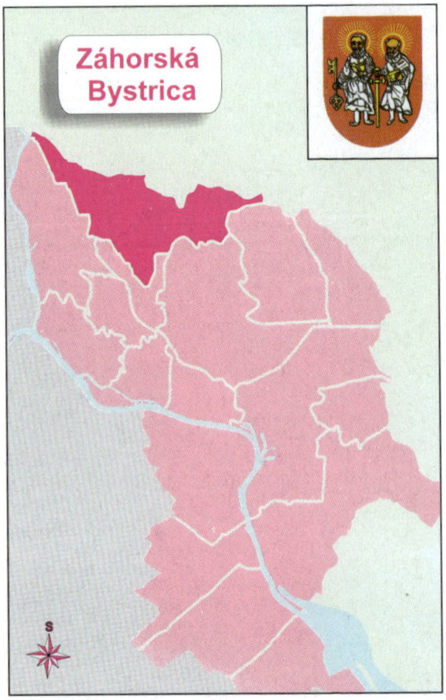

Left: Rustical house in Záhorská Bystrica
Right: Záhorská Bystrica
The Karpatia club

The Baroque-Neo Classical Roman Catholic **church of Sts. Peter and Paul the Apostles** is the historic monument, which survived in Záhorská Bystrica. It was built in the years 1830-1834 on older foundations. The Baroque **chapel** next to the road leading to the villages is from the late 18th century. Its facade was changed in the 20th century. The Roman Catholic **parsonage**, a one-storeyed Baroque building from 1737 is another sacred monument. The **Carpatia** co-operative founded in Záhorská Bystrica in 1967 deals with the breeding and training of horses and in the south-western end of the village is the modern complex of buildings of the private **TV station Markíza**.

Devínska Nová Ves

Altitude:	140 m
Area:	6.5 km^2
Population:	7,050

The urban district **Devínska Nová Ves** lies on the north-western edge of Bratislava. Its western border coincides with the state frontier with Austria that in fact is in the middle of the river Morava. In the south the territory of this urban district enters the area of Devínska Kobyla.

The settlement of Devínska Nová Ves is very old and dates back to the Neolithic. Objects from the Iron and Bronze Ages are not missing either. Unique finds docu-

menting the Slav and Avar settlements are especially precious. One of the oldest and most important **burial places** was found precisely in the territory of Devínska Nová Ves. Some historians associate it with **Samo's Empire**, which was the first union of Slav tribes in the territory of modern Slovakia, founded by the Frankish merchant Samo in 623. 856 skeleton and 27 cremation graves were found in the burial place used in the 7th to 9th century. The archaeologists discovered equestrian graves (warriors buried with their horses). Varied finds in single graves offer an idea of the life of contemporary people and extremely interesting study material for historians.

The first reference to Devínska Nová Ves is from 1435. A document of the Pressburg chapter mentions Ján of Nová Ves. The village was called *Wyfalw, Wyfakllu*, in Hungarian *Dévényújfalu* and in German *Theben Neudorf*. It was one of the serf villages of the Devín estate. Further written references to the village appeared in relation to the Turkish threat in the mid-16th century. Spanish soldiers also passed through and sacked several villages including Devínska Nová Ves. Then the Croatian colonists came. In the 16th century the village was called Chorvátska Nová Ves. The village belonged to the Counts of Sv. Jur and Pezinok and also the Pressburg orders such as the Jesuits, Ursulines and Paulines of Marianka owned some property there. There was a customs point in the village in the 16th century, which controlled the export of timber and cattle to Austria. The first industrial firms were founded in the village in the 19th century. These were a lime works, a brickyard and a distillery. But the village was stricken by several disasters. Napoleonic troops crossed the river Morava after they occupied Austria and devastated Devínska Nová Ves while progressing to Pressburg at the beginning of the 19th century. The plague epidemic of 1831 killed 107 people, and also the fires of 1849, 1866, and 1880 partially destroyed the village. Construction of a horse railway was a great event. The railway led from Pressburg over the bridge in Devínska Nová Ves to Schlosshof and Vienna. The regular connection existed since 1838. Ten years later the Pressburg-Devínska Nová Ves-Marchegg-Vienna line was opened. The beginnings of workers' movement, not only in Slovakia but also in the whole Austro-Hungarian monarchy, are connected with Devínska Nová Ves. For instance, when the **congress of the Austrian social democratic party** (1875) in Marchegg was broken up, its delegates met in Devínska Nová Ves. The village progressively developed into a small town, which was annexed to Bratislava in 1972.

The originally Renaissance Roman Catholic **Church of the Holy Spirit** built in the early 16th century and later adapted, is the cultural monument, which deserves attention. The Neo Classical structure of the **customs station** from the 18th century was recently adapted to the town hall. The building of the **steam engine-operated brickyard** founded in 1891 is historically

Right: Sandberg
Devínska Nová Ves

interesting. It produced shingles, ornamental bricks and tiles. It employed 200 workers and its equipment was fairly modern for that time. A clay pit and several big quarries belonged to the brickyard. On the river terraces formed by the rivers Danube and Morava a big car factory called Bratislavské automobilové závody was built in the years 1971-1974. Now it belongs to the **Volkswagen** company. Two new housing estates **Kostolné** and **Podhorské** with flats for eleven thousand inhabitants were built in the 1980's. Devínska Nová Ves is a community, which conserved its **Croatian ethnicity**, and the Croatian language is still spoken. In August 1989 the first **Festival of the Croatian Songs and Dances** was organized there and since then Croatians from Slovakia, Austria, Hungary and their homeland Croatia meet every year in Devínska Nová Ves. The village has got two **folk ensembles** of its own - *Rosica* and *Grbačieta.*

The **National Nature Reserve of Devíska Kobyla** is a unique locality of special fauna and flora is. It lies in part of the Devínske Karpaty Mountains on an area 101 hectares between Devínska Nová Ves, Dúbravka and Devín; 234 species of mushrooms, 110 species of lichens, 100 species of mosses, and 1,100 plant species confirm the originality of this place. Xerophytes and thermophiles with precious and protected plant species and animals live on the southern and south-western slopes of Devínska Kobyla. The forests on the south-western slopes are the remains of the original thermopile oak growths. An **instructive path** leading through the reserve provides visitors with information about the occurrence of special vegetation and wild life. It has got seven stops with information panels. The most interesting locality of the National Nature Reserve Devínska Kobyla is the sand profile on the **Sandberg** mountain. There are rock remains of the Tertiary sea with horizontal layers, the age of which is estimated at 14 to 16 million years (→ 7). Another **instructive route** was prepared in 1996 over the flood plain of the Morava which runs along the river Morava from Devín to Devínska Nová Ves and ends in Vysoká pri Morave (outside Bratislava). The 23 km long route has 16 information boards.

Devín

Altitude:	140 m
Area:	6.5 km^2
Population:	7,050

The urban district **Devín** lies below the Devín Castle at the confluence of the Danube and Morava. Devín is ten kilometres away from Bratislava. The village with castle lies on the spot where the Danube enters the Devínska brána (Devín Gate). On the opposite bank of the Danube is the Austrian historic town of Hainburg.

In the territory of the urban district Devín, Aenolithic settlement of people of the furrowed pottery, settlement of Unětice and Magyar cultures from the Bronze Age, a Hallstadt settlement, Celtic *oppidum* and the Roman military station were found. The soldiers of the XIVth Roman legion staying in Carnuntum built the station in the early 2nd century on the castle hill. The Romans built the foundations of another station and an earthen rampart in the fourth century during the reign of the Emperor Valentinian I.

A unique loaf of bread

In 1986 in the eastern part of Devín Castle a settlement structure dated by finds of pottery to the 5th century was discovered. It included a hole of a destroyed furnace full of carbonated grain. But the most precious find was the one of the carbonated loaf of bred. Its diameter is 23 cm and thickness 6.5 cm. Its original weight when fresh must have been around one kilogram. The surface of the bread is broken. It was made of wheat with an admixture of rye. Beside the bread and grain single pieces of bread and bread crust were also found. The bread was broken in pieces, as the Romans were accustomed to eat it. The find of the bread loaf in Slovakia is unique. It is precious evidence of an advanced food production technology from the migration period.

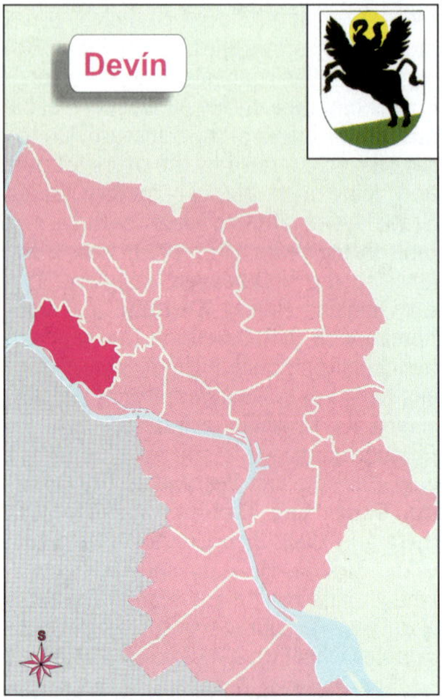

But Devín and above all Devín Castle played their most important roles several centuries later. In the time of the Great Moravian Empire the Castle was the most important fort of the Slavs in their fight against the expansive Frankish Empire. The castle is probably first mentioned under the name *Dowina* in the Fulda annals from 864. In other place "Rastislav's fort indescribable and among others unseen" protecting the Empire against the raids of the Bavarians is mentioned. So far it is not definitely clear whether both mentions refer to the same locality. Besides the castle height there is also the possibility that Rastislav's castle stood on the site of one of the two hill forts above today's Devínska Nová Ves. The fort on the Devín rock hill was an important fort of the Great Moravian defensive system. The Slav population lived in the castle even after the fall of Great Moravia. The cemetery, which was in use until the end of the 11th century, proves it. When after the fall of the Great Moravian Empire the frontier changed, Devín lost its strategic importance. It entered the history for the second time when the Hungarians and Austrians fought over the Devín Gate in the 13th century. A castle was built in the top of the rock between the 13th and 15th century. Its owners were changing and the fort was gradually expanded. The family of Garay owned the castle in the first half of the 15th century,

Right: Devín Castle seen from Sandberg
The Moravian gate of Devin Castle

then in 1460 the Counts of Sv. Jur and Pezinok took it over followed by the Báthorys in the years 1527-1605, and finally by the Pálffy's from 1605. The Castle became inhabitable in the 18th century and fell into decay, which was finished in 1809 when Napoleonic troops, blew it up. In the first half of the 19th century Devín Castle became the symbol of fight for freedom of the Slovaks. On Sunday April 24th 1836 Ľudovít Štúr in company of his fifteen disciples ascended to the Castle of Devín. This **memorable walk** of Štúr's group was the symbol of the past glory of the Great Moravian Empire, which they considered the most important period of the national history of the Slovaks.

Devín Castle standing on a massive rock hill above the confluence of the Danube and Morava is an unusually impressive landmark. Its ground plan is very irregular and adapted to the shape of the rock it stands on. On the western side a steep rock face overtowers the confluence of rivers and behind it is a lower hill with mildly inclined slopes. The whole castle area consisting of a foreground, lower, middle, and upper castle is enclosed by continuous walls with three gates. The northern side which was considerably more vulnerable than the southern one is protected by a long **northern rampart**. It was made already in the time of the Emperor Valentinian I in the 4th century. Timber palisades reinforced the fort in the 10th century and in the 15th century the rampart was opened to provide a shortcut between Devín Castle and the serf town through the northern **Devínska brána gate**. Today we enter the castle through the western **Moravian Gate**. The southern gate protected by a pair of semicircular bastions was built in the 15th century on an older Great Moravian rampart. Close behind the gate and on the right side of the path is a precious archaeological monument from the Roman period of Devín's history. The ground plan of the **remains of a bulky stone building** from the 4th century suggests a Classical tomb. Fragments of wall with preserved plasters up to 85 cm tall and the original floor were found there. Especially the **iron cross** is interesting. If it is the Christian symbol then it is the oldest sacred monument found in the territory of Slovakia. Left from the path and near the Moravská brána gate Old Slavic graves from the 10th and 11th centuries were found. The path divides into two on the ridge of the castle hill. The left branch leads to the place where stood a **Great Moravian church** in the 9th century. One can see its rectangular ground plan with an apsid and a small model on a plinth shows what the church might have looked like. The archaeologists also found **re-**

Left: The Virgin Tower
Right: The middle castle
The upper castle
The village Devín

mains of a hut from the period of migration of people under the north-western corner of the **church foundations**. South of this church another smaller sacred building from the 11th and 12th century and **cemetery** with graves from the 10th to 13th centuries were found. East of the Great Moravian church is the eastern **Pressburg gate** in the Renaissance style. The first branch of the path leads to the conserved ruins of the middle and upper part of the **medieval castle**, which was smaller than the Great Moravian fort. In the first half of the 15th century the Gothic **Garay palace** with two stories was built and the Renaissance palace and fortifications were added in the 16th century. Some vaulted spaces of this palace are today used for exhibitions. The origin of the 55 metres deep **castle well**, which is on the courtyard of the middle castle, is linked to the period when Garay was the owner of the castle. Archaeologists found **remains of Roman architecture** under debris near the well. The structure built of quarry stone had about 4 or 5 rooms. Near the well is also a terrace with view of the abandoned **amphitheatre**, the Danube and the mountain of Braunsberg in Austria. In the wonderful setting above the bicolour confluence of the Danube and Morava an elegant tower with battlements stands out. It is the **Virgin tower**.

A bridge over a moat and stairs lead to the top platform with remnants of a guard tower from the 13th century rebuilt in the 15th century with panoramic view of the surroundings.

The Virgin Tower Legend

The legend is about knight Nicholas: lord of Devín Castle who went to seek his bride as far as Carinthia, and it was the virgin Margaret of a rich Carinthian family he chose. The father of the girl refused Nicholas's offer, but the knight kidnapped Margaret. The virgin Margaret did not object because she liked the knight's courting and Castle of Devín too when she saw it. But before the wedding was prepared, Margaret's uncle, the Abbot of Isenburg visited Devín and took Margaret home with him back to Carinthia. Sir Nicholas pursued the uncle's trail and won his bride back after a short fight. Immediately after Nicholas returned to Devín the wedding was prepared and held. But the Abbot Rafael cheated the guards and assaulted the castle. The Carinthians outnumbered the warriors defending Devín Castle and compelled Nicholas to retreat to the slim tower above the confluence of the Danube and Morava, where he was killed. His young bride jumped into the Danube. The muddy water of the river buried the virgin Margaret on her wedding day and since then the tower standing on the rock has borne the name The Virgin Tower.

The community of **Devín** probably originated from a serf village under the castle. But maybe it is older than the castle itself. It was first mentioned in an document from 1254 in connection with the vineyards of the Pilis Abbey. It was referred to as *Villa Thebyn* in 1327. Out of several names the Slovak name Devín (in German *Theben*) eventually survived. The village was granted the privilege of market in the 15th century and developed into a small yeoman town. By the beginning of the 17th century Ján Keglevich acquired Devín and in 1616 he faced an armed conflict with his serfs. The rebellion of the Devín people against their landlord was the reaction to abolition of their privileges and hard serf duties The first fishermen's guild was founded here in the 17th century and it associated the fishermen of Devín and the surrounding villages. More guilds were founded in the 18th century for boatsmen, vintners, pottery-makers and tailors. At the beginning of the 19th century there was a tax station and a yarn producing factory in Devín. In the first half of the 20th century Devín was the favourite place for trippers above all for its famous red-current wine and fish. Part of the village was adjudicated to Austria in 1922. In the years 1938-1945 Devín belonged to the German Reich and in 1946 it was annexed to Bratislava, though it preserved its rural character until today.

The most valuable historic monument is the Roman Catholic **church of the Virgin Mary**. Originally it was built in the Gothic style in the first half of the 14th century. It was restored in the Baroque and Neo Classical taste in the years 1677-1772. There are **two manor houses** in Devín. The first in the Late Renaissance style was built in the first half of the 17th century and the second was built in the second half of the 17th century in the Early Baroque style.

The Northern Suburbs

The north-eastern part of Greater Bratislava consists of three urban districts, the outer edges of which reach as far as the forests of the Little Carpathians. Rača is in the north, Vajnory in the east and the suburb of Nové Mesto the closest to the city centre. The northern suburbs include plains and the slopes of the mountain range. Older rural settlements or their remains alternate here with residential quarters or industrial areas.

Nové Mesto

Altitude:	135 m
Area:	37.5 km^2
Population:	32,500

The urban district of **Nové Mesto** or the New Town links Rača and Vajnory with the city centre. It originated by building on agricultural land. It also encompasses extensive forested territory of the Little Carpathians including the Horná Mlynská dolina valley. A special part of this territory consists of the quarters of Kramáre and Koliba. The axis of the central part of Nové Mesto is the Račianska ulica street starting in the centre of Bratislava and running to the quarters of Rača in the north. Similar axis in the east is Vajnorská ulica street connecting the centre with Vajnory in the north-east. In the north of the area between these two key streets lies the industrial zone of Istrochem. The south-eastern limits of the urban district Nové Mesto are represented by Trnavská cesta road and Rožňavská ulica street separating it from the urban district Ružinov. In the south Nové Mesto borders on Staré Mesto or the Old Town.

No compact settlement existed in the territory of today's Nové Mesto. For centuries there were only isolated houses or

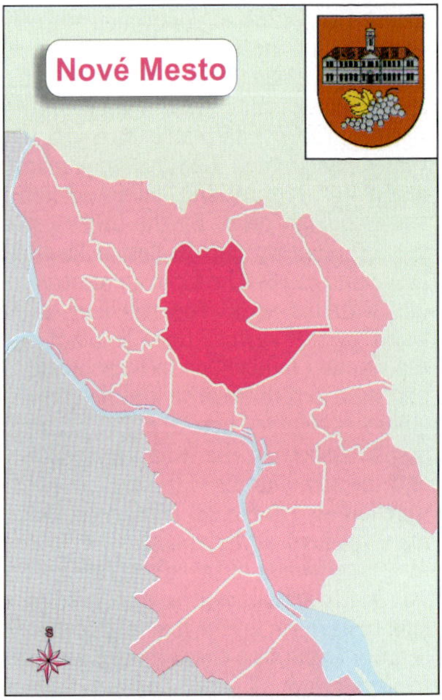

farms amidst meadows and fields. Two roads crossed the area. One of them, Račianska ran from Pressburg through Rača to Modra, and Vajnorská road connected Pressburg with Vajnory. On the edge of the Nové Mesto and along the now disappeared Mlynské rameno arm of the Danube there ran another road, Trnavská, heading to Trnava and Nitra. The brickyards in the open agricultural landscape and quarries on the edge of the Little Carpathians were sources of economic activity. The forests remained more or less intact and human activity concentrated on felling, hunting and collection of forest fruits. The Malá Mlynská dolina valley with water mills and a disappeared medieval settlement of Sellendorf was an exception.

Urbanization of today's Nové Mesto started on the site of two toll stations, where the mentioned medieval roads crossed the outer defensive ramparts of Pressburg. Two squares that originated around them still bear the word "mýto" (toll) in their names: Račianske mýto

Right: Trnavské Mýto square
The horse railway station

and Trnavské mýto. **Trnavské mýto** is today a busy crossroads of four Bratislava's principal streets. It developed around the toll station standing on the crossroads of Vajnorská and Trnavská. There was a cross and statue of St. John Nepomuk in 1783. In the first half of the 19th century the space around the toll station and the local inn changed into a cattle market. The importance of Trnavská toll station increased when a **horse railway station** on the track from Pressburg to Svätý Jur and Trnava was also built next to it in 1840. Fortunately, the railway station building, very modern for that time, escaped demolition in the 1980's. This building with a typical tower on the corner of Krížna and Legionárska streets is depicted on the coat of arms of the urban district of Nové Mesto. The **Stein Brewery** was built by the station in the year 1872-1873, and it still produces the favourite Stein beer. One can have a pint in the Pivovarská restaurant in front of the brewery. Trnavské mýto though, is better known among the citizens of Bratislava as the place, where the principal or central market place existed. When it was moved to another place, the people continued to use the name "the central market place" for the area. Today there is an **in-door market** in a modern building from 1983 although it stands on the opposite side of Trnavské mýto square. The site of the former market place is occupied by the likewise modern building of **Dom odborov Istropolis** or the trade union centre. It was built in stages in the years 1973-1981. Trade unions retained a part of this complex, but its main part was taken over by the city, which exploits it for cultural and social events. The theatre hall of **Istropolis** is one of the biggest in the city. **Dom techniky** or Technical House with another theatre hall (a permanent stage of **Radošinske Naive Theatre**) is also part of this complex with entrance its from Škultétyho street.

The wide meadows and fields with isolated farms between Vajnorská and Trnavská cesta roads were built up only recently, in the course of the 20th century. Only the name of one of those farms called Jurajov dvor survived. In the area of *Ziegelfeld*, the German for Brick Field in the neighbouring Pasienky were brickyards. However, Bratislava lost Petržalka during the Second World War and the city was deprived of almost all of its sport grounds and football stadiums. Consequently, in the years 1939-1940 new sport area in **Tehelné pole** and later also in **Pasienky** was started. The **swimming pool** called **Tehelné pole** on

ulica Odbojárov street was the first to be finished. But the **football stadium of ŠK Slovan Bratislava** is the biggest sport structure there. It was built in the years 1939-1944. The local sport club Slovan achieved great success winning in 1969 the European Cup. The players of the "blue" team were also the key members of the Czechoslovak football representation in 1976, when the team won the title of European Champion. Another combined athletics and football stadium was built in neighbouring Pasienky, belonging to the first league football team of **Inter Bratislava**. The stadium of "black and yellow" team with the first artificial tartan track in Slovakia hosts also the world top athletes participating every summer in the popular light athletic meeting called **Grand Prix Bratislava**. The **Winter Stadium of Ondrej Nepela** stretches between Odbojárska and Trnavská streets. It was built in 1938 and twenty years later also roofed. The second ice-rink sharing the roof with the Winter Stadium was built in 1973 on the occasion of the world championship in figure-skating. The ice hockey club of Slovan using the Winter Stadium raised important individuals, some of them known all over the world, such as brothers Štastní, Vlado Dzurilla, Jozef Golonka or Dušan Pašek. A tennis area (1944), bicycle stadium (1946), sports hall and skittle facilities (1962), in-door swimming pool Pasienky (1973), and another hall Mladosť (1987) were gradually added to the complex. Although sport facilities prevail in the area, the residential complex of **Nová doba**, very modern for the time when it originated, was also built on the corner of Vajnorská and Bajkalská streets in the years 1932-1933. Beyond the Pasienky area is the artificial **lake Kuchajda**, originally a gravel pit.

Račianske mýto is a complicated crossroads where as many as seven streets meet. A toll station stood there as early as 1767. The first blocks of flats were built near the corner with **Legionárska street** following the design of K. Šilinger in 1924. The flats in the neighbouring **street Šancová** built in 1931 belonged to the **Unitas company**. The architects of this interesting architectural complex were F. Weinwurm and I. Vécsi. The north-western part of Račianské mýto is still vacant. The site of the closed Blumentálsky cemetery has been a municipal park since 1974. The road to Modra via Rača and Pezinok started close to the former toll station. It was the predecessor of today's very long **Račianska street**. This is the industrial area of the city, gradually built in the second half of the 19th century. The **Danubius Electric factory** is closest to it and it originated in 1902 as the **Siemens-Scuckert** factory producing electric engines. On the opposite side of Račianska street residential complexes were built in several stages. (1927). The blocks called **Legiodomy,** now Ursínyiho

Left: The Winter Stadium of Ondrej Nepela
Right: Environs of Račianska ulica street

street, designed by D. Jurkovič and J. Pacl were built in inter-war period. Further north, the territory between Račianska and Vajnorská, belonged to the army. First there was the building of the **infantry barracks** on what is now Kutuzovova street which simply maintained the three hundred year tradition of putting military camps on the local meadows. On the eastern end of the barracks an unusually tall cylindrical building was built in 1977. The students of the **Military College** inhabit *Kukurica* or the Corn Cob. The industrial zone continues beyond the barracks and occupies the area east of Račianska ulica. The sweet smell of chocolate in the southern part of the zone suggests the presence of the chocolate factory **Figaro Jacobs Suchard**. The German share-holding company of Stollwerck brothers, who successfully exported its products all over Europe, was founded in 1896. The sweet factory became famous among the children for its caramel sweets colloquially called "štolverky". The immediate neighbour of the **Figaro factory** was the mill Shindler and Jedlin. When it burnt down in 1927 the same company built a new one. **Eltos** with electric ware (formerly Tungsram and Tesla) and **Palma-Tumys** producing vegetable oils follow. The biggest firm in this part of industrial zone is the chemical company Istrochem. It carries on with the activity of the famous *Dynamitka* that was built on waterlogged meadows south of Rača in 1873. Shortly after the factory founded by the Hamburg company **Dynamit Nobel** developed into one of the biggest industrial firms in the Monarchy. The first stage of its construction finished in 1892. It followed designs of the Pressburg builders the Feiglers who preferred the historicizing style. Before 1910 in total 69 industrial and service buildings in the area of about 40 hectares were built. Construction of the factory was accompanied by that of the workers colony and during the Second World War also a big sugar factory was added to the complex.

Several buildings used for the educational purpose stand in Račianska ulica street. There are several medium level professional schools. In 1953 the student dormitories **Mladá garda** were built opposite the Eltos company, to plans by the architect E. Belluš. Urbanization of the western side of Račianska neighbours with a belt of vineyards, which cover the south-eastern slopes of the Little Carpathians. On the slope of Briežky Mt. one can admire a valuable **technical monument Rösslerov lom** or Rössler's quarry. Historic documents refer to the quarry as early as 1405 and it was used until the 20th century. By the end of the 19th century the terrestrial funicular was used for the first time in Slovakia for the work in this quarry.

More than a half of the area of the urban district of Nové mesto is occupied by the landscape park called **Bratislavský lesný park**. This indeed large (17 square kilometres) recreation area on the territory of Bratislava is the forested territory of the southern part of

the Little Carpathians. It is divided by Lamačská brána Gate into two independent parts. The one in the south consists of the massive mountain Devínska Kobyla. The northern part is bigger and borders on the Nové Mesto. This part consists mostly of meadows and broadleaved forest, which offer possibilities of relaxing in a pleasant setting. The area has numerous marked hiking footpaths and tourist amenities. The citizens of Bratislava have used the area since the first half of the 19th century, and the most popular spot was **Železná studnička** (The Iron Well). In 1826 construction of spa started at Železná studnička. The spa, which was given the name of Emperor Ferdinand V and was later bought by the rich Pressburg businessman Palugyay, exploited two local springs of ferrous water. But the importance of the spa diminished and the place became more popular as a recreational area. In 1890 it became the venue of the **May-Day celebrations** in Pressburg, the day, on which the workers of several local factories concentrated here. The **monument** from 1971 recalls the event.

The road starting at Železná Studnička heads to the north-west and runs along the Bystrička brook to the former game-keeper's house **Kačín**. It is a favourite picnic place and the destination of family trips. Near Kačín one can see what is called the **Written Stone**. It commemorates an event in 1600. The town of Pressburg was in dispute with Palatine Mikuláš Pálffy. This important Hungarian baron and hero of the Turkish wars owned the large estate of Pajštún and Stupava adjoining the property of the free royal borough of Pressburg. The cause of the argument was the frontier between the properties and it had to be solved by the Emperor Rudolf II himself who designated the rock existing amidst the Little Carpathian forests as the point dividing the two estates. The marks of the quarreling parties and the year 1600 are carved in it.

A road and hiking path run along the Horná Mlynská dolina valley. Close to the demolished eighth mill called **Klepáč** is a baroque **pillar**. Below Klepáč is the lower pair of **lakes**, which animate the natural setting of the valley. Below them the valley opens into the wide **Partizánska lúka meadow**, the place full of Bratislavians during weekends. The lower part of the valley is cut by **Červený most** (Red Bridge), an iron construction painted in red. Originally there was an older bridge built in 1848 on the oldest steam railway line in Hungary. The predecessor of the present Red Bridge was made of stones and red bricks. It bridged the Horná Mlynská dolina valley with eight arches a total of 215 metres long. The trains crossed the valley 17 metres above the riverbed of the Vydrica. The retreating German army destroyed the old bridge in April 1945. A fragment of one pillar is all what is left. Near the

Left: Commemorating pillar on the Kamzík Mt.
Right: Kramáre and Kamzík Mountain
Železná studnička

bridge is **Kramerov lom** (Kramer's quarry) where stone was extracted from the 16th century. In 1956 a military ammunition store was made there. The entrance into the Horná Mlynská dolina valley is at the place called **Patrónka,** which is the territory below Červený most and outside the administrative territory of Nové Mesto. Its name is derived from Roth's ammunition factory founded in 1874. In time of the First World War it employed as many as three thousand workers. The present Patrónka is a big crossroads framed by modern buildings behind which is the area of the **Slovak Academy of Sciences**.

The massive mountain of **Kamzík** (439 m) in the southern part of the Little Carpathians is a place frequently visited by Bratislava trippers. It is easily accessible by an asphalt road from Koliba. The name of the mountain originated from German *Gemsenberg*. At the crossroads next to its top is a **pillar** from 1683, which recalls the last stay of Turkish troops and their collaborators in the environs of the town immediately before the famous defeat at Vienna. Another **monument** standing below Kamzík in turn commemorates the last battle of the Prussian-Austrian war in 1866, which took place in the forests on the slopes of Kamzík. However, the main tourist attraction of Kamzík is the 200 metres tall **TV tower** built in 1974 on its top. The revolving restaurant on top of the tower offers panoramic view of the environs reaching, in fair weather as far as the Neusiedel lake and the Alps in Austria. On the eastern side of Kamzík is the

meadow called **Cvičná lúka** or the Exercise Meadow. Standing near the stalls with refreshments one gets a fine view of the wide plains of the Danube lowland. Cvičná lúka with its ski track is an ideal slope for the beginner skiers and sledders. The summer sled bob track attracts the trippers in summer.

Two new city quarters originated on the southern slope of Kamzík. More easterly is the villa quarter **Koliba**. Archaeological finds prove that this locality was inhabited by the Celts. In the Middle Ages Koliba was covered by vineyards with scattered huts. Urbanization of this area started only by the end of the 19th century. When the first halls of **film studios** were built in the forest of Koliba in 1948, the locality became the centre of the film industry in Slovakia. Construction was concluded in 1974. **The Slovak Hydrometeorological Institute** also has its seat in Koliba.

The quarter of **Kramáre** is situated above the railway tunnel on the track of the Main Station-Lamač. The forest called *Chormer* and part of the administrative territory of the disappeared settlement of Sellendorf in the Horná Mlynská dolina valley was mentioned in 1375. The name of the settlement may be connected with the hammer mill to which the road coinciding with present Magurská ulica street led. The smelting plant in this locality was in operation until 1929. In 1936 the hospital of infectious diseases was built in the part of Kramáre called **Krásna Hôrka**. More **buildings associated with health-care** including the Medical Research Institute and of the Ministry of Health of the Slovak Republic followed. The biggest building of this complex is the **Hospital of Academician Dérer with the polyclinic** on Limbová street.

Rača

Altitude:	135 m
Area:	37.5 km^2
Population:	32,500

North of Nové Mesto is the urban district **Rača** (170 m above sea level, population 21,000). It is about 8 kilometre away from the city centre. The administrative territory of Rača stretches over an area of 23.9 km. In the west it includes part of the forested massive of the Little Carpathians and in the east it borders on Vajnory.

The history of Rača is archaeologically documented already from the Neolithic with the particular, that in its territory several remarkable objects were found: a stone axe dated to the turn of the 2nd and 3rd millennium BC, ornamental bronze rings from Celtic period, etc. The first written reference to Rača is from the first half of the 13th century. A document act from 1237 mentions the settlement *Okol*, which was in the area of the present railway station and its population was Slavic. The name of Old Slavic origin testifies to it. The word *okol* or *okolica* used to denote the fences in which cattle was kept. Yeoman Racha gave his name to the part of Okol and it appeared for the first time in the 13th century. Although the new settlement of Rača based on the territory of Okol had a Slavic name, its population were Germans invited here after the Tartar invasion.

The history of Rača is closely linked to its **viticultural traditions**. The local vineyards are referred to in the oldest historic document from 1237. Many of Rača's vineyards were owned by burghers of Pressburg, even by some Austrians. They were called "guests" and paid to the yeomen of Rača fees for their vineyards. The wine growing reached its apex in the 15th century. In 1419 twelve thousand buckets of wine (1 bucket = 54 litres) were harvested in Rača and neighbouring Vajnory. In Rača alone 7,305 buckets of wine, were produced which equalled double the amount produced in the surrounding villages. The medieval

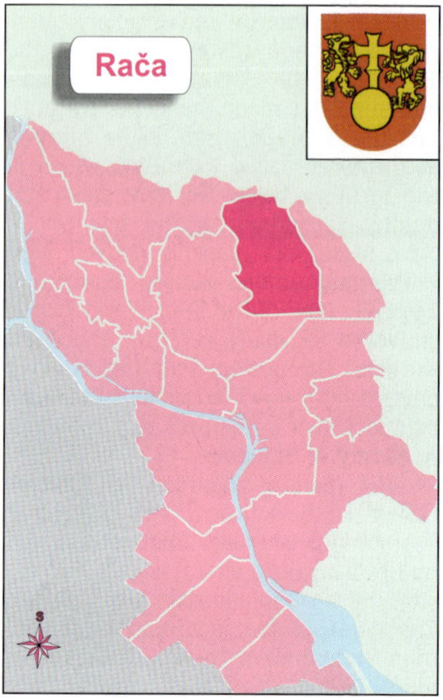

Right: Rača

prosperity of viticulture can be attributed to favourable climatic conditions. Warmer climate supported expansion of vineyards even to elevated positions in the Little Carpathians. There are still heaps of stones removed from vineyards called "hroble" to be seen high above the existing lower limit of the forest.

Medicinal wine

Rača wine was always one of the best quality wines produced in the region of the Little Carpathians. It was also always somewhat more expensive than the rest of them. The vintners of the surrounding villages used to buy Rača wine to mix it with their own in order to improve its taste. Račišdorf (now Rača) wines were often sold as dessert wines. They were successfully exported as far as Silesia. They would certainly have found clients in Austria, if not for various customs and import restricting measures. Pressburg did not support the trade in the excellent Rača wine because then nobody would buy Pressburg wine, which was not as good. The famous connoisseur of Hungarian viticulture Matej Bel estimated Rača wine high above that of Pressburg. He especially appreciated its taste, aroma and medicinal effects. The good reputation of the wine of the local vineyards was also propagated by the Pálffy family, who owned the village for a long time. Count Mikuláš Pálffy was a great fan of Rača wine. Thanks to his contact it was also sold in foreign market. It arrived at the Imperial court in Vienna as well. Legend has it that Maria Theresia liked Rača wine. Once, when Her Majesty fell ill while staying in the Austrian Alps, she was sent an efficient medicine. It was a consignment of Red Frankovka from the Rača priest and worked. The Queen liked the wine a lot and as a token of gratitude Maria Theresia pardoned the people of Rača the due tax from the harvest and promoted the priest to noble estate in 1776. Frankovka was never missing on the tables of the Imperial court from that time.

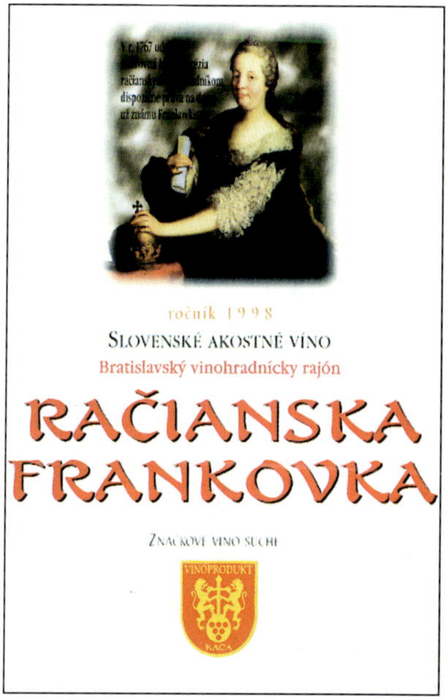

The property relations and owners in Rača were frequently changing. The village belonged to the Counts of Jur and Pezinok in the years 1512-1515. The Báthory family acquired Rača in 1527, but the state judge Mikuláš Báthory pawned his part of the property to the castellan of Devín, Michal Bay, for five thousand guldens as a reward for good service in 1581. Bay became owner of the pawned land two years after. The village had 120 houses in 1533. The population is not quoted but the number of houses suggests that Rača was bigger then Prača (Vajnory) or Devín. Along the

permanent inhabitants a great number of seasonal workers called "tovarichári" came to Rača to help the local vintners with hard work in the vineyards.

In the latter half of the 16th century the first **Croatian immigrants** came to Rača. The oldest record of their presence in the village is from 1578. Croatians of Rača in contrast to their compatriots settled in other villages around Pressburg were assimilated. Only the names reveal the Croatian origin of some people. Ján Keglevich became the new landlord of Rača by the beginning of the 17th century . The serfs of Devín later joined by those of Rača rebelled against this cruel landlord in 1616. The best known owners of Rača though, were the Pálffys from the Malacky branch of this rich Hungarian family. Palatine Pavol Pálffy acquired Rača together with Devín in 1635 and his heirs retained the property until the 20th century. Rača with its

Left: St. Philip and St. James church
Right: The vineyards of Rača

229 serf houses was the biggest settlement near Pressburg in 1768. Slovaks prevailed and that is why the local school also taught in Slovak apart from German. The fact that the Slovaks prevailed in Rača manifested itself above all in the revolutionary years of 1848-1849 when they gave support to the **Slovak uprising**. The village gathered a hundred volunteers and provided refuge to the Slovak Voluntary Corps for a short time. The units staying in Rača were visited by the chief commanders Ľudovít Štúr and Michal Hodža on June 30th of 1849.

The population of Rača increased in the second half of the 19th century, from 2,408 in 1870 to 3,843 in early 20th century. The stimulus of development was the railway. First it was the horse railway connecting Pressburg with Trnava (1840) and then in 1873 Rača was connected to Leopoldov by the steam railway. A colony of railway workers was built around Rača railway station and it became the core of what is called Nová Rača. The structure of population changed as well. Especially the number of workers was increasing while that of vintners was constantly dropping.

Rača has undergone enormous changes in the course of the 20th century. New housing estates were started: Krasňany (1955-1960), Experimental housing estate (1962), Barónka (1969-1975), Komisárky (1971-1976), and Záhumenice (1978-1980). Rača became administratively part of Bratislava on April 1st 1946. Rača has got a number of industrial firms: Vinárske závody which originated from the confiscated property of the German viticultural association, Kozmetika, Meopta, the plant producing optic apparatuses, etc. Rača had also famous table tennis and field hockey players.

A visit to Rača is an excellent opportunity to see a typical Little Carpathian viticultural village in its almost intact form. The oldest core of the village extends from Námestie hrdinov square to

Evangelical church. Right in the square and on Alstrova ulica street are several **yeoman curias**. Historically the most valuable building in Rača is the **Roman-Catholic parish church of St. Philip and St. James** with a massive rectangular tower ending in a tall prismoid roof. The church was built before 1390 in the Gothic style. It was given Renaissance form in 1629 and Baroque reconstruction was carried out in 1732. The **Evangelical church** is much younger. Pressburg builder B. Pandl built it in the years 1834-1835. The tower was built only in 1905. At the opposite end of the village only **St. Anna's chapel** survived from several old buildings. There are also typical **rural houses** in Rača. They are mostly concentrated on Alstrova street. When the street row of houses was full, the new houses were built behind with entrances from long yards. In some yards one can see five or six houses built in a row. The peasant houses of Rača were adapted to their main occupation – wine production. They had to have enough room for pressing and storage of wine. Some vintners emptied the front room of the house to use it as a tavern. Rača is rich in various folk traditions. It is rare to meet people wearing folk costumes, but they do put them on at the time of the traditional vintage.

"Vajnléze" ***of Rača***

When the last grapes were brought down from the vineyards, the next Sunday was the day when vajnléze *or the wine feast was organized in the village. Young people wearing their best clothes gathered in the yard of the curia on Barónka hill to prepare allegorical carts and a garnish made of grapes. In the afternoon the ceremonious procession with horses adorned with ribbons set in motion. On the way down the village young boys and girls would offer wine to the public. Only later the older citizens carrying traditional viticultural tools joined the procession, which stopped in front of the inn, where the dancing party was to be held. The dancing halls in the inn At* Brichta *or* At Mészaros *were also lavishly adorned with bunches of grapes and ribbons. Anyone who wanted to taste the grapes hanging around had to do it unnoticed, because if the "guard" caught him "stealing" grapes he would be punished by a fine. Successful harvest was concluded by a thanksgiving ceremony in the Evangelical church, where all sorts of fruit, vegetable, grapes and wine were displayed on a table. The priest would thank God for the good harvest and bless the displayed fruit.*

Rača is the starting point for hiking and skiing trips to the wider area around the **game-keeper's lodge Biely kríž** (500 m above sea level) lying in the north of the park. High situated clearing with a game-keeper's lodge and surrounding beech forest is an ideal picnic spot. Next to the game-keeper's lodge is the crossroads of three marked hiking footpaths leading to several attractive tourist landmarks of the Little Carpathians.

Vajnory

Altitude:	131 m
Area:	13.5 km^2
Population:	3,450

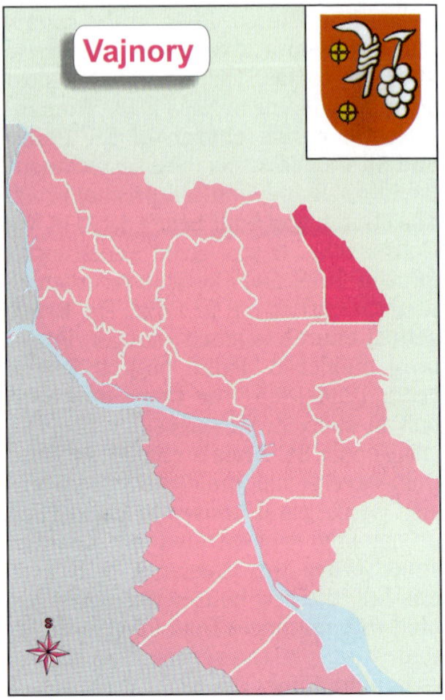

The urban district **Vajnory** is on the north-western edge of Bratislava, about 10 km away from the city centre. In the north-west a narrow protuberance of its area enters the south-eastern slopes of the Little Carpathians. In the south it reaches the road to Senec. The north-eastern and eastern borders of the administrative area of Vajnory coincides with that of Greater Bratislava.

The history of Vajnory goes back at least to the Great Moravian period. In the territory of today's Vajnory two little settlements existed with the Old Slavic names *Prača* and *Dvorník*. Their inhabitants were probably subjects of the fort on Bratislava castle hill. Archaeologists have documented two localities. One of them is near the railway station of Vajnory where an **Old Slavic burial place** dated to the 8th century was found. The second is immediately beyond the border of the administrative area of the village near the farm Triblavina, where the archaeologists discovered a **Great Moravian settlement**. The community *Dvorník* could have been this settlement. As its name suggests (*dvor* = yard) its people might have served the feudal lord of the Bratislava hill fort. The name *Prača* (*prak* = catapult) indicates that warriors using catapult or people producing this efficient weapon lived there.

Sometime in the 12th century Hungarians also settled this area as the oldest known written document of 1208 contains name the *Sceleus* which is the Latin version of the Hungarian name Szöllős (vineyard). Historians associate it with Dvorník. Apart from the neighbouring Rača, a document from 1237 also mentions the settlement *Parache* which is obviously modification of *Prača*. The document mentions the owner of the village, the Archbishop of Esztergom. According to another document of Archbishop of Esztergom Lodomeir from 1297, *Praca* became the property of the Cistercian monastery from Heiligenkreuz, as a result of a property exchange. In connection with the activity of this order in Pressburg, in 1307 the German form of Vajnory *Weinarn* appeared for the first time. Cistercians **leased their serf village to the city of Pressburg**. Vajnory was a profitable property at that time and other owners also had their vineyards in its administrative area, for example the Counts of Svätý Jur or burghers of Trnava. Negotiations between Pressburg and the monks of Heiligenkreuz concerning purchase of Prača-Vajnory took several decades and ended only in 1525 by an agreement sealed by King Louis II. Pressburg kept the property until the abolition of serfdom in 1848.

The city of Pressburg was represented in the village by an administrator

Right: The taverns in Vajnory

called the *išpán*. He supervised collection of taxes in kind and in cash, he managed the works on the landlord's plots. But he was not supposed to interfere with the life of the village. The public matters were dealt with by the village administration consisting of a mayor and four to five aldermen. Vajnory suffered a lot from fighting and rebellions. In the mid-16th century, for instance, Spanish soldiers were accommodated there but they eventually sacked the village. The mercenaries fighting in the Rebellions of Estates during the agitated 17th century behaved in the same way. Vajnory had about 320 inhabitants by that time. The population number increased with arrival of the Croatian immigrants before the end of the 17th century to about 490. In the 18th century the position of Vajnory and its population improved in spite of the fact that Pressburg tried to exploit it as much as possible. The people of Vajnory were always able to balance high taxes with high productivity, especially in good years,

Vajnory was the village with the highest number of Slovaks compared to the rest of the villages around Pressburg. The local geographical nomenclature, surviving documents written in the Biblical Czech language, and the names of the people prove it. For example: In 1910 1,863 inhabitants lived in Vajnory, 1,761 adhered to Slovak nationality, 92 were Magyars and 10 Germans. This was the environment where the priest **Ferdinand Juriga** (1874-1950), an important representative of the Slovak politics of the first half of the 20th century

was born. He was the only Slovak deputy in Hungarian Parliament before the Monarchy disintegrated. Juriga together with Andrej Hlinka founded the Slovak People's Party.

The airport of Vajnory

On the meadows west from Vajnory the oldest airport of Slovakia was founded. When on 4th May 1919 the military aircraft with General Milan Rastislav Štefánik on board was prepared to land, the airport was a kind of adapted meadow. However, Štefánik never reached his destination as the aircraft crashed at Ivanka pri Dunaji. The causes of the accident remained unexplained. On 23rd October 1923 the first regular air line of Czechoslovakia began to operate. Czechoslovak airlines were flying between the Prague airport at Kbely and the Bratislava airport at Vajnory. The former military aircraft A-14 type Brandenburg was flying 180 kilometres/hour, and a flight to Prague took 3 hours. Today a long-distance bus is able to arrive in Prague in

the same time. The airport of Vajnory is still open and it is used by the Slovak sport aeroclubs.

The people of Vajnory were economically oriented towards the Pressburg market also after the abolition of serfdom. They sold their crops and other products in the town and bought there what they needed. The Pressburg aldermen sold an estate, pond and lands in Vajnory owned by the town to Móric Sprinzl. The businessman founded a farm and distillery in the village. The farm provided jobs for many villagers. After the Second World War Vajnory became part of Bratislava. It was included into what is called Greater Bratislava along with other villages on April 1st 1946. The social structure of population changed with the change of regime and conditions. In 1958 only 600 from the three thousand inhabitants of Vajnory worked in agriculture including viticulture. Many people made use of improved road and railway communication with Bratislava and took up jobs in services and industry.

Although Vajnory became part of the city, it preserved its traditional rural character. The oldest peasant houses of Vajnory are from the early 19th century. The Roman-Catholic **church of St. Ladislav** was built in the 14th century in the Gothic style. A new nave was added to it in 1771. The main altar dedicated to the patron saint of the village is from the late 19th century. Roľnícka ulica street is the main street of the village and narrow houses with long yards skirt it. One of the Vajnory houses on Roľnícka ulica street was adapted as an ethnographic exhibition in 1966. The **Vajnorský ľudový dom** (The Folk House of Vajnory) (No. 185) is not only a representative example of a traditional dwelling of a vintner of Vajnory, it also offers wonderful products of folk painters in its interior. One can see there various folk paintings with varied patterns of ornament. Especially the kitchens were decorated. The paintings are the works of the natives. One of the last living artists was Katarína Bruderová, who painted houses of Vajnory in the first half of the 20th century. Pottery and embroidery supplement the interior of the typical house. The colourful local folk costume is also the pride of Vajnory. In spite of its close proximity to the metropolis, the village still preserves many folk customs. Vajnory also has **Vajnorák**, the oldest **brass band** in Slovakia founded in 1866.

Left: St.Ladislav church

The Eastern Suburbs

East of Bratislava centre are three urban districts. Ružinov is nearer to centre, while Vrakuňa and Podunajské Biskupice are on its eastern edge. The eastern suburbs extend on a flat landscape where mosaics of former villages, large housing estates, industrial zones, but also gardens, fields and floodplain woods alternate.

Ružinov

Altitude:	133 m
Area:	39.7 km^2
Population:	73,000

Ružinov is the second largest urban district as far as the area and population are concerned. The name of this part is comparatively young and in its German form *Rosenheim* it appeared only in the early 20th century. Prievoz is also an appropriate name as it denoted the oldest settlement in the territory of Ružinov, but it is only a part of Ružinov.

The territory of present-day Ružinov was once a large island called Mlynské nivy. Around today's Pribinova ulica were also Bažantí and Prostredný islands and north of Zimný prístav port was Svinský island. Beyond Pressburg two small fords crossed the Malý Dunaj river. Both were part of an important trade road, called Dunajská heading from Pressburg over Žitný ostrov to Komárno and Buda. The upper ford was near the village that was first mentioned as *Obern Urfar* in 1374. This was the settlement, which later developed into **Prievoz**. King Vladislav donated this village to the Rozgoň family in 1441 and later it remained the property of Pressburg Castle until the abolition of serfdom. Then it was referred to as *Felrew*, a corruption of the Hungarian name *Förév* and translation from German *Ober Ufer*. German Lutherans formed

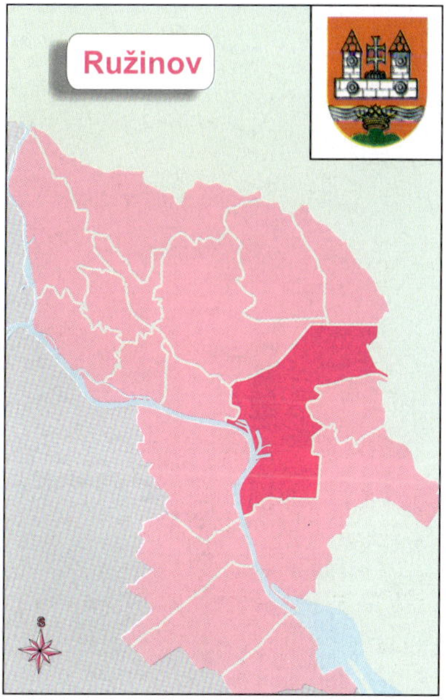

the majority of the population in the 17th and 18th centuries. The administrative territory also included Ovsište on the other side of the Danube until 1933. On April 1st 1946 when it was adjoined to Greater Bratislava, the population of Prievoz was 8,500.

The cultural monument of Prievoz is the **Csáky's manor house** built around 1900. Part of it is a later built **oratory of The Sacred Heart of Jesus** administered by the female congregation of St. Francis of Assisi and today it is the parish church. At present the manor house is the hospital and Franciscan female monastery. There is also **Evangelical church** in Prievoz built in the 1930's. Prievoz was the only village now included in Bratislava, which had a **town hall** of its own standing on the Radničné námestie square.

The past of Ružinov is closely connected with cultivation of vegetable and fruit. Extensive orchards and gardens spread on the plain north of Prievoz. A road, predecessor of the pre-

sent **Záhradnícka ulica street**, led to gardens mostly owned by **Bulgarian cultivators**. They were the main suppliers of fruit and vegetables to the Bratislava markets. They were also the main marketers in the former Centrálne trhovisko market (today Trnavské mýto) which was nicknamed "the wooden village". They are still found in the **Central market place**, which moved to **Miletičova ulica street**. The same as the old, the new market has its original atmosphere that deserves a visit even if there is no intention of shopping. It is very busy on Saturday mornings. The shoppers and sellers alternate and apart from fresh vegetable, fruit and flowers one can buy all kinds of cheap consumer goods. Fermented cabbage and sour cucumbers called *kvašáky* brought from the Záhorie region are an inseparable part of the market in autumn. When all the shopping is done, one should also taste good wine accompanied by the local speciality, which is a pancake made of raised paste with garlic (lokša in Slovak) or *cigánska* (the roasted pork chop).

The territory of today's Ružinov has experienced great changes recently. When the Danube was finally controlled and the danger of flooding of the orchards and gardens was averted in the twentieth century, the area became interesting for architects and builders. The first worker's colonies originated here in inter-war period. West of Prievoz were the Hubertova and Klingerova colonies. Next to the textile factory on the northern end of Miletičova street another colony was built and the *Dornkapplen* colony has existed on the territory of present **Trnávka** since the twenties. The colony provided living to the working class in small houses with a piece of garden. The Masarykova colony was added in the thirties. The Salesian order decided to construct a church in the area and the oratory with the **Don Bosco's Church** were started in 1937 in Trnávka. Gabriel Schreiber prepared the designs. As the Salesians went short of money they built only a part of the three-nave church with presbytery before 1938. The church was rebuilt in 1968 and widened. The Salesians of Bratislava also built the Salesian monastery in Miletičova street in the time of the First Republic. It was con-

Left: Csáky's manor house in Prievoz
Right: Don Bosco's church
Štrkovecké jazero pond

fiscated in the fifties and after the Velvet Revolution, the **Salesians** restored their **monastery** standing on the corner of a busy crossroads and added to it a modern church.

The urban fabric between the city centre and Prievoz now called **Nivy** was started in 1910 when the first blocks around Dulovo námestie square were built. Architect Emil Belluš designed eight houses on an H-shaped ground plan. In the fifties construction concentrated around Dulovo námestie square and Miletičova street. The first post-war housing estate was built along **Svätoplukova ulica street** and it is called **500 flats**. The central architecture of **Dulovo námestie square** is the building of the **Dukla Hotel** built in the years 1956-1959 following the design of Štefan Svetko. In the early sixties the housing estate **Ružová dolina** was built and the biggest urbanistic project realized in the territory of the urban district **Ružinov** was the series of Greater Bratislava housing estates: Štrkovec, Ostredky trávniky and Pošeň which took in about fifty thousand inhabitants. They were built between the years 1962 and 1970. The fifth quarter, **Starý Ružinov**, was built as the last one in the eastern part of Záhradnícka ulica in the eighties. Ružinov progressively acquired several modern service structures such as the **Bratislava Hotel** (1974), The **Winter Stadium of Vlado Dzurilla** (1979), and the **Junior Hotel** (1982), the **department store of Ružinov** (1984), **House of Culture of Ružinov** (1985), a **hospital with poly-**

clinic (1985), several shopping centres and administrative buildings.

In the southern part of **Ružinovská ulica street** a **park** was founded, and designed by Ferdinand Milučký. The the park originally bore the name of the Slovak politician Karol Šmidke, but its present name is the **Park of Andrej Hlinka** (1864-1938). Recreational activities of the quarter concentrate around **Štrkovecké jazero pond**, known for its swans. In June every year the race of unconventional vessels is organized on the pond.

Formation of the industrial basis in the territory of the urban district Ružinov started sometime in the 19th century. The first industrial structure in the eastern outskirts of Pressburg was **Klinger's factory** producing linen goods. In 1894 the businessman Oto Bondy founded the **Kablo factory** on today's Továrenská ulica street. It is still producing cables and isolators. The firm **Gumon** has a similar programme of production. It is situated on

the corner of Košická and Mlynské nivy street and it was founded in 1911. In its time it was the only factory in the Kingdom of Hungary, which produced rubber for electric equipment. In the neighbourhood of "káblovka", the **municipal power plant** started experimental production of electricity in 1901. Not far from Trnavské mýto, the cotton factories **Danubius** opened in 1909. The building of the factory will be now restored as a shopping centre.

The biggest industrial plant east of the city centre was started in 1895 on the plots in the locality called Mlynské záhrady. Advantageous position near the river port decided that the Budapest share holding company **Apollo** built an important crude oil refinery there. Construction of the first buildings was finished in April 1896. The refinery processed in the first years of its existence about 35 thousand metric tons of crude oil a year. During the Second World War Apollo became an important strategic company of the military industry of Nazi Germany. In 1944, when the eastern front drew closer to the eastern frontiers of Slovakia the **mass bombing** of Germany and its satellites became more intensive. Bratislava experienced the heaviest air raid in the morning of **June 16th 1944**. The attack was directed to the refinery, which immediately changed into an island of black smoke and fire. In several horrible minutes 133 people were killed, including 78 employees of the factory. The air raid destroyed eighty percent of the Apollo refinery. An accident in 1958 precipitated the end of the old refinery on Košická ulica street. In the meantime, in 1951 construction of a new petrochemical plant **Slovnaft** in the locality **Vlčie hrdlo** was started. The crude oil arrived via the **pipe line** called **Družba** to the new plant on February 22nd 1962. Production was considerably expanded in the seventies. But the location of Slovnaft in the upper part of Žitný ostrov proved to be very wrong. Oil and other pollutants seeped into the local sources of drinking water. Drinking water sources in Vlčie hrdlo supplying a large part of Bratislava had to be closed and the population supplied from cisterns. This emergency situation was solved only thanks to huge investments into the buffering zones preventing the escape of pollutants into the gravel and sand layers and by building new water sources in the villages of Hamuliakovo and Ostrovné lúčky. In early 1980's Slovnaft built a new and modern compound, which facilitated production of lead-free petrol and a more rational production of other petrochemical products.

Left: The Monument of M. R. Štefánik
Right: Winter port

The former Apollo factory originally situated north of the Winter Port was given a new function by the city architects and administratively it was included in the Staré Mesto quarter. On the corner of Košická and Pribinova streets printing and journalist activities concentrated. The building of the Presscentrum has been used since 1980 and it contains the majority of newspaper and journal editorial offices. Next to the **Presscentrum** is the biggest printing house of newspapers and journals in Slovakia, the **Danubiaprint**, and the building of the **Press Agency of the Slovak Republic** (Tlačová agentúra Slovenskej republiky). Further to west is the building site of the **new Slovak National The-**

atre. One of the buildings owned by the municipal transport company houses the popular theatre stage of Bratislava, the **Stoka Theatre**.

The supraregional transport function of the eastern suburbs is also important. They contain the bus terminal, the airport and the river port. The modern **bus terminal Mlynské Nivy** was built near the busy crossroads of Karadžičova and Mlynské Nivy streets in the years 1975-1983. The city continues its old tradition of international trade mediated by the Danube river transport since the Middle Ages. **Starý prístav** (the Old Port) spreads between the Danube channel and Pribinova street. East from Košická is **Zimný prístav** (the Winter Port) with two artificial pools for ships, which anchored there in winter. As the Old Port became too small for the developing river traffic on the Danube, the New Port was started in Pálenisko with two rectangular basins and a repair depot in 1975. Near **Nový prístav** (the New Port) is the two storied **Prístavný most** (the Port Bridge) over the Danube. It is the part of the southern by-pass motorway around Bratislava.

The **Airport of M. R. Štefánik** is situated on the north-eastern edge of the urban district Ružinov. It is partly on the territory of the village Ivánka pri Dunaji. It was opened in 1950. A new building of the airport was added to the area in 1970. In front of the older building stands the **monument** to the Slovak inventor **Štefan Banič** (1870-1941), who invented the parachute. It is no accident that the airport bears the name of the important Slovak politician and scientist **Milan Rastislav Štefánik** (1880-1919). Štefánik tragically died in an air crash on May 4th 1919. His plane fell on the field east of the present airport. In the north of the airport is the Bratislava's largest artificial **lake Zlaté piesky**. It originated by extraction of gravel in locality called Krížové polia. The lake was adapted as a natural bathing pool in 1964. It became one of the largest sport and recreation areas of the city with tourist facilities and accommodation.

Vrakuňa

Altitude:	132 m
Area:	10.3 km^2
Population:	18,500

The urban district **Vrakuňa** spreads on the eastern edge of Greater Bratislava. The urban fabric connected Vrakuňa with the contiguous urban district of Podunajské Biskupice. This common settlement is in the uppermost part of Žitný ostrov. In the west it borders on the urban district Ružinov.

The oldest document proving the existence of Vrakuňa dates from 1279. In another written document from 1290 a settlement called *Vereknye* is mentioned. The settlement originated next to the ford over the Danube arm. Later there was a port used by the peo-

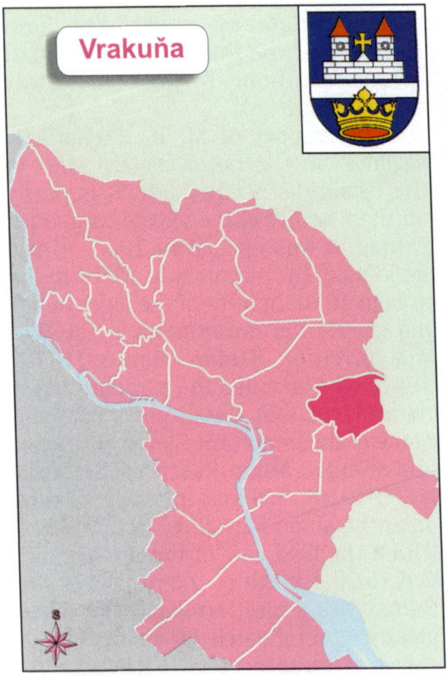

ple of Pressburg. Collected tolls are mentioned in 1306. Starting by 1356, the name of *Frettendorf* referring to Vrakuňa is mentioned. Pressburg was offered the opportunity to buy this serf village in 1356 and partially applied it in 1392. The family of Rozgoň purchased the village in 1436 and in 1449 the ford of Vrakuňa became the property of Pressburg Castle. Vrakuňa was a small settlement with population of 120 in 1631 and 470 two centuries later. They were mostly farmers, hauliers and fishermen. When Vrakuňa was annexed to Bratislava its population was 2,300.

Vrakuňa did not have a church of its own until recently. It had only a **chapel** of **the Holy Name of the Virgin Mary** standing by the road and built in 1879. The single-nave rectangular building has a Prussian vault. It also has a little rectangular tower and on the main altar is the oil painting of the Immaculate Conception from 1879 by Károly Jakobey. The modern **church of the Holy Name of the Virgin Mary** next to the chapel was built in 1994. Besides the family houses in the territory of Vrakuňa there are also modern housing estates. The axis of the new part of Vrakuňa is **Rajecká ulica street** with pedestrian zone and shops. On the western edge of Vrakuňa's territory is **Ružinov cemetery**, the largest in Bratislava. It was opened in 1982 and the entrance is from Popradská ulica street. On the left **bank of the Malý Dunaj** or the Little Danube is the quarter called Nová Vrakuňa consisting mostly of family houses, which originated on the land formerly belonging to the Pálffys. In the south of Vrakuňa is the **landscape park of Vrakunský les**.

Left: The landscape park of Vrakunský les

The Queen of the Danube

The legend has that once upon time amidst the floodplain forest of the

Danube a splendid palace existed. It was inhabited by water nixies with such intensive blue eyes that they passed that colour to the waters of the Danube. Jug, the butcher's hand living in the village fell in love with one of them called Rosava. As he could not resist his passion, he set off to the forest following the voice of his heart. He got lost and wandered among the willow trees until he finally saw Rosava's sisters dancing on a clearing . The water nixies were teasing and dancing with Jug and inviting him ever deeper into the dark forest as they tried to get rid of the uninvited intruder. Jug was dancing with water nixies and perhaps he would die of so much dance if not for Rosava. The boy was taken to the Queen sitting in the middle of the Water Palace. Rosava was defending him and begged for mercy. The Queen hesitated because she feared humans as the greatest enemies of her green realm. However, the brave Jug's speech when he asked for permission to marry Rosava and take her to his home convinced the Danube Queen. But it was Rosava who refused the offer as she knew that Jug in spite of his good and loving heart could not protect her against all vicious people. The water nixies accompanied Jug to the village and he never saw them again as they moved to the Black Sea. The water of Danube lost its beautiful blue colour after their departure nixies. Only when the blue skies find their reflection in the Danube people remember the beautiful blue-eyed water nixies which use to live there in the past.

Podunajské Biskupice

Altitude:	134 m
Area:	42,5 km²
Population:	20,500

The urban district **Podunajské Biskupice** lies south of Vrakuňa and east of Ružinov. In the south, the administrative territory of Podunajské Biskupice reaches as far as the Gabčíkovo dam. Biskupice borders on the area of Slovnaft in the south and on the villages of Žitný ostrov in the east.

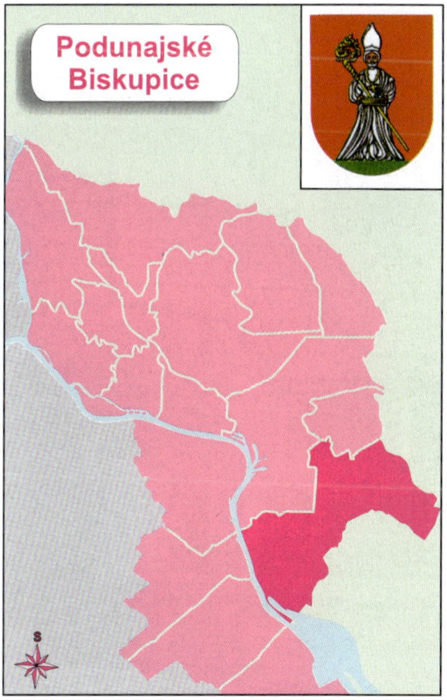

The Biskupice mile stone

The Romans were known as excellent road builders. Their roads survived for ages and some of them are still used. Along the Roman roads with hard surfaces the orientation mile stones quoting the number of miles to the nearest town were set. The central mile stone called milliarium aureum *was placed in the Forum Romanum in Rome and it quoted the distances to the important cities of the Roman Empire. One of the Roman mile stones was also found in the territory of today's Podunajské Biskupice. It was moved to Esztergom. The mile stone of Biskupice quoted the distance of 16 Roman miles and it is precisely the distance of Podunajské Biskupice from the capital of the former Pannonia, Carnuntum.*

According to the archaeological finds, the territory of Biskupice was already settled in the Roman and Great Moravian eras. The medieval settlement probably existed here in the 11th century. Originally it was shared by the Archbishopric of Esztergom and the Pressburg Chapter. In the early 14th century the only owner of Podunajské Biskupice was the Archbishop of Esztergom. In 1441 the village was attacked by the mercenaries of Ján Jiskra of Brandýs and the village improved its defence by construction of a fort. A document from 1450 denotes Biskupice as *oppidum*, a small serf town. Archbishop Mikuláš Oláh granted the town the market privilege in 1450. The town used to have two coats of arms. The older one contained the traditional patron saint of the Esztergom Archdiocese, St. Vojtech and later it was a new coat of arms with St. Nicholas. Reformation never reached Biskupice and the local population always adhered to the Roman Catholic confession. An important battle took place near the village on August 25th 1620, when the Imperial troops faced the rebellious army of the noble Gabriel Bethlen. The Transylvanian prince was defeated which meant peace for Pressburg and its environs. The village had 120 houses populated by 700 people in 1643. But two hundred years later its population grew to

Left: St. Nicolas' church
Trojičné námestie square
Museum of Trade
Right: The hospital in Podunajské Biskupice

1,218 and the number of houses was 212. Podunajské Biskupice was administratively incorporated into Greater Bratislava in 1972. Then it has population of 7,500. In the last quarter of century the population has more than doubled as a result of the construction of a pair of housing estates in the 1970's. The housing estate of **Medzi jarkami** for 5,800 people was built in the years 1973-1976 and another housing estate of **Dolné hony** inhabited by 18,000 people was added to in the years 1974-1979.

The most important cultural and historic monument of the village is the Roman Catholic **parish church of St. Nicholas**. It was built before 1250. It was originally a Gothic church, but was several times rebuilt. It was severely destroyed during the Turkish wars and had to be almost entirely reconstructed. In 1750 its interior was adapted in the Baroque taste, and shortly after an Archbishop's oratory was added to it. Re-Gothisizing interventions were made in 1901 and the reconstruction of 1937-1938 meant the addition of two lateral structures. The original Gothic details of the St. Nicholas church partially survived in the tower and the sacristy, where there are two reliefs depicting the Lamb of God and Christ's Head. The presbytery contains the copy of the Baroque sculpture of the sitting Madonna. Inside one of the church walls a stone with Roman inscription from Carnuntum was found. On Krajinská street is a Neo-Classic **manor house** with a **chapel** from the 18th century. In the 19th century it was rebuilt as a **hospital**, which exists there also today. The remains of another **manor house** are in the locality **Lieskovec** south of the Slovnaft area. Originally it stood amidst the disappeared **Archbishop's park**.

The Southern suburbs

The southern suburbs in the Transdanubian (seen from the city centre) part of Bratislava occupy an area of 94 square kilometres, or an exact quarter of the total area of the city. The main riverbed of the Danube in the north and the east limits its territory. The southern and western limits of Transdanubian Bratislava are in fact the state frontiers in the south with Hungary and in the west with Austria. The territory of Bratislava lying beyond the Danube is divided into four urban districts, which have been developing as independent communities. The northernmost one of them is Petržalka neighbouring with Jarovce in the south. Southeast of Jarovce is the Rusovce village and Čunovo is in the extreme south.

Development of the territory lying on the "other" bank of the Danube was long and complicated. Wars, rebellions and plague epidemics, shifts of state frontiers, first between the Kingdom of Hungary and Austria, then between Hungary and former Czechoslovakia, were the adverse sides of its history. Rusovce, Jarovce, Čunovo became part of Mosony County in the 11th century. Petržalka, in turn, was part of Bratislava County. The first three communities were adjudicated to Hungary after the First World War, while Petržalka was annexed to Czechoslovakia. Moreover, Petržalka, the same as Devín, became part of the Nazi German Reich. After the war in 1946 Petržalka became the urban district of Bratislava. Rusovce, Jarovce and Čunovo were first included in Czechoslovakia on the basis of the Paris Convention from October 1947, and maintained the status of independent villages within the Bratislava district for another 25 years. They were added to Bratislava only after 1972.

Right: The building of Technopol
The New Bridge and housing estate

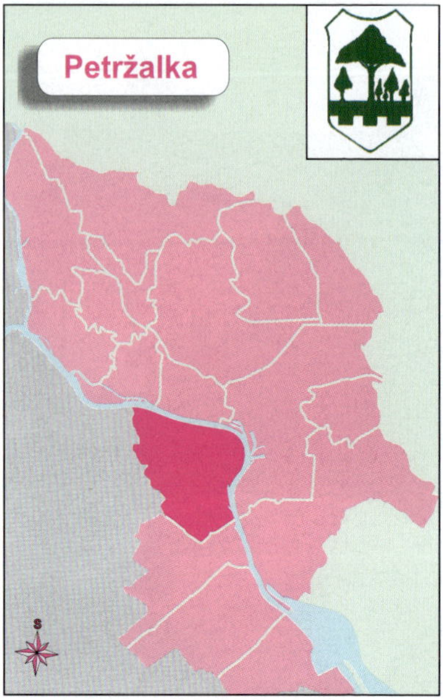

Today the four communities are urban districts in the district of Bratislava V.

Petržalka

Altitude:	135 m
Area:	28.7 km^2
Population:	125,300

The urban district **Petržalka** if it was independent settlement, would represent the third largest city in Slovakia. The result of enormous building activity on the right bank of the Danube can be best appreciated from the southern terrace of Bratislava Castle. This "concrete jungle" is home of every fourth Bratislavian.

The settlements in the territory of today's Petržalka originated in the past on a slightly elevated aggradation rampart of the Danube out of reach of the floods. The founders of the community situated it between the old Danube arms, called Pečnianske and Chorvátske. The oldest known description of today's administrative territory of Petržalka is that of King Andrew II from 1225. According to this document a settlement of Pechenegs lay directly opposite the ford. The task of these traditional guards of the frontiers of the Kingdom of Hungary was to protect one of the few comfortable passages over the Danube. Their settlement presumably disappeared several years after and during the reign of King Belo IV, who had displaced the Pechenegs. A homestead of German colonists replaced the former community. It is referred to by the name *Flezyndorf.* In late 13th century the Pressburg chapter obtained this land and that is the reason why the place of the former homestead is now called **Kapitulský dvor** (Chapter Yard).

In the 15th century a new settlement sprung up on the territory of Petržalka. German colonists created a community called *Engerau* (The Narrow Flood Plain) or *Unger Au* (The Hungarian Grove). The Hungarian community preferred the name *Ligetfalu*. It became the basic settlement unit of future Petržalka. The village was first situated on lands, which were part of the Devín estate. It had about 30 homesteads by the end of the 16th century. The Pálffy's acquired it in 1635 and it was about this time that the first Croatian colonists came to the prevailingly German village.

The Pressburg chapter had the first sacred building, a single-nave church, built on its lands in the village of *Flezyndorf* in 1672. There were also an inn, a well, and a port in the village. The inn

was never short of clients. Merchants and other travellers were moving around the ford and the provisional bridges over the Danube. At the time of coronations held in Pressburg the place became especially busy. There was a camp of luxurious tents where the noble visitors, including princes and kings, attendants of this event were waiting for the ceremony. Nevertheless, the whimsical Danube represented a permanent threat for the communities living on its right bank. In 1771 Maria Theresia ordered construction of anti-flood dikes. These prepared the ground for the building of a new royal road to Vienna, the predecessor of the existing Viedenská cesta road. Documents from 1786 quote that there were 90 houses and 118 families in the village of *Engerau* on Pálffy's property. The inhabitants of Engerau were mostly living on haulage and crafts.

Petržalka became the green hinterland of Pressburg and a very popular one in the course of history. The citizens

of Pressburg imitated the lordly pastimes seen in Paris, London or Vienna. Especially the ceremonious opening of the Bridge of Francis Joseph (today the Old Bridge) on New Year's Eve of 1890 is memorable. The Emperor himself opened the traffic on the first fixed bridge across the river. From 1914 the local electric railway connecting Pressburg with Vienna was using this bridge as well. The Vienna tram, as it was nicknamed by the Bratislavians, crossed Petržalka, Hainburg and Petronell to end its journey in Vienna. Its home depot was in Kittsee in Austria. The Vienna tram was stopped in 1938 and after the Second World War only the city trams crossed the Old Bridge to Petržalka. Later trains used the bridge, but today the railway track is not used.

In August 1919 (eight months later than the city) Petržalka became part of the newly created Czechoslovak Republic. In the inter-war period (1930) there were 1,571 houses with 14,164 inhabitants in Petržalka. In spite of preserving its rural character with low houses and gardens, the first factories also appeared in Petržalka. Its people got the opportunity to work in the local factory Matador (rubber production) and Sphinx (kitchen ware). Small factory of Harsch brothers produced timber boards, Winter's factory made varnishes and paints, and Wienmann's factory produced driving belts. Omnia was active in wood processing and Avenarius produced paints.

The park of Petržalka, today called **Sad Janka Kráľa**, possesses a kind of primacy. Few of the European metropols can say that they have the oldest public park. The citizens of Pressburg had the revolutionary idea of founding a garden for all, accessible to the general public, not only to the privileged classes, in the 1770's. They chose for the purpose the alluvial forest on the right bank of the Danube lying right opposite the historic city centre. A public collection gathered the means necessary for felling trees. The trees were felled in a way, which created the pattern of an eight-tip star along which later rows of trees were planted. The park was called *Sternallee* (A Star Tree Row). But the following decades were not too favourable for further development of the park. It was repeatedly destroyed by floods and in the agitated years of the Napoleonic wars the city did not have enough money for its maintenance. Ballus' book from 1825 does not mention any city park at all. The part was renewed only a year later by planting greenery in connection with construction of a café house. The space became a park in the proper sense of the word only in 1832 thanks to Mayor Anton Námer and the name of the park was then *Burger Au* (Municipal plains). The park flourished under the adminis-

Left: Sad Janka Kráľa park
Right: Leberfinger restaurant
The garden arbour in the Sad Janka Kráľa park

tration of František Floridus Romer, Professor of the Royal Academy and owner of a famous botanical collection. The park acquired many still existing exotic wood species, including wonderful ginkgo and plane trees, which judging by their size, must have been planted around the early 19th century. Members of the Pressburg Beauty Association took care of the park after 1868. Their main objective was to create sport and recreational facilities that included construction of the building of a sports union and a rowing club. There was also a menagerie after the First World War. Rosary containing about 3,000 varieties of roses was the attraction of the 1930's.

About a hundred years before that (in July 1828) the structure of an open-air **theatre Arena** was built on the right bank of the Danube. Theatre in Italy inspired its designers. Different genres were on the programme of Arena: dramas, operas and musicals. The shows were held in summer on Sundays and feast days. The public had the opportunity to watch famous artists from Vienna or Budapest. In 1899 a new building was erected on the site of the original Arena Theatre and it has survived until today. The world famous mime Milan Sládek with his ensemble is now trying to restore old theatre traditions. The attractive and frequently visited **building of Au Café** used to stand not far from the propeller port. It was built in 1826. Situation of this café was not accidental. It was near the bridge and the customs house and its aim was to make the waiting more pleasant for the travelling

public. The café was known for good music and a perfect service. It was pulled down in the sixties. A little bit lower down the stream was a **municipal inn** known under the name **Leberfinger**, after its last owner, where concerts were held twice a week. Although it was out of operation for a long time, it was reopened recently. There is a pension for elderly actors in the building as well. Below the Old Bridge the public **swimming pool** called **Lido** was built in 1934. The area contained various sport grounds.

Sad Janka Kráľa park was profoundly reconstructed in the 1960's. All undesired vegetation was removed and the result was more space that enhanced the beauty of the big old trees. The park now has several sculptures. One of them is the **statue of Janko Kráľ** (by F. Gibala). The **statue** of the Hungarian revolutionary **Sándor Petőfi** was moved here from the former Promenade (today Hviezdoslavovo námestie square). The unique garden arbour,

originally the **tower of the Franciscan church** is also impressive. The wonderful Gothic tower used to be one of the most beautiful in the Kingdom of Hungary. But it suffered from an earthquake so that it was dismantled and reerected on the place where it stands now.

Petržalka has always been a locality with sport facilities. Traditional sport practiced in Petržalka was rowing and several rowing clubs existed on the right bank of the Danube. **Prešporský veslársky klub** (The Rowing Club of Pressburg) was founded as the first in the Kingdom of Hungary in 1862 and it was then a modern sports club. Buildings of the Slovak and German rowing clubs survived until today. Petržalka also had the football stadium of Červená hviezda, which belonged to the Czechoslovak football elite of the second half of the 1950's. As a result of its unusually large dimensions people called it "the airport". However, this stadium and other sports facilities were built up by blocks of houses in the 1980' and Petržalka has now only one football league stadium called **Artmédia Petržalka**.

Old Petržalka as remembered by the medium and old generation of Bratislavians has practically disappeared in the process of urbanization. One of the few buildings left is the Roman-Catholic **church of the Exaltation of the Holy Cross**. It stands to the north-west of the Panónska cesta road. It was built in 1932 to plans by V. Karfík. Two years later it became the seat of the newly created parish of Petržalka. This church was built because an older church from1672 was pulled down when Viedenská cesta road had to be widened. The businessman Tomáš Bata contributed to the construction of the new church, which was built in incredible six months. The existing interior contains the original pews and the organ made in Rigler's workshop. The Pressburg sculptor Aloiz Rigele made the **statue of Christ Crucified**. The most precious monuments are in the park in front of the church. One of them is the **statue of the Virgin Mary** standing on a stone Baroque pillar from the 18th century moved here from the Viedenská cesta road. The **statue of St. John of Nepomuk** moved here from the park near the Danube is another. The first houses of the gigantic **housing estate Petržalka** were started in 1976. Since then every year about 6,000 new flats were added to the vast area on the right bank of the Danube. About 10,000 workers were employed in its construction. Gradually 120,000 inhabitants moved onto the right bank of the Danube. There is probably no housing estate of comparable size in the whole of Europe. In the north-west of Petržalka's administrative territory is **Incheba**, an extensive multi-functional exhibition area. The most of is structures are finished and operating. Various exhibitions including the **International**

Left: Artmedia Stadium in Petržalka
Right: Gerulata

Chemical Fair of Incheba are held in its premises. **Sports events**, for instance international lawn tennis matches are also held here. The area also has its **hotel**.

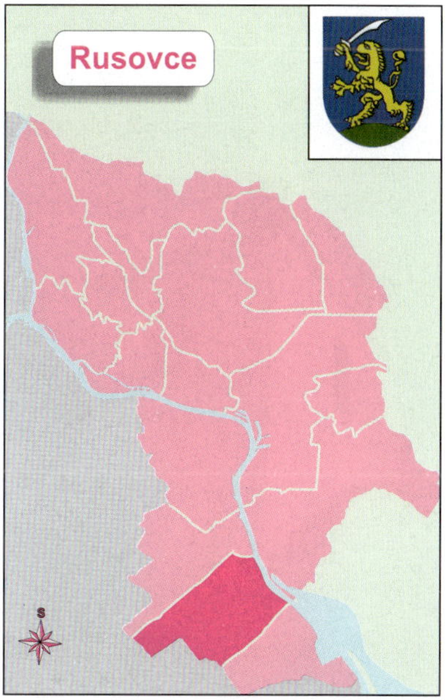

Rusovce

Altitude:	135 m
Area:	25.6 km²
Population:	1,700

Rusovce is the biggest of the three urban districts of the other bank of the Danube lying south of Petržalka. Rusovce is a very old community. Though its territory was settled already in the Older Bronze Age it became most notable in the first four centuries when the northern frontiers of the Roman Empire moved to the middle section of the Danube. The territory of today's Rusovce found itself in the Roman province of Pannonia administered from Carnuntum. Romans built there the military camp of **Gerulata** as a part of the *Limes Romanus* defensive system, securing the northern limit of the Empire against the raids of German tribes. Romans left numerous traces of their stay in Rusovce. Archaeologist gradually disclosed various remains of architecture, such as the ruins of the Roman forum, a well, remains of furnaces, tombstones and altar stones, but also individual bricks and shingles with symbols of the XIVth Roman legion. Four cemeteries, a great amount of coins, fragments of pottery, utensils of everyday use made of bronze and iron were found here. Especially prccious was the find of a deformed helmet of the Roman officer who was probably killed in the war with Markomani. The antique history of Rusovce is documented in the exhibition of the **Municipal Museum Múzeum antiky – Gerulata** (open only in summer).

The territory of today's Rusovce was also settled after Roman Gerulata disappeared. The presence of a Slav-Avar burial place from the 8th century and 150 graves of the early feudal cemetery from the 11th to 12th century prove it. The medieval village on the territory of Rusovce is first referred to in a document from 1208. Its name was *Wuiswar* or *Vruzwar* in the oldest historic sources. Historians associate the name with Russians who were entrusted with the defence of the early feudal fort by the old Magyars against the Franks. In the 14th and 15th century the German name *Karlburg* and the Hungarian name *Oroszvár* (The Russian Castle)

were used. Both names in their modified forms were used until the second half of the 20th century when the present name Rusovce originated

The village thrived on its advantageous situation on a trade road. It is referred to as an *oppidum* or small town. King Belo IV of Hungary donated it to Comes Herrard of Trenčín in 1266. It became a trade centre with a customs house already in the 14th century. During the 16th century immigrants from Croatia fleeing from the Turks came to Rusovce. Their descendants were assimilated in the following centuries. In the 17th century the rural community changed into a small serf town with market privilege. In 1742 a numerous Jewish community with their own administrator is mentioned. The villages were the property of the Zichy family then, and of the Lónayis in the 19th century. There were 223 houses with 2,003 inhabitants in 1787. The villagers lived on agriculture and haulage. A great part of lands was owned by the Lónayi family, until it was parcelled after the Second World War and given to displaced people who came here after the departure of 150 German families. The remaining land became the basis of the newly founded state property farm.

The ground plan of Rusovce has a typical spindle-shaped form, which was enlarged by modern urbanization. The older generation of houses is from the 19th and early 20th centuries. The architectural feature of Rusovce is the Neo-Classical **manor house** built in 1840 on the site of an older manor house from 1521. The manor house acquired its attractive facade by application of the Romanticizing style of what is called the Windsor type imitating English Gothic. It has towers, battlements and a central risalite with terrace. In front of the manor house is the **statue of a lion** standing on a pillar. The manor house has got a big **park**, composition of its wood species is not especially varied but the trees are tall with big crowns. Oaks and plane trees prevail. The manor house serves the **folk ensemble SĽUK**, which moved here in 1951. The village of Rusovce has got two churches. The **St. Vít and Modesta church** is older and stands on the edge of the park. It was built in 1613 in the Renaissance style using the remains of an older Romanesque church from 1208. The church was rebuilt in the historicizing Neo Romanesque taste in the second half of the 19th century. The second, Roman Catholic parish **church of St. Maria Magdalene in Rusovce** is from 1662 and it is built in then fashionable Early Baroque style. The main altar of Maria Magdalene made of wood is from the mid-17th century. The Late Renaissance sculptures of St. Stephen, St. Ladislav and the kings of the Old Testament, David and Salamon adorn it. The lateral altars display the traits of transi-

Left: St. Vít and Modesta church
Right: Folk architecture in Jarovce

tion of the Renaissance to the Baroque style. They were made in the second half of the 17th century and in the first half of the 18th century. The Renaissance-Baroque pulpit and the stone font are from the same time. The chapel in former homestead Laura is from the end of the 19th century.

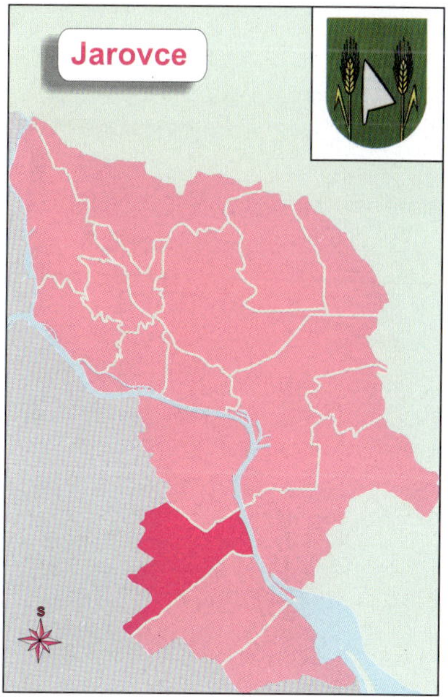

Jarovce

Altitude:	135 m
Area:	25.6 km^2
Population:	1,700

The village of **Jarovce** stretches along the south-west of the right bank of the Danube and is one of the oldest, judging from the existing historic documents, in this area. It was mentioned already in 1208 as *Villa Ban* in connection with the fact that it was donated to the Benedictine monastery at Lebény, in Hungary. The name *Jahrendorf* is mentioned in 1436. The oldest documents referring to the village in connection with arrival of the Croatian immigrants are from the 16th century. The presence of Croatians in the village is obvious also from the older names *Horvátfal* (1522) and *Kroatisch-Jahrendorf* used since the 18th century. The record of the canon's visit from 1659 proves that all inhabitants of Jarovce in that time were Croatians except for one immigrant. Turkish troops burnt the village in 1527, but it was comparatively quickly renewed and in 1542 it had 13 homesteads. But a new disaster came in 1551 when fire destroyed almost all houses. There was a customs house in Jarovce, owned then by the Esterházy family, in the 16th century. In 1787, 597 inhabitants lived in 72 houses. The third fire came in 1910 when half of the village burnt down. The villagers were mostly farmers. Some of them worked in the local brickyard, which produced until 1930.

The Roman Catholic **church of St. Nicolas** was built in 1764-1765 in the Late Baroque style. The sponsor of the building was Count Esterházy. The monumental tower of the church was built in 1884. German troops blew it up on April 3rd 1945. The existing tower was built in the years 1969-1970. The single-nave church with a semicircular presbytery contains the original furniture from the 18th century. The wooden Late Gothic sculpture of the Madonna is older, as it dates from the late 15th century. The main altar of St. Nicolas and the two lateral altars are from the early 20th century. The wooden Baroque sculpture *Ecce homo* is from the late 17th century.

Folk architecture from the 19th and the beginning of the 20th century survived on Mandľová ulica street. Years 1850, 1865, 1885, and 1895 are carved on the facades of the oldest houses. The typical folk houses of Jarovce are clay structures. The walls are built from burned or unburned clay. In reconstruction of the village after the 1910 fire, the unburned bricks were used. In the nomenclature of the construction and decoration components the original Croatian words have survived until the present time.

Čunovo

Altitude: 130 m
Area: 18.6 km^2
Population: 800

Čunovo was in the past an independent village and now it is the remotest part of Bratislava on the right bank of the Danube. The settlement of the territory of this village is archaeologically documented from the Roman and Old Slavonic periods. Inhumation graves from the 2nd to the 4th centuries and several centuries younger Slav-Avar burial place were found here. The first written reference to Čunovo is from the first half

Left: St. Nicolas church in Jarovce
Rural house in Jarovce

of the 13th century. A document from 1232 mentions the village named *Chun*. Only in the 15th century (1451) also the German name Sandorf appears, which probably suggests the prevalence of the German ethnicity in this region. Until then it was inhabited by a mostly Slav population, which was assimilated first by the Hungarian and later by German ethnicities.

The plague epidemic of 1409-1410 reduced the population of Čunovo. The war between King Mattias Corvinus and the Emperor Fridrich of Germany did not avoid the village either. Fighting and direct consequences of the stay of both armies on its territory had its disastrous consequences on the village and its population. In the 15th century Čunovo was part of the Magyaróvár estate owned by the Counts of Sv. Jur and Pezinok. Croatians driven out of their homeland by the Turks first came to Čunovo by the early 16th century and later formed the main ethnicity of the village. The influx of the refugees from the "Lower Land" became even more intense after the unfortunate defeat at Mohács in 1526. The landlords provided them space to settle in the Austrian-Hungarian boundary area, which also contributed to the defence of the frontiers. **Croatians** received the abandoned and devastated land to restore its productiveness. The village was owned by various owners then and the best known of them were the Horváth's. In the 17th century, Catholic Croatians prevailed over the minority of Protestant Germans. The people lived on farming and forest works. They kept cattle and horses, though they repeatedly faced devastating floods. In the second half of the 18th century the village had two landlords, Count Szapáry and yeoman Sándor. The hard life became more bearable thanks to the reforms of Maria Theresia. The first census organised during the reign of Joseph II in the years 1784-1787 shows that there were 99 houses populated by 716 people in

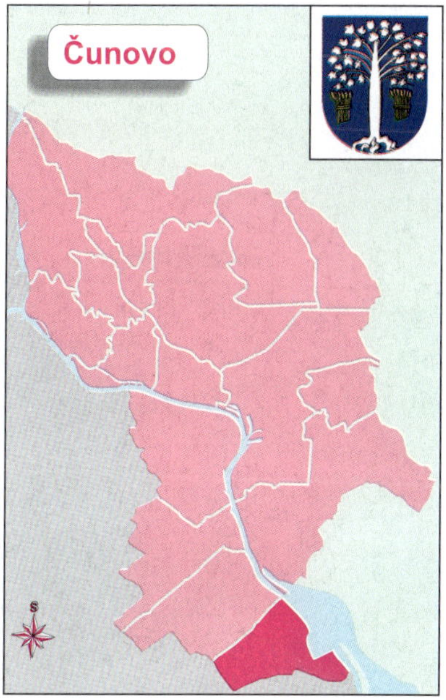

Čunovo. Although the population dropped later, the Croatian-German character of the population was maintained. In the 19th century there were three mills in the village and the farmers began to grow fruit trees. After the abolition of serfdom in 1848 the lands of Čunovo passed into the estate obtained by the families of Szapáry, Zichy, and Zsitvay in 1851. The Čunovo estate survived almost a century. It was parcelled only in 1927 when Count Lónay owned it. After disintegration of monarchy in 1918 Čunovo was adjudicated along with Rusovce and Jarovce to Hungary. It became part of Rajka district in Mosony County. It had 687 inhabitants in 1930. Croatians prevailed over 126 Germans and 160 Hungarians. In inter-war period many villagers commuted to Austria where they found better work opportunities. After the Second World War Čunovo belonged to Hungary for a short time. The result of the peace negotiations between Czechoslovakia and Hungary which took place in Paris, was

the extension of Bratislava's hinterland lying on the left bank of the Danube and Čunovo, Rusovce, and Jarovce were annexed to it.

The most valuable historical monuments of the village is the Neo-Classical **curia** from the end of the 18th century and the Roman-Catholic **Church of St. Michael** built in 1783 in the Late Baroque taste. In its interior are the Late Baroque altar, Neo-Classical pulpit and an organ from the 18th century. The Gothic **chalice** from the second half of the 15th century is also valuable. On the main altar is the statue of the patron saint of the church and parish of St. Michael the Archangel.

North of the villages is the **Nature Reserve Ostrovné lúčky**. The locality is notable for occurrence of precious plant species, especially the orchids. Part of Ostrovné lúčky is a multicultural growth of Canadian poplar planted here in 1958. Attraction of the environs of Čunovo is the **Gabčíkovo dam** and a **modern water sport area**. **Mini-Slovakia** is a recently founded gallery containing miniature copies of the most important cultural and historical monuments existing in Slovakia.

Left: The water sport area in Čunovo
The gallery of Mini-Slovakia

Hiking tours

Bratislavians are very lucky as the thick woods of the Little Carpathians cover almost a quarter of the area of their city. Thanks to it they can easily abandon the nuisance of the metropolis counting about half a million inhabitants and escape within a short time to the wonderful natural landscape. The Little Carpathians are short, but unusually picturesque mountains, attractive in any season.

We are offering three all-day hiking tours, which in essence cover all attractive spots of the mountain range. All of them follow routes, which do not abandon the limits of Greater Bratislava. They start and end at the points accessible by the public transport and are suitable for all, old or young hikers. More eager tourists will certainly gladly try the basic routes with the option of expansion to destinations lying beyond the limits of the city, such as the Pajštún Castle, the pilgrim village of Marianka, or even the Pezinská Baba Saddle. Occasional hikers will perhaps prefer the shorter options, which leave more time for mushroom picking, picnics or simple relaxation in fresh air. The three hiking tours run in the territory of protected landscape, the trip to the Devínske Karpaty Mts. even runs through the strictly protected area of a nature reserve, where the movement and stay of tourists is limited by the guidelines of nature protection, which must be observed. Remember: Nature belongs to all of us!

1. The Devínske Karpaty Mountains

The most beautiful natural setting in the territory of Bratislava
Dúbravka – Devínska Kobyla – Sandberg – Devín – Devín Castle – Devínska Nová Ves

Situation: The Devínske Karpaty Mts., the southernmost part of the Little Carpathians.
Starting point: Dúbravka, the urban district of Bratislava at the eastern foot of the Devínska Kobyla Mt. The trip starts at the bus stop on Čiernohorská ulica street.
Finishing point: Devínska Nová Ves, urban district of Bratislava on the northern foot of the Devínska Kobyla Mt. The trip ends at the bus stop on Eisnerova ulica street.
Schedule: Dúbravka – saddle below Švábovský vrch hill ½ h – crossroads below Devínska Kobyla ¾ h – Devínska Kobyla ¼ h – crossroads below Devínska Kobyla ¼ h – Sandberg ¾ h – Waitov lom quarry ½ h – Devín ¾ h – Devín Castle ¼ h – Devínska Nová Ves 1¼ h. Total 5¼ hours.
Elevation gain: 375 m

Grade: Moderately demanding tour running on well-marked hiking paths. Ascent to Devínska Kobyla is not toilsome as it is gradual and gentle. It starts in Dúbravka, which is the highest situated part of Bratislava. About 2 hours necessary for the visit of Devín Castle should be added to the total time needed for the trip.

Map: Turistická mapa Malé Karpaty – Bratislava 1:50 000 (sheet 127). Edition of summer hiking maps published by VKÚ, š. p., Harmanec

Basic route: A tour in Devínske Karpaty Mts. offers a visit to the part of Bratislava, which is generally considered the most beautiful. Unique views of picturesque landscape alternate with traces of remote past while staying in a valuable natural setting with rare plants and wild life.

Start at the bus stop in **Dúbravka** (250 m above sea level) and continue on Jadranská ulica framed by the traditional rural houses. You are following the blue hiking mark (the path No. 2436). Passing by the church on Strmé sady street you come to Plachého ulica, which continues up to **Švábsky vrch hill** (360 m a.s.l.). The first section of asphalt road through the wood is not marked. The path enters wide meadows at the saddle above the round top of Dúbravská hlavica hill (357 m a.s.l.). Here it joins the red hiking mark (international long-distance route No E 8, or 0701). Not far from the **mountain hotel** bearing an unusual name **Áno, prosím** (Yes, please) the red route crosses with the yellow-marked hiking path. The red path later enters the wood again where it becomes slightly steeper. It avoids the top of the Devínska Kobyla Mt. North of it the asphalt road changes to a forest path, which joins the green-marked hiking route after about a kilometre. If you turn left **at the crossroads** (about 450 m a.s.l.) you will easily reach the highest point of the tour, which is about 30 m lower than the near-by top of **Devínska Kobyla** (514 m a.s.l.), which is closed to the public. The highest point of Devínska Kobyla lies amidst woods so there is no view of the surrounding landscape. But you will get a fine view of the Devín Castle and Braunsberg in Austria from the place, where an arbour used to stand. The basic route goes back to the crossroads of the green and red hiking routes and continues on the path heading north following the green

mark. The forest opens to clearings in places with view of the Záhorská nížina lowland. Coming closer to Devínska Nová Ves the open landscape fully displays its beauty. On the western side and immediately in the vicinity of Devínska Nová Ves **Devínska Kobyla instructive path** joins the basic route. It will take you to **Sandberg** (210 m a.s.l.), the world famous palaeontological locality. After seeing it you continue on the blue hiking route (No. 2461) heading to the south. The path runs in meadows alternating with young wood growth. On its left side there are unique views of Marchfeld in Austria and Devín Castle. The route runs along the lower plateau of the big **Waitov lom quarry** (230 m a.s.l.). The route to **Devín** (150 m a.s.l.) leads across gardens on the southern slope of the Devínska Kobyla hill. You will get to **Devín Castle** passing by the cemetery and turning right onto the road leading to a large parking lot below the castle. After the visit of the Castle area starts the last section of the tour. The point is right next to the **confluence of the Danube and Morava** (139 m a.s.l.), which you reach by passing through the southern gate. The final stretch leads on asphalt path that is a part of **instructive path through the floodplain of the Morava**. The instructive path ends in the village of Vysoká pri Morave. **Devínska Nová Ves** (145 m a.s.l.) is the final point of this route.

2. Around the Horná Mlynská dolina valley

A pleasant walk in forest landscape of the Little Carpathians around the attractive Horná Mlynská dolina valley.

Červený most bridge — Kamzík — Pekná cesta road — Horná Vydrica — Kačín — Červený most bridge

Situation: The southernmost part of the Pezinské Karpaty Mts., the Little Carpathians.
Starting and finishing point: Červený most bridge, the final stop of trolley bus in front of the entry to the Military Hospital.
Schedule: Červený most – Kamzík 3 h – Cvičná lúka meadow 1 h – Tri duby ¾ h – Krásny vrch ½ h – Horná Vydrica ¼ h – Malinský vrch ¼ h – crossroads at Sekyl ½ h – Cimbal – ½ h Kačín ¼ h – Červený most 1½ h. Total 6½ hours.
Elevation gain: 264 m

Grade: Moderately demanding tour for its length. But it can easily be reduced. A part of the route is on unmarked paths that require attention for orientation in the terrain.

Map: Turistická mapa Malé Karpaty – Bratislava 1:50 000 (sheet 127). Edition of summer hiking maps published by VKÚ, š. p., Harmanec

Basic route: This is an ideal tour for anybody, who seeks a pleasant stay in the woods. Practically the whole route runs in the Little Carpathian forest landscape full of natural smells and sounds. It passes by the Horná Mlynská dolina valley. The route cuts the valley in its spring part with beautiful meanders.

The hiking tour starts in front of the entry to the **Military Hospital** (Nemocnica Mi-

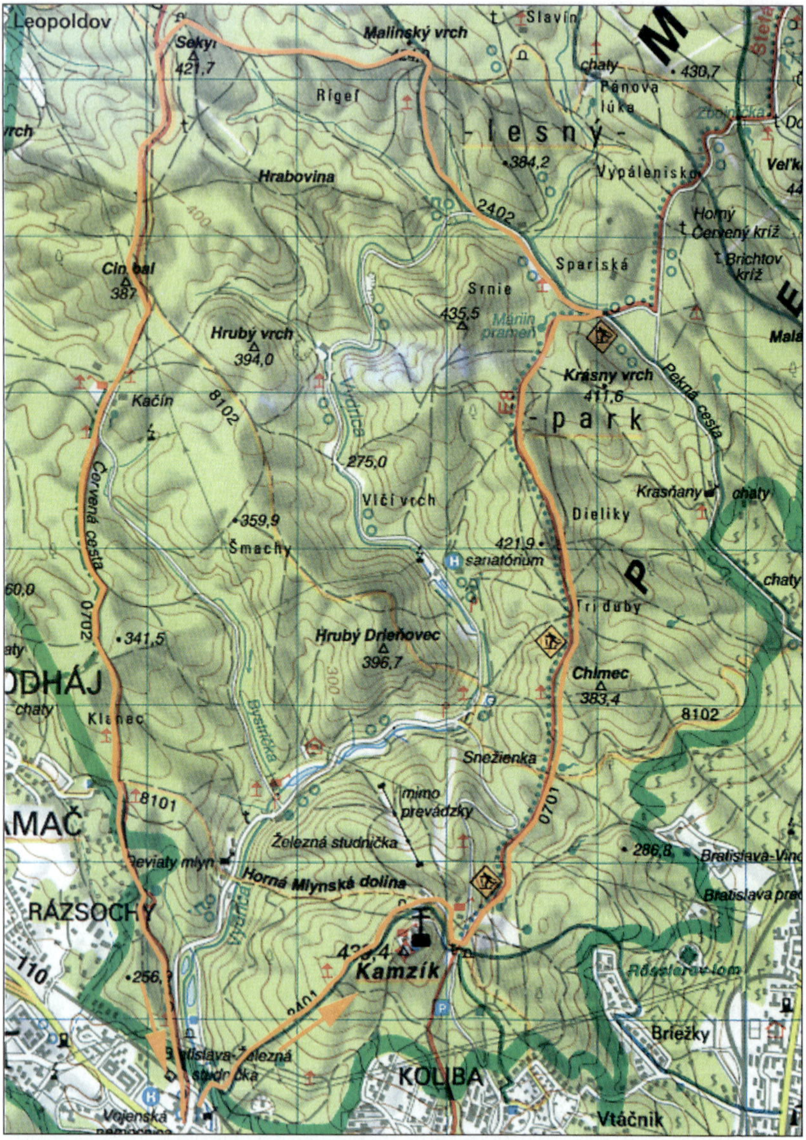

nisterstva obrany) (175 m a.s.l.). Following the blue mark of the path No. 2401 you pass under the iron construction of the **Červený most bridge** into the recreational area of Partizánska lúka meadow. The asphalt path will take you across the floodplain of the Vydrica brook. Under the little well and close to Červený most bridge there is a path ascending the slope above the spring. Later it joins the forest road, which ascends to the slope of Kamzík hill. The footpath will take you to a wide clearing where is a unique view

of the southern part of Bratislava. This is about the only view on the route. The clearing lies on the edge of the plateau, which also includes the top part of the **Kamzík hill** (439 m a.s.l.) with the TV tower. The blue-marked footpath avoids the top of the hill and passes by the newly built West Hotel heading to the upper edge of **Cvičná lúka meadow** (400 m a.s.l.) Standing above the meadow, which is full of skiers in winter and fans of the bob track in summer one can admire the wide Danube plain stretching east of Rača and Krasňany quarters. The local stand offers the last opportunity of a little snack and a view of open landscape before you reach the aim of the tour. The red-marked hiking route (E 8, or 0701) continues along the edge of Cvičná lúka meadow and gently ascends on the plateau-like ridge towards the wooden shelter under the Chlmec hill (383 m a.s.l.) and carries on to **Tri duby** (350 m a.s.l.). Before you reach the crossroads on Pekná cesta road you can drink from **Maria's spring** offering cold and refreshing spring water. The asphalt road marked in blue (No. 2402) continues from the crossroads. After passing by the military structure called **U Slivu** (327 m a.s.l.), the path runs along the Vydrica brook for a while. Moderate ascent in a comparatively thin wood with high oaks leads to the **Malinský vrch hill** (424 m a.s.l.). Then you will abandon the marked route and proceed to the left onto an unmarked forest road. You need not fear going astray. The road branches in two after about a hundred metres and our branch is on the left. The route passes by a bulky oak and heads through the middle of a flat ridge to the west. You will have to stick to this road until reaching a fork of two roads. Your road is on the right. It passes by a round hill and joins the red-marked hiking route No. 0702 next to the little road chapel. Hikers call it Červená cesta road. It will take you in no time under the top of **Sekyl** (400 m a.s.l.), where the route crosses the yellow-marked hiking route No. 8102. Beyond the round top of **Cimbal** (387 m a.s.l.) the yellow-marked route turns left and ours is the forest road marked only in red. It slightly descends to the **Kačín hill** (330 m a.s.l.), which is a favourite picnic spot of the Bratislavians. The route carries on the asphalt road, which branches next to a tourist shelter. The red mark sends you to its right branch that keeps its southern direction. On the **Klanec hill** (314 m a.s.l.) the yellow-marked hiking route No 8101 connecting Železná studnička (left) with Lamač (right) cuts our road. The final descent to Horná Mlynská dolina valley will take you to the aim of the tour. It is a short walk from **Červený most** to the trolley bus stop in front of the **Military Hospital** (175 m a.s.l.).

3. The Rača circle

Refreshing wander around the northern part of the Bratislava landscape park with picnic.
Rača — Malá Baňa — Zbojníčka — Pánova lúka meadow — gamekeeper's lodge Biely kríž — Rača

Situation: The south-eastern part of the Pezinské Karpaty Mts., the Little Carpathians
Starting and finishing point: Rača, urban district of Bratislava accessible by the public transport.

Schedule: Rača – Malá Baňa 3 h – crossroads with the red route ½ h – Zbojníčka ¼ h – Pánova lúka meadow ¼ h– Bystrické ½ h – Biely kríž 1¼ h - Rača. Total 5 hours.
Elevation gain: 328 m.

Grade: Slightly demanding tour running mostly in forest with easy orientation on marked hiking with an option of a picnic.

Map: Turistická mapa Malé Karpaty – Bratislava 1:50 000 (sheet 127). Edition of summer hiking maps published by VKÚ, š. p., Harmanec

Basic route: The environs of Rača are a favourite tourist area. Wonderful forest landscape is criss-crossed by hiking paths. The forest clearings and meadows are ideal for picnics.

Start at the tram stop in **Rača** (170 m a.s.l.) on Detvianska ulica street and set off towards the north. Turn left on Námestie hrdinov square following the blue hiking mark (No. 2403) and the Alstrova ulica framed by traditional vintner houses will take you to the first crossroads. The street on the right heads to the **out-door swimming pool of Zbojníčka**. There is a parking lot next to Zbojníčka where one turns left onto the hiking

footpath ascending to the slope of the Knižkova dolina valley. After a moderate ascent you will get near the round hill of **Malá Baňa** (361 m a.s.l.). Its top is accessible by a short retour. The quarry immediately below the top opens a unique view of the slopes of the Little Carpathians with Veľká Baňa hill (444 m a.s.l.) towering above Knižkova dolina valley. You will go back to your path that continues on the flat forested ridge towards **crossroads** with the red-marked footpath (E 8 or 0701). Going north-east on the forest asphalt road you get to the popular little well called Zbojníčka (400 m a.s.l.). Refreshed you can continue on the yellow hiking path (8126) heading to the **Pánova lúka meadow** (380 m a.s.l.). The fresh meadow amidst the woods is the first good opportunity for a picnic. The basic route leads from Pánova lúka to the north into the spring part of the Vydrica brook. The blue marked path (2403) crosses the old shallow valley. The place called **Bystrické** (420 m a.s.l) is the crossroads of several hiking footpaths that lead either to Marianka or Borinka. Yours is the yellow-marked path (8103) leading to the meadow next to the **gamekeeper's lodge Biely kríž** (498 m a.s.l.). This highest point of the route too is a good place to relax and have a picnic. The final stretch of the tour leads on the asphalt road marked in blue (No. 2403). The road ends in **Rača**. A good conclusion of the nice trip can be a visit to one of the local taverns, where one can taste the fine wines of Rača.

Bike Tours

It is proved that the bicycle is the most ecological, most economical and in the cities the quickest transport means for distances below 3-5 kilometres. It does not have to be necessarily only the means of active relaxation or improvement of health condition, but also a suitable everyday vehicle used for transport to school, work or shopping, provided the organization of the particular city allows it. But it is not the case of Bratislava. Apart from some exceptions concentrated on the right bank of the Danube, in Petržalka, no separated and reasonably drawn routes for bikers exist in Bratislava. Although there was an effort of the citizens to change this unfavourable situation nothing or very little was done in the respect, though projects exist. Many principal communications (such as Trnavská, Ružinovská and Račianska streets) offer enough space for drawing bike lanes. The environs of Bratislava are ideal for biking in an open landscape outside the city, which could be linked with the ones running through the city. Let us hope that the responsible bodies will not only adopt but also implement the idea of introducing bike lanes into the territorial planning and Bratislava will join hundreds of other European cities with a friendly approach to the bike fans.

We offer here three bike tours leading partially through the city and ending in its outskirts. The prevailing part of the city's terrain is unusually suitable for biking. The choice of bike tours in the environs of Bratislava is varied. It is given by the situation of the city on the limits of the Little Carpathians and two lowlands: the Danube and Záhorská nížina. As well as the classic easy, typical family trips on the floodplains of the Danube or Morava, there are also more demanding bike tours in the Little Carpathians where the elevation gain of the highest sections of the tours compared to the Danube embankment is as much as 270 m and the ascents (or descents as you like) reach in places 10%. The Little Carpathians offer many possibilities in gently undulating to mildly dissected landscape. In any case, one should always bear in mind that one rides in protected landscape and that other bikers or hikers frequent the roads, which requires tolerance.

Our choice of the routes is also suitable for the city bikes. Those who are interested in more bike tours should read the guide book by T. Hučko, published in Pedál Publishing House in 1998 under the title "Okolo Bratislavy" (Around Bratislava) describing more than 700 km of bike tours within and outside the city limits.

1. Petržalská

2. Devínsko - pomoravská

3. Malokarpatská

1. The Route of Petržalka

Route: Border crossing Berg - Pečniansky les wood - pass under the Bratislava bridges - the eastern edge of Petržalka - around the waste water cleansing station (ČOV) - on the dike to Čunovo.
Length of the route: 22 kilometres
Elevation gain: the route descends from 139 m to 130 m above sea level
Brief description: The route follows almost the whole of the right bank section of the Danube on the territory of Slovakia, and follows its main stream with the exception of the first stretch. It is especially suitable for children as it leads on the dike except for a several hundred meter long stretch.
Map: The detailed bike map of Bratislava-Podunajsko in scale 1:100 000 (sheet 7), edition of bike touring maps published by VKÚ, š. p., Harmanec.

Detailed description: The route starts on the Slovak side of the customs point **Petržalka-Berg**. The whole route is part of the **Danube bike route** leading from Passau in Germany, over Vienna in Austria and Bratislava ending in Budapest in Hungary.

The first, about 700 m long section runs on a busy principal access road to the border crossing. Before the first crossroads with motorway turn left and proceed on the concrete pavement along the motorway, which is on your right. You are entering the **Pečniansky les forest**, one of the few remnants of the Danube alluvial forest. You are getting closer to the Danube. The parallel communication crosses the **Lafranconi bridge** further to the left side of the Danube (option to turn off to Mlynská dolina valley, Devín, the Little Carpathians and the housing estates in the western part of the city). However, before reaching the bridge you will take the sharp turn right under the bridge onto the dike which runs for another about 1.8 km in alluvial forest. Beyond the tall building of the **Incheba fair area** you will abandon the dike, pass onto Viedenská cesta road (beware of traffic which is luckily not too dense here) and heading to the left you will pass under the pylon of the New Bridge. A little rest on a bench on the embankment is the opportunity to get the most beautiful and perhaps the most typical view of the dominant buildings of Bratislava: Castle, the Parliament, St. Martin's Minster and the hotels on Rázusovo embankment on the opposite bank of the river. The view from the Bystrica restaurant on the top of the pylon of the bridge is even more attractive.

Continue on Viedenská cesta road on the right bank of the Danube between the embankment on your right and Sad Janka Kráľa park on your right. After about 800 m you will reach the crossroads, the fun-fair, and the parking lot under the **Old Bridge.** Crossing the bridge to the opposite side of the river is possible, but not recommendable for the bike track coincides with that for pedestrians.

Next to the fan-fair turn left to the river and continue under the bridge on Klokočova street and the Danube dike along the river. You are passing by the **open-air swimming pool Lido**. The dike slightly turns to the right and follows the sharp bend of the river below Bratislava. After about a kilometre and half you will pass under the last Bratislava bridge, **Prístavný most** or the Port Bridge. Here to you can cross the river and go to the quarter of Prievoz or continue to the housing estates in the eastern part of the city. The following section of the track, like the preceding ones are easy for orientation. Continue on the

Danube dike. On the right side is the area of the Economic University and the housing estate of Petržalka on your left are the floodplain forests. The dike slightly turns to both sides. After about 3.6 km you reach the south-eastern edge of Petržalka near the gravel extraction plant and the waste water cleansing station. Continue up to the village of **Rusovce** (about 4 kilometres from the waste water cleansing station). The Danube on your left is constricted into the **dam of Hrušovo**, part of the Gabčíkovo dam. This part of the track is a real paradise for the bikers. In fine weather hundreds of bikers and roller-skaters of all age categories frequent it. Mutual tolerance will make the trip pleasant for all.

If you want to get close to the main stream of the Danube, turn left off the dike near the snack stand before arriving at Rusovce and go along the **Jarovské rameno arm** and further on the road directly along the Danube. You will come back to the original route after about 4.5 kilometres. Another 6 kilometres will bring you to the aim of the route in the village of **Čunovo**. You will get into the village by turning off the dike to the right. Turn left at the crossroads and you will arrive at the structure that dams the old Danube channel with water sport area. (beware for the vehicles of the building site and follow the road signs and warnings!). The Danube branches at this spot into the old channel (down the stream on the right) and the feeding channel of the Gabčíkovo dam. This is also the place of Bratislava's limit, which coincides with the Slovak-Hungarian state frontier. You can continue out of Bratislava to **Vojka** (15 km) or to **Gabčíkovo** (20 km).

2. Devín and along the Morava

Route: Karlova Ves - Devín - Devínska Nová Ves - Devínske Jazero
Length of the route: 19 kilometres
Elevation gain: the route ascends from 136 m to 170 m above sea level.
Brief description: A comfortable trip. The first stretch is on the road and passing Devín it coincides with the instructive path through the Morava floodplain. This stretch is very suitable for the family trips. The whole route runs along asphalt roads.
Map: The detailed bike map of Bratislava-Podunajsko in scale 1:100 000 (sheet 7), edition of bike touring maps published by VKÚ, š. p., Harmanec.

Detailed description: The trip starts next to the **restaurant Riviéra**, on the crossroads on the southern or "lower" end of the Karlova Ves quarter. First you will pass by the **Sihoť water works** on your left and continue on Devínska cesta road between the foot of the Devínska Kobyla Mountain and the arm of the Danube. The first almost 1,000 metres up to the viaduct leading to the Dlhé diely housing estate are busy but there is no danger provided you are careful. The route carries on across gardens and along a quarry on the right side up to the **village of Devín**, 7.5 km away from Riviéra. On the crossroads at the beginning of the village continue right ahead on the Slovanské nábrežie embankment up to the rock of Devín castle. This is where **the instructive path in the floodplain o f Morava** starts. The overall length of the instructive path is 21 kilometres and it has 16 information boards describing the natural and historical features of the surrounding landscape. The instructive path was made thanks to the initiative of the non-govermental conservationist or-

ganizations, their fans and enthusiasts. Practically the whole instructive path runs in the boundary belt along the Slovak-Austrian frontier, which was strictly guarded until 1989. Ironically, this politically motivated "protection" in fact prevented the damage to the precious riparian ecosystems. Then you continue up the stream of the Morava, which flows into the Danube precisely in this place. The route runs on the dike of the Morava. The foot of Devínska Kobyla Mt. is on our right the whole time before we arrive at Devínska Nová Ves. Soon the **Nature Reserve of Sandberg** emerges. On the left side on the opposite bank of the river is the village of Markthof in Austria. Further north the castle of Schlosshof is seen. This part of the route is comparatively busy with numerous bikers and pedestrians. If the Morava is too high some stretches of the route are unpassable. After about 3.5 km you will get to the southern edge of the village of **Devínska Nová Ves.** There are several ways how to get into the village. Before arriving at the little bridge over the **Stará mláka** brook (beyond the information board No. 5) the road divides in two. Both of them lead to **Devínske Jazero**, the aim of the tour. If you turn left and abandon the instructive path passing onto the asphalt road by the co-operative farm, you will pass under the railway track heading to Marchegg and continuing beside the railway track to Kúty, after 6 km you will come back again to the instructive path immediately before the aim of the route. There are interesting remains of fortifications along this part of the track built here as part of the defence system of Czechoslovakia against the expected German invasion in the thirties. But a much more interesting alternative way of entering Devínska Nová Ves is the one, which continues along the instructive path. After about four kilometres pass under the railway track to Marchegg and stick to the river on your left. After 3.5 km you will reach a crossroads with a parking lot, the end of our route. One can continue turning left and after a 9 km ride arrive at **Vysoká pri Morave** across the Nature Reserve Dolný les reaching the end of the instructive path or by turning right reach the centre of the town of **Stupava**.

3. The Little Carpathian route

Route: Patrónka (Červený most) - Železná studnička - Spariská - Krasňany. Option: Spariská - Dolný Červený kríž - Rača.
Length of the route: 14 kilometres, option 16.5 kilometres
Elevation gain: the route ascends by 170 m or 230 m (from 180 m above sea level to 350 or to 410 m a.s.l. on optional route).
Brief description: A dissected route for ascents and steep descents requiring a certain experience and good physical condition. It runs in the valley of the Vydrica, which is the most comfortable access to the main ridge of the Little Carpathians.
Map: The detailed bike map of Bratislava-Podunajsko with a scale of 1:100 000 (sheet 7), edition of bike touring maps published by VKÚ, š. p., Harmanec.

Detailed description: The trip starts in front of the **Military Hospital** (Nemocnica Ministerstva obrany) by the public transport stop. Pass under the railway viaduct known as the **Červený most** bridge and continue in the valley of the Vydrica around **Partizánska lúka meadow** on a mildly ascending road. You will reach **Železná studnička** after about 2.3 km passing by the turn off to Kačín. Continue straight ahead in the valley of the Vydrica passing by Snežienka (the former lower station of the ski lift to Kamzík Mt.) and around the Rehabilitation Centre of the Heart Diseases for about 5.7 kilometres before arriving at the locality **U Slivu**, where you join the blue marked route. The valley of the Vydrica turns to the right here and again to the left after about 500 metres. Continue straight ahead following the blue mark, and leaving behind the valley of the Vydrica you arrive at **Spariská** (350 m a.s.l.) the highest point of the route ending in Krasňany (at the crossroads with the red-marked path turning left is the option of the route ending in Rača). Stick to the blue mark. After about 700 metres on flat terrain comes a steep descent (by 180 m over 2,500 m) passing through the forest and amidst vineyards ending in Pekná cesta road in **Krasňany**.

If you choose the option of Rača, turn left in Spariská and follow the red mark. A moderate ascent about 1,700 long around Horný Červený Kríž to Dolný Červený kríž up to about 410 m above sea level will bring you to the highest point of the route. The red hiking mark turns left and you continue straight ahead and after a while you will come to a steeply descending stretch (by 200 m over 2,100 m). Here you reach the blue hiking mark which will take you through the vineyards with dispersed huts in the locality of Kopanice to the historic centre of **Rača**.

Accommodation

Bratislava hotels are comparatively expensive though the locals pay half the price paid by foreigners. Regarding the limited number of hotels existing in Bratislava they are mostly booked up especially in the high tourist season and during fairs, or national or international events. Then there is no other way than to try private pensions or hostels.

The old hotels in the city centre were restored and along with the new ones they rank among the luxurious European establishments not only as far as their service is concerned, but also in price. Cheaper hotels are farther from the centre and the small hotels and pensions are also in peripheral parts of the city.

The hotels in Bratislava are classified into five categories. We have also classified the accommodation into five groups for easier orientation: luxurious four-star hotels, three-star hotels for demanding clients, two-star standard hotels, single-star simple hotels and cheap accommodation.

Luxurious hotels are equipped with modern technological appliances and an exclusive interior. All rooms have their bathrooms and separate lavatories, there is a TV set with satellite or cable transmission, a radio set, refrigerator, telephone and safe. A luxurious hotel provides almost all kinds of hotel service, including those of a personal nature, special services for travelling businessmen and business services. The offer of luxurious accommodation includes the Holiday Inn Hotel situated a bit outside the centre with a wide spectre of provided service: swimming pool, sauna, fitness centre, modern congress rooms, restaurant with excellent gastronomic specialities, and parking. The Devín Hotel situated right in the historic centre on the Danube embankment is also included among the luxurious establishments. It is an older hotel bearing the name of

Luxurious hotels

Hotel Devín,
Riečna 4,
☎ 54 43 08 51

Hotel Danube,
Rybné nám. 1,
☎ 59 34 08 34

Hotel Perugia,
Zelená 5,
☎ 54 43 18 24

Hotel Forum,
Hodžovo nám. 2,
☎ 59 34 81 11

Hotel Holiday Inn,
Bajkalská 25/a,
☎ 48 24 51 11

Hotel West,
Kamzík - les,
☎ 54 78 86 92

High standard hotels

Hotel Bratislava,
Seberíniho 9,
☎ 43 33 65 80

Hotel Dukla,
Dulovo nám. 1,
☎ 55 96 89 33

Hotel Incheba,
Viedenská cesta,
☎ 80 20 00

Hotel Kyjev,
Rajská 2,
☎ 52 92 20 41

Hotel Miva,
Bzovícka 38,
☎ 63 82 10 52

Castle of Devín. The completely modernized hotel offers accommodation in 100 air-conditioned rooms with classic interiors and a choice of single- or double rooms, or suits. The price includes breakfast served in the form of what is called "Swedish table". The hotel has got an exquisite French restaurant, a café with restaurant, aperitif bar, congress centre and luxurious salon.

In the immediate neighbourhood is the new Danube Hotel with appropriate comfort of equipment and service - car hire, parking, shops, conference rooms and the like. The Forum hotel, also located in the centre, is ideal for businessman and business events. It has got 219 rooms and 11 suits, three restaurants, cafés, a casino, bar, night club, fitness centre, sauna, swimming pool, solarium and a congress hall. The Perugia hotel is smaller and cosier one right in the centre of the pedestrian zone. It offers pleasant ambience and an outstanding cuisine. The first class West Hotel situated amidst the greenery of the Little Carpathians offers all that a modern and luxurious hotel should: single and double-bed rooms, suits and penthouses - luxuriously furnished apartments with a kitchenette and a complete service - an ideal solution for demanding clients staying away from their homes for a long time. There are also the Mexican restaurant, sauna, swimming pool, solarium and congress room. The environs of the hotel offer a choice of hiking or bike tours, a ski lift in winter and a summer bob track.

We also have included in the **category of hotels for demanding clients** the ones with smart, comfortable, and higher-standard equipment providing a wide spectrum of hotel and other services satisfying the personal or business demands of the guests. All rooms in these hotels have their own bathrooms and lavatories, colour TV

Hotel Tatra,
Nám. 1. mája 5,
☎ 52 92 21 11

Hotel Nr. 16,
Partizánska 16/a,
☎ 54 41 16 72

Hotel ~ Penzión Arcus,
Moskovská 5,
☎ 55 57 25 22

Penzión Grémium,
Gorkého 11,
☎ 54 13 10 26

Botel Fairway,
Nábr. L. Svobodu,
☎ 54 41 22 07

Botel Gracia,
Rázusovo nábr.,
☎ 54 43 21 31

Hotel Sorea,
Kráľovské údolie 6,
☎ 54 41 44 42

SIMPLE ACCOMMODATION ESTABLISHMENTS

Hotel Astra,
Prievozská 14/a,
☎ 53 41 40 16

Hotel Družba,
Botanická 33,
☎ 72 00 65

Hotel Flóra,
Zlaté piesky,
☎ 44 25 79 88

Hotel Junior,
Drieňová 14,
☎ 43 33 80 00

Hotel Nivy,
Záhradnícka 93,
☎ 55 57 03 90

Hotel Rapid,
Telocvičná 11,
☎ 43 41 02 57

Hotel Turist,
Ondavská 5,
☎ 55 57 27 89

Hotel Doprastav,
Košická 52,
☎ 55 57 43 13

Motel Evona,
Senecká cesta 2,
☎ 44 45 65 38

Karpatia
Poľný mlyn 1,
Záhorská Bystrica,
☎ 64 77 60 29

Youth hostels

Študentský domov J. Hronca,
Bernolákova 1,
☎ 52 49 77 23

ŠD M. Nešpora,
Svoradova 13,
☎ 54 41 53 86

ŠD Mladá garda,
Račianska 103,
☎ 44 25 31 36

ŠD Mladosť,
Staré grunty 36,
☎ 65 42 12 03

ŠD N. Belojanisa,
Wilsonova 6,
☎ 52 49 77 35

Kemp - Chatová osada Zlaté piesky,
Senecká cesta 2,
☎ 44 25 73 73

and radio sets, refrigerator, and telephone. They include the Kyjev Hotel in the city centre next to Tesco's department store. It offers an above-standard service such as trips, sport activities and meetings. Another hotel in the centre and next to the Presidential Palace is the Tatra Hotel. In the chamber ambience of the villa quarter below Bratislava Castle is No. 16 Hotel. Foreign visitors seek out this first class hotel above all. In the vicinity of the Slovak-Austrian frontier in the quarter of Petržalka is the modern Miva Hotel with a cafe, pizza restaurant, and supermarket. It provides top quality services satisfying the travelling businessman above all. The fair complex of Incheba contains a hotel bearing the same name used by the visitors to the Bratislava international fairs. This category includes the hotels on the other bank of the Danube: the Sorea Hotel and the ones rather retired from the centre such as Dukla and Bratislava Hotels. Gracia and Fairway are boat hotels; Arcus and Gremium are pensions, which contribute to the choice.

The **standard hotels** provide the service corresponding to this attribute. We have included in this group simple hotels and pensions. Such accommodation is normally outside the city centre in remote suburbs. The prices of accommodation and services are lower.

The **one-star or no star hotels** are even cheaper category. In spite of the lower standard of services provided they are also popular among visitors. A good example is the Doprastav Hotel situated in the wider centre of Bratislava not far from the Central Outdoor Market. Youth hostels are establishments offering cheap accommodation in clean and simple rooms with several beds and common bathrooms. They are suitable for short-term stays of larger groups of guests, above all young people.

Hotel	1	2	3	4	5	6	7	8
Danube	540	80	120	40	230	240	600	•••••
Forum	450	180	60		200	300	400	•••••
Devín	104	50	70		147	250	400	•••••
Holiday Inn	350	110	120			280	300	•••••
No 16	31	20						•••••
Perugia	26	40			60		250	•••••
Miva	33	40	20		75	20	150	••••
West	78	46	21		40	150	300	••••
Tatra	116	72	15		200		250	••••
Nivy	500	130			50			••••
Botel Fairway	53	60	60		12	150	250	••••
Botel Gracia	47	60					250	••••
Chez David	18	50					250	••••
Bratislava	628	100	100				250	•••
Echo	60	80		15	25	30	250	•••
Incheba	76	80	40	40	50	150	200	•••
Sorea	130	120	150	40	150	120	180	•••
Astra	84	80		30	50			•••
Rapid	55	100	40		50	80	140	•••
Remy	94	60				70		•••
Turist	195	80		30	30	80	180	•••
Penzión Arcus	28							•••
Penzión Grémium	9	42	100		22		200	•••
Dom športu	120	250	60		290			•••
Barónka	245	100	20	70	30	120	200	••
Áno prosím	132	100		50	250	150	250	••
TOP	56				40	100	120	••
ŠD J. Hronca	328		20	30	50	75	150	••
ŠD Mladosť	432					60	80	••
ŠD N. Belojanisa	200					80	110	•
ŠD Mladá garda	500		30	40	500			•
ŠD M. Nešpora	155			100				•
Javorina	102	90		30	35			•

Kapacita	1 Ubytovanie	2 Reštaurácia	3 Kaviareň	4 Vináreň	5 Kongresová sála
Capacity	1 Accomodation	2 Restaurant	3 Café	4 Wine Bar	5 Congress room
Kapazität	1 Unterkunft	2 Restaurant	3 Café	4 Weinstube	5 Kongreßsall
Férőhely	1 Szállás	2 Vendéglőt	3 Kávéház	4 Borozó	5 Kongresszterem

Orientačná cena	6 Raňajky	7 Obed	8 Ubytovanie	•	< 500 Sk
Orientational price	6 Breakfast	7 Lunch	8 Accomodation	••	500 – 1000 Sk
Orientierungspreis	6 Frühstück	7 Mittagessen	8 Unterkunft	•••	1001 – 2000 Sk
Megközelítő ár	6 Reggeli	7 Ebéd	8 Szállás	••••	2001 – 3000 Sk
				•••••	> 3000 Sk

Restaurants

Arkádia,
Zámocké schody 3,
☎ 54 43 56 50

Harmónia,
Ventúrska 9,
☎ 54 43 16 83

Maria Theresia,
Palisády 50,
☎ 52 92 55 90

Aušpic,
Viedenská cesta 24,
☎ 62 25 09 16

Biela pani,
Jozefská 11,
☎ 54 43 50 34

Červený rak,
Michalská 26,
☎ 54 43 13 75

Leberfinger,
Viedenská cesta 257,
☎ 62 31 75 90

Reduta,
Medená 3,
☎ 54 43 52 42

Divný Janko,
Jozefská 2,
☎ 54 43 04 18

Rybársky cech,
Žižkova 1,
☎ 54 41 30 49

Slovenská reštaurácia,
Hviezdoslavovo nám. 20,
☎ 54 43 48 83

Terno,
Nám. SNP 30,
☎ 54 43 53 89

U Liszta,
Klariská 1,
☎ 54 41 25 40

Food and beverages

An immediate and simple way of becoming familiar with the nature of any town is by tasting the local food. Bratislava offers numerous opportunities for this.

The original cuisine of Bratislava is varied, fancy, and tasty thanks to the gastronomic influences of the surrounding European regions. As far as the food customs are concerned, certain principles are adhered to: breakfast is rather modest, lunch is served comparatively early: between 11:00 and 13:00 and consists mostly of two dishes. Dinner is served from 17:00 and it is more substantial. Some restaurants serve meals anytime until late evening hours.

Details are not less important: an aperitif before the meal, which is usually accompanied by beer, wine or in the event of some celebrations a bottle of Champagne. Dessert is followed by a cup of coffee, occasionally a glass of cognac. Fast food is also represented in Bratislava (establishments of McDonald's).

Let the waiters advise you before ordering a meal and try some of the local specialities. Although the Bratislava restaurants tend to offer foreign meals, traditional Slovak or Bratislava meals also appear on their menus.

The majority of the restaurants are in the city centre but it is also worth going a little further to the remoter parts where you can

find outstanding food for more acceptable prices. The cheapest food is available from stands (*buffets*) with refreshment offering sausages, frankfurters, buns and sandwiches. The common Slovak meals are offered by inns and taverns though they mostly live on tapped beer or wine.

Restaurants

The best ones are those that cater for foreign clients. They are much more expensive than the popular establishments but their service and cuisine are of top quality. In such restaurants they find you a place, they offer you hors d'oeuvres and do not be surprised if you find various surplus charges on your bill, such as cutlery, milk, bread, butter or ketchup. If you want to have a special meal in a smart ambience go for instance to the Harmónia restaurant and if you want to experience old aristocratic manners, perfect service with all details, chose Maria Theresia restaurant in the centre. It is one of the best in Bratislava.

A different, Baroque or Rococo atmosphere from Mozart's time is found in the luxurious restaurant of the Reduta with an offer of Austro-Hungarian specialities and a wide choice of international cuisine satisfying not only your stomach but also your eyes.

A Slovak restaurant in the traditional folk style with authentic wooden furniture and the typical Slovak meals from different regions is located on Hviezdoslavovo námestie square. The varied menu offers a great choice of quality meals, for instance, the Slovak cabbage, bean, and mushroom soups, potato dumplings; authentic Slovak dumplings with salted cheese and a great variety of fish specialities. By the way, the visitors of Bratislava keen on fish meals should visit the renovated and modernized Fish Guild (Rybársky cech) catering excellent fish meals including the Hungarian fish soup called *Halászlé* and different sea and river fish meals. The

class of the restaurant is confirmed, beside other things, also by the fact that they use silver cutlery.

Snack bars are cheaper and quicker and some of them offer a lot of varied little snacks to be taken in the company of friends or colleagues.

Cafés

More comfort and a pleasant atmosphere is offered by the cafés. Some of them boast a long tradition

CAFÉS

Bystrica,
Nový most,
☎ 62 31 77 46

Kaffe Mayer,
Hlavné nám. 4,
☎ 54 41 17 41

Jazz Café,
Ventúrska 5,
☎ 54 43 46 61

Galéria Café,
Panská 12,
☎ 54 43 12 28

Korzo - kaviareň,
Hviezdoslavovo nám. 11,
☎ 54 43 17 96

Piano bar,
Laurinská 11,
☎ 54 41 58 80

Café Regina,
Hurbanovo nám. 7,
☎ 54 41 64 31

U anjelov,
Laurinská 19,
☎ 54 43 27 24

U mamičky,
Majakovského 9,
☎ 54 43 46 18

PIZZERIAS

La Tratoria,
Ferienčíkova 3,
☎ 52 96 16 20

Pizza Bolero,
Starohájska cesta 35,
☎ 62 41 16 00

Pizza Caesar,
Rovniankova 9,
☎ 63 83 98 39

Pizzeria - Restaurant Corleone, Hviezdoslavovo nám. 21, ☎ 54 43 55 48

Pizza Dano, Hálova 5, ☎ 62 24 23 89

Pizza House, Hviezdoslavovo nám. 15, ☎ 54 43 18 40

Pizza Hut, Drevená 8, ☎ 54 41 76 66

Pizzeria Alviano, Rybničná 13, ☎ 43 71 15 05

Pizzeria Ciao, Trnavská cesta 37, ☎ 44 37 33 67

Pizzeria Diabolíno, Balkánska 150, ☎ 62 85 96 64

Pizzeria Dominika, Vlastenecké nám. 3, ☎ 62 24 21 70

Pizzeria La Mamma, Škultétyho 10, ☎ 44 37 19 38

Pizzeria Romantika, Gaštanová 6, ☎ 54 77 76 74

Pizzeria Saranda Ristorante, Dr. V. Clementisa, ☎ 43 33 50 29

EXOTIC AND FOREIGN RESTAURANTS

Bambusová záhrada, Františkánske nám. 3, ☎ 54 43 24 26

and are proud of the fact that famous figures from various spheres were visited them including intellectuals, artists, students, and bohemians. Former "legends" among the cafés are trying to restore their past glory: Grand, Astorka, Múzejka, Berlínka, Tatra, Alžbetka or Štefanka and Savoy Carlton are among them. Many achieved the top European level and all of them have a wide choice ranging from simple cakes and sandwiches to complete meals. A visitor to Bratislava should not miss the café of Bystrica above the New Bridge with unique view of the city. Especially in the night the city evokes a romantic atmosphere. Lovers of sweets and pastries or tarts should go to the classic Viennese café and sweetshop Café Mayer. The Piano bar is in the style of the thirties or forties in the centre of the Old Town. This establishment arranged in artistic spirit with pleasant and discreet music offers an original atmosphere. If that does not satisfy you and you want to feel like in heaven go to the café U anjelov (At the Angels), a perfect café with first class service, personal approach, little specialities topped by an excellent coffee. Those who want to avoid the busy city streets should try Regina Café next to the Michalská brána gate with a wide offer and good service and the opportunity to meet some famous Bratislava figures.

Pizzerias

They have a place among the favourite restau-

rants of the Bratislavians and the tourists. There are several in the city centre and all of them offer typical Italian meals: several kinds of spaghettis and pizzas and a variety of vegetable salads. Such meal should be accompanied by a good Italian wine and why not a portion of seducing ice cream. One of the best pizzerias in Bratislava is Corleone Pizzeria, which also offers other than Italian specialities. Pizza House is in the same locality with a wide offer of pasta meals served by quick and polite staff in a cultivated atmosphere. Typical Italian restaurant is La Trattoria on the edge of the Old Town, which apart from the Italian meals serves marine fish, and a good choice of light Italian wines.

Exotic and foreign restaurants

You can eat Chinese, Japanese, Thai or Mexican meals in Bratislava. Especially the number of Chinese restaurants has increased recently. The tasty Chinese food is available for example in Jasmín restaurant right below Bratislava Castle famous for its high quality. Traditional Chinese meals including shrimp or sour soups, baked Pekinese duck or kung-pao are prepared here. There are other Chinese restaurants such as Palatín and Bambusová záhrada in the city centre, which attract the guests with their calm and pleasant ambience, exclusive meals and special menus with an additional take-away service. Unique and original restaurants are the

Japanese Sushi bar and restaurant Tokyo offering Japanese and Thai cuisine. The busy atmosphere of Mexico can be experienced in the restaurant serving Mexican food. Its name Hystéria is an appropriate one because there is always temperamental youth having a good time with hot Mexican gravies and tapped beer.

Čárda Kormorán on the bank of the Petržalka lake Draždiak brought an atmosphere of the typical Hungarian csardas dance music

Čárda Kormorán,
Veľký Draždiak,
☎ 63 82 82 52

Čínska reštaurácia Shanghai,
Prievozská 14/A,
☎ 53 41 50 79

Čínska reštaurácia,
Laurinská 3,
☎ 54 43 38 65

Delfín,
Ružová dolina 18,
☎ 53 41 55 57

Francúzska reštaurácia,
Riečna 4,
☎ 54 43 08 51

Jadran Gril - gyros,
Rybárska brána,
☎ 54 43 12 83

Hysteria pub,
Odbojárov 9,
☎ 44 45 44 95

Japonská reštaurácia Tokyo,
Stromová 16,
☎ 54 77 54 06

McDonald's,
Nám. SNP 14,
☎ 52 92 19 27

McDonald's,
Obchodná 58,
☎ 52 73 13 28

Palatín,
Laurinská 3,
☎ 54 43 38 65

Reštaurácia a kaviareň Perla,
Mariánska 11,
☎ 52 96 44 93

Reštaurácia Chez David,
Zámocká 13,
☎ 54 41 38 24

Reštaurácia Jasmín,
Židovská 7,
☎ 54 41 51 82

Spaghetti & co.,
Gorkého 1,
☎ 54 43 23 03

Sushi bar,
Panská 27,
☎ 54 43 49 82

U vychádzajúceho slnka,
Dobšinského 18,
☎ 52 49 20 22

WINE BARS

Šenkvická viecha,
Panenská 33,
☎ 54 41 90 24

Bakchus,
Hlboká cesta 5,
☎ 52 49 41 78

Hradná vináreň,
Bratislavský hrad,
☎ 59 34 13 58

Kláštorná vináreň,
Františkánska 2,
☎ 54 43 04 30

Modrá hviezda,
Beblavého 14,
☎ 54 43 27 47

U Dežmára,
Klariská 1,
☎ 54 43 15 11

U zlatého jeleňa,
Vysoká 32,
☎ 52 93 22 32

Veľkí františkáni,
Františkánske nám. 10,
☎ 54 43 30 73

Malí františkáni,
Nám. SNP 24,
☎ 54 43 25 36

and a choice of excellent Hungarian food to the city.

If you seek perfect atmosphere and are fan of authentic French food, visit the Devín Hotel and its French restaurant. You can accompany the prepared meals by some older year of French wine and enjoy a high level service. Greek food is available in the restaurant Delfín or in Jadran grill-gorys. Swedish meals are served in the snack bar of the Ikea department store, the Balkans are represented by the restaurant of the Miva Hotel or in U mamičky in the wonderful environment of a garden with a swimming pool above Bratislava Castle.

The taverns and wine bars

A good wine should accompany a good meal. The viticultural traditions of Bratislava date to the Roman era of the region, which was always favourable to grape growing and production of excellent and fine wines. The taverns of Bratislava were special in the sense that they sold wine only in the grape-picking season and only in the houses of vintners. The old Pressburg taverns disappeared, but the good Little Carpathian or Bratislava wines are still here and have preserved their traditional sparkle. The best known Bratislava wine bars include first of all Kláštorná vináreň, Šenkvická viecha, Veľkí Františkáni or Malí Františkáni while the last mentioned is the one most similar to the old taverns. Kláštorná is a typical tavern in cellars and apart from the wines of domestic and foreign production it also serves food. Veľkí Františkáni also has a restaurant in folk style and it is popular among the young people, while university students prefer Šenkvická viecha with its cheap but excellent bean or tripe soups and the "cattle goulash".

Pubs

Beer is the most sought after and popular beverage. Its rich history and tradition in the neighbouring Bohemia has been adopted also in Slovakia. The typical bitter flavour of beer tastes best in a pub.

The Old Malthouse colloquially called Mamut (The Mammoth) is the largest beer hall in Bratislava, which offers numerous trademarks of beer. It consists of several rooms including the Bingo hall, billiard tables, a restaurant offering grilled meals or baked ribs, plain hash and crumbs, sausages, etc. The newly established Kelt pub with imitated Celtic decoration is also a favourite one.

The original interior of Irish pub, The Dubliner, with its unique Irish atmosphere and an offer of typical Irish meals enriched the Old Town and quickly won its fans among the Bratislavians and the foreign visitors of the city.

Harley Davidson Pub is the name of a very specific pub in the boundary of the urban districts of Vrakuňa and Ružinov. Its regular guests are the fans of good and high-performing motorbikes and the related way of life. The interior of the pub is divided into several parts where you can listen to the music of some popular group or watch strip tease both female and male, in a friendly atmosphere.

PUBS

Corgoň,
Šustekova 17,
☎ 62 31 86 91

Harley Davidson,
Rebarborová 1,
☎ 43 19 10 95

Irish pub,
Sedlárska 6,
☎ 54 41 07 06

Jadran ASI,
Nevädzová 5,
☎ 43 33 08 09

KGB,
Obchodná 52,
☎ 52 73 12 79

Stará sladovňa,
Cintorínska 32,
☎ 52 92 11 51

U Jozefa,
Klenová 20,
☎ 54 77 12 21

U lipy,
Daliborovo nám. 3,
☎ 63 45 11 94

Camel Pub,
Ventúrska 4,
☎ 54 41 84 64

Hockey Club,
Ondavská 3,
☎ 55 56 79 68

Kelt,
Hviezdoslavovo nám. 26,
☎ 54 41 15 89

17's,
Hviezdoslavovo nám. 17,
☎ 54 43 51 35

Antiques

Antikva,
Prepoštská 4,
☎ 54 43 33 75,
open
Mo-Fri, 10-16.30

Galéria Antika Dorota,
Mýtna 31,
☎ 52 49 75 76,
open
Mo-Thurs, 10-17.30

Galéria Maráky,
Panská 17,
☎ 54 43 26 61,
open
Tue-Fri, 10-13, 14-18,
Sa 10-13

Art Decoration,
Kozia 15,
☎ 54 41 23 70,
open
Mo-Fri, 12-18

Secession,
Palackého 8,
☎ 54 43 16 90,
open
Mo-Fri, 10-11.45,
13-17.30

Stanley Art,
Ventúrska 12,
☎ 54 41 15 25,
open
Mo-Fri, 10-18.30

Books

Artfórum,
Kozia 20,
☎ 54 41 72 32,
open
Mo-Fri, 10-19,
Sa-Sun, 9-13

Gump,
Uršulínska 9,
☎ 54 41 15 76,
open
Mo-Fri, 9-19,
Sa 10-20,
Sun 14-20

Luxor,
Štúrova 3,
☎ 52 96 78 81,
open
Mo-Fri, 9-19,
Sa 9-14

Shopping

Statistics say that the purchasing power of the citizens of Bratislava is the best in Slovakia. This is also the reason Bratislava has got a number of shopping centres, department stores, small and big shops with luxurious or cheap goods of all kinds. But Bratislava is not a cheap city at all. Economizing Bratislavians have got used to do their shopping at time of sales and special offers of some shopping centres.

Obchodná, Michalská, Laurinská streets, the passages and big department stores and shopping centres represent the shopping "paradise" of the city. One can also visit the outdoor and indoor markets offering everything ranging from fresh vegetable and fruit to imported clothes and handmade products.

The shops are normally open from 9:00 to 18:00, Saturdays only in the morning. But there are exceptions as many shops depend on tourists and adapt their opening hours to the demand. The big department stores such as Tesco, IKEA and Soravia open continuously from Monday to Sunday.

Antiques

They are concentrated mostly in the Old town and one can admire and buy there wonderful and mute witnesses of history – Middle Ages, Neo Classicism, Impressionism or Futurism. Collectors should go to Galéria Antika Dorota, Galéria Maraky, Art Decorations, Stanley art or Secession offering some remarkable end-of-the-century objects.

Books

A varied offer of books of different genres can be found in the bookshops. The largest and the most interesting ones are in the centre including the foreign literature bookshops. The newly opened Luxor bookshop on Štúrova ulica is the largest of the city. Its luxurious setting with many thematic departments also offers "luxurious" and good books. Artfórum and Gump specialize in non-commercial literature and are the favourite ones in Bratislava. You will find here philosophical, artistic, politological books, good journals, fiction, poetry, compact discs, and even comics. Ex Libris bookshop is in line with the two last mentioned. Big Ben Book Shop is a specialised bookshop selling English literature. Second-hand books, old and precious prints, rare editions are sold in Steiner and spe-

cialized literature, maps or atlases are found in Edia. The Dobrá kniha bookshop sells religious books.

Souvenirs and gifts

If you are one of those who like lovely hand made folk or handicraft ware even in the present time of mass production, Bratislava has something to offer. Typical Slovak hand made products, embroidery, leather or wrought iron and carved wood artefacts are sold in the shops Folk Folk and ÚĽUV in the centre. If you are interested in trademark and luxurious gifts, glass and porcelain, visit the shops Krištáľ Sklo Porcelán, Porcela Plus Slovakia, Moser, SM Glass Store, all of them in the centre and you will certainly choose from cut class vases, glasses, ash-trays, bowls or little statues, cups, etc. Specialized wine shops with a varied choice of wine from all over the world offer a different kind of gift. You will find them in the Old Town and the largest are Vinotéka San Francisco and Vinotéka Sv. Urbana. If you are not quite sure what kind of gift you are looking for go to Twiggy, Aleana-etno shop, Wiedler, Galéria Vivo in the centre and chose something original and specific from the domestic and imported production.

Shopping centres

All in one and the broadest assortment of goods is offered by the large modern department stores and shopping centres, the number of which is constantly increasing, above all in the periphery. One of the largest shopping centres in now under construction next to the football stadium of AŠK Inter and it will also have recreational facilities.

The most popular department stores in the centre are Tesco and Dunaj with the contiguous Dom odievania. A new and smart CITY Center was recently opened in Obchodná ulica street with quality goods. IKEA sells furniture and items of interior decoration. It is outside the

SOUVENIRS AND GIFTS

Folk Folk,
Rybárska brána,
☎ 54 43 48 74,
open
Mo-Thurs, 10-18,
Pi 10-19,
Sa 10-18,
Sun 10-17

ÚĽUV,
Michalská 4,
☎ 54 43 22 88,
open
Mo-Fri, 10-18,
Sa 9-13

Krištáľ Sklo Porcelán,
Poštová 3,
☎ 52 96 76 83,
open
Mo-Fri, 10-18,
Sa 9-13

Porcela Plus Slovakia,
Štúrova 9,
☎ 52 96 74 03,
open
Mo-Fri, 10-18,
Sa 9-13

Moser,
Zelená 1-3,
☎ 54 43 55 10,
open
Mo-Fri, 10-18,
Sa 9-13

Lýdia Krištáľ, Porcelán,
Panská 6,
☎ 54 41 85 39,
open
Mo-Fri, 9-18,
Sa 9-13,
Sun 15-18

SM Glass Store,
Laurinská 6,
☎ 54 41 29 26,
open
Mo-Fri, 9.30-19,
Sa 9.30-14.30,
Sun 13-18

Vinotéka sv. Urbana,
Klobučnícka 4,
☎ 54 43 25 37,
open
Mo-Fri, 10-18,
Sa 10-14

Twigi,
Klariská 7,
☎ 54 43 38 06,
open
Mon-Sa, 10-19,
Sun 14-19

Wiedler,
Hlavné nám. 4,
☎ 54 41 18 43,
open
Mo-Fri, 10-19,
Sa 10-18,
Sun 11-19

SHOPPING CENTRES

Tesco,
Kamenné nám. 1,
open
Mon-St, 8-19,
Thur 8-20,
Fri 8-21,
Sa 8-17,
Sun 9-17

OD Dunaj,
Nám. SNP 30,
☎ 54 43 08 89,
open
Mo-Fri, 9-19,
Sa 9-14

CITY Center,
Obchodná 58,
open
Mo-Fri, 10-19,
Sa 9.30-14

IKEA,
Tomášikova 46,
☎ 43 29 38 30,
open
Mon-Sun, 10-20

Baumax,
Rožňavská 4,
☎ 48 27 83 10,
open
Mon-Sa, 8-19.30,
Sun 9-19.30

Shopping Park Soravia,
Rožňavská 34,
☎ 43 41 08 07,
open
Mo-Fri, 9-20,
Sa 9-18,
Sun 10-17

centre on the road to Piešťany. A bit farther on the same road is Baumax selling the household and garden utensils and out on the edge of the city is a new shopping complex SP Soravia.

Outdoor and indoor markets

The outdoor markets of Bratislava have a unique atmosphere with a mixture of smells, sounds, colours and forms. You can buy there fresh vegetable and fruit, poultry, flowers, clothes, and electronic appliances. One large outdoor market is in Miletičova and two huge indoor markets are in Trnavské mýto square and in the centre on the SNP square.

Entertainment

Bratislava has not got anything that might be called a quarter dedicated to entertainment, but in spite of this there is a considerable offer. Lovers of movies, theatre, music or dance will find what are they looking for.

The survey of cultural and social events, cinema or theatre programmes is normally announced in the daily newspapers or specialized bulletin *Kam v Bratislave* or you can go and inquire at the Bratislava Information Service. Entrance cards are sold directly at the cash boxes or you can purchase them in advance. Groups can ask for reservations in writing, telephone ordering is not possible yet.

Theatres

Bratislava has a comparatively great number of theatres for a small city. The majority of being rather permanent theatres are in the centre. The theatre season starts usually in September and ends in June. July and August are the time of theatre vacations. One can attend open-air performances in summertime, which are usually held in the historic courtyards of old Bratislava or in parks and gardens. Most of the shows start at 19:00 and be prepared for the fact they are generally sold out.

The stars of the Slovak theatre can be seen live on the stages of the Slovak National Theatre, the Theatre of P. O. Hviezdoslav and in Malá scéna of the SND.

A specific and attractive atmosphere is found in the theatre shows of the chamber Theatre Astorka Korzo of the Slovak National Theatre.

The L+S Studio in Tatra Passage with shows made for the two personalities of Slovak comedy Milan Lasica and Július Satinský have their steady fans thanks to their intellectual and poetic humour and the top artistic performance of the pair. The West Theatre with casual and commercial programme is in the centre. The Aréna Theatre of the world famous mime Milan Sládek has an attractive position on the Danube embankment in the Sad Janka Kráľa park.

Other small theatres found their home in various cultural establishments, for instance Divadielko a.ha works in the local cultural centres, the popular Radošinské Naive Theátre usually appears in one of the theatre halls of Istropolis, and the STOKA theatre is active in the former trade union club close to the Danube.

Theatres

Divadlo P. O. Hviezdoslava,
Laurinská 21,
☎ 54 43 30 83

Nová scéna,
Kollárovo nám. 20,
☎ 52 92 57 41

Malá scéna,
Dostojevského rad 7,
☎ 52 92 37 75

Divadlo Astorka, Korzo 90,
Suché mýto 17,
☎ 54 43 20 93

Divadlo West,
Kolárska 3,
tel. 52 96 58 32

Divadlo GUnaGU,
(Klub Čierny havran),
Biela 6,
☎ 54 43 29 42

Divadlo Stoka,
Pribinova 1,
☎ 52 92 44 63

Divadlo Aréna,
Viedenská cesta 10,
☎ 54 43 38 67,
(pokladnica PKO)

Radošinské naivné divadlo,
Škultétyho 5,
☎ 55 56 35 08

Štúdio S,
Nám. 1. mája 5,
☎ 52 96 75 52

Divadlo a.ha.,
Školská 14,
☎ 0905 43 53 22

Štátne bábkové divadlo,
Dunajská 36,
☎ 52 92 36 68

Concerts, opera and ballet

Slovenské národné divadlo,
Hviezdoslavovo nám. 1,
☎ 54 43 30 83

Slovenská filharmónia,
Medená 3,
☎ 54 43 33 51-3

Klub Jazz-Avi,
K. Adlera 22,
☎ 64 36 89 96

CINEMAS

Hviezda,
Nám. 1. mája 11,
☎ 52 96 74 71

Mladosť,
Hviezdoslavovo nám. 17,
☎ 54 43 50 03

YMCA,
Karpatská 2,
☎ 52 49 87 88

Obzor,
Radlinského 18,
☎ 52 49 75 22

Tatra,
Nám. 1. mája 7,
☎ 52 96 89 94

Charlie centrum,
Špitálska 4,
☎ 52 96 33 96

Istropolis,
Trnavské mýto 1,
☎ 50 22 82 41

Istota,
Karloveská 4,
☎ 60 29 72 83

DISCOS AND NIGHT CLUBS

Casiopea night club,
Nobelova 32

Bajkal,
Bajkalská 27

Hotel Forum night club,
Hodžovo nám. 2,
☎ 59 34 89 36

Hysteria pub,
Odbojárov 9,
☎ 44 45 44 95

Concerts, opera and ballet

Bratislava is also called the city of music although a short-term visitor cannot always personally experience it. Enormous demand results in the tickets being are sold out long before the events.

The focus of Bratislava music life is the Slovak National Theatre. The opera of Bratislava is much sought after because of its top singers represented by such figures as Peter Dvorský, Ľubica Rybárska, and Michal Babjak whose quality is also recognized abroad. The majority of the opera shows of the SND (Slovak National Theatre) are performed in their original languages, which is appreciated above all by foreigners. In the immediate vicinity of the historic building of the SND is Reduta, the concert hall of the Slovak Philharmonic Orchestra. The offer of musicals is varied, and successful shows are sold out on the day when the sale of the tickets starts. Jazz concerts are organized by Jazz-Avi regularly on Tuesdays and Thursdays. Once a year in autumn International Jazz Days are held in Bratislava and their level is excellent. The main event of classic music is the Bratislava Music Festival also held in autumn.

Cinemas

All larger cinemas are in the city centre. Their programme consists mostly of popular Hollywood films. Small club-type cinemas though, also offer more serious and recognized movies. You will find detailed information of the movie programme in the weekly *Kam v Bratislave* or the *Metropol*, the journal published twice a month. Both are sold at newspaper stands.

Discos and night clubs

Although the nightlife of Bratislava lags behind that of other European metropols there are some opportunities to have fun and dance all night.

The most popular and the oldest establishment of this type is Jalta in the centre, which apart from a musical program offers striptease shows.

One of the largest entertainment centres of Bratislava, Bajkal offers a varied program. It is open the whole week and there is the exclusive Raiders café with pleasant music, the Indian salon and Extreme Club. For its capacity of 800 persons it is probably the largest entertainment centre in Slovakia. You can visit it on Fridays and Saturdays from 20:00 to 06:00 hours. A favourite club for its pop-

ular house parties moderated by the Bratislava and foreign DJ's is the U-Club. Further from the centre, in the 3rd Bratislava district there are two popular establishments under a common roof: Cassiopeia nightclub and Queen's club. The first is a big modern disco established in the former cinema and the latter is a smaller stylish club organising various music parties.

Casinos

If you have still some money left and want to take a risk in American of French roulette, blackjack or boule you can visit one of the Bratislava casinos. Some are in the building of Reduta, in Park Casino or the casino of the Forum Hotel.

Sport and recreation areas

Sport, bathing, and recreation have their centres outside the city and in the periphery. The Zlaté piesky lake with tennis courts, volleyball grounds, table tennis, football and billiard is the most popular among Bratislavians. Kuchajda is a similar lake, which originated after extraction of gravel and it has boat leasing and volleyball grounds, the artificial lake of Štrkovec likewise has grounds for ball games, tennis, soft-tennis, table tennis and hall football. You can swim in the indoor swimming pool of Športová hala and Športová hala Mladosť in Pasienky equipped with a fitness centre and sauna.

The most popular and most visited sport events are the football and ice hockey matches. The clubs of Bratislava are among the best of Slovakia and they can be watched at the football stadiums of Tehelné pole, Pasienky and indoor ice-rings of Ondrej Nepela and Vladimír Dzurilla.

Jalta bar,
Gorkého 15,
☎ 54 43 04 88

Smirnoff,
Šafárikovo nám. 7,
☎ 52 92 54 72

Steps,
Panenská 27,
☎ 54 43 07 51

Queens Pub,
Nobelova 32

U-Club,
Nábr. L. Svobodu,
☎ 0905 27 49 06

Casinos

Kasíno Park,
Hviezdoslavovo nám. 21,
☎ 54 43 16 69

Kasíno Fórum,
Hodžovo nám. 2,
☎ 59 34 01 11

Kasíno Reduta,
Mostová 3,
☎ 54 43 20 21

Swimming pools

Delfín,
Ružová dolina 18,
☎ 53 41 55 53

Krytá plaváreň,
Junácka 4,
☎ 44 25 67 69

ŠK Iskra Matadorfix,
Údernícka 20,
☎ 63 83 05 24

Rosnička (STARZ),
Dolné Krčace,
☎ 64 36 09 60

Tehelné pole (STARZ),
Odbojárov 9,
☎ 44 37 28 28

Zlaté piesky,
Senecká cesta 2,
☎ 44 25 70 18

IMPORTANT INFORMATION

Bratislava Information Service, Klobučnícka 2, ☎ 161 86, 54 43 43 70, 54 43 37 15
Police ☎ 158
Fire unit ☎ 150
Pharmacies with emergency service
Nám. SNP 20, ☎ 54 43 29 52
Ružinovská 12, ☎ 43 33 11 43
Líščie údolie 57, ☎ 65 42 58 66, 65 42 59 62
Strečnianska 1, ☎ 63 83 58 68
Bus terminal, Mlynské nivy ☎ 0984 22 22 22
Main railway station ☎ 50 58 44 84
M. R. Štefánik Airport, Bratislava Ivánka ☎ 48 57 33 53
Danube Passenger Harbour ☎ 52 93 22 26
Telephone enquiry ☎ 120, 121
Road administration (Improper parking) ☎ 45 24 99 11, 0905 62 31 21

AIRLINES
AEROFLOT, Laurinská 13, ☎ 54 43 51 92
AUSTRIAN AIRLINES, Rybné nám. 1, ☎ 54 41 16 26
BRITISH AIRWAYS, Štefánikova 22, ☎ 52 49 98 01-2
CZECH AIRLINES, Štúrova 13, ☎ 52 96 10 38
DELTA AIRLINES, Rajská 2, ☎ 52 92 09 40
LOT, Polish Airlines, Špitálska 51, ☎ 52 96 40 07
LUFTHANSA LAUDA AIR, Štúrova 4, ☎ 52 96 78 07
SLOVAK AERLINES, Trnavská 56, ☎ 44 45 60 01, 44 45 40 64
AIR FRANCE, Prievozská 6/A, ☎ 53 41 98 12

BANKS AND FINANCIAL INSTITUTIONS
We recommend changing money in banks and exchange offices.
Exchange offices are placed in hotels, tourist bureau's, and at border crossing check points.

BANKS AND EXCHANGE OFFICES
Ľudová banka, Vysoká 9, ☎ 59 65 11 11
Československá obchodná banka, Michalská 18, ☎ 59 34 51 11
Banka Austria, Mostová 6, ☎ 59 69 11 11
City bank, Viedenská cesta 5, ☎ 68 27 81 11
Credit Lyonnais bank Slovakia, Klemensova 2/A, ☎ 59 26 21 11
Devín banka, Františkánske nám. 8, ☎ 54 43 10 70
Internationale Nederlanden Bank, Kolárska 6, ☎ 59 34 61 11
Investičná a rozvojová banka, Štúrova 5, ☎ 59 79 11 11
Istrobanka, Laurinská 1, ☎ 59 39 71 11
Konsolidačná banka Bratislava, Cintorínska 21, ☎ 52 92 13 87
Poštová banka, Gorkého 3, ☎ 59 60 31 11
Poľnobanka, Vajnorská 21, ☎ 49 50 21 11
Prvá stavebná sporiteľňa, Bajkalská cesta 30, ☎ 58 23 11 11
Slovenská sporiteľňa, Nám. SNP 18, ☎ 59 77 11 11
Slovenská záručná a rozvojová banka, Štefánikova 27, ☎ 57 29 21 11
Stavebná sporiteľňa Wüstenrot, Grösslingova 77, ☎ 59 27 51 11
Tatra banka, Vajanského nábrežie 5, ☎ 68 65 11 11
Všeobecná úverová banka, Nám. SNP 19, ☎ 59 55 11 11

CAR RENTALS
ADECAR, Hybešova 36, ☎ 44 88 15 72
AUTOPROGRES, Karpatské nám. 23, ☎ 44 88 66 50
HERZ - TRADEX, Airport, ☎ 43 29 14 82
LE - CAR, Starohradská 10, ☎ 63 83 42 68, 6 381 05 83
PROFIT - CAR, Hagarova 9, ☎ 44 88 50 03
SLOVCAR, Gagarinova 17, ☎ 43 41 18 49, 43 41 18 50
STOP - CAR, Púpavova 33, ☎ 65 42 72 01
STOP - PAL - CAR ☎ 65 42 72 02, 65 42 72 20
TOLEDO CAR, Saratovská 12, ☎ 64 28 44 95
VRÁBLIK RENT A CAR, Čiernovodská 6, ☎ 45 24 74 07

CROSS BORDER CHECK POINTS
To Austria:
Bratislava Petržalka - Berg, ☎ 63 83 85 43
Jarovce - Kittsee, ☎ 62 86 01 19 (lorries up to 3,5 tons)
Bratislava - harbour, ☎ 52 93 22 26
To Hungary:
Rusovce - Rajka, ☎ 62 85 91 98

FOREIGN REPRESENTATIVES
Apostolic nunciature (The Holy See Embassy)
Uršulínska 3, 811 01 Bratislava, ☎54 79 35 28
Embassy of the Republic of Bulgaria
Kuzmányho 1, 811 06 Bratislava, ☎ 54 43 59 71, 54 41 53 08
Embassy of the Kingdom of Belgium
F. Kráľa 5, 811 05 Bratislava, ☎ 52 49 13 38
Embassy of the Czech Republic
29. augusta 5, P. O. Box 208, 810 00 Bratislava, ☎ 52 93 12 04, 52 93 12 05
General Honorary Consulate of the Kingdom of Denmark
Ventúrska 12, 815 16 Bratislava, ☎ 54 41 84 70-1
Embassy of the Republic of France
Hlavné nám. 7, 812 83 Bratislava, ☎ 54 43 57 45
Embassy of Greece
Panská 14, 811 01 Bratislava, ☎ 54 43 41 43
Embassy of the Kingdom of Holland
Fraňa Kráľa 5, 811 05 Bratislava, ☎ 52 49 15 77
Embassy of the Republic of Croatia
Mišíkova 21, 811 19 Bratislava, ☎ 54 43 36 47
Consulate of the Canadian embassy for technical co-operation
Mišíkova 28 D, 811 03 Bratislava, ☎ 52 44 21 75
Honorary Consulate of the Grand Duchy of Luxembourg
Bajkalská 25, 827 18 Bratislava, ☎ 53 41 85 85
Embassy of the Republic of Hungary
Sedlárska 3, 814 25 Bratislava, ☎ 54 43 05 41
Embassy of the Republic of Poland
Hummelova 4, 811 01 Bratislava, ☎ 54 41 31 74
Embassy of the Republic of Austria
Ventúrska 10, 811 03 Bratislava, ☎ 54 43 29 85
Embassy of the Republic of Romania
Fraňa Kráľa 11, 811 05 Bratislava, ☎ 52 49 16 65, 52 49 35 62
Embassy of the Russian Federation
Godrova 4, 811 06 Bratislava, ☎ 54 41 34 68, 54 43 49 10
Embassy of the Republic of Slovenia
Moyzesova 4, 813 15 Bratislava, ☎ 57 27 43 30

Embassy of the United Kingdom of Great Britain and Northern Ireland
Panská 16, 811 01 Bratislava, ☎ 54 41 96 32, 54 41 96 33, 54 41 76 89
Embassy of the United States of America
Hviezdoslavovo nám. 4, 811 02 Bratislava, ☎ 54 43 08 61, 54 43 33 38,
Embassy of the Federal Republic Germany
Hviezdoslavovo nám. 10, 813 03 Bratislava, ☎ 54 41 96 40, 54 41 96 34
Embassy of the Kingdom of Spain
Prepoštská 10, 811 01 Bratislava, ☎ 54 41 57 26, 53 15 724-26
General Honorary Consulate of Sweden
Lermontovova 15, 811 05 Bratislava, ☎ 54 43 39 00, 54 11 54 62
Embassy of the Republic of Italy
Červeňova 19, 811 03 Bratislava, ☎ 54 41 31 95
Embassy of the Republic of Turkey
Holubyho 11, 811 03 Bratislava, ☎ 54 41 55 04, 54 41 56 06,
Embassy of the Republic of Ukraine
Radvanská 35, 811 01 Bratislava, ☎ 54 43 16 72, 54 43 18 90

FOREIGN CENTRES FOR CULTURE
British Council, Panská 17, ☎ 54 43 11 85, 54 43 17 93
Bulgarian information and cultural centre, Jesenského 7, ☎ 54 41 01 40
Czech centre, Nám. SNP 12, ☎ 59 21 42 01
French Institute, Sedlárska 7, ☎ 54 43 48 10 , 54 43 46 62
Goethe Institute, Konventná 1, ☎ 54 41 42 59, 54 41 52 81
Polish Institute, Nám. SNP 27, ☎ 54 43 20 13

GALLERIES
GALLERY OF BRATISLAVA
Primatial Palace (Primaciálny palác), Primaciálne nám.1.
Permanent exposition. Tapestries and paintings. European paintings of past centuries. Collection of English tapestries from 17 century.
Open Tuesday - Sunday 10 a.m. - 5 p.m.
Mirbach Palace (Mirbachov palác), Františkánske nám. 11, ☎ 54 43 15 56
Permanent exposition. Mid European baroque painting, graphics and sculptures.
Open Tuesday - Sunday 10 a.m. - 5 p.m..
Pálffy Palace (Pálffyho palác), Panská 19, ☎ 54 43 36 27
Permanent exposition. Founding personalities of the modern Slovak paintings and sculptures. Slovak paintings and sculptures at the turn of the 20th century. Gothic table painting and plastic. Central European paintings and sculptures.
Open Tuesday - Sunday 10 a.m. - 5 p.m.

SLOVAK NATIONAL GALLERY
Water Barracks (Vodné kasárne), Rázusovo nábr.2, ☎ 54 43 42 76
Permanent exposition. Old and Modern Slovak Arts, Gothic arts of Slovakia. Baroque Arts of Slovakia. Icons. Slovak Paintings and sculptures of 19th century. Modern Slovak painting and sculpture of the first half of 20th century.
Esterházy Palace (Esterházyho palác), Námestie Ľ. Štúra 4, ☎ 54 43 20 81
Permanent exposition. Old European arts from the collection of SNG.
Open Tuesday - Sunday 10 a.m. - 6 p.m.
Gallery NOVA (Galéria Nova), Baštová 2, ☎ 54 43 30 39
Open Tuesday - Sunday 1 p.m. - 6 p.m.
Gallery Médium, Hviezdoslavovo nám. 18, ☎ 54 43 22 51
Gallery of Photography PROFIL Prepoštská 4,
Open Tuesday - Sunday 1 p.m. - 6 p.m.

Gallery of Štefan Nemčok, Štefánikova 25, ☎ 52 44 27 77
Open Tuesday - Sunday 10 a.m. - 6 p.m.
The House of Arts (Dom umenia), Nám. SNP 12, ☎ 52 96 44 58
The place is leased for exhibition purposes.
Open Tuesday - Sunday 9 a.m. - 6 p.m.
K.F.A. Gallery, Karpatská 11, ☎ 52 49 70 30
Open Monday - Friday 9 a.m. - 5 p.m.
Perugia Gallery, Zelená 5, ☎ 0903 77 37 37
Gallery Michalský dvor, Michalská 3, ☎ 54 41 10 79
Open Tuesday - Sunday 1 p.m. - 6 p.m.
Gallery DONNER, Klobučnícka 4, ☎ 54 43 37 53
ULUV, Obchodná 64, ☎ 53 33 20 35
Gallery SPP, Drevená 4, ☎ 54 13 12 54
Open Tuesday - Sunday 10 a.m. - 6 p.m.
Gallery Ardan, Lermontovova 14, ☎ 0905 44 31 06, 52 49 32 35
Open Tuesday - Saturday 4 p.m. - 7 p.m.
Gallery SFVU, Michalská 7, ☎ 54 43 32 29
Open Monday - Friday 9 a.m. - 5 p.m.
Gallery Grémium, Gorkého 11, ☎ 54 43 06 53
Open Monday - Friday 9.30 a.m. - 6 p.m. , Saturday 9.30 a.m. - 1 p.m.
Gallery X - STYLE , Zámočnícka 5
Open Monday - Friday 11 a.m. - 6 p.m., Saturday 10 a.m. - 2 p.m.
Gallery Gerulata, Hodžovo nám. 3
Open Tuesday - Sunday 12a.m. - 6 p.m.
Gallery Café, Panská 12, ☎ 54 43 12 28
Open Monday - Friday 9 a.m. - 11 p.m., Saturday 9 a.m. - 1 p.m.
BIBIANA, Panská 41, ☎ 54 43 35 50
Open Tuesday - Sunday 10 a.m. - 6 p.m.

GARDENS AND PARKS

Botanical Garden of UK, Botanická 3, ☎ 65 42 03 51, 65 42 54 40
Forest park, Železná studnička
Janko Kráľ park, Petržalka
Lunapark, Petržalka
Medical garden, Ul. 29. augusta
Landscape park, Búdková cesta
Zoological garden, Mlynská dolina 1, ☎ 65 42 28 48, 65 42 28 23

INDOOR SPORTS STADIUMS

Indoor Stadium Mladosť, Trnavská cesta 31, ☎ 44 37 23 04
Indoor Stadium STARZ, Drieňová 11/a, ☎ 43 33 79 84
Indoor Stadium, Harmincova, ☎ 64 36 61 71
Indoor Stadium Pasienky, Trnavská 29,, ☎ 44 37 21 27
Indoor Stadium PKO, Nábr. arm. gen. L. Svobodu, ☎ 54 41 60 40

INSURANCE OFFICES

Allianz, Záhradnícka 151, ☎ 55 46 48 55
Amslico, Hviezdoslavovo nám. 20, ☎ 59 36 31 11
Europian Travelling (Európska cestovná poisťovňa), Ventúrska 12, ☎ 54 41 84 66
Kooperativa, Štefanovičova 4, ☎ 57 29 91 11
Nationale Nederlanden, Kolárska 6, ☎ 59 34 64 12, 59 34 64 60
Otčina, Lazaretská 15, ☎ 59 30 30 11, Križna 52 , ☎ 55 57 58 36, 55 57 58 32
Slovak Insurance (Slovenská poisťovňa), Dostojevského rad 4, ☎ 59 63 11 12
Kontinuita, Dr. Klementisa 10, ☎ 48 28 23 42-43

Social Insurance (Sociálna poisťovňa), 29 augusta 10, ☎ 38 48 111
Transportation Insurance (Dopravná poisťovňa), Levická 3,
☎ 55 56 46 28, 55 42 32 36
Union, Tolstého 7, ☎ 54 43 22 04, 54 43 42 25
Universal Bank Insurance (Univerzálna banková poisťovňa), Košická 52,
☎ 50 23 04 23
Universal Healthcare Insurance (Všeobecná zdravotná poisťovňa), Bárdošova 2,
☎ 54 77 10 00
Universal Social Insurance Tatry (Všeobecná sociálna poisťovňa Tatry), Miletičova 40,
☎ 55 56 59 85

INTERNATIONAL ORGANIZATIONS
Delegation of the European Commission
Panská 3-5, 810 00 Bratislava, ☎ 54 43 17 18, 54 43 17 27
European Bank for Reconstruction and Development
Grösslingova 4, 814 18 Bratislava, ☎ 52 92 14 51
Information and documentation centre of European Council
Klariská 5, 810 00 Bratislava, ☎ 54 43 57 52,
International Financial Corporation (IFC)
Francisciho 4, 811 08 Bratislava, ☎ 52 93 16 81,
International organisation for migration
Pribinova 25, 810 11 Bratislava, ☎ 50 63 33 20,
United Nations High Commission for Refugees
Štúrova 6, 811 02 Bratislava, ☎ 31 78 75, 31 78 76,

MUSEUMS
SLOVAK NATIONAL MUSEUM

Museum of Natural Science (Prírodovedné múzeum), Vajanského nábr. 2,
☎ 59 34 91 41
Mineralogy. Flora and fauna of Slovakia. Fauna of Seas. Mushrooms around us. Variations of the world of flora.
Open Tuesday - Sunday 9 a.m. - 5 p.m.
Historical Museum - Castle (Historické múzeum - hrad), ☎ 59 34 16 26
The stone witness. Overview of recent research and prospective of reconstruction of Bratislava castle. Natural Historical Monument. Historical furniture. Historical weapons. Jewels of the ancient past of Slovakia.
Open Tuesday - Friday 9 a.m. - 5 p.m.
Music Museum - Castle (Hudobné múzeum - hrad), ☎ 54 41 33 49, 54 41 43 00
Bastion Luginsland Exhibition of musical instruments.
Open Tuesday - Sunday 9 a.m. - 5 p.m.
Archeological Museum (Archeologické múzeum), Žižkova 12, ☎ 54 41 36 80
Jewels of the ancient past of Slovakia. Celtics and Slovakia. Antic.
Open Tuesday - Sunday 9 a.m. - 5 p.m.
Museum of Jewish Culture (Múzeum židovskej kultúry), Židovská 17, ☎ 54 41 85 07
Open daily except Saturday from 11 a.m. - 5 p.m.
Museum of non European Cultures (Múzeum mimoeurópskych kultúr), Židovská 18
African arts.
Open Tuesday - Sunday 9 a.m. - 5 p.m.
CITY MUSEUM (MESTSKÉ MÚZEUM), Primaciálne nám. 3, ☎ 54 43 47 42
Exposition of the history of Bratislava, Old City Hall (Expozícia dejín Bratislavy), Primaciálne nám. 1
Open Tuesday - Sunday 10 a.m. - 5 p.m.

Exposition of weapons and town fortifications (Expozícia zbraní a mestského opevnenia), Michalská veža
Open Wednesday - Monday 9 a.m. - 4.30 p.m.
Exposition of Viticulture (Expozícia vinohradnícka-vinárska), Radničná 1
Open Wednesday - Monday 9 a.m. - 4.30 p.m.
Exposition of feudal justice, Old Town Hall (Expozícia feudálnej justície), Primaciálne nám. 3
Open Wednesday - Monday 10 a.m. - 5 p.m..
Pharmaceutical exposition (Farmaceutická expozícia), Lekáreň Červený rak, Michalská ulica 26
Open Wednesday - Monday 9.30 a.m. - 4.30 p.m.
Exposition of arts and crafts (Expozícia umeleckých remesiel), Beblavého 1
Open Wednesday - Monday 9.30 a.m.- 4.30 p.m.
Music exposition - The house of J. N. Hummel (Hudobná expozícia - rodný dom J. N. Hummela), Klobučnícka 2
Open Tuesday - Sunday 12 a.m. - 5 p.m.
Exposition of historical watches (Expozícia historických hodín), Židovská 1, Dom u dobrého pastiera
Open Wednesday - Monday 9 a.m. - 4.30 p.m.
THE CASTLE DEVÍN (Devín - hrad), ☎ 65 73 01 05
Open daily except Monday from 10 a.m. - 5 p.m.
MUSEUM OF J. JESENSKÝ, Somolického 2, ☎ 54 43 47 42.
Open Monday - Friday 8 a.m. - 1 p.m.
MUSEUM OF POLICE SR (Múzeum polície), Gunduličova 2, ☎ 50 56 66 98
Open Tuesday - Saturday 10 a.m. - 5 p.m.
MUSEUM OF COMMERCE (Živé múzeum obchodu), Sasinkova 19, ☎ 55 41 57 21
Open Monday - Friday 9 a.m. - 9 p.m.
MUSEUM ĽUDOVÝ DOM, Roľnícka ul. 181-185, Vajnory, ☎ 54 43 47 42
It is necessaries to book in advance at city part administration.
MUSEUM OF ANTIQUE, Rusovce, ☎ 62 85 93 32
Open from 1st. May daily except Mondays from 10 a.m. - 5 p.m.

PUBLIC TRANSPORTATION

The public transportation includes buses, trams, and trolley busses. One way ticket costs 12.- Sk and one can buy it in newspaper stands and machines, placed on some stops of public transportation. A day ticket (24 hour) costs 60.- Sk . A weekly ticket costs 200.- Sk. Tickets are sold at the Main Railway Station and in the passage of Mierové square.

STADIUMS

Cycling Stadium , Kalinčiakova, ☎ 44 37 27 09
Winter Indoor Stadium O. Nepelu, Odbojárov 9, ☎ 44 37 28 28
Winter Indoor Stadium V. Dzurillu, Ružinovská 4, ☎ 43 33 64 47

TAXI

B. P. taxi coop ☎ 163 33, 65 42 21 11, 65 42 33 33
FUN TAXI ☎ 161 61, 54 77 74 77
HAPL TAXI ☎ 161 11, 44 45 20 00, 44 25 33 33, 44 25 88 88,
MERCEDES TAXI ☎ 62 80 19 62, 62 80 35 55, 62 80 36 66
OTTO TAXI ☎ 54 77 75 77
PROFI TAXI ☎ 162 22, 32 12 12
PSK TAXI ☎ 54 77 71 11
TAXI BP Service ☎ 65 42 55 55, 65 42 22 22, 65 42 22 86
V. I. P. ☎ 160 00, 55 41 41 41
YELLOW EXPRESS ☎ 44 44 11 11

Index of streets

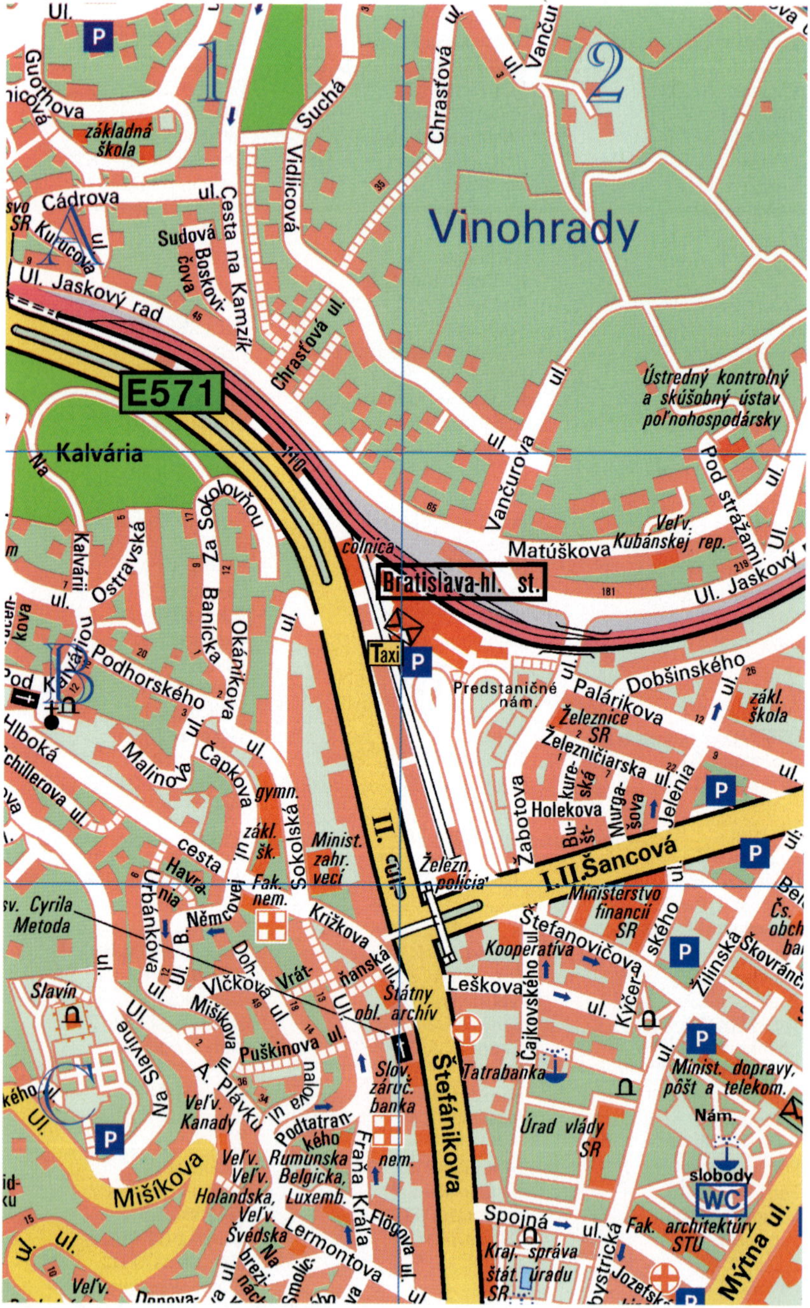
Vinohrady
E571
Kalvária
Bratislava-hl. st.
colnica
Taxi
Predstaničné nám.
Ústredný kontrolný a skúšobný ústav poľnohospodársky
Matúškova
Veľv. Kubánskej rep.
Ul. Jaskový rad
Cádrova
Sudová
Cesta na Kamzík
Vidlicová
Suchá
Chrasťová
Vančurova
Pod Strážami
Pod Kalváriou
Podhorského
Ostravská
Za Sokolovňou
Banícka
Okánikova
Čapkova
Malinová
Hlboká
Schillerova
Palárikova
Dobšinského
Železničiarska ul.
Železnice SR
Holekova
Žabotova
Murgašova
Jelenia
I.II.Šancová
Ministerstvo financií SR
Štefanovičova
Kooperatíva
Leškova
Kýčerského
Čajkovského ul.
Tatrabanka
Úrad vlády SR
Minist. dopravy, pôšt a telekom.
Nám. slobody
WC
Fak. architektúry STU
Mýtna ul.
Spojná ul.
Kraj. správa štát. úradu SR
Jozefská
Banskobystrická
Žilinská
Škovránčia
Štefánikova
Štátny obl. archív
Slov. záruč. banka
Podtatranského
Puškinova ul.
Vlčkova
Mišíkova
Dohnányho
Vrátňanská
Križkova
Minist. zahr. vecí
Sokolská
gymn.
zákl. šk.
Fak. nem.
Havlíčkova
Urbánkova
Němcovej
Sv. Cyrila Metoda
Slavín
Na Slavíne
A. Plávku
Veľv. Kanady
Veľv. Rumunska
Veľv. Belgicka
Holandska, Luxemb.
Veľv. Švédska
Lermontova
Flöglova ul.
Fraňa Kráľa
Mišíkova
základná škola
Guothova
Kuzmányho
zákl. škola

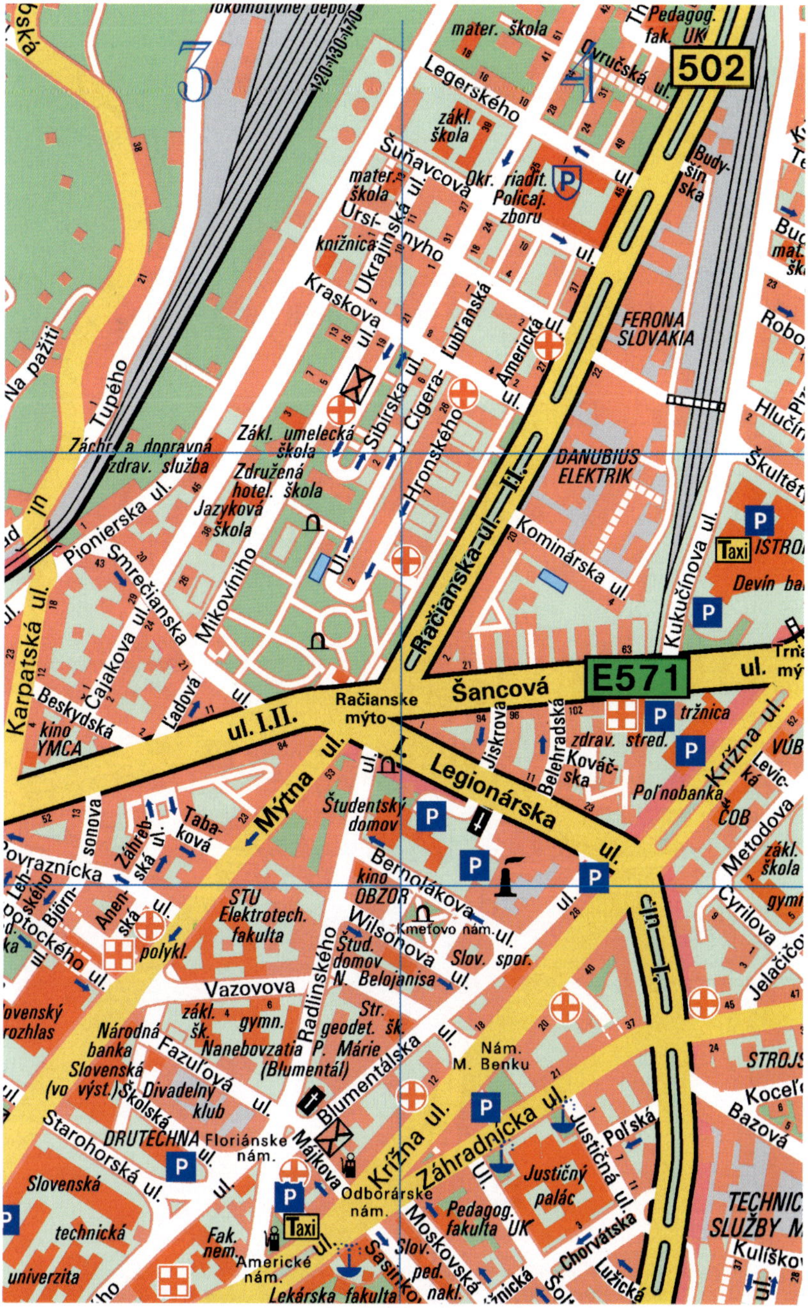
3
4
502
E571
Legerského
Suňavcova
Okr. riadit. Policaj. zboru
Ursínyho
Ukrajinská ul.
Kraskova ul.
Sibírska ul.
J. Cígera-Hronského
Ľubľanská
Americká ul.
FERONA SLOVAKIA
DANUBIUS ELEKTRIK
Račianska ul. I.II.
Kominárska ul.
Kukučínova ul.
Šancová ul.
Račianske mýto
ul. I.II.
Mýtna ul.
Legionárska ul.
Jiskrova
Belehradská
zdrav. stred.
tržnica
Kováčska
Poľnobanka
Križna ul.
Metodova
Cyrilova
Pionierska ul.
Smrečianska
Čajakova ul.
Ladová
Mikovíniho
Karpatská ul.
Beskydská
kino YMCA
Tupého
Na pažiti
Záchr. a dopravná zdrav. služba
Zákl. umelecká škola
Združená hotel. škola
Jazyková škola
Tabaková
Záhrebská ul.
Povraznícka
Študentský domov
Bernolákova
kino OBZOR
Kmeťovo nám.
Wilsonova
Slov. spor.
Štud. domov N. Belojanisa
Vazovova
STU Elektrotech. fakulta
polykl.
Radlinského
Str. geodet. šk.
Zákl. šk.
gymn.
Národná banka Slovenská (vo výst.)
Nanebovzatia P. Márie (Blumentál)
Fazuľová
Divadelný klub
Školská
Blumentálska
Nám. M. Benku
Križna ul.
Záhradnícka ul.
Justičná ul.
Justičný palác
Poľská
Chorvátska
Lužická
Pedagog. fakulta UK
Moskovská
Sasinkova
Lekárska fakulta
Americké nám.
Fak. nem.
Odborárske nám.
Floriánske nám.
Majkova
DRUTECHNA
Starohorská ul.
Slovenská technická univerzita
Slovenský rozhlas
Taxi
ISTRO
Devín
VÚB
ČOB
mater. škola
zákl. škola
Pedagog. fak. UK
Ovručská ul.
Budyšínska
STROJ
TECHNIC. SLUŽBY
Kuliško
Koceľ
Bazová
Jelačičova
Trnavské mýto
Škultéty
Hlučín
Robo
knižnica

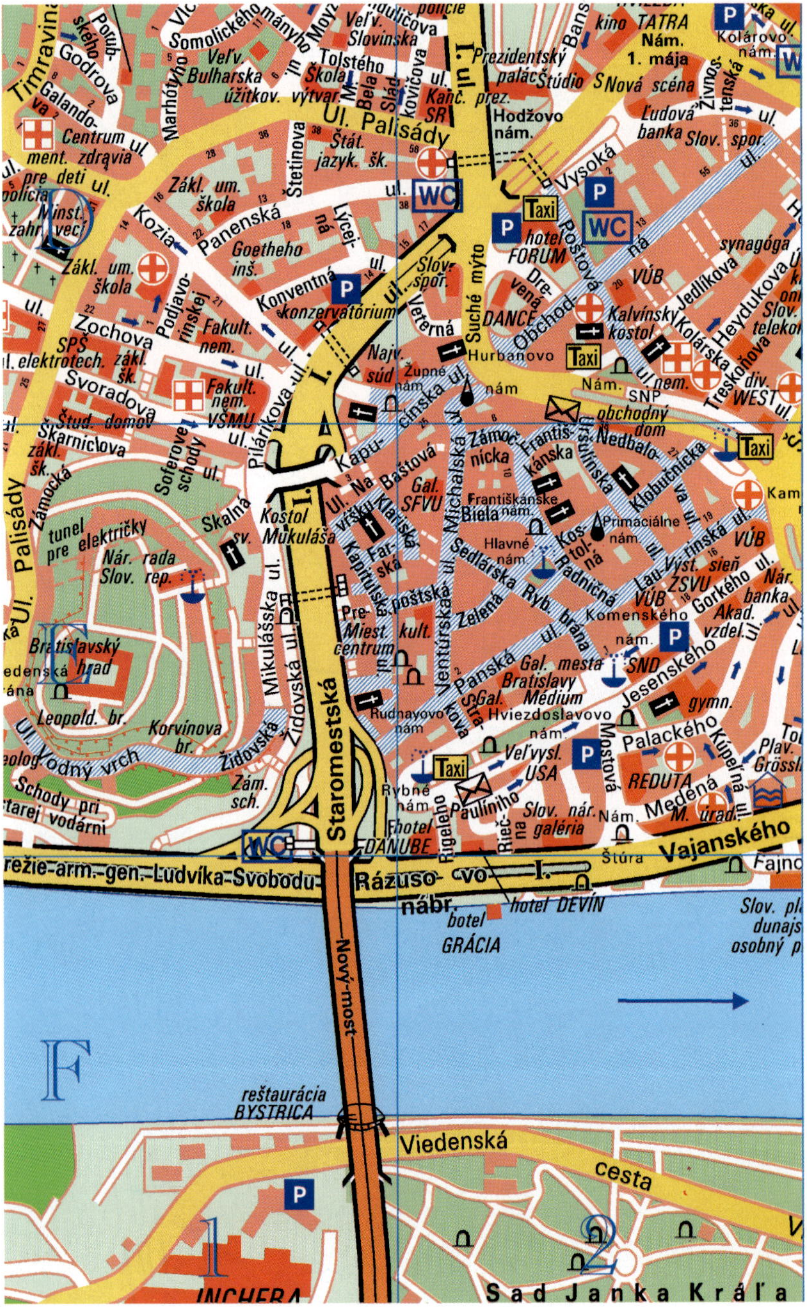
Timravina
Godrova
Galandova
Centrum ment. zdravia pre deti
Minst. zahr. vecí
Somolického
Mánesovo
Veľv. Bulharska
Marhótypho
Tolstého
Škola úžitkov. výtvar.
Veľv. Slovinská
Kozičova
Prezidentský palác
Štúdio S
Nová scéna
kino TATRA
Nám. 1. mája
Kolárovo nám.
Živnostenská
Ul. Palisády
Štát. jazyk. šk.
Hodžovo nám.
Ľudová banka
Slov. spor.
Vysoká
Štetinova
Zákl. um. škola
Panenská
Kozia
Goetheho inš.
Konventná
konzervatórium
Lýceálna
Slov. spor.
Suché mýto
hotel FORUM
Rostova
Obchodná
Dunajská
synagóga
Jedlíkova
Heydukova
Slov. telekom
Zákl. um. škola
Podjavorinskej
Fakult. nem.
Zochova
SPŠ elektrotech.
zákl. šk.
Svoradova
Štud. domov
Najv. súd
Župné nám.
Veterná
Drevená
DANCE
Kalvínsky kostol
Kolárska
Treskoňova
Hurbanovo nám.
Nám. SNP
obchodný dom
WEST
Fakult. nem. VŠMU
Škarniclova
Pilárikova
Kapucínska
Zámocká
Šoferove schody
Skalná
Kostol sv. Mikuláša
Na vŕšku
Baštová
Gal. SFVU
Michalská
Zámočnícka
Františkánska
Nedbalova
Klobučnícka
Františkánske nám.
Biela
Primaciálne nám.
Uršulínska
Kostolná
Hlavné nám.
Radničná
Laurinská
Výst. sieň ZSVU
VÚB
Gorkého
Nár. banka
Akad. vzdel.
tunel pre električky
Nár. rada Slov. rep.
Kapitulská
Farská
Klariská
Sedlárska
Rybárska brána
Zelená
Poštská
Komenského nám.
Ventúrska
Pre-Miest. kult. centrum
Panská
Gal. mesta Bratislavy
Mikulášska
Židovská
Bratislavský hrad
Leopold. br.
Korvínova br.
Vodný vrch
Schody pri starej vodárni
Staromestská
Zám. sch.
Rudnayovo nám.
Gal. Médium
Hviezdoslavovo nám.
Mostová
Palackého
Jesenského
gymn.
Kúpeľná
Veľvysl. USA
REDUTA
Medená
M. úrad
Plav. Grössling
Rybné nám.
Rigeleho
Paulíniho
Riečna
Slov. nár. galéria
Nám. Štúra
Vajanského
hotel DANUBE
nábr. arm. gen. Ludvíka Svobodu
Rázusovo nábr.
botel GRÁCIA
hotel DEVÍN
Slov. pl. dunajs. osobný p.
Nový most
reštaurácia BYSTRICA
Viedenská cesta
Sad Janka Kráľa
INCHEBA
D
E
F
1
2
WC
P
Taxi

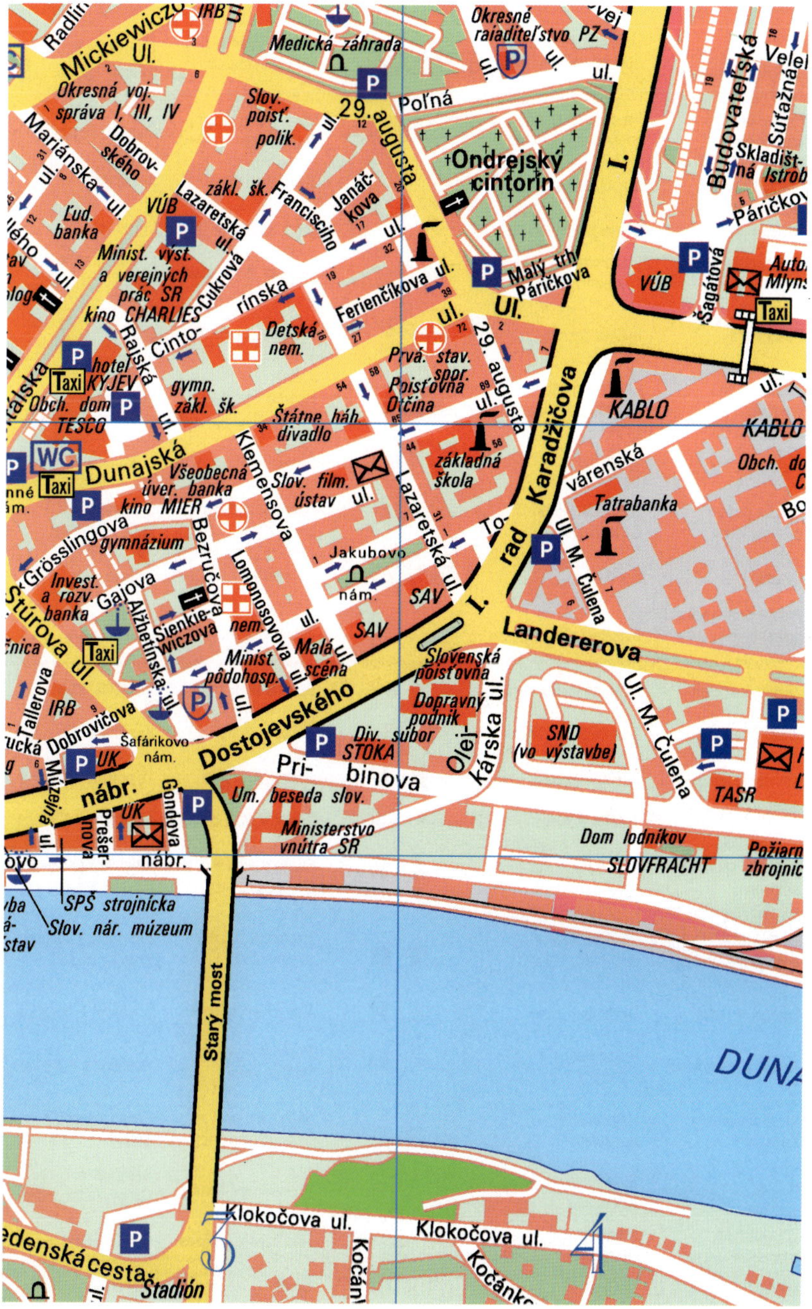
Mickiewiczova ul.
IRB
Medická záhrada
Okresné riaditeľstvo PZ
Okresná voj. správa I, III, IV
Slov. poisť. polik.
29. augusta
Poľná
Ondrejský cintorín
Mariánska ul.
Dobrovského
Ľud. banka
VÚB
Lazaretská ul.
zákl. šk.
Františkánske
Janáčkova
Budovateľská
Súťažná
Skladištná
Istrobanka
Páričkova
Minist. výst. a verejných prác SR
Cukrová
Cintorínska
Feriencíkova ul.
Malý trh
Páričkova
Šagátova
Auto
VÚB
Taxi
kino CHARLIES
Rajská
Detská nem.
Prvá stav. spor.
Poisťovňa Otčina
hotel KYJEV
Taxi
Obch. dom TESCO
gymn. zákl. šk.
Štátne háb. divadlo
KABLO
KABLO
Obch. dom
WC
Taxi
Dunajská
Všeobecná úver. banka
kino MIER
Klemensova
Slov. film. ústav
Lazaretská ul.
základná škola
Karadžičova
várenská
Tatrabanka
Grösslingova
gymnázium
Bezručova
Lomonosovova
Jakubovo nám.
SAV
I. rad
Ul. M. Čulena
Invest. a rozv. banka
Gajova
Alžbetínska ul.
Sienkiewiczova
nem.
SAV
Landererova
Štúrova ul.
Taxi
Tallerova
Minist. pôdohosp.
Malá scéna
Slovenská poisťovňa
Dopravný podnik
Olejkárska ul.
IRB
Dobrovičova
Šafárikovo nám.
Dostojevského
Div. súbor STOKA
SND (vo výstavbe)
Ul. M. Čulena
UK
Múzejná ul.
nábr.
UK
Prešernova
Gondova
Pribinova
Um. beseda slov.
TASR
Ministerstvo vnútra SR
Dom lodníkov
SLOVFRACHT
Požiarna zbrojnica
nábr.
SPŠ strojnícka
Slov. nár. múzeum
Starý most
DUNA
Klokočova ul.
Klokočova ul.
Kočánkova
Viedenská cesta
Štadión
3
4

Viacpruhová cesta; európske označenie	Mehrspurige Straße; Europastraßen-nummer	E571	Dual carriageway; european road No	Többsávos út; európai útjelzés
Hlavné prejazdné cesty s číslom	Hauptdurchfahrts-straßen mit Nummer	61	Main through roads with number	Sugárút útszámmal
Prejazdné cesty	Durchfahrtsstraßen		Through roads	Átkelő utak
Ostatné cesty	Sonstige Straßen		Minor road	Egyéb utak
Jednosmerná ulica, schody	Einbahnstraße, Treppe		Oneway street, steps	Egyirányú utca, lépcsők
Pešia zóna	Fußgängerzone		Pedestrian area	Sétány
Železnica so stanicou	Eisenbahn mit Bahnhof	Rusovce	Railway with station	Vasút állomással
Les	Wald		Forest	Erdő
Ihrisko; park, zelená plocha	Sportplatz; Park, Grünanlage		Sport-ground; Park, grean area	Sportpálya; Park, zöldterület
Cintorín	Friedhof		Cemetery	Temető
Plochy priemyselných podnikov	Industriegelände		Industrial area	Ipari területek
Zastavané plochy	Bebaute Fläche		Built-up area	Beépített terület
Verejné budovy	Öffentliche Gebäude	Dom kultúry	Public building	Középület
Kostol • Kaplnka	Kirche • Kapelle		Church • Chapel	Templom • Kápolna
Vežovitá stavba • Pošta	Turm • Postamt		Tower • Post-office	Torony • Posta
Čerpacia stanica • Autoservis	Tankstelle • Autore-paraturwerkstätte		Filling station • Car repair shop	Üzemanyagtöltő állomás • Autószervíz
Zmenáreň • Informačná kancelária	Wechselstube • Informationsbüro	Z	Exchange-office • Inquiry office	Pénzváltó • Idegen-forgalmi Hivatal
Pomník • Hotel	Denkmal • Hotel		Monument • Hotel	Emlékmű • Szálloda
Polícia • Parkovisko	Polizeistation • Parkplatz		Policestation • Parking-area	Rendőrség • Parkoló
Krytá plaváreň • Kúpalisko	Hallenbad • Badeplatz		Swimming-pool • Schwimming-bath	Fedett uszoda • Strand
Fontána • Lekáreň	Springbrunnen • Apotheke		Fountain • Chemist	Szökőkút • Gyógyszertár, patika
Zdravotnícke zariadenie	Krankenhaus, Heilanstalt		Health-care facilities	Gyógyintézet
Mierka	Maßstab	1:10 000	Scale	Mérték

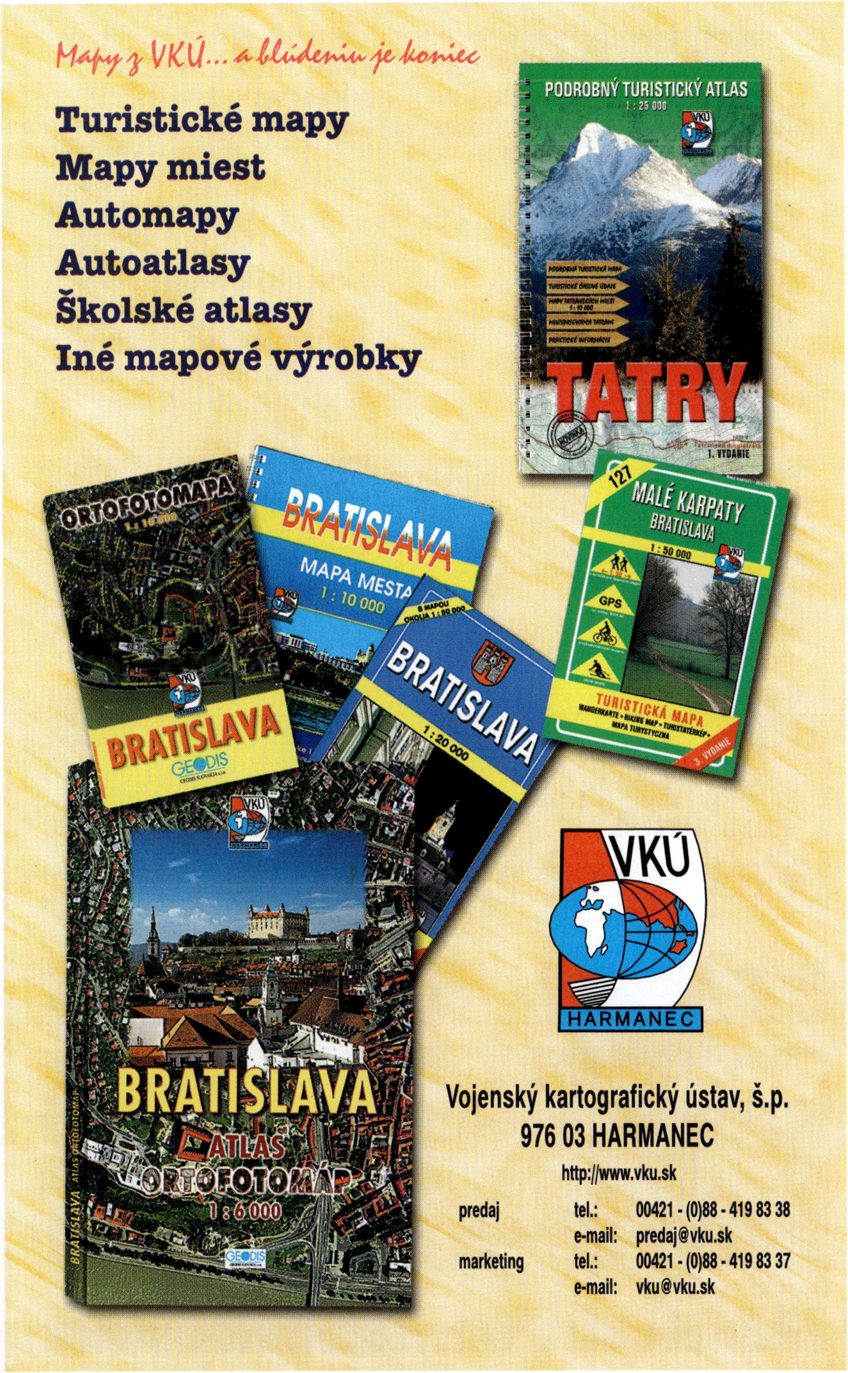
Mapy z VKÚ... a blúdeniu je koniec
Turistické mapy
Mapy miest
Automapy
Autoatlasy
Školské atlasy
Iné mapové výrobky
PODROBNÝ TURISTICKÝ ATLAS
1 : 25 000
TATRY
1. VYDANIE
ORTOFOTOMAPA
BRATISLAVA
GEODIS
BRATISLAVA
MAPA MESTA
1 : 10 000
BRATISLAVA
1 : 20 000
127
MALÉ KARPATY
BRATISLAVA
1 : 50 000
GPS
TURISTICKÁ MAPA
3. VYDANIE
BRATISLAVA
ATLAS
ORTOFOTOMÁP
1 : 6 000
VKÚ
HARMANEC
Vojenský kartografický ústav, š.p.
976 03 HARMANEC
http://www.vku.sk
predaj tel.: 00421 - (0)88 - 419 83 38
e-mail: predaj@vku.sk
marketing tel.: 00421 - (0)88 - 419 83 37
e-mail: vku@vku.sk

Vydavateľstvo DAJAMA
Ľubľanská 2, 831 02 Bratislava
Tel./Fax +421 7 442 53 182, 642 87 098
e-mail: geonad@internet.sk
http//:www.dajama.sk